INTRODUCING THE THEATRE

Ellen Terry as Lady Macbeth (1888) from the painting by J. S. Sargent, R.A.
(*see page* 250).

INTRODUCING THE THEATRE

TOGETHER WITH A DISCUSSION ON THE
FACTORS WHICH MAKE FOR
"GOOD THEATRE"

BY

ERNEST SHORT

EYRE & SPOTTISWOODE
LONDON

This book, first published in 1949, is printed in Great Britain
for Eyre & Spottiswood (Publishers) Ltd, 15 Bedford Street, London, W.C.2,
by The Broadwater Press Ltd, Welwyn Garden City, Herts.

CONTENTS

v

CONTENTS

v

ILLUSTRATIONS

INTRODUCING THE THEATRE

INTRODUCTION

I N this book I propose to pass in review the plays and theatrical
entertainments of the past half-century or so, which, so far as
I can judge, have given most pleasure to English audiences.
What follows is in no sense a history of the modern stage in
England. Rather, it is a discussion of ways and means. My
primary interest is with the ways and means which have made
for "good theatre" in my day and generation.

And, by "theatre", I do not mean "drama". My concern is
rather with the very varied arts of the playhouse, as opposed to
that of the playwright's study. The distinction is important.
When Matthew Arnold in 1879 wrote, "In England, we have no
drama at all," he did not imply that there was no English
"theatre". Marie Wilton, Nellie Farren, Henry Irving, and
Ellen Terry were there to give any such proposition the lie. The
discussion we have in mind relates to the theatre symbolized by
Byam Shaw's act-drop at the London Coliseum, dating from
Edwardian times, which pleasantly mingled Wagner, Elgar, and
Arthur Sullivan, and, because it included Pinero and Beerbohm
Tree, did not omit W. S. Gilbert, Cissie Loftus, and George
Robey. The fact that James Agate, writing from critical heights
established by Hazlitt, described *Rose Marie* as "the whoppingest
of monuments to inanity" is no reason for ignoring the entertainment and failing to analyse the reasons for its success. *Rose Marie*
registered 851 performances at Drury Lane and is still remembered, evidence enough that it was very acceptable "theatre".

Even Plato, who will not be accused of undue partiality towards the lighter stage, reminds us (Jowett, *The Laws*, Book VII,
816) that it is necessary to consider and know uncomely persons and thoughts and those which are intended to produce
laughter in comedy. The reason he advanced was that "serious
things cannot be understood without laughable things, nor
opposites at all without opposites, if a man is really to have intelligence of either." James Agate himself put the matter in its right
proportion when he said, "I have managed to preserve intact a
nursery sense of the theatre." There we have the proper approach.

I

The thrills to be recalled and understood are the elemental ones which follow the lifting of a curtain and give rise to laughter, or, what is so nearly akin to laughter in a theatre, tears.

The art of the theatre began with anecdotage, the first art which pre-supposed and, indeed, necessitated an audience. As Bergson pointed out, laughter is always the laughter of a group and the bigger the group the louder the laughter. As it operates in the theatre, the law is, "the fuller the house, the more uncontrolled is the laughter." Laughter-creation, in fact, is a primary factor in the theatre. It may arise from a comedy of situation or a comedy of character, but always the dramatic element is there. Indeed, a talented comedian is continually exploiting opportunities in which the situation emphasizes characterization or characterization enriches situation. Thus the mock-dignity of the stage butler is doubly comic when the situation fits the fun. The Yorkshireman, Sydney Howard, who was a heavily built man and a slow mover, was born to be a musical comedy or revue butler. Who will forget him at the telephone, when the service bell rang and the habitant of Room 226 asked for his early cup of tea and a newspaper?

"Will you have it hot, sir?"

And the final, "I wonder who that was?" when Sydney put down the receiver and lifted his wondering gaze towards the ceiling.

The laughter which associates itself with butlers and footmen arises from friction with a traditional social code and, incidentally, this is why the author of *The Chiltern Hundreds* (1947) selected a butler as the proper guardian of ancestral traditions and all they stand for in England. How excellent Michael Shepley was as Beecham, the butler, who so unexpectedly found himself in (and out of) the House of Commons!

This is a typical example. Similar memories, duly related to the fundamentals in drama and the art of acting, will lead to a consideration of the factors which make for success or failure in the theatre. What forms should the artistry of the stage take if the rewarding tears, or, in the alternative, smiles, chuckles, and full-throated laughter are to arise? What should be the special contributions of the various craftsmen who contribute to a highly complex unity. In the theatre, what is the function of the dramatist, what of the player, what of the producer? And why stop at these? There are also the costume-designer, the scene-painter, the electrician and the maker and mender of "props". All have contributed to our happy evenings.

In these memories lies the underlying justification for our book. It is to be a source of pleasant and memorable recollections, but it is to be hoped that it may add something to pleasures in prospect, for every iota of understanding will help enjoyment. If its conclusions cannot be accepted as final, what matter?

With the plays of Ibsen in mind, William Archer once spoke of a dramatist taking a cutting from the tree of life, planting it in the rich soil of his imagination, and letting it ramify and burgeon as it would. Such a test may justly be applied to dramatic master-pieces, though it will bear small relation to the greater number of the plays and players which will figure in the following pages. Nevertheless, what theatre-lovers have witnessed during the past fifty or sixty years can only be described as the rise of a new "theatre". The size of modern playhouses and the number and variety of the plays which claim the attention in themselves con-stitute a new problem. If dramatic ballet and wireless plays be included, we may well be witnessing a revolution in popular entertainment which will rank with the invention of the printed book and news-sheet in its effects upon political, economic, and social life. The experience of half a century suggests that the semi-educated (and the majority in every democratic com-munity which is numbered by the million is necessarily semi-educated) cannot learn wisdom or gain vision from the printed word alone. Those capable of grasping the significance of the printed word are few in comparison with those who can gain understanding from a picture, whether it be in the newspaper, on the screen or on the stage. What the theatre can offer is a vivid and vital expression of the mingled comedy and tragedy which constitute modern life, and the community which neglects such an aid to a full life is foolish.

To-day, the cinema public is larger than that of the theatre, but I attribute this primarily to the relative cheapness and com-fort of the picture-houses. The distinctive theatrical thrill is an impression of imaginative illusion, whereas the appeal of the cinema lies in a sense of actuality based upon the accepted integrity of the camera record. The picture page of a popular newspaper is persuasive for the same reason. The press photographer, we tell ourselves, was there.

My firm conviction is that, though the modern theatre may take somewhat longer to establish itself in popular favour, its future is assured. Be that as it may, this book is addressed to the keen playgoer. He, at any rate, will not admit that his favoured art cannot live in competition with the cinema. If there are doubters the survey which follows should persuade them that the stage to-day is displaying that capacity to react to ever-changing circumstances which is the surest test of vitality.

One other preliminary consideration: any careful study of the factors which underly the distinctively theatrical thrills will almost certainly focus attention upon the nature and reactions of audiences which furnish the real material presented for analysis. It is conceivable that a dramatist might write a play for his own edification and pleasure. It is almost impossible that he could stage it in a playhouse and persuade a critical public to enjoy it. Always, the factors which make for good "theatre" must be considered in relation to audiences. Theodor Lipps devised the theory of *einfühlung* to cover the reactions of the spectator to all the states of experience, sub-conscious as well as those on the plane of thought, which are active when a work of art is appraised. Applied to the theatre, the theory tells us that looking is not enough. Even sympathy ("feeling with" the actor or dramatist) will not suffice for full understanding and pleasure. Empathy ("feeling into") is called for. In other words, each member of an audience is required to project himself into any play so that he may share the *raptus* which the dramatist experienced when he made his first contact with a worthy theme and the thrill of the player when he realized how the words of the dramatist would come to life through his own craft-skill.

Nothing less than this "feeling into" a play or a piece of acting will yield the genuine theatrical thrill, which Plato described as "playing the tragic or comic poet in your own person". The ideal playgoer must lend himself to an elaborate self-deception and thus share in the creative effort of those who made the play. And, be it remembered, the ideal spectator adds not a little to the creative process not only from his own store of memories and

Roman Theatre,
Verulamium (*see
page* 10).

A summer theatre of the sixteenth century (Holland). From the painting by Pieter Breughel the Younger (*see page* 13).

emotions but from his insight into the processes of organization and synthesis. Full understanding, indeed, would seem to imply that the spectator can re-enact the whole process of creation which brought the entertainment into being, whether by dramatist, producer, or player. This ideal is plainly unobtainable, but it is the aim of this book to set out and illustrate the factors involved.

Victor Hugo, in the Preface to *Cromwell* (1827), wrote:

"The Stage is an optical point. Everything that exists in the world, in history, in life, in man—should be and can be reflected therein. Aided by her magic wand, Art turns the leaves of the ages, clothes the whole with a form at once poetical and natural and imparts to it that vitality of truth and brilliancy which gives birth to illusion, that prestige of reality which arouses the enthusiasm of the spectator. . . Thus the aim of Art is almost divine, to bring to life again, if it is writing history; to create, if it is writing poetry."

If half of this be true, our inquiry promises at least some amusing and instructive hours; so "Overtures and Beginners, please!"

CHAPTER I

THE THEATRICAL TRADITION

M Y primary concern is with the theatre of the past half-century, the plays and players you and I may have seen. Nevertheless, some thought must be given to the tradition upon which the modern stage bases its practice and technique.

It all began when the first funny story went the round of the tribal camp and established the reputation of some great unknown as a "comic". From anecdotage to story-telling was a short step, and, at this point, tears were mingled with laughter. When mimicry was added to assist illusion, the elements of drama were there. The art form was completed when rhythmic utterance and the ordered movements of actors and dancers were added to the characterization and narrative of a story-teller, whose words as leader were answered by a chorus of followers. Add an audience and the theatre was in being.

Day-dreaming, anecdotage, idle song and dance were latent in human communities from early times. Even anecdotage was not without an element of mimicry, and mimicry took on the colour of artistry through the ritual of sympathetic magic which associated itself with successful hunting and hopes for harvest in primitive agricultural communities. The paintings of the Altamira cavemen display clear evidence of a desire to propitiate the powers of life and death by assuming their imagined characteristics and a similar element can be traced in most magical rites.

The theatre of to-day has developed through two thousand years and more from beginnings which still exercise an influence upon our stage. The element of mimicry, the principles of story-telling, the part to be played by a chorus, the relation of the leading actors to the supporting players—a hundred problems of the kind have been tried out, until the comedies, tragedies, and farces which we recognize as belonging to our own times became possible. In effect, what happened was that numerous arts were welded into a new whole, The Theatre, and this is why Charlotte Cushman, with her intense love of the theatre, could say without exaggeration:

"I love all arts equally, only putting my own above the others, just because in it I recognize the union and culmination of all. To me it seems as if, when God conceived the world, that was Poetry. He formed it and that was Sculpture: He coloured it and that was Painting: He peopled it with living beings and that was grand, divine, eternal Drama."

It would seem that the mimetic instinct is ingrained in the human kind, and Greek tragedy and comedy alike had their origin in the instinct. The magical rites in honour of Dionysus, the wine god, became tragedy or comedy when critical and cultivated audiences superseded the chance gatherings of villagers or townsfolk in spring, the time when the earth appeared to be receiving a new measure of the power from which arise both death and generation. The *phallos* itself which loomed so largely in Greek comedy was an accepted symbol of the generative energy of the world, as Iamblichus pointed out as long ago as the fourth century B.C. Whereas the physical accompaniments of tragedy were a bodily shiver which associated itself with fear and the flow of tears which arises from pity, comedy was associated with the sense of well-being which follows heightened sex, in which the thrill of satisfaction and the phenomena of smiles and laughter are curiously mingled. To this day the distinction between tragedy and comedy is the presence of fear and pity as opposed to the presence of laughter, a laughter which in very many forms of comedy is not without sexual accompaniments.

Nor is this all. From the first there was an element of exaggeration in the mimicry, as there had been in the "funny story", for ritual was based upon mimicry of imagined gods and heroes, or, if not gods and heroes, then the demonic forces which seemed to be responsible for generation in man and nature. Imagine such a mysterious spirit, impersonated by a tribesman fully aware that he is working upon the emotions of a crowd. When, with due gesture and dance, this leader cries "Awas", the crowd falls back, until what seems to be a friendly spirit takes up the dance, and the crowd recovers poise.

Already the influence of hearers or spectators was apparent. It reached a climax when chance hearers or spectators, who had been attracted by a religious rite, were transformed into an audience, ready and anxious to be edified or amused by what they recognized as a work of art. As for the elements of acting, they included the temporary identification of the actor with the imagined character he was impersonating. In order that this identification should be complete, a sequence of images had to arise in the imagination of the player, and these images, in turn, aroused gestures, changes of vocal inflection and other muscular reactions, which make up a full impersonation.

The Greek Tradition

Historically, the theatre, as an organic whole, had its beginnings in Ancient Greece, the origins of tragedy being the improvisations of the leader in the rhapsodical dithyramb sung in honour of Dionysus. The rites were enacted during the annual festivals of the god, the principal ones being the Lenaea, the festival of the wine-press in January, and the great Dionysia in March. In course of time the dithyrambic chorus came to consist of fifty singers and dancers, but, by 487 B.C., the chorus in an Athenian tragedy had been reduced to twelve, doubtless because a cycle of four plays now made up a typical day in a dramatic festival. Instead of fifty players for what seemed a single performance there were twelve or fifteen for each of the four plays constituting a cycle. When Thespis elaborated the rôle of the leader, making him an actor, whose words answered and amplified the songs of the chanting chorus, primitive tragedy was in being. Aeschylus was content with two actors and a chorus, while Sophocles and Euripides had three, who shared the speaking parts. Aristotle tells us that Sophocles also invented scenery. A dressing-room for players dates from about 465 B.C. Soon such properties as a crane for snatching a player from the stage or suspending a deity in mid-air were added, and about 425 B.C. a permanent stone background superseded the temporary wooden stage of the early theatre. It had doors for the entry or exit of players and represented a palace, a temple, or a market-place, as the dramatist required.

A Greek stage was considerably longer than the thirty or so feet of a modern theatre and in this respect the performance resembled that in an open-air theatre, such as Regent's Park, London. It was the size of the theatre which called for the use of masks, as the large mouths of the masks had some of the qualities of the megaphone. Bell-shaped vessels of bronze, placed in niches around the hill-side theatre, eliminated echo and thus improved the acoustics. A semi-circle in the natural slope of a hill not only made the seating of large audiences relatively simple, but assisted easy hearing. The seats in the various tiers were approached by steps cut in the hillside and a horizontal gangway divided the auditorium into two or more parts. The blue of the Attic sky, the lovely toned marble of the ringed orchestra, the tiers upon tiers of robed spectators, completed a setting as beautiful as ever graced a work of art. Wearing a lofty headdress (the *onkos*), which towered above a mask, and thick soled boots (the *cothurnus*), a leading actor was an imposing figure, appearing, perhaps, seven feet high, in comparison with the singers and dancers in the ringed dancing-floor, the *orchestra* below. The actors' shoulders were freely padded, so bodily sub-stance was added to the artificial height.

The mask, *cothurnus*, and *onkos* are accepted stage practice in China to this day. In the Greco-Roman Theatre, in the second century A.D., forty-four different masculine masks and twenty-five feminine masks were enumerated, the feminine masks being white in contrast to those of the men, which were brownish. Of the forty-four masculine masks, seventeen were used for tragic rôles and twenty-seven for comic parts. Masks are neglected to-day in the British theatre, though Priestley used them with effect in *Johnson Over Jordan* and Charles Cochran played with the device in revue. It may be that the increasing size of the modern playhouse will encourage the re-introduction of symbolic masks.

Owing to the origins of tragedy no money-making element obtruded itself in the Greek theatre. Plays were not put on "for a run". Each cycle was designed for a single performance at a semi-religious festival, much as T. S. Eliot or Dorothy Sayers might write a poetical play around the life-story of a saint for a festival performance in the Chapter House at Canterbury or some other Cathedral. For a long time there was not even a charge for a seat, and in the fifth century B.C. the admission fee was only a couple of obols. Well-to-do citizens, as an honourable duty, met the cost of training the chorus and providing the costumes and properties for a dramatist who considered himself fortunate in being permitted to write a cycle for a coming festival. There might be added the final honour of victory in the competition for the first prize.

Apart from Aristophanes and occasional performances of Roman comedies at public schools or universities, playgoers to-day are chiefly concerned with Greek tragedies as they are presented in translations. These offer exceptional opportunities for acting and may achieve a high degree of beauty, but an evening with Euripides, Sophocles, or Aeschylus, under, say, the guidance of Gilbert Murray, or even an afternoon in the open-air theatre at Bradfield, bears but a faint resemblance to a day in the theatre of Dionysus at Athens four hundred years before Christ. An Athenian audience was exclusively male and a beginning was made at dawn. Not one Greek play, as the modern habit is, but a cycle of three tragedies and a satyric comedy were presented, so each performance continued until nightfall. Whereas the theme in a Greek play is necessarily unfamiliar to modern audiences, to Athenian playgoers it was as well known as the recension of a Bible story would be to-day. And because the story was familiar, a Greek tragedian made a point, as Dryden showed in his *Essay of Dramatic Poesy*, of setting "the audience, as it were, at the post where the race is to be concluded", thus saving spectators the tedious expectation of seeing the course set out. The result was that attention was focused upon the dramatist's treatment of the theme, the poetry and power of his writing, and the speaking and chanting of players and chorus. The Greek tragedian was under no temptation to play to "a gallery", the assumption being that work would be judged by the stern code proper to the performance of a rite in honour of a deity. When Aeschylus, in the *Oresteia*, brought the Furies themselves into the circular orchestra the tragedy was fulfilled. Terror-stricken,

Orestes clings to the statue of Athena and cries to the goddess for aid, and the illusion for an Athenian audience was the deeper because, in the interval before the coming of the goddess, the Furies had chanted the ritual hymn which by tradition preceded the tearing of a living victim to pieces.

Lacking the intensity of imagination which arises from contact with actual faith, a modern audience may well find a performance of Eugene O'Neill's *Mourning Becomes Electra* a more fitting introduction to the realities of Greek tragedy than any translation can be. The modern dramatist supplies the story which an Athenian audience took for granted, including an elaborate plot leading up to his central theme. An Athenian, like a Londoner in Shakespeare's time, was quite capable of supplying the scenic background from his imagination. Grant these fundamental differences, the tragedy of the Mannon clan bears a close resemblance to that which embodies the murder of Agamemnon and Clytemnestra.

Sophocles, as a typical Greek tragedian, was not interested in the problem of changing and developing personality which obsessed the Renaissance, and so the characters in a Sophoclean play are relatively static. Consequently, when Shakespeare and the Elizabethan dramatists presented their characters, much more complicated methods and many more changes of background were called for, and facial expression and gesticulation were used much more freely. To-day, we have passed still further from the heroic which interested both Greek and Renaissance theatre-goers. Our concern is with the presentation and analysis of men and women of our own time and stature, and this has brought in its train new acting methods, novel presentations of plot, realistic costumes and naturalistic scenery which a Greek would have neither welcomed nor understood. All these factors make for a more concentrated form of story-telling than Eugene O'Neill could employ in his modern version of the Greek tragedy and make *Mourning Becomes Electra* a valuable illustration of the changes in the theatrical tradition since Greek times.

Greek comedy had a somewhat different origin from tragedy. It arose from the communal processions in honour of Dionysus, which ended, naturally enough, with phallic songs and dance.

Our word comedy is derived from the Greek κῶμος meaning a revel, with the addition of ᾠδή (song), and the art form arose when the back-chat exchanged between the leading singers and the audience of townsfolk was added to the original song and dance. This back-chat, when given artistic form by such a poet as Aristophanes, added a satiric quality to Greek drama, which modern comedy still tends to retain. The chorus, in particular, was much more than a traditional survival. Rather it was an all-important element in Aristophanic comedy and it is noteworthy that W. S. Gilbert utilized the chorus in full measure when he created Savoy opera, the nearest thing to the plays of Aristophanes in English drama.

As Nietsche said, the Greek chorus stood for "the lyric cry", representing what Schiller had described as "the living rampart against reality". To this E. S. Dallas added, in *The Gay Science*: "The chorus are always present watching events, talking to the actors, talking to the audience, talking to themselves—all through the play: indeed, pouring forth a continual stream of musical chatter. And what are the chorus? The only intelligible explanation which has been given is that they represent the spectator. The spectator is introduced into the play and made to take part in it."

We shall see how far-reaching was this association between players and spectators in all future drama. For the rest, the leaders in the Dionysiac processions were heavily disguised and, in comedy, these disguises took the form of the comic masks, together with the *phallos* and substantial pads which gave stomach and buttocks laughable proportions.

The later Greek dramatists introduced romantic love into their comedies, and Plautus, a Roman, exploited the familiar plot of latter-day comedy, "boy meets girl, girl loses boy, boy gets girl." As the romantic themes were exhausted, Roman comedy tended to degenerate into licentiousness and buffoonery, an exception being the plays of Terence, in which the wit and sense of style suggest that they were written for a small and instructed audience. Other differences from the Greek were built-up architectural backgrounds to the Roman stages, while the players were slaves and, with the exception of the famous Roscius, did not win the popular esteem actors had had in Greece.

The Mediaeval Tradition

The earliest recognizable form in which English drama displayed itself was in village *ludi* with their mimetic dances, and in traditional folk drama of the *St George and the Dragon* type, such as Thomas Hardy described in *The Return of the Native*. Later an element of ordered acting was introduced by the Church. Just as Greek tragedy and comedy developed from popular pantomime and dance, so the mediaeval mysteries developed from the mumming of peasants and religious playlets acted by choir boys and priests in parish and abbey churches. The institution of the feast of Corpus Christi in 1264 resulted in annual dramatic festivals and cycles of plays extending over four or five days, in which each scene was mounted on a wheeled cart which moved through a town from one open space to another. Wealthy citizens contributed towards the cost, perhaps on the understanding that the pageant would stop opposite their home or shop. In Fouquet's well-known picture of the martyrdom of St Apollonia, a man in clerical uniform, holding a book of the words, is not only prompting the players but signals when it is the turn of an actor to come on to the stage. He was the mediaeval equivalent of the modern producer, and, doubtless, was responsible for rehearsals.

But the significant thing is that the rebirth of the theatre in mediaeval times had associations with ritual comparable with those in Hellenic times. In place of the ritual of the Wine God or the Spirit of Spring, there was the ritual of the Sepulchre at Eastertide. At first this was enacted around the high altar at the east end of the church. Later, an Easter Sepulchre, a representation of Christ's tomb, was an architectural feature in many churches. At times, a sculptor added a Christ rising from the tomb, or an angel pointing to the empty tomb, with the words, *Non est hic*. Such an Easter Sepulchre served as a background for a couple of players enacting a simple Passion play.

Much more important historically, however, were the pageants given by guildsmen in the market-places. In time, the scenic and mechanical effects became highly ingenious and effective, particularly those associated with representations of Paradise and Hell. We read of "a Hevyne which would open", and of "a bad angyl" who entered "into Hell with thondyr". In

1520 "a skin of parchment and gunpowder" was one of the properties which added realism to a Hell scene at Kingston-on-Thames. Demons carried "black rods full of squibs" or long flaming spurs, on which were thrown handfuls of powdered resinous pitch from which issued terrible flame and smoke. *Machines* of this kind, taken over from the old-time mystery plays, had an important place in many Elizabethan and Jacobean productions. As for the mediaeval stage dresses, Adam and Eve wore skin tights of "whytt lether", doubtless to suggest their naked innocence. The stage directions in a Cornish play told the stage manager to have "ffig leaves redy to cover ther members" and, later, "garmentis of skynnes" (Alladyrce Nicoll, *Development of the Theatre*, p. 76). Nor should the importance of the miming "fool" be forgotten, the more because he was the forerunner of Shakespeare's clowns. The amateur guild-actors were only too glad to enliven their displays with some professional talent drawn from the travelling *jongleurs*.

The Renaissance Tradition

All of this implies that, in mediaeval and Renaissance times, players and public were in much closer communion than they are to-day. Indeed, Mr John Munro reminds me that a marked characteristic of early English drama was this bringing of audiences and players as closely together as possible. In the first English comedy known to be free of biblical or allegorical content, *Fulgens and Lucrece*, written by Medwell for Cardinal Morton before 1500, two of the players are ostensibly from the audience. The aside and the soliloquy were other methods of putting the audience in a privileged position in regard to the play. Another method was to allow privileged members of the audience to sit upon the stage, and of this the modern stage boxes are a vestige. Onlookers crowded so closely to the stage that there was little of the mystery which modern audiences would associate with a supposedly unknown world behind the footlights. Still another method has been to include characters in the play who are themselves an audience and speak for it. This is the method used in *The Knight of the Burning Pestle*, in *The Taming of the Shrew*, and other plays.

There is a tendency to revive such practices nowadays. The method of presenting part of a play from the auditorium was incorporated in *White Horse Inn* at the Coliseum and reached a climax of effectiveness when Charles Cochran staged *The Miracle* at Olympia, converting the vast hall into something suggesting a mediaeval cathedral. Audiences were left with a sense of having been in the actual place which the dramatist devised for the miracle of his story. Similarly, Granville-Barker, in his Shakespearean productions between 1911 and 1914, added a projecting "apron" to the Savoy proscenium and thus brought his players into closer contact with onlookers in the stalls, as well as securing more space for his stage spectacles. In vaudeville, too, a platform stage, extending well into the stalls, is used upon occasion. Lightly-clad dancers move up and down the joy plank, the producer's intention being to persuade the occupants of stalls and pit that they are enjoying more intimacy with the beauties of the stage than is customary and, in this sense, are active participants in the evening's entertainment. Robert Morley's pleasant innovation in *Edward, My Son*, when from time to time he stepped completely out of the stage picture and addressed a few confidential remarks to the audience, will be fresh in the memory.

The progress of Elizabethan tragedy and comedy from such a morality as *Everyman*, or such a "merry interlude" as *Ralph Roister Doister*, which Udall wrote for the boys of Eton College, need not be stressed. A connecting link with Shakespearean tragedy was such a thriller as Kyd's *The Spanish Tragedy*, with its ghosts and its violent deaths, but the origins were numerous and complicated, as Thorndike shows in his *Tragedy* and Cunliffe in *Early English Tragedies*.

Owing to the operation of the sharing system, the more successful actors of Elizabethan times were men of substance. At theatres, such as the Globe and the Blackfriars, the leading members of the company received a fixed percentage of the receipts. They provided their own dresses and properties and drew their shares of the takings daily after each performance, the wages of the attendants and stage-hands having first been deducted. Not until the eighteenth century did the theatrical manager arise, who accepted the risk of failure or success and in exchange gave his players weekly salaries, supplemented by occasional "benefits". The facts are set out in Chambers's *Elizabethan Stage*. The first company of Elizabethan players of which we have knowledge are the Servants of the Earl of Leicester the evidence being a patent granted to James Burbage in 1574. Four years later we come upon a record of the Children of Paul's, who began by acting mysteries and moralities. The Children of the Chapel Royal and the Children of the Revels were other early companies and all Lyly's plays and some of the plays of Ben Jonson were acted by them. Some well-known adult players of the Elizabethan and Jacobean stage learnt their trade in these companies of boy players. As a result of the growing interest in the drama no fewer than seventeen theatres were built in the London area between 1570 and 1629, when the growth of Puritanism was a prelude to the decline of drama which characterized the period of the Civil War and the rule of Cromwell.

It is not my purpose to sketch, even in the most summary fashion, the origins of modern drama in Elizabethan times. As has been said, the Renaissance dramatists tended to create individual characters and relied upon invented plots rather than upon the traditional myths of the Greeks or the Bible stories of mediaeval times. It is, however, of interest to recall the reversion of Ben Jonson, a classicist, to the type-characters of Terence, as opposed to the more highly individualized characters of Shakespeare. As he shows in *Every Man in his Humour*, Ben Jonson accepted the mediaeval theory of "humours" and regarded "the natural moistures of the brain" as determining a man's nature. Given too much of one "humour", a man was necessarily an eccentric, perhaps choleric, greedy, or testy, and the action arose from exaggerating the effects of the "humour". Ben Jonson explained:

> As when some one peculiar quality
> Doth so possess a man that it doth draw
> All his affects, his spirits and his powers
> In their confluctions all to runne one way,
> This may be truly said to be a Humer.

Hence Cutbeard was a barber, Madrigal, a poetaster, and Lickfinger, a cook. The point is interesting as the distinction between individualized characters and typical abstractions is still in being and distinguishes one class of comedy writers from that which is more interested in creating individuals.

The Restoration Tradition

When the London theatres reopened in 1660 after the Cromwellian interlude, the open-to-the-sky playhouse known to Shakespeare was a thing of the past. The new theatre resembled not the Globe which was the summer house of the Burbage-Shakespeare company, but the Blackfriars, their winter house. This was roofed and had artificial lighting. After the Restoration, plays were given on stages not only framed by a proscenium but shut off from the audience by a curtain which rose and fell to mark the beginning and end of each scene or act. This was the period when Sir William Davenant (1605-68), himself a writer of Court masques and operas, established the Drury Lane and Covent Garden Theatres, both of which have a history connecting them directly with the stage of our own times.

The curtained hall with a raised dais and the permanent architectural scenery had a longer history on the Continent than in England. The earliest Renaissance theatre was designed by Alberti in 1452 for Pope Nicholas V, and classical plays by Plautus and Terence were given in Roman theatres before the end of the century. The publication of a treatise by Vitruvius enabled the Renaissance architects to construct what they regarded as replicas of Roman theatres, in particular Palladio's theatre at Vicenza, which was opened in 1584 and included a permanent architectural background which served as scenery, after the Roman fashion.

When English plays were first acted in a closed building, such as the Blackfriars Theatre, chandeliers with candles were used, some hanging from the roof, others on either side of the stage. A candle-snuffer also attended to the guttering tallow-dips. "Snuffers! Snuffers!" was a frequent cry in London theatres from the time of Burbage to those of Edmund Kean. In the following 150 years the development of the proscenium frame, realistic scenery, and historical costumes changed the whole approach to drama and acting. At last, the fore-stage disappeared, only to be

revived occasionally in our own day by such students of the old-
time drama as William Poel and Robert Atkins.

But this was not all. Women were now appearing in London
in the feminine roles, in place of boys. In France, women had
appeared occasionally in mystery plays, taking silent parts such
as Eve, Bathsheba, Susanna, or the Virgin Mary. By 1545 Marie
Fairet was playing in plays derived from Latin sources, though
the majority of French farces were too indecent for women to
appear in them. In Italy, the Roman girl, Flaminia (about 1565)
is the first professional actress of whom a definite record remains,
but, soon, every company of comedy players in Italy had its
leading lady. Isabella Andrerni, born at Padua in 1562, became
Europe's most famous *prima donna innamorata*. She could dance
and sing, but her speciality was improvised comedy, based upon
an outlined plot, displayed in the wings. She might impersonate,
for example, a sprightly heroine, who engaged in all sorts of intrigues before she found her lover at curtain fall; or she might
dress as a man or be mistaken for a courtesan, as the rough plot
ordained. Isabella's example made possible the acting triumphs
of the French players, Madeleine and Armande Béjart, in
Molière comedy, and the women who played in the early Restoration comedies and tragedies in England.

When the comedies of manners and intrigue by Congreve,
Wycherley, and Vanbrugh were presented, it was in relatively
small theatres, where the action was increasingly thrust back
from the audience. The introduction of a proscenium, floats, and
a dividing curtain finally ended the illusion that players and
auditors were any longer participating in a common rite, an
illusion which was complete in Greek times, was potent in connection with the semi-religious dramas of the later Middle Ages,
and had not entirely disappeared in Elizabethan times.

The earliest movable scenery in English drama was made by
John Webb for Davenant's opera, *The Siege of Rhodes*. Properties
were moved in full view of the audience, liveried attendants coming in to move chairs and tables. Under the influence of the
Court masque, such scenery became more and more elaborate
and naturalistic. If realistic scenery was a relatively late-comer
in the English stage, so were historically accurate costumes. In
Elizabethan stage production there were gorgeous dresses in

plenty, but they were not historical. Their rich material and beauty of colour constituted their justification. As late as the time of David Garrick, Lady Macbeth appeared at Drury Lane in a big hoop and wig, and Macbeth wore a gorgeous Court suit, with ruffles, breeches and a powdered wig. At the Théâtre Français in Paris, the players wore curled and powdered wigs, even if the part was Oedipus or Julius Caesar, for was it not an essential in the Court dress of the eighteenth century? Madame Favart was an innovator in respect of costume, when she donned a real Turkish dress in the part of a Turkish princess, or played Queen Dido, in distress over the loss of Aeneas, clad only in a chemise. In England, when Charles Kemble played Macbeth in a Highland kilt, tartan, and bonnet, he was regarded as a rebel against established tradition. Only after Charles Kean's production of *King John* at Drury Lane in 1823, for which Planché designed the costumes, was historical realism in the background to drama regarded as an essential in successful stage productions.

Apart from the principals, the casual employment in the Elizabethan and post-Renaissance stage did not encourage a high level of professional accomplishment, so it is not surprising that the "prompter" was to the fore. In Elizabethan times, the open stage made "prompting" difficult, but a "book-holder" stood in the tiring-room and could prompt a failing memory on the open stage. After the Restoration, and with the creation of the private playhouse, the prompter achieved the position which made Sheridan say, "a steady prompter is the corner-stone in a well-regulated playhouse." Apart from a book of the words, the Restoration prompter had a bell and a whistle. With the bell he signalled to the musicians when their aid was needed, and with the whistle he indicated to the stage hands that a change of scene was imminent.

The methods of collecting audiences were equally primitive. Newspaper criticism and advertisements prior to the nineteenth century were not available, so bill-posting and processions with drums and trumpets were the accepted method "for the calling of peopell together". In 1600 we read of Henslowe buying "a drum and two trumpets to go into the country", these being judged essential during a provincial tour. As late as the eighteenth century "drum and trumpet" advertising continued in England. Sarah Kemble (Mrs Siddons), as a small child marched stiff and straight at the head of her father's company, with hands upraised, balancing a small drum on the crown of her head, while a player walking behind beat a skilful tattoo upon the sheepskin.

The Nineteenth Century

So we come to the era immediately preceding the theatre of to-day. It does not furnish material for an encouraging picture. During the hundred years between 1750 and 1850, middle-class audiences were making their first contact with the English theatre since Shakespearean times. Coarse melodrama and knockabout farce constituted the staple dramatic fare, apart from the masterpieces of Goldsmith and Sheridan and revivals of a few classical plays which offered big rôles to a Garrick, a Siddons, a Kean, or a Macready. Moreover, the new middle-class audiences called for larger theatres, so that the seating arrangements at Covent Garden and Drury Lane, the historic homes of drama in the West End of London, removed playgoers still more from the players on the stage and made the subtle inter-play of wit which characterized the comedies of Congreve and the rest no longer possible. What was best in English drama was regarded rather as "literature" than as living "theatre", so much so that Coleridge and Charles Lamb tended to criticize Elizabethan plays as presentations of poetical passages and character studies. Wordsworth wrote *The Borderers* and Keats and Armitage Brown collaborated in a play which was accepted by Drury Lane, while Shelley's *The Cenci* dates from 1819, but none of them are alive to-day, except as literature. Thomas Lovell Beddoes, in 1825, did not exaggerate when he wrote, "The man who is to awaken the drama must be a bold trampling fellow."

A melodrama is in origin a drama with music. Opera is drama set to music, a very different thing. Being a drama of situation, based primarily upon the determination to astonish, melodrama has always hovered between the exaggeration of farce and the fantasies of romance. Unlike the hero or heroine of tragedy, the creatures of melodrama have never been victims either of over-

A Mediaeval Mystery Play, as shown in Carpaccio's "Assumption of the Virgin" (*see page* 14).

A performance of
Sheridan's *School
for Scandal* in 1777
at the Drury
Lane Theatre
(*see page* 230).

riding fate (as in Greece) or of conflict in character and circumstance (as in Shakespearean tragedy). There was, indeed, justification for the slow music which served as a prelude to the suffering of hero or heroine in melodrama. Provided the situations created the all-important sense of wonder and suspense, the musical background enforced a mood fitted for the acceptance of a fable which, by hypothesis, was going to make big demands upon credulity, and was likely to be unacceptable to any except unsophisticated audiences.

Much was achieved as a consequence of the ending of the long monopoly enjoyed by the so-called Patent Houses. Covent Garden and Drury Lane owed their existence to patents granted by Charles II in 1663. With the Patent Houses must be grouped "the little theatre" in the Haymarket which enjoyed a renewable licence, first granted to Samuel Foote in 1766. These three playhouses enjoyed a monopoly of legitimate drama, including Shakespeare, Sheridan, and Congreve, so that "minor theatres" were limited by law to concerts, farces, and variety entertainments. In 1843, Parliament removed the restrictions by abolishing the monopoly of the Patent Houses.

One of the few pieces which recall the drama of the 1820's is Pierce Egan's *Tom and Jerry*, with its amusing picture of "The Corinthians". A decade or two later came Sheridan Knowles's *The Hunchback* and Bulwer Lytton's *Lady of Lyons* and *Money*. These, together with numerous dramatizations of Dickens's novels, were the pick of the basket.

Until 1833, when Parliament passed the Author's Act, writers of plays had no recognized rights in the property they had created. The only hold an author had upon his property lay in the fact that a manager had to purchase the manuscript of a play before he could produce it. Douglas Jerrold received no more than £70 when he sold the manuscript of *Black-Eyed Susan* to Elliston in 1829. This was Jerrold's sole reward for what proved to be a big money-maker, as its first run was for 150 nights. In the sphere of economics, the reform which brought about existing conditions was the passing of the American Copyright Bill in 1891, which assured the author protection in America as well as in Britain.

With royalties for the writers of successful plays and profits for

c

successful managements all over the English-speaking world, the commerical theatre came to its own. Slowly, the Bohemian elements vanished. Dramatists, players, producers, scene painters, and costumiers all added their quota of invention and experience. During the nineteenth century the scenery was largely painted and there were few, if any, of the solid "sets" which add so much interest to modern theatrical production. A host of technical innovations have followed.

In the 'sixties, the curtain of a West End theatre rose about 6.30 and the entertainment was not over until about 11.30 p.m. A typical playbill included a one-act comedy, perhaps a musical extravaganza, and a melodrama which provided the *pièce de résistance*. Many of the audience brought their evening meal with them. If not, there was a possible supper in the form of Whitstable oysters and porter, the oysters being on sale at street stalls and costing no more than 8d. a dozen.

Considered as a social institution, it is to be noted that, early in the nineteenth century, London theatres were regarded as a recognized resort of prostitutes. As late as 1844 a writer in *The Theatrical Journal* wrote of "great public brothels". Part of the service which Macready rendered to the stage of his day was his vigorous action in making the saloon in his theatre "a fit resort for any gentleman or lady". In mid-Victorian times a flavour of rogue and vagabond still hung around many London theatres and this persisted until Madame Vestris, the Bancrofts, Henry Irving, and the Gilbert and Sullivan management inaugurated their remarkable reforms. The British theatre until the 'sixties and 'seventies was primarily an entertainment for men. Largely owing to Henry Irving at the Lyceum, the Bancrofts at the Prince of Wales's and the Haymarket, the Kendals and John Hare at the St James's, and Gilbert and Sullivan at the Savoy, women in the 'eighties were attracted in ever-increasing numbers to the West End theatres. Thus, by slow but sure degrees, potential audiences were doubled because the men of the 'nineties brought their wives, sisters, daughters, and sweethearts to the theatre, instead of regarding "the Play" as primarily a masculine amusement and not very respectable at that.

Between 1843 and 1865 no new theatre was opened in London. Thereafter, they came in a full spate. The Prince of Wales's was opened in 1865, the Holborn in 1866, the Old Queen's in 1867, the Globe and the Old Gaiety in 1868, the Charing Cross in 1869, the Vaudeville in 1870, the Court and the Opéra Comique in 1871, the rebuilt Haymarket in 1879, the Old Prince's in 1880, the Criterion in 1874, and the Old Savoy in 1881.

Very memorable was the day when Marie Wilton, in company with H. J. Byron, the playwright, paid a visit to "The Dust Hole" off Tottenham Court Road and determined to convert what had been the "Queen's" into the Prince of Wales's Theatre. Miss Wilton borrowed £1,000 from a brother-in-law and began by putting in upholstered stalls and carpets. When the playwright Byron was in alliance with Marie Wilton at the Prince of Wales's, the pair used to carry home their shares of the takings each night, tied up in a pocket handkerchief. Only when the weight of coppers and silver was too great did little Marie Wilton suggest to Byron that a bank account might be desirable. Marie Wilton married Squire Bancroft and it was the Bancroft management which first tucked the orchestra under the stage. It did much to popularize the matinée and paid full salaries to every one concerned in it.

When it is added that the Bancroft management originated the "ten-shilling stalls", and established the precedent of "one play a night", the debt the modern theatre owes to Marie Wilton is plain. Her first play was a Byron burlesque but the decisive change came when she accepted Robertson's *Society* with the remark, "It's better to be dangerous than to be dull." Clement Scott, who saw the first night on 11 November 1865, tells of the delight of playgoers when Bancroft, well-dressed and with his cheery enthusiasm and boyish manner, made love to a pretty girl. Hitherto, stage lovers had tended to be sixty years of age and "dressed like waiters at a penny-ice shop". Sir Squire and Lady Bancroft in fact inaugurated a revolution in comedy production which was the counterpart of Irving's work at the Lyceum in romantic drama and Shakespearean plays. Scenery-doors which opened, furniture of the period, stage carpets, and ceilings were among the Bancroft changes. As a result, a school of natural acting and natural play-writing became possible.

Tom Robertson, by the way, was equally gifted as dramatist and producer. W. S. Gilbert, himself a master of stage manage-

Design, by Our Church-and-Stage-Guilded Youth, for a Stained-Glass Window, to be put up in the Church of SS. Maria, Bancroftius, et Caecilus, at Pontresina.

24

ment, frequently attended Robertson's rehearsals and said: "I look upon stage management, as now understood, as having been absolutely invented by Tom Robertson."

On the producing side, John Hare used to say that Robertson had the gift of conveying to his players an immediate insight into the characters assigned to them. In Clement Scott's words, "Robertson seemed to read his plays and act them at the same time."

And the crowning wonder was that adequate rehearsals, stage carpets and ceilings, clear diction and good manners in conduct and costume did not land managements in the Bankruptcy Court. The Bancrofts were still in the 'forties when they retired with a fortune of £180,000. Garrick left £120,000, but with this exception no estate of an actor-manager approached that of Squire Bancroft until earnings from films radically altered the standard of remuneration.

What emerges from this necessarily hasty survey of the European stage over two thousand years is that, whenever a fresh body of ideas arises, accepted theatrical tradition and technique must be changed. Dramatists and actors alike must find forms better fitted to express the new thought and give the new characters life. Just as the rationalists who followed in the wake of Ibsen discarded the aside and the soliloquy, so dramatists who are exploring the world of the sub-conscious to-day are finding unexpected virtues in the aside and the soliloquy, unreal as these seemed fifty years ago. Eugene O'Neill wrote in this connection: "It is only by some form of 'super-naturalism' that we may express in the theatre what we comprehend intuitively of that self-obsession which is the particular discount we moderns have to pay for the loan of life."

The chief difference between drama in the second half of the nineteenth century and that mid-way through the twentieth century, is that, to-day, the typical dramatist is less interested in exciting situation than was formerly the case. Instead, he works upon a generalized idea, seeking characters, dialogue, and a setting which will express it. One reason is that the multiplicity of facts put before the public in books, magazines, newspapers, the wireless, and the cinema are forcing the dramatist, like the journalist and the broadcaster, to become a popularizer and interpreter of the ever-changing world of fact and idea.

CHAPTER 2

THE PLAYHOUSE

FEW factors are more fundamental in the theatre than those associated directly with the playhouse. We have noted the special conditions arising from the open-air stage of the Greeks and the semi-open-air stage of Elizabethan times. Such factors as the size of a modern theatre, or the tradition it may have established through association with a particular type of entertainment, call for similar understanding if the playbills of the recent past and the productions of to-day are to reveal their full significance. Indeed, these factors have greater importance than ever owing to the heavy capital expenditure arising from competition with the "talkies".

When Oswald Stoll staged *White Horse Inn* the Coliseum was the chosen theatre. It seats about 2,200 and Stoll knew that only his outsize theatre could justify an outsize chorus and the big amount which had to be spent upon scenery and costumes if a musical comedy was to rival a spectacular film. Moreover, all Oswald Stoll's contacts had been with the popular theatre. As a boy he helped his mother in managing the Old Parthenon music-hall in Liverpool and went on to develop the two-shows-a-night system, later extended to the theatres which the Stoll organizations established all over Britain in partnership with Edward Moss.

The problem which Sir Oswald Stoll faced when he produced *White Horse Inn* is continually before the managements of the larger London theatres. It was the problem which the owners of the Dominion Theatre at the corner of Tottenham Court Road and Oxford Street failed to solve. It had seating accommodation fully as large as the Coliseum and was intended to be a super-theatre suited for spectacular musical comedies and revues. So large is the Dominion that a management once paid Maurice Chevalier £4,000 a week for a two weeks' season. Chevalier was earning £80,000 a year from such films as *The Love Parade* or *The Innocents of Paris*, so the fee had to be large. With stalls at 14s. 6d. apiece and two performances a day, the Dominion estimated that £20,000 would come into the box-office, so there seemed to be a margin of profit even when Maurice Chevalier had taken his inordinate share. Unhappily, there was only one Maurice Chevalier and his charm only crowded the Dominion for a week or two. Lupino Lane in *Silver Wings*, singing "When I am with you, I'm happy, and, when I'm without you, I'm blue," is one of the few memories which theatre-goers cherish from the Dominion association with vaudeville. All too quickly it passed into the devouring maw of the cinema.

The saddening fact means no more in the realm of artistry than Henry Irving's dictum: "The drama must succeed as a business, if it is not to fail as an art." Lewis Waller coined a variant when he asked plaintively, "What shall it profit a manager if he fills his whole pit but has to paper his stalls?" Managers who forget the truth suffer, even if they do not suffer in the same degree as the confiding investors who put up the money for bricks and mortar in the first instance.

Noel Coward's *Cavalcade* took the form it did precisely because it was designed for the largest theatre in London. Drury Lane seats about 2,350. Similarly, when *Oklahoma!* reached London in 1947, it had 1,400 performances on Broadway to its credit and more than two million New Yorkers had paid to see it, in addition to 1,918,000 in American provincial cities. Plainly, a smaller theatre would not only have been unsuitable for so colourful a production, but it could not have hoped to cater for the big audiences that were to be expected. It is noteworthy that Noel Coward's *Pacific, 1860* was too flimsy in structure and on too small a scale to serve Drury Lane. Coward laid his background in one of those fancy-fed Pacific islands which are the counterpart in musical comedy of the Ruritanias of the romantic novelist. To Samolo came a vaudeville star and the exchange of kisses with the hero quickly called for a choice between love and a professional career. Daphne Anderson, singing, "I wish I wasn't quite such a big girl" and other pleasant trifles in *Pacific, 1860* would doubtless have earned a year's run at a rather smaller theatre, but not at Drury Lane.

For a musical show which calls for rather less spectacle than *Oklahoma!* a London theatre should seat about 1,200 nightly. When George Edwardes took over Daly's in 1893 and began to stage the memorable series of comic operas which included *The Geisha* and *The Merry Widow*, the theatre held 1,225 people, while His Majesty's, where *Chu Chin Chow* had its record run, holds 1,320, rather fewer than the London Hippodrome, where Ivor Novello presented his romantic comic-operas. The Adelphi, with

Mr Punch Pays Tribute to a Great Trio

seating accommodation ranging from 1,100 to 1,200, depending upon the number of stalls as opposed to pit seats, is ideal for a modern musical show. Until W. H. Berry came upon the scene at the Adelphi, the house was popularly associated with melodrama, and particularly with the brand which William Terriss dispensed so successfully in the 'nineties. After Terriss's murder the Adelphi drifted along uneasily, until Bill Berry entered upon the two-thousand appearances which made him murmur, "I suppose I go with the gas brackets."

The larger musical shows are so costly nowadays that they cannot pay their way in smaller theatres. These must be content to stage intimate revue if the management is interested in music. A musical comedy or romance must attract at least £2,000 a week if the cast, the orchestra, and the back-stage staff are to be paid. Only then does the management begin to pay off initial costs and earn a real profit. When Gilbert and Sullivan and D'Oyly Carte were each earning £20,000 a year at the Savoy, the weekly expenses totalled about £800. When George Edwardes took over the Old Gaiety and produced *The Shop Girl* he was not unhappy if the takings were £1,000 a week. A management would be facing certain bankruptcy on a similar basis to-day.

I have insisted upon the desirability of fitting the theatre precisely to the type of play. Nevertheless, important as the right theatre is, the right management may be equally important. When Charles Cochran made up his mind to make the Pavilion a centre for spectacular revue, and transferred the nucleus of his company from the Ambassadors', he was faced with the very small Pavilion stage. Indeed, the solitary entrance to the stage was so small that women wearing hooped gowns could not enter. Yet Cochran's productions at the Pavilion made an average profit of £15,000 and only one of them actually lost money. If ever there was a natural showman it was Charles Cochran. When the script of *The Better 'Ole* came into his hands in 1917 and he decided to produce the play, his comment was, "It's a question of getting the right theatre." The showman's genius displayed itself when he added, "I should like the Oxford music hall. That is a theatre with an atmosphere redolent of Old Bill and beer." The Oxford it was and Bairnsfather's "Fragment from France" registered 811 performances. The Oxford had arisen from the inn-yard of the Boar and Castle, hence the good brown ale atmosphere.

The Lyric Theatre, as the name suggests, was built in 1888 out of the profits earned by the opera *Dorothy*, and seats almost 1,300. The Prince of Wales's (1,200) and, of course, the Gaiety, with 1,250 seats, are other theatres suitable for substantial musical shows. So was the old Empire, with its 1,340 seats. The Savoy, in the palmy days of Gilbert and Sullivan, seated about 1,080. A larger theatre would be needed to-day. Indeed, some very successful Gilbert and Sullivan revivals were staged at the Prince's Theatre in Shaftesbury Avenue, which holds 1,850.

Of such kind are the factors which largely determine the length of a run, the price of tickets, the salaries of actors and actresses, what will stand revival, and what new plays have some chance of making money at the theatre selected for their production.

The Comedy Houses

The Criterion, holding 560, is a delightful house for light comedy. It was built in 1874 by Spiers and Pond on the site of the Piccadilly dancing saloon. Attached to the theatre was the Long Bar, where the "Criterion Boys" congregated. Not a few of them were known to the police. The first lessee of the Criterion was William Duck, who paid Spiers and Pond a beggarly £50 a week. Charles Wyndham took the lease from Duck and the palmy days of the Criterion opened, at first with farces, such as *Brighton*. Later, the Criterion was the home of *David Garrick* which alone must have given the management a net profit of £100,000, as Wyndham paid no royalties, having bought the play outright from Robertson.

The Criterion was reconstructed in 1903 and since then has had Terence Rattigan's *French Without Tears*, with a run of 1,030 performances, to its credit. The Criterion, however, is on the small side, and when Sir Charles and Mary Moore built a theatre, Wyndham's, more precisely suited to their needs, they arranged a seating accommodation of 730. The building of Wyndham's was not a lone venture. With it was associated a somewhat larger theatre on an adjoining site, the New. This has seats for 940 and served perfectly for such a production as Shaw's *St Joan*, John Gielgud's production of *Richard of Bordeaux*, and the memorable Old Vic revivals in the mid-'forties, with Sir Laurence Olivier and Sir Ralph Richardson as the stars, were later triumphs. The Criterion, Wyndham's, and the New maintained their connection with the Wyndham family, being managed by Howard Wyndham, a son of Sir Charles by his first wife, and Sir Bronson Albery, a son of Mary Moore.

The Duchess, which was built in 1929 and seats 494, is akin to the Criterion as a house eminently suitable for comedies with small and relatively inexpensive casts. It can claim the larger part of credit for the record run of Noel Coward's *Blithe Spirit* (1,997 performances), though the play was produced at the Piccadilly. The Court, with seats for 642, was another ideal house for light comedy and farce, as was Terry's Theatre in the Strand, with seats for 665. The Pinero farces and comedies, among them *The Magistrate*, *The Times*, and *Sweet Lavender*, were given at the Court and Terry's, while the Court was also the scene of the Vedrenne-Barker management between 1905 and 1908, which included Shaw's *You Never Can Tell* and *John Bull's Other Island*.

For Mayfair drama which calls for more elaborate dressing and more costly scenery, a rather larger house, such as the St James's, is needed. When Sir George Alexander ruled at the St James's the theatre held 1,200, but Alexander did not confine his productions to modern comedy and though his Shakespearean productions did not compete with the spectacles staged by Irving and Forbes-Robertson at the Lyceum or by Tree at His Majesty's, they were fully worthy. Rather more than 1,800 made a full house when Irving, Ellen Terry, Forbes-Robertson, and Mrs Patrick Campbell were the attractions at the Lyceum, while Tree could welcome 1,320 to His Majesty's.

At first sight the St James's Theatre would seem somewhat apart from recognizable theatre-land, but it came into being long before Shaftesbury Avenue arose. John Braham, the singer and composer of "The Death of Nelson", bought a hotel and spent £26,000 upon a theatre primarily for his wife. The venture failed and Braham lost about £80,000. Indeed, the St James's was a dire failure until Mitchell, the Bond Street librarian, leased it and presented the great Rachel in a series of French plays. Then Mr John Wood brought the theatre into the limelight. Its real fame dates from between 1879 and 1888, when Hare and the Kendals managed the St James's. They paid a rental of £30 a week, that is to say £1,560 a year, and the Kendals were on the salary list for £25 a week, as was Hare, though Madge Kendal was the real draw. An early production, *Impulse*, adapted from the French, made £30,000 profit, after a nine months' run.

Alexander took over the St James's on 31 January 1891 and continued there until March 1918. He rarely produced a play which did not pay its way, though he experimented with sixty-two full-length plays. The St James's has not enjoyed such a management since Alexander's death.

The advantages arising from associating a definite type of entertainment with a particular theatre can be illustrated from the success attending the decade when Cyril Maude and Winifred Emery were the stars at the Haymarket. They had been playing at the Comedy, when Comyns Carr was in control, with aid from his clever wife and Stuart Ogilvie. Pinero's *Benefit of the Doubt* was one of the Comedy productions. When the venture failed, Cyril Maude and Winifred Emery contemplated management at the Garrick. Frederick Harrison, however, who had been unlucky in partnership with Forbes-Robertson, had a better idea. He suggested Cyril Maude and himself should lease the Haymarket, which he knew intimately as he had been there as Tree's business manager. When Tree built His Majesty's with the profits made from *Trilby*, the Haymarket was ready to receive the Maudes and they began with *Under the Red Robe*, a stirring romance by Stanley Weyman, in which Herbert Waring was brilliant as Gil de Berault. There followed twenty outstanding successes, including *She Stoops to Conquer*, *The Rivals*, and *The School for Scandal* in a single season.

The Garrick, which W. S. Gilbert built for John Hare from the profits he made from Savoy opera, is another house usually associated with comedy. Its triumphs include the memorable star-cast production of *Diplomacy*, for which Hare tempted the Bancrofts to return to the stage. Here, too, Arthur Bourchier and Violet Vanbrugh staged a number of Sutro comedies early in the century. It holds 1,250 people when full.

A speculator named Sefton Parry built the Avenue, now the Playhouse, believing the site was certain to be taken over by an extension of the railway station, and it opened in 1882 with a revival of *Madame Favart*, Fred Leslie being in the cast, together with Florence St John and Marius. A year or two later Arthur Roberts was playing there as Joe Tarradiddle in Offenbach's *La Vie*. Later came notable managements under Charles Hawtrey and Cyril Maude. The latter rebuilt the Avenue and renamed it the Playhouse. Noteworthy, too, were the days when Frank Curzon held the lease, with Gladys Cooper as his partner. Their

revival of *The Second Mrs Tanqueray* will not be forgotten. The
Playhouse needs a policy suited to its size. It is as cosy and comfortable a theatre as any in London.

The Stoll, with seats for 2,090, which has staged successful ice
spectacles, the Victoria Palace, where 1,500 nightly moved their
feet to the rhythms of "The Lambeth Walk", the Shaftesbury,
where 1,300 more did the same service when the *Belle of New
York* was making theatrical history, are other theatres which call
for mention in this connection. It may be added that Covent
Garden as a theatre seated 1,950, the Old Alhambra 1,650, and
the Old Vic in Waterloo Road, 1,454.

Intimate Revue

The theatres suited for intimate revue are the Ambassadors'
(490 seats), the Vaudeville (650 seats), and the Little Theatre
(375 seats). The Vaudeville was opened in 1870 and for some
time was the oldest theatre in London, except Drury Lane and
the Haymarket. The first management was that of the well-
known trio, David James, H. J. Montague, and Tom Thorne.
When they opened the Vaudeville the theatre cost £30 a week to
run and the Bar alone paid all expenses. This was one reason for
the popularity of the Vaudeville in the last quarter of the nineteenth century. Experiments were possible, without bankruptcy
necessarily following a failure. H. J. Byron's farce, *Our Boys*, was
an early success, with David James, as Perkyn Middlewick, the
retired butterman. At the Vaudeville, too, in its early days,
Henry Irving made a memorable appearance as Digby Grant in
Two Roses, one of his comedy triumphs. In 1892, the Gatti
brothers purchased the Vaudeville and its modern history began,
the years in which Seymour Hicks and Ellaline Terriss were the
bright and particular stars leading to the revues associated with
André Charlot, which gave Bea Lillie and Gertrude Lawrence
their early opportunities.

To the Ambassadors' belong Charles Cochran's early experiments in revue at the beginning of the first World War, while the
Little Theatre, which dates back to 1910, associated itself with
the Herbert Farjeon revues which took their name and character

from the tiny theatre. The Whitehall, which was built in 1930 and seats 620, could be converted into a very acceptable home for intimate revue of the Gate Theatre type. So might the Fortune Theatre in Drury Lane, which seats about 500 people and is approximately the size of the Ambassadors'. The Fortune was opened in 1928 and was valued at £100,000. It belied its name and soon was on offer at a price which did little more than cover the debenture-holders.

If seating capacity and kindred money problems are important in the world of the theatre, so is the comfort, physical and psychological, of playgoers. Kyrle Bellew, Arthur Bourchier's second wife, bought a long lease of the Strand Theatre in Aldwych towards the end of the first World War, after it had suffered numerous vicissitudes. Being a woman, Kyrle Bellew's main idea was to make her theatre a happy one for women. She experimented with lighting and flowers, particularly with lighting. "What is the reaction of a woman who suddenly realizes that the wrong lighting is ruining a pretty frock?" Directly Kyrle Bellew put the question, she realized that no woman would really enjoy a play unless good lighting gave her complexion and frock their chance. So at the Strand, in the 'thirties, the lighting of the auditorium was made perfect and complexions and dresses alike were just right.

The Commercial Managements

There are many more theatres than there were 150 years ago and the playgoing public has greatly increased, but it is not a fact that the financial rewards due to successful ventures have greatly changed. After Charles Kean played Shylock at Drury Lane for the first time on that memorable 27th of January 1814, the season lasted sixty-eight nights and the receipts averaged £484 9s. od. a night, the gross takings totalling £32,942. Nor were Kean's takings a record. Ten years earlier, William Henry Best had played twenty-eight times at Drury Lane and his aggregate takings were £57,210, that is £614 a night, or £130 more than those of Charles Kean.

What has changed for the players has been the fortunes to be made in acting for the films and, on the production side, the huge sums of capital required owing to the growing cost of playhouses. No longer can an actor-manager afford to control and manage his own theatre as Irving did, as Tree did, as Alexander did. To-day, in the majority of cases, a string of theatres is controlled by men who necessarily regard theatrical productions as potential money-makers, rather than as aids to a fuller artistry.

Between the two wars the name H. M. Tennent graced many a theatrical programme. Mr Tennent was a producing manager, representing substantial monied interests, and after his death the business continued as H. M. Tennent Ltd, with Mr Hugh Beaumont and Mr A. Stewart Cruikshank in control. In a single month (June 1943) H. M. Tennent (Productions) Ltd was responsible for eight London theatres. Here is the tally: Aldwych, Lillian Hellman's *Watch on the Rhine;* Apollo, Terence Rattigan's *Flare Path;* Cambridge, Shaw's *Heartbreak House;* Duchess, Coward's *Blithe Spirit;* Globe, Priestley's *They Came to a City;* Haymarket, Noel Coward's *Eight Thirty;* Phoenix, Congreve's *Love for Love;* St James's, Turgenev's *A Month in the Country.* Surely as business propositions go, a very worthy tally. *Robert's Wife,* Coward's *Operette,* Dodie Smith's *Dear Octopus,* and *Thunder Rock* are other plays we owe to the Tennent organizations.

Firth Shephard was another business manager who controlled a considerable section of the London stage, particularly on the lighter side. Mr Shephard began his career as a *siffleur;* he whistled for a living at masonic and other convivial functions, in days when entertainers could pick up a few shillings and even an occasional guinea at such work. From this stage work he passed on to authorship, particularly the lighter type of revue. *Shephard's Pie* of 1925 and *Lady Luck* of 1927 are to his credit. He wrote *Lady Luck* in collaboration with Greatrex Newman. By 1928, Mr Shephard was in partnership with Leslie Henson and, after 1935, in management on his own account. *The Housemaster, Going Greek,* and *Arsenic and Old Lace* are typical Firth Shephard successes. "See a Shephard Show" is advice which audiences accepted with alacrity for over a decade, though usually without any understanding of the significance of the fact from the standpoint of the economics of a fully worthy "theatre".

When Sir Oswald Stoll passed away, the Stoll Theatres

Corporation came under the control of Prince Littler and, in 1943, His Majesty's, the Adelphi, the St James's, the Lyric, the Apollo, and the Cambridge were all under Littler's control, with Jack Hylton owner of a substantial number of shares and thus participating in the management. In addition, Stoll Theatres Corporation, with an issued capital of £2,102,417, owned or controlled the London Coliseum, the Stoll Theatre, Kingsway, and a long series of "Palaces", "Empires", and "Hippodromes" all over the country. Nor does the Littler interest end with Prince Littler. There is Emile Littler, with his pantomimes, and Blanche Littler, who is joint managing director of Prince Littler Theatres and Tours Ltd.

Again, Tom Arnold was originally a clerk in the office of the De Frece music-hall circuit. He entered on a large scale into theatrical business as a touring manager, chiefly with musical shows. These eventually numbered more than a hundred. When Julian Wylie died in 1934 Tom Arnold acquired his pantomime properties and he also manages the Ivor Novello productions. A lease of the Palace Theatre is one of Mr Arnold's activities.

Lee Ephraim hails from Hopkinsville, Kentucky, and came to England in 1909, becoming managing director of Daniel Mayer Co. Ltd, and thus responsible for such shows as *Havoc* (1924) and *Rose Marie* (1925). When Ephraim left the Mayer Company, he formed Lee Ephraim Co. Ltd and produced *Sunny* at the Hippodrome, *The Desert Song* at Drury Lane, *Blue Eyes* at the Piccadilly, *Lilac Time* at Daly's, *Funny Face* at the Prince's, and *Gay Divorce* at the Palace, a truly varied bunch.

Gilbert Miller, like Lee Ephraim, is an American but he had early associations with Charles Hawtrey and Henry Ainley, when the latter was an actor-manager at the St James's. *The Green Goddess*, *The Last of Mrs Cheyney*, *Interference*, *The Late Christopher Bean*, *Berkeley Square*, *Tovarich*, and *Victoria Regina* were among the Gilbert Miller productions, apart from those in the United States. He controls the St James's Theatre as I write.

Jack Waller began as an instrumentalist in a minstrel troupe and for several years was a music-hall entertainer of recognized talent. He became proprietor of the Seven Butterflies concert party in 1910 and twelve years later entered into the memorable partnership with Herbert Clayton, which gave London *No, No,*

Nanette, *Mercenary Mary*, *Hit the Deck*, and *Silver Wings*. After the Clayton partnership was dissolved Jack Waller produced *He Wanted Adventure* and *Please Teacher*. Here is a manager of full competence, who can select and train a chorus and has the widest experience of management—in fact, a man of the theatre.

A deep and abiding enthusiasm for the theatre is, of course, sufficient justification for embarking upon theatrical ventures, and Anmer Hall is a man with such an enthusiasm. Though a chairman of rubber companies and ex-master of the Clothworkers Company, Anmer Hall (Alderson Horne) has found time not only to act but to produce plays. In particular, he had a lease of the Westminster between 1931 and 1947, his productions including Bridie's *The Anatomist* and *Tobias and the Angel* and Eugene O'Neill's *Anna Christie* and *Mourning Becomes Electra*.

Sydney Carroll is another former producer who has brought more than a knowledge of the theatre to management. Boundless enthusiasm was Sydney Carroll's asset. Sir Barry Jackson and Alec Rea, Basil Dean's partner in Reandean, and later the moving spirit in Reandco, have a similar justification for theatrical management. At one time a successful shipowner and merchant in Liverpool, Alec Rea came to the stage as Chairman of the Liverpool Repertory Theatre.

London Suburban Production Houses

Between 1924 and 1939, some of the most promising London productions were introduced at small suburban theatres, such as the Embassy, the "Q", or the Mercury, Notting Hill. The Mercury was opened on the strength of a welcome £10,000 which Ashley Dukes, scholar, dramatist, and critic, made out of his delightful romance, *The Man With a Load of Mischief*, as he tells us in his autobiography, *The Scene is Changed*. Incidentally, this charming volume includes a telling and connected argument in favour of the revival of poetic drama in Britain, an argument which has since been reinforced by the production in 1945 of *This Way to the Tomb*, the modern morality which brought Ronald Duncan and Benjamin Britten into partnership.

A parish hall and a couple of adjoining houses just off Notting

D

Hill Gate were converted into a bijou playhouse, and a talk with W. B. Yeats and T. S. Eliot persuaded Ashley Dukes to run the Mercury as a Poets' Theatre. Eliot's *Murder in the Cathedral* was the opening venture at the Mercury. After its first production in the Chapter House at Canterbury, critics were quick to recognize the worth and originality of the play. The Mercury version was rather more elaborate than that given at Canterbury and the element of a chronicle play was less evident. It thus became the plainer that Eliot, as poet, had a message for his own age. Indeed, the speeches of the Four Knights towards the end of the play seemed as up-to-date in their appeal as the Epilogue of *Saint Joan* had seemed in 1924. The Knights spoke to the people of Britain as Fascist or Nazi totalitarians would have done, if a twentieth-century Lincoln had been murdered by four plain Englishmen, "who put their country first". The Mercury only has about 150 seats, yet Eliot's play completed a run of nine months and was seen by 20,000 people, and since then it has been seen all over the world. Moreover the success of *Murder in the Cathedral* encouraged a number of young writers to explore the possibilities of poetic symbolism as a medium for the expression of twentieth-century experience. The matter is discussed more fully in a later chapter. Incidentally, T. S. Eliot's lead encouraged experiments in the versification of the rhythms of latter-day speech, a very different thing from mere variants upon the blank verse formula which had served Shakespeare and his Elizabethan contemporaries well enough, but had shown itself to have little more than survival value apart from Elizabethan drama. Auden and Isherwood, with their expressionistic plays, and Sean O'Casey, with *Within the Gates*, were among those who made verse experiments and associated them with post-war themes, seeking to attune the reactions of audiences to the old-time appeal.

Nearer the theatrical centre is the Arts Theatre, in Newport Street, off Leicester Square. Founded in 1942 by Alec Clunes, the Arts enrolled over 20,000 associate-members in six years, apart from 4,500 full club members. Mr Clunes is entitled to claim that he founded the Arts Theatre as it had only 250 members when he took it over. *Awake and Sing* by Clifford Odets was the first production, and plays by James Bridie, John

Masefield, Somerset Maugham, Pinero, Sheridan, J. M. Synge, Eugene O'Neill, and Peter Ustinov have followed. The five shillings subscriptions of the 20,000 associate-members make relatively cheap seats possible and assured audiences enable the Arts to experiment not only with new plays but with lesser known actors and actresses. All members of the company receive £5 a week regardless of their standing in the profession and the average run is only three weeks.

Still in the thirties, Alec Clunes comes of theatrical stock and was a member of the Old Vic company for a time. His Hamlet, in a revival at the Arts Theatre in 1945, revealed an actor of parts, to be added to his gifts as director and producer. That a non-commercial venture of this type should have such success is a portent of importance for the future of the British Stage.

If the venture at the Arts Theatre is full of promise, that at the Old Vic and Sadler's Wells can claim astonishing achievement. The credit belongs in the first place to Dame Lilian Baylis, but there must be added a tribute to talents and enthusiasms as varied as those of Rosina Filippi, Matheson Lang, Ben Greet, G. R. Foss, Robert Atkins, and Tyrone Guthrie. Both the theatres have a history of more than a century. The beginnings of Sadler's Wells date back to the seventeenth century, when a man named Sadler exploited a mineral spring near Islington, in rivalry with those at Epsom and Tunbridge Wells. In 1683 there was a "musick house" which helped to popularize the medicinal side of the business. Similarly, the Old Vic in Georgian and Victorian times added semi-theatrical entertainments to a general business as a coffee tavern. A new era opened when Dame Lilian Baylis took over the Old Vic in 1897, bent upon doing something for the culture of South London, in association with the more prosaic task of furnishing coffee at reasonable prices to the people of Lambeth. A modest beginning. The venture revealed its full potentialities when Dame Lilian, in the 'twenties, rebuilt Sadler's Wells to serve as "The Old Vic of North London".

The achievements of Dame Lilian and her associates can best be judged from the fact that every play of Shakespeare has been given by a first-rate company, though, in 1913, Rosina Filippi with difficulty found means to present a Shakespeare play one night a week for a single month. During the first World War Shakespeare established himself in South London and there followed the inter-war years when most of the stars of to-day were glad and proud to play at modest salaries in support of Dame Lilian's noble endeavour. To-day, the Old Vic and Sadler's Wells venture, regarded as a great whole, is very near to being a national theatre and this with all the virtues of free enterprise. Dame Sybil Thorndike, Sir Laurence Olivier, Sir Ralph Richardson, and John Gielgud are only a few of the players who have added to their own stature as artists, while supporting this best of all theatrical ventures in our islands. "Nothing venture, nothing have!"

The "try-out" houses, most of which are in the near suburbs, are necessarily small. The Arts Theatre, which may be described as a West End "try-out" house, though this does less than justice to the big experiment, seats 334. The Westminster, with 580 seats, is another West End theatre suitable for productions which appeal to a limited number of playgoers. At the "Q" Theatre, Kew, which seats 497, Jack de Lion produced more than a hundred plays within two years, ten of which later justified revival at larger West End theatres. The rule at the "Q" was a new production every week. It was too many.

At the Embassy, Swiss Cottage, where 678 people can find seats, Ronald Adam began in 1932 with a capital of £87 and in four years a hundred plays were produced, of which twenty were transferred to West End theatres. What unrecognized dramatists thought of the Embassy management is suggested by the fact that Mr Adam was asked to read 1,500 plays in a single year. The Embassy was originally the Hampstead Conservatoire of Music and it was converted into a theatre when the success of Sir Nigel Playfair at Hammersmith suggested that the fortunes of suburban theatres might be growing. Ronald Adam found he could produce a full-length play and run it for a fortnight at the cost of approximately £750, a small sum compared with most West End try-outs. *Miracle at Verdun*, with its thirteen scenes and its hundred characters, *Ten Minute Alibi*, and *The Dominant Sex* were among the Embassy successes. All would have been easy if the Embassy management had drawn the profits upon its West End ventures, instead of a modest commission. *Ten Minute Alibi* brought £15,000 clear profit to the original backer, who chanced also to be a millionaire.

The Embassy was badly blitzed and, after the second World War, it was taken over by Anthony Hawtrey, a son of Sir Charles. In three years Hawtrey produced thirty-five plays at the Embassy, a number of which were translated to the West End for a further run. A club and a dramatic school are attached to the Embassy.

The Everyman, Hampstead, began as a drill-hall, but the guidance of Norman Macdermott and Malcolm Morley in the 'twenties converted it into an accepted London theatre. It is not without significance that Macdermott ignored any temptation to put down Turkey or Persian carpets in auditorium or foyer and asked his clientele to be content with inexpensive and lasting coconut matting. What he had in mind was a small and intimate try-out house, whence promising plays could be transferred to the recognized West End theatres, if they were successful in Hampstead. Moreover, Macdermott and Malcolm Morley recognized that the same law applied to the body of players upon whom they could draw. They also had to be keen, and prove their keenness by their willingness to accept a fixed £5 a week during the Hampstead run, regardless of their position in the profession. Of course, when a play went on to a West End theatre, normal salaries were resumed. One outstanding virtue in the Everyman experiment was that it revealed that many players of worth were willing to take a chance with a promising play. Lilian Braithwaite's appearance in Noel Coward's *The Vortex* was only one example.

The Lyric, Hammersmith, is an outstanding example of a theatre, well away from Shaftesbury Avenue, attracting sufficient audiences year after year to justify a management bent upon giving Londoners its best. When Nigel Playfair produced *The Beggar's Opera* playgoers travelled to Hammersmith five and ten times. They gave a welcome only less hearty to Edith Evans and Robert Loraine in a Congreve comedy. Yet no theatre could have shown less promise of burgeoning into the equivalent of a West End house. Playfair began by interesting Arnold Bennett in the venture and the novelist persuaded several of his friends to subscribe £1,000 apiece. Bennett, however, refused to risk any of his own money. "Time is money," he said. "I risk my time in theatres and I won't risk both time and money." Instead, he became chairman of Playfair's board of directors and served in the capacity for seven years. A week's takings at the Lyric could produce a maximum of £1,200, and during the three and a half years run of *The Beggar's Opera* the company played to an average of £900 a week. The success of *Abraham Lincoln* was no less decisive and it placed the Lyric on London's theatrical map.

Provincial Repertory

Sir Barry Jackson was a business man and blessed with ample means and as a man of business he established the Birmingham Repertory Company just before the War of 1914 and it remained his sole responsibility until the civic authorities lent their aid to the venture. Prior to the war of 1939 the general policy was to present eight plays in a season, two being classics, two revivals of well-known modern plays, two completely new plays, and two oddments. Thus *A Midsummer Night's Dream* and *The School for Scandal* were produced as the classics in one season, Mr Bridie's *The Anatomist* being a revival and Miss Mary Sheridan's *The Courageous Sex* the new original play. An ardent playgoer from childhood, Barry Jackson saw Miss Horniman's productions at Manchester and registered a mental vow to do a similar service for his own city, Birmingham. The earliest performances of the Birmingham Players were given in the dining room at "The Grange"—the home of Jackson's parents. Foote's *The Liar* was given in 1903 and *Twelfth Night* in 1904, *The Interlude of Youth* (a morality) following in 1907, with Drinkwater and Barry Jackson in the cast. This led to a public performance in a mission hall and the Pilgrim Players were inaugurated. Jackson designed the dresses and scenery, *Eager Heart* being an early production. The names of actors were not printed on the early programmes, and the company painted their own scenery, usually on Sunday mornings.

A more professional element was introduced when Barry Jackson utilized the Edgbaston Assembly Rooms, which seated 400, and produced *The Two Gentlemen of Verona. The Importance of*

Being Earnest followed in 1908, *Eager Heart* being the customary Christmas fare. In all thirty-five performances were given in 1910-11, a remarkable achievement, as the players were making a living in business. Moreover, the hall was seldom more than half full and Jackson had to make good considerable deficiencies. By 1911 a touring party was added to the labours of the Pilgrim Players, some travelling to the villages on bicycles and some in Jackson's car. There were also pastoral performances during the summer.

By 1913 Barry Jackson had decided to build his own theatre and the career of the Pilgrim Players ended, being replaced by Birmingham Repertory, with John Drinkwater as general manager. Bache Matthews, who has written the story of the venture, was its business manager. Galsworthy's *The Pigeon* was the first modern play produced, and *Candida* followed, with Madge Mackintosh as Candida. Hankin's *The Cassilis Engagement* was also revived nine times, Maeterlinck's *The Death of Tintagiles*, Schnitzler's *A Farewell Supper*, and Chapin's *Augustus in Search of a Father* made up a triple bill in 1913-14. The opening of the first World War brought difficulties in its train, but twenty-two new plays were produced, Ion Swinley being with the company for a time. By 1918-19 William J. Rea was in the company and *Abraham Lincoln* was produced. It ran for a month and, in February 1919, went to the Lyric, Hammersmith, and ran for 466 performances. Boughton's *The Immortal Hour* came in 1920-21, and forty-two performances were given before Jackson put it on at the Regent, London. In all 421 performances of this musical drama were given, with Gwen Ffrangcon-Davies as Etain. Nor must *The Farmer's Wife* be forgotten. It was produced during the war, with Hardwicke as Churdles Ash, the sharp-tongued old misogynist. *The Farmer's Wife* in due course came to London. At the Court Theatre it went slowly at first. Then suddenly "House Full" notices were displayed and eventually it reached 1,300 performances. Here was evidence of outstanding achievement, yet it is the barest outline of the achievements of Birmingham Repertory. *Cymbeline* in modern dress was given in 1922-23, the first "Shakespeare" in plus-fours. The King wore the uniform of a field-marshal and in the wager scene the guests were in evening dress. Imogen was a boy in knickerbockers and a cap in her disguise. Shaw was so pleased with the company's work in his *Heartbreak House* that he agreed to *Back to Methuselah* being attempted.

The Malvern Festival was an extension of the Birmingham Repertory Company's activities. Here, Sir Barry Jackson's purpose was to unite the characteristics of a garden party, a picnic, and a healthy summer holiday, with investigation into modern drama. In the Malvern Hills, the Repertory Company were to do for Shaw and other British dramatists what the Stratford Memorial Theatre was doing for Shakespeare or Bayreuth for Wagner. Apart from the plays, there were lectures by Professor Bonamy Dobrée, Professor Allardyce Nicoll, and others. Moreover, Shaw himself was often present and could be relied upon to endow any such gathering with a measure of enthusiasm. Primarily, the Malvern Festival, like the Three Choirs Festival at Gloucester, Worcester, or Hereford, was devised for earnest students, so Sir Barry Jackson occasionally introduced such a curiosity of the drama as an "Interlude" by John Heywood, thus illustrating the growth of the English theatre. And the financial results were all that enthusiasm could hope for? By no means. Again and again Barry Jackson had to dip into his pocket and, at last, he passed on to Stratford-upon-Avon. But solid work had been done and years of enthusiastic effort had shown that substantial achievement was possible in spite of economic difficulties.

The Shakespeare Theatre at Stratford-upon-Avon has been an unfortunate venture. After the first theatre on the site was burnt, the trustees (it was an error of judgement) offered the commission to design and build the new playhouse to public competition. Naturally none of the established theatrical architects chose to risk their professional reputations; and only semi-amateurs in a highly technical job chose to compete. The result was what might have been foreseen. None of the designs were satisfactory, so what seemed the least objectionable was chosen. To-day, players agree that the Shakespeare Theatre is an uncomfortable house, while the exterior gives the impression of a grandiose factory rather than a place in which dramas of immortal genius might be enacted. But, from the standpoint of the theatre, it is the interior that is all-important. The lie of the stage in relation to the audience is such that it is difficult in the extreme to make contact with the auditorium and establish the all-important intimacy. A primary essential in theatre designing is to bring the audience into the closest possible association with the players, compatible with a proper view of the stage. This cannot but involve putting a section of the audience into the space ordinarily occupied by the boxes in the theatre of tradition. A stretch of bare wall on either side of the stage, as at Stratford, is deadening to emotional acting. When bad acoustics are added, the handicaps under which actors and actresses labour at Stratford are plain. What should have been a splendid adventure has proved to be a barren search for the unachievable.

Manchester, of course, was the preserve of Miss Horniman, of happy memory, whose good deeds were by no means confined to the Old Vic and Sadler's Wells. In Manchester, Miss Horniman gave Iden Payne a lot of money and told him to go ahead. He took a small theatre in the Midland Hotel and in 1907 produced eight plays in five weeks. Next year Miss Horniman took the Gaiety Theatre and Iden Payne produced for eighteen weeks.

From the pioneer work at Manchester came Liverpool Repertory, where the moving spirit was Alec Rea, a Liverpool shipbroker, who became chairman of the Liverpool Repertory Theatre. Basil Dean was a member of Miss Horniman's Company in Manchester and became the first producer at Liverpool. Success followed when Alec Rea's business capacity supplemented the technical skill and enthusiasm for the theatre of Basil Dean.

Following Basil Dean, William Armstrong was for years the guiding spirit in Liverpool Repertory, his directorship beginning in 1923. Part of Mr Armstrong's managerial policy was to produce at least a dozen one-act plays in a season, usually by untried dramatists. In 1940, Mr Armstrong was able to record:

"For years we were financially successful, and in spite of weekly expenses of £500, made a regular profit. But this miracle was not achieved by deserting 'rep.' and exploiting London successes. Some of our biggest financial successes were plays like Sherwood's *The Road to Rome*, Sierra's *The Kingdom of God*, Mrs Schauffler's *Parnell*, Priestley's *Time and the Conways*, and Huxley's *The World of Light*."

Bristol has a long theatrical history, so it was fitting that it should lead the way in the direction of municipal drama. At the Bristol Theatre Royal, Mrs Siddons, the Kembles, the Keans, and Macready appeared. Later Mrs Bancroft, Mrs Kendal, Kate and Ellen Terry were members of the Bristol stock company, and the city just missed its opportunity of giving Henry Irving his first chance. In the present century a repertory theatre was established with aid from the Bristol Corporation which provided the theatre, while the local Rotary Club organized the sale of blocks of tickets and made themselves responsible for finding the money necessary to run the theatre. A beginning was made with R. C. Carton's *Other People's Worries*. Later came plays by Galsworthy, Sutro, and St John Ervine. The municipal theatre at Bristol, once the little Colston Hall, holds about 500 people.

The Leeds Civic Playhouse was another vigorous institution. Amongst other things it presented morality plays in market squares, using a motor-lorry as a stage. Among the plays thus given were Laurence Housman's *Little Plays of St Francis*, each lasting about half an hour, and three plays constituting an evening's entertainment. Here again the actors and actresses were amateurs, unless a part of exceptional difficulty was essayed. Six plays were given annually and each ran a week. Mr Masefield's *Good Friday*, the *Oepidus Rex* of Sophocles, and *The Dybbuk* were among the productions.

The Castle Theatre, Farnham, is another example of the welcome decentralization which is revolutionizing the world of the theatre in Britain. Opened as a private membership playhouse in December 1939, it built up a reputation during the difficult war years, until it had the support of three thousand members. The building goes back to the sixteenth century and the theatre only holds 150 people, yet *Arsenic and Old Lace*, *Candida*, *Dr Clutterbuck*, *Twelfth Night*, and *Hamlet* were given in a single season, the latter after but one week's rehearsal. A spirit of enterprise coupled with courage can do wonders in a repertory theatre. An interesting experiment of the second World War period was the Travelling Repertory Theatre, with headquarters at Dartington Hall, in Devonshire. It was organized by a group of unemployed actors and actresses, who started with no capital.

Shaw's *Arms and the Man* and plays by Sean O'Casey were given in bombed towns and to audiences of evacuees.

At the Royalty, Glasgow, Alfred Wareing established one of the earliest repertory companies, as a counterblast to the touring companies which faithfully reproduced London successes, with actors and actresses drilled to imitate London originals, look for look, gesture for gesture. Milton Rosmer also produced at Glasgow, and Lewis Casson, Jean Cadell, and Nicholas Hannen were among the popular players in the years before 1914. After the War came the Scottish National Players, who not only had a regular season in Glasgow but organized a camping tour in August, thus combining a healthful holiday with profits. It has been said that Glasgow repertory was killed by the immense success of J. J. Bell's *Wee MacGregor*, thus furnishing an example of the truth behind Sir Herbert Tree's quip:

"When is a repertory theatre not a repertory theatre?"

"When it's a success!"

An astonishing example of great results achieved by meagre means is furnished by the Maddermarket Theatre at Norwich. In the 'twenties the players were a modest amateur dramatic society, who gave their entertainments in the old Norwich Musick House, so called because the city "waits" assembled there at Christmas time. When this building was condemned as unsafe, the little company purchased what was originally a Roman Catholic church, built in the Georgian style with a gallery running around three sides. This gallery was left and the rest refurnished as an Elizabethan playhouse, with an "apron stage". The site and rebuilding cost £3,000, the players doing not a little of the carpentry and all the painting themselves. Here, for three years, the Norwich Players produced Shakespeare's plays and other classics without running into debt; in itself, no small feat. The method adopted was to devote three weeks to rehearsals and then give public performances for a week. Thus a fresh Shakespeare play could be given every month. In all, 80 plays were presented in thirteen years. By 1948, 300 plays had been presented, including Shakespeare in its entirety. The "apron" stage was 34 feet wide and 20 feet deep, and the curtain at the back of the stage could be lowered, so that the action was continuous in front of the curtain. By this means *Hamlet*, as Shakespeare left it, was played in less than three hours.

The Maddermarket, Norwich, owes almost everything to Mr Nugent Monck. Before the first World War, in 1911, he was an impecunious actor, glad to have a chance of renting a cottage for which he paid six shillings a week and where he could produce plays in an upper room, with the help of an enthusiastic body of amateurs. Three years later the Norwich Players began to act in the Musick House, which had seats for exactly ninety-nine spectators. After the first World War Mr Monck began again, and, by 1921, he was able to build a theatre of his own, now known as the Maddermarket, madder being a root used for dyeing wool when Norwich was a centre of the textile trade. Here there were seats for about 220 people, and Mr Monck produced not only Shakespeare but Euripides, Webster, Wycherley, Congreve, and Dryden, as well as numerous modern plays. Nine productions a year cost Mr Monck about £1,000, while the takings were about £1,400 a year. The odd £400 provided salaries for the three main organizers. As for the rest, when off-duty, they were school teachers, bank clerks, shop assistants, and even school-boys.

It is not true that in play-production a large capital is the primary essential. The Maddermarket gives the lie to the statement. The primary necessity is a whole-hearted devotion to the theatre as art and as craft. The high rentals and a heavy entertainment tax seem to make a big initial capital essential in the West End of London, but in the suburbs and provinces enthusiasm is producing results from which a coming generation will assuredly profit.

CHAPTER 3

THE DRAMATIST GETS TO WORK

W E have our playhouse and its potential audience, but the play is lacking. For a play, a dramatist is a primary necessity. Even in the days when Italian comedians and comediennes improvised upon set themes, an author had to lay out the bones of a story and suggest the general lines upon which the plot would move. In the modern theatre the author is at times a factor of relatively small importance, and, in musical shows, he is frequently replaced by a committee, signifying, as committees do, "many, but not much." In the beginning, however, the dramatist is invariably the master of ceremonies. He it is who calls the tune and, willy-nilly, players and audiences must dance to his measure.

If there is an exception to the law that, in the beginning, the dramatist is all-important it is in revues, such as Albert de Courville produced at the Hippodrome in and about the years of the first World War. Here the spectacle was the all important element. It cost most. "The book", said de Courville "is the last, not the first thing, in revue." De Courville's big worry was a leading lady with personality enough to give point to the spectacles. Numerous gifts are called for. Beauty has its value, but personality is more important, if outsize audiences are to be impressed. Elsie Janis had the needful talents, so had "Vi" Loraine. Ethel Levey, too, in several de Courville productions displayed the gifts in full measure. To the leading lady had to be added a comedian broad enough in method to make outsize audiences laugh, a George Robey, for example. For the rest de Courville relied upon numerous changes in *venue* and "ran things through" so quickly that criticism was lulled.

If this book were concerned with the drama rather than the theatre, our approach to the factor, dramatist, would be different. *Vis-à-vis* the theatre, however, the author's task is, primarily,

49

to provide opportunities for acting. As the author only reaches his audience through a body of complementary artists, the author who underrates their importance does so at his peril. The beginning is a nebulous idea, almost, but not quite, devoid of form, and may be described as incarnation. It is the moment when the theme gives the first promise of embodiment in the flesh-stuff of the players, coupled with the belief that, given a competent company, the craft at the dramatist's command will suffice for the task. Already a process of elaboration and construction has begun, for the would-be author has made some contact, at least imaginatively, with the myriad potentialities associated with the theme and has won a measure of assurance that a truly expressive formal pattern can be found.

No small part of an author's task lies in reconciling the formal qualities which make a play of worth with the multitudinous incidents and characters which cannot but present themselves for possible representation. During the stage of embryonic life the artist-craftsman is mingling his imaginative and craft capabilities with the numberless possibilities suggested by his theme. In a play, as in a symphony, delight arises from the surprising confluence of parts which might, normally, be supposed to be the world asunder. Here lies the real test of the dramatist's skill.

The Well-Made Play

There are unhappy associations with the phrase "well-made" as applied to plays. Fifty years ago, Bernard Shaw was almost the only playwright who did not accept the principle that a dramatist was well advised to follow an old and well-tested principle, whereby exposition of the theme was followed by the development of a plot, while the plot, in turn, was raised to a crisis, which ushered in the concluding curtains. Old Alexandre Dumas told his boy, aged twenty, that the secret of successful play-writing lay in this—Act One, clear; Act Three, short; and everywhere, interest.

The material calling for dramatic treatment to-day is far more complex than it was and the cinema and broadcasting have accustomed theatre audiences to vastly more complicated methods of story-telling and character presentation, involving, maybe, switches forward or switches backward, which makers of the old-time "well-made" play would have disdained. Nevertheless, it is difficult to escape from the rude common sense of Tom Taylor, a very competent craftsman in mid-Victorian times, when he said: "In the first act you tell 'em what you're going to do; in the second act you do it; and, in the third, you tell 'em you've done it."

Eugène Scribe, who died in 1861, wrote more than 300 plays and they were given, not only in Paris, but all over Europe. Born in the theatrical world, Scribe was writing plays of sorts in boyhood and when he reached manhood he was already a master in stage-carpentry and the creation of the puppets, whom the bourgeoisie of his time were likely to applaud. Like old Dumas, Scribe laid special stress upon clarity of exposition and in his anxiety that audiences should know precisely what he had to "tell 'em", he covered every essential point in his story three times—once for the intelligent and attentive, secondly for the intelligent but inattentive, and thirdly, for the non-intelligent and inattentive.

C. E. Montague, speaking a generation after Dumas, Tom Taylor, and Eugène Scribe, and being a critic of considerably more insight than any of them, carried the argument a stage further when he said that the mark of a well-made play was "to be great in minor respects and minor in great ones". Montague, of course, was thinking of comedies of the Scribe type or melodramas such as Tom Taylor or Sardou constructed and not of masterpieces of construction such as *Oedipus Rex* or *Othello*. Being himself both intelligent and attentive, Montague was apt to be bored by two hammerings home of the same impression. In other words, what Montague judged to be wrong with Scribe was the machine-like element in his technique. Too often, Scribe achieved his exposition by such an obvious device as a dialogue between a couple of servants dusting the furniture.

Even granting C. E. Montague his point of view, it can scarcely be denied that in working-up situations, giving actors and actresses full opportunities, and preserving a plausibility sufficient to carry audiences with them, those who accepted the canons of a well-made play achieved considerable success. Certainly, a

wealth of ingenious invention went to the making of a first-rate
Sardou play, as a bare sketch of the plot of *Fedora* shows. Surprise,
suspense, and passion which achieved climax after climax—all
were marshalled with rare skill.

The Princess Fedora has a lover, Vladimir, and at the opening
of the first act she comes to his home. She is anxious, for he has
failed to keep an evening appointment. Quickly we see there is
only too good reason for Fedora's fears. The wheels of Vladimir's
coach are heard and a police officer appears. A scurry of foot-
steps in the adjoining bedroom, and the murmur of frightened
servants tell Fedora that her lover has returned, "Yes, but if not
dead, then dying."

The Princess runs to the bedroom door and sees the surgeons
at their ugly work. Vladimir has been murdered. Over his body
she swears she will be revenged. Before the curtain falls, Fedora
has a clue to the murderer—Count Loris Ivanoff, a Nihilist suspect. And all this in a single breathless act.

Some months pass and Princess Fedora meets Count Loris in
Paris. He has heard nothing of Fedora's *affaire* with the dead
Vladimir, and makes love so pleasantly that the Princess has her
first doubts. She mentions the name, "Vladimir Garishkine!"
and Loris admits that he is suspected of the murder.

"Ah, but you are innocent!"

"Yes!"

Nevertheless, the Princess is not convinced. Why has Loris run
away from St Petersburg? The man takes her by the hand, looks
into her eyes, and asks if she loves him wholly. In her burning
desire to know more, the Princess avows her love, until Loris
admits that he was the man who shot Vladimir. In a fury of
indignation Fedora breaks from him.

"Assassin! Assassin!"

"No," is the reply. "Vladimir's death was righteous punishment."

With this avowal, Fedora feels that she still does not know the
full facts. Using the wiles of a Delilah, she pleads for the truth, the
whole truth.

"Why did you kill him? Tell me!"

"To-morrow!"

"No, to-night! I am going home. Follow presently. The

The Tale of Two Cities by Charles Dickens, Lyceum Theatre (1860) (*see page* 21).

A Victorian Melodrama, *The Lights o' London*, by George R. Sims, The Princess's Theatre (1881) (*see page 22*).

wicket gate leading into the garden will be unfastened. I shall be alone."

At curtain-fall Loris covers Fedora's hands with kisses, but, as the door closes upon him, Fedora springs to her feet. There is triumph in her cry. "Ah, bandit! Je te tiens!"

FEDORA

The Two Fedoras
"Very Like! Very Like!" is Mr Punch's comment, quoting from "Hamlet"

But Sardou's aim is to pile passion upon passion and surprise upon surprise. First Fedora calls in an officer of the secret police and tells him of Ivanoff's coming. Her purpose is that, when she has learnt how Vladimir died, Loris shall be delivered into the police ambush. But at this point Sardou's invention takes another turn. The story as the Princess hears it is very different from what Fedora looked for. Vladimir was the lover of Loris's wife and Fedora is shown letters of whirling passion, written at the very time Vladimir was accepting Fedora's own kisses. As Fedora sees the new situation, she is sending Loris to certain

E

death. To save her lover, the Princess throws herself into his arms and embraces him.

"Stay!" she whispers.

But Sardou has to fill his last act, and he builds upon the fact that Fedora's revenge was fashioned only too surely; the Russian police arrest a brother of Loris, then his mother. It is now the man who is seeking revenge. Already Loris knows that some woman has been spying upon him and when he denounces her, Fedora pleads passionately for the unknown woman, until her very vehemence reveals the truth:

"C'était donc toi," cries Loris.

For a moment the passionate lover becomes an avenging devil. He seizes Fedora by the throat, but believing she will die at his hands, she has taken poison. Thus she falls into the arms of her horrified lover. Loris lifts the dying woman on to the couch, and, as a concluding horror, the dead body rolls again on to the floor. A typical Bernhardt death.

It would not be difficult to find disfiguring coincidences in Sardou's plot, but they did not seem important when La Grande Sarah was playing the name-part. With poor support from company, scenery, and production, she could give Sardou's inventions a semblance of reality, at any rate until the theatre lights were lowered for the last time and one was again in the cool air of outer night where free thought was possible. Mrs Bernard Beere was the only English actress who could play Fedora with the passion and power the part called for, and, good as she was, she lacked the genius of the French woman. Had restraint and repose been added to Mrs Bernard Beere's technique, she would have been a tragic actress of the first order. Her stage presence was beautiful in a high degree and her diction well-nigh perfect. Mrs Bernard Beere played Fedora when the Bancrofts produced the play at the Haymarket in 1883. Twelve years later Beerbohm Tree revived *Fedora* for Mrs Patrick Campbell at the Haymarket, himself playing Loris. Mrs Campbell was beautiful as Fedora but not markedly successful. She gave up the part to Mrs Tree.

It is worthy of note that the craft-skill required to fit Sarah Bernhardt with such parts as *Fedora* or *La Tosca* extended beyond the first production in Paris. Plays suited for the divine Sarah had also to serve touring towns all over England and America. In *Tosca* there was a great fête in the Farnese Palace, where Tosca sang, but when the play was given on tour a few supers had

Sarah Bernhardt, in the 'eighties

to suffice. It is a tribute to Sardou's talent that the thrills of *Tosca* and *Fedora* remained effective under depressing conditions.

The Budding Dramatist

An early acquaintance with the fundamentals of any art is acknowledged to be an advantage to any executant artist. Music is a case in point. So are painting, sculpture, and story-telling, as it displayed itself in the Brontë family. It would be strange if the general rule did not apply to play-making and play-acting, inasmuch as many children are by nature play-makers, play-actors, and even play-producers. May I give an example, which is instructive even if it includes an element of the apocryphal?

A mother, at a time when her three small children were supposed to be enjoying a mid-day rest, heard noises in the night nursery. Tip-toeing upstairs, she found Annie aged six and Jack aged four sitting in a state of nature on the floor. As for Number 1, aged eight, he was strolling up and down, wearing a large bath towel and his father's top-hat.

"Anne, what does this mean?"

"Please, Mummy, we are Adam and Eve in the Garden of Eden."

"And, James, what are you?"

"I'm God," said Number 1, "taking a walk in the cool of the evening."

Play-acting and play-production in this immature form is common in the nursery. John van Druten displayed a direct interest in the theatre at a very early age. In his amusing autobiography, *The Way to the Present*, he disclosed that, with the aid of school friends, he ran theatres in an imagined country to the number of thirty.

"We must have invented titles for at least a thousand plays, as well as the names, histories, personalities, and appearances of about three hundred actors and actresses, all of whom were as vividly alive to me as the people of the London stage."

When van Druten wrote *Gertie Maude* he introduced a young girl Sheila with just this primitive passion for the theatre. She had her toy stage. She collected the *Play Pictorials* of the period. She enjoyed an imagined life in the theatre world which was fully as vital as her dealings with the grown-up world of reality. In the day-nursery scene, we watched Sheila in the semi-darkness crouched behind a table and reaching up her hand now and again to move the paper figures on the mimic stage.

Sheila (improvising) (woman's voice): Oh, Basil, forgive me; oh, forgive me! (*man's voice*): There are some things that can't be forgiven. (*She reaches to the figure of the woman.*) (*in her own voice*). Oh, there goes the table.

Doris (the nurse in Sheila's audience): Sheila, you must be quick. It's bed-time.

As a school-boy James Barrie was not only an ardent playgoer, but displayed a very early interest in stagecraft. His favourite place was an end seat in the front row of the pit. There were no stalls in the Dumfries playhouse. From this vantage-point the budding playwright could see into the wings and guess at what was going on "behind". While still a school-boy Barrie wrote his first play, *Bandalero the Bandit*.

Alfred Sutro, a typical creator of "well-made" plays, was a scenario-maker. He told William Archer: "Before I start writing the dialogue of a play, I make sure that I shall have an absolutely free hand over the entrances and exits: in other words, that there is ample and legitimate reason for each character appearing in any particular scene, and ample motive for his leaving it. I write a play straight ahead from beginning to end, taking practically as long over the first act as over the last three." In this connection Granville Barker said: "I always write the beginning of a play first and the end last; but as to writing 'straight ahead'—it sounds like what one may be able to do in Heaven." William Archer, who was interested in the problem, has told us that most of the dramatists whom he consulted were opposed to the principle of "roughing-out" the big scenes first, and then imbedding them, as it were, in their context. Sir Arthur Pinero went the length of saying: "I can never go on to page 2 until I am sure that page 1 is as right as I can make it. Indeed, when an act is finished, I send it at once to the printers, confident that I shall not have to go back upon it."

Mention has been made of van Druten's early preoccupation with the stage, and it is interesting to note how this coloured his growing insight into life and made him conceive characters in dramatic terms, rather than those of the novel. Van Druten was twenty-two when the Stage Society produced *Young Woodley*, though he was twenty-seven before it had its first run at the Savoy. From that time onwards, his success was unimpeded. A plot for van Druten is an interesting concatenation of characters. Accordingly, he is not fundamentally a story-teller, though doubtless he would admit that a water-tight plot is vastly convenient even to the dramatist who specializes in personalities. No easy aids to dramatic effect for van Druten, such as asides or soliloquies. He is a realist, and for this reason owes much to his early producers, in particular to Miss Auriol Lee. When *The Voice of the Turtle* was heard in the theatreland which van Druten's waking hours are always exploring, Sally Middleton, a small-part American actress, flashed into van Druten's mind. Soon the idea of beau-snatching in this environment raised the problem of the sleeping arrangements in the bed-sitting room and kitchened flat in which such ladies live while "resting". When Bill, the boy friend of a couple of the actresses, was added, van Druten had his play and it pleased him that a single set and three characters sufficed to display the clash he had in mind. But more of this later.

John van Druten's *I Remember Mama* is another example of the almost plotless drama, which stands for the negation of the well-made play of the accepted nineteenth-century pattern. *I Remember Mama* was an adaptation of Kathryn Forbes's novel, *Mama's Bank Account*, which told of a Norwegian family, with a home in San Francisco at the beginning of the twentieth century. The father was a carpenter; Katrin, the eldest daughter, wanted to be a writer; Dagmar, the youngest, longed to be a veterinary surgeon. A doctor brother, three aunts, and Uncle Chris were other members of the family over which Mama presided, the guiding star in every crisis. As Dagmar says, "Mother can fix anything."

Van Druten fashioned his stage picture of the Norwegian family with the aid of Katrin, the writer. She was the *commère* of the play and sat at the side of the stage reading from the notes she is making for her story *Mama's Bank Account*. As Katrin reads her story, it is enacted on one of three revolving stages which van Druten employed. From time to time Katrin leaves her writing desk and takes her place with the rest of her family in the numberless episodes which constitute the play and justify the revolving stages. Thus we are shown the hospital ward in which Dagmar is having her mastoid operation and into which Mama has penetrated by disguising herself as a "char". Again, the ubiquitous Mama is seen selling cookery recipes to a fashionable woman novelist, thus giving Katrin her chance of literary success. The interesting point is that such a story could never be told if the Victorian formula of three or four acts of cause and effect had been followed.

What does one mean by character creation as applied to playwriting? Speaking of her part, Anastasia Rakonitz, the possessive mother in the Jewish play, *The Matriarch*, Mrs Patrick Campbell said to the authoress, "I like this part, Peter. I can turn round in it."

Edith Evans might have made the same remark about Agatha Payne in *The Old Ladies*, as Rodney Ackland transmuted it from the novel of Hugh Walpole. The novelist himself tells us that Agatha Payne was "not a cleanly old woman. Her splendid hair, as black now as forty years ago, was tumbled about her head carelessly and stuck into it askew was a cheap black comb, studded with black diamonds. Her colour was swarthy, brown under the deep red of her cheeks and there was a faint moustache on her upper lip. But she must have been handsome once, a fine bold girl in those years long ago." Reading on, it was plain that Walpole's theme was greed for beauty, as manifested in the character of Agatha Payne. Quickly, Edith Evans saw that here was that rare thing, a character in which an actress of worth could turn round.

The opening scene was laid at Christmas-time and Lucy Amorest (Mary Jerrold) had provided a Christmas tree for two other lonely and elderly spinsters May Beringer (Jean Cadell) and the gipsy-like Agatha Payne. Greed is the ruling passion of Agatha Payne; the lust of possession of the beautiful. In the play, this takes the form of the lovely bit of polished amber in May Beringer's dingy bed-sitting room. The amber is the sole remaining thing of beauty in the possession of the three lonely women. The growing desire and the implacable determination to possess are expressed in Agatha Payne's outburst: "What do you know of lust or desire? If I had only half an hour to live I would want the sensation of owning that beautiful thing."

The fat, heavy body of the old gipsy in the shapeless maroon-coloured dressing-gown of the first act and the dirty yellow velvet robe with the menacing sequins of the last scene; Agatha's love for raspberry jam, sticky nougat, and well-sugared cocoa; Miss Evans did not miss a point. But, never forget, without the tremulous May Beringer of Jean Cadell and the happy Lucy Amorest of Mary Jerrold, the Agatha Payne of Edith Evans might have been a very different thing.

It is interesting to compare the highly dramatic contrasts of character which made for the success of *The Old Ladies* with van Druten's treatment of interlocked characters in *Old Acquaintance* which was given at the Apollo during the second World War. The playwright built up his acts out of the friendship of a couple

of women who happened to have been at school together. This and
no more. Katherine (Edith Evans) was a maker of good novels
whose books "sold well", while Mildred (Marian Spencer) was a
poor novelist whose books "sold" even better. Plainly, there was
no story here, so the play arose from the clash of character.
Katherine has integrity though her standards in sexual affairs
are dubious, or at any rate seem so when the unspoilt girl Deirdre
(Muriel Pavlow) comes into her life. Deirdre is Mildred's
daughter. Katherine loses a lover and Mildred a daughter
before curtain-fall, but they remain friends.

An interesting development of the interlocked characters
motif is to be found in Knoblock's *My Lady's Dress* or Schnitzler's
A Round Divorce. Schnitzler linked a street-walker with a soldier;
the soldier with a parlour-maid; the parlour-maid with a gentleman; the gentleman with a young wife; the young wife with her
husband; the husband with a girl friend; the girl friend with a
poet; the poet with an actress; the actress with a nobleman and
the nobleman once more with the street-walker.

Character Creation

Story-telling has always been in the forefront of the human
consolations, and, on the stage, the main narrative of the
dramatist is reinforced ten-fold by the revelations each of the
characters are making regarding themselves. Consider the
implications of this pleasant story of a small girl, ten or there-
abouts, who was taken to the Old Vic (then in Waterloo Road)
to see *The Merchant of Venice*. She sat enthralled, until the Casket
Scene reached its climax. Then, at the point where Bassanio
turned from Portia to find the casket which was to give happiness
to both, the Portia kissed her Bassanio.

"Daddy," whispered the little girl, breathlessly, "she has
told him; she has told him!"

In its relation to the story-telling element, character creation
on the stage—whether by dramatist or player—is in the nature
of the overtones in music which add quality and depth to the
original note. Which is why many dramatists create their
characters first, in order to assure themselves that the overtones

will be there when the suitable story has been found. Pinero once said, "The beginning of a play to me is a little world of people. I live with them, get familiar with them and they tell me the story." Or again, "I call my characters together and then stand by and look at them or listen to them."

Similarly, for Terence Rattigan a play arises from characters in a given environment. He does not believe in working up to a dramatic situation, and this primary interest accounts for his outstanding achievement to the present being his creation of Crocker-Harris, the schoolmaster in *The Browning Version.* Rattigan gave himself no more than one hour but the result was an unforgettable piece of acting and an hour of "theatre" which every playgoer who saw it will treasure in memory. Nothing that can be called a theme and a modicum of plot, yet Crocker-Harris comes to life in Eric Portman's capable hands. The man was a first-class classical scholar in his undergraduate days, but has been a failure ever since. When the curtain rises he is facing his last day at the public school, where he has worked for years. There is no pension in prospect; the prospect is £200 a year, teaching the elements of Latin and Greek to youngsters in a preparatory school. For the rest, Crocker-Harris is married to a shrewish sensualist, who is carrying on an *affaire* with another master, an *affaire* which gives symbolic significance to a line from *The Agamemnon*, which a lazy boy translates, "boasting over her husband's body". But what brings a catch in the throat and tears to the eyes is that this lovable man has not a friend in the world. Neither boys nor colleagues care in the least that he is leaving. Yet you and I, watching Eric Portman in the theatre, know that here is one of Nature's gentlemen, even if he be a human misfit. This is the dramatic situation and it has arisen from a character fully imagined by dramatist and actor.

This does not mean that character is all-important. Rather it implies that, if the characters are rightly conceived in their relationship one to another, Rattigan feels assured of his plot. Plot as he sees it arises from characters, background, and theme, though *The Winslow Boy* was an exception to Rattigan's rule. Here the dramatist's problem was to write a play around an exciting episode of actual fact, the Archer-Shee case, in which a young naval cadet was wrongfully accused of theft and only the efforts of his family, coupled with the acumen of a great lawyer, saved the lad from ruin. Remembering the success of the cross-examination scene in *Mrs Dane's Defence*, Rattigan felt he would be on sure ground in the opening scenes, in which the boy's guilt or innocence were in question. The dramatist's real difficulties were to arise later. Rattigan confessed that he made a number of bad shots before he got far enough away from the newspaper story to create a play which would carry conviction. In the end, *The Winslow Boy* was less a dramatic representation of the Archer-Shee case, than a series of characters who were allowed to tell a story suitable for the three hours' traffic of the stage. In particular Rattigan had several acts to fill and the details of a protracted legal battle seemed very unpromising material. Doubtless Mr Rattigan considered the reactions of the case upon the father or mother. In fact, he chose to focus attention upon a sister who had lost her lover in consequence of the scandal.

In this matter of character creation and plot-making, we are fortunate in having a full and frank analysis of his own reactions from John Galsworthy. For Galsworthy, plot was character and dialogue was character. He was assured that people act and speak as they do at any given time because of what they are. So long as he was on intimate terms with his characters Galsworthy felt safe. He wrote when the mood to create was upon him and pre-ferred the inspiration distilled when pen touched paper. As he said, when walking or shaving, plots or characters would just jolt forward. The words in which the jolts expressed themselves came when Galsworthy took up his fountain-pen and prepared for work.

Clyde Fitch, the American dramatist, said much the same thing when he confessed that he was often astonished at the way his characters developed. "I tried to make them do certain things. They did others."

In his Romanes Lecture on *The Creation of Character in Literature*, Galsworthy went a step further when he said that the vitality and freedom of character creation derives, as a rule, from the subconscious mind instinctively supplying the conscious mind with the material it requires. He continued: "I sink into my morning chair, a blotter on my knee, the last words or deed of some character in ink before my eyes, a pen in my hand, a pipe in my mouth and nothing in my head.

"I sit. I don't intend: I don't expect: I don't even hope. I read over the last pages. Gradually my mind seems to leave the chair, and be where my character is acting or speaking, leg raised, waiting to come down, lips opened ready to say something.

"Suddenly my pen jots down a movement or remark, another, another, and goes on doing this, haltingly, perhaps for an hour or two. When the result is read through it surprises one, by seeming to come out of what went before, and by ministering to some sort of possible future.

"Those pages, adding tissue to character, have been supplied from the store-cupboard of the subconscious, in response to the appeal of one's conscious directive sense, and in service to the saving grace of one's theme, using that word in its widest sense."

Ibsen was a careful craftsman and precise in a high degree. His method was to write one play every two years and to publish it regularly in the second week of January every second year. The facts are given in a volume, *From Ibsen's Workshop*. He devoted a year brooding over the theme, the characters and the incidents, and a year to writing and rewriting. Always, there was a year of waiting and watching, followed by a six or seven months' burst of intensive creation. Ibsen knew all about the earlier life of his characters. Nora, for example, was spoiled in childhood. Oddly enough, Ibsen always had a number of toys on his desk, a bean from Switzerland, an ivory elephant, a tin soldier, and a china cat. Apparently, he used the toys as counters in composition. His table was the floor-plan of his stage. Oddly enough, J. B. Priestley has confessed that his grey-matter is energized by typewriters, preferably well-endowed with gadgets. At one time Priestley had nine typewriters in his Highgate study. In his pocket, and a constant companion, was a small, shiny, black notebook, in which the dramatist was wont to jot down ideas, and the germs of ideas, as they flashed into consciousness. "The fifteen plays I have written began their life in that note-book," said Priestley on one occasion.

If the primary inspiration varies greatly from dramatist to dramatist, so do the writing methods. Sardou, a master of the machine-made play, relied upon an elaborate scenario and worked closely to it when writing the individual scenes. The preparation of a dossier might occupy years, memoirs and histories being ransacked, noted, and cross-indexed. Then Sardou would construct his scenario and, at last, write his play. Edward Knoblock, another clever technician, also made no attempt to set down dialogue until he had an elaborate scenario to guide him. This scenario not only set out every entrance and exit in a play but gave in detail the drift of the speeches. Galsworthy, on the contrary, not only did not find the preliminary note-taking essential, but did not even prepare a scenario. Similarly, Dumas fils, who wrote *La Dame aux Camélias*, considered it a waste of time to construct a detailed scenario. In his preface to *La Princesse Georges*, Dumas wrote, "You should not begin your work, until you have your concluding scene, movement and speech clear in your mind. How can you tell what road you ought to take until you know where you are going?" Dumas fils was fond of revealing the secrets of the workshop in the Prefaces to his plays. Of *Le Supplice d'une Femme* he wrote, "Any one can relate a dramatic situation. The art lies in preparing it; in getting it accepted; in making it plausible, especially in untying the knot."

Pinero, who was a confirmed note-taker, said, "Cause-effect! Cause-effect! Two of the most substantial parts of the fabric which go to make up a fine play are logic and intuition. Without logic you cannot construct a play. Without intuition, you cannot write it."

Somerset Maugham's method was to devise an anecdote and then search for the characters and environment fitted to exploit it, always remembering that each play had to run at least a hundred nights, if it was to pay its way. Nevertheless, as a man of the world, with a wide experience of men and women, Somerset Maugham takes his character-creation very seriously, even if it is secondary in point of time. Maugham's sense of the theatre is so keen that he insists upon his public being interested in his situation, rather than merely chuckling over his smart sayings. He cuts witty dialogue of the Wilde-Lonsdale type ruthlessly. Noel Coward, as he reached maturity, also came to the conclusion that a higher value should be put upon situation in drama than upon the laughter-creating worth of smart dialogue and epigrammatic lines. Somerset Maugham found play-writing more amusing than novel-writing. "If you have the knack it is very easy. If you have not got the knack, you had better not do it." Hastily, Maugham added, "I do not mean that if you have the knack you can do it without effort. That would be absurd." But more of this hereafter.

Some of the most informing glimpses into a dramatist's workshop (his mind) come from Bernard Shaw. Shaw had been reading a passage in *A History of the Late Nineteenth Century Drama* by Allardyce Nicoll and complained that it "fairly made him jump". Nicoll had rashly assumed that Shaw learnt his art from Pinero, Jones, Carton, Grundy, and Wilde, and the gad-fly out of Dublin resented the implications. The fact was that Shaw regarded himself as furiously opposed to the methods and principles of these predecessors. Theirs were "constructed" plays; well-made plays, based upon the practice of Scribe, which Shaw compared derisively to cats' cradles, clockwork mice, and the like.

"Instead of planning my plays I let them grow as they came and hardly ever wrote a page knowing what the next page would be."

As against the Victorians, Shaw's secondary glory was that he scorned the police-news and crude sexual adventure without which he believed his competitors were helpless. Nevertheless, Shaw was far too shrewd a dramatist to ignore the essentials which two thousand years and more had revealed and which had not really changed since Greek times, when Aristotle defined the six constituent parts thus: (1) plot, (2) *ethos* or moral bent, (3) intellect, that is to say the way in which the characters think, (4) voice or diction, (5) melody (in the chorus, etc.), and (6) spectacle.

Shaw doubtless persuaded himself that his mind moved in the direction of natural story-telling and character-creation, but in fact, he did not forget the lessons of tradition. If a single characteristic had to sum up his work it would be that, of all the dramatists of his time, he was most profoundly conscious of his art in relation to his period. Indeed, there are admirers of Shaw who value the Prefaces which discuss these relationships fully as much as the plays themselves. In some sense or another every dramatist who seeks a wide influence must be profoundly conscious of his period. Otherwise, how can he make full contact with the audiences who are the final shapers of the art of the theatre?

And, of course, there is the dream play, the equivalent of Coleridge's *Kubla Khan* in the realm of poetry. William Archer (and I never knew a critic with a more dour approach to the arts) used to say that his own play *The Green Goddess*, came to him in a dream. St John Ervine claimed a similar origin for a promising plot, though the play itself failed to materialize. On the day of the dream a young man had been hanged for murdering a girl in Richmond Park and when Mr Ervine got to bed that night he dreamed he was standing in the dock at Old Bailey, awaiting sentence of death. He was innocent (there was no doubt about that), but the jury had given their verdict. When the Clerk of the Court asked whether the prisoner had anything to say, Ervine replied, "Yes, I have a lot to say," and proceeded to deliver a remarkable impromptu speech, directed against the jury. This is what Mr Ervine says he said in the dream:

"You have found me guilty of a crime which I did not commit, and have resolved to hang me. I do not blame you for that. The evidence against me is black, although it is entirely circumstantial, and if I were a member of the jury and one of you were the prisoner, I should find you guilty on the evidence. But I did not commit this crime, nor do I know who did, nor is there any clear proof that I committed it. I cannot expect you to believe my bare word against evidence that seems convincing, but I beg of you this one thing, that, if I am hanged, all of you, when my innocence is established, as it will be one day, will swear that never again, if you can help it, will any man or woman be hanged in this country on circumstantial evidence alone!"

Argument and oratory were unavailing. Sentence was pronounced, the Court of Appeal paid no heed to the prisoner, the petition to the Home Secretary was fruitless, and in due course Mr Ervine (in his dream) was hanged. As he dropped to death and saw the rope straightening itself out, he anxiously awaited "the very nasty jerk", but the expected pain did not materialize. As though under laughing gas or chloroform, he passed from mortal existence.

It was at this point that Mr Ervine's play came to life. As the sleeper watched the swaying body, he saw the Soul leaving on its last journey. It was the very spit of the living form, clothed in a similar blue serge suit and differing only from the body in seeming of lighter texture. It was floating in the air and to the dreamer there was a stupendous change. Misery, as by magic, vanished; in its place the soul moved through an atmosphere of indescribable joy. "Thank God, I'm finished with you!" ejaculated the dreamer and at this point he awoke. Ervine's regret was that he did not sleep on and know what followed when the Soul left "that dreadful cellar" and entered upon its new world, for what the dream suggested was not the tragedy of a wrongful sentence but a sequence of spiritual adventures, involving the discovery of a soul in eternity comparable with the body Mr Ervine had discovered in his earthly passage from birth to the gallows.

St John Ervine's *Jane Clegg* was first produced by Miss Horniman at the Gaiety, Manchester, and had a lower-middle class background. Jane, played by Sybil Thorndike, is Henry Clegg's wife.

In the first few sentences, the dramatist sounded the keynote which was maintained throughout the play.

Mrs Clegg: I can't think wot's keepin' 'Enry.

Jane Clegg (without looking up from her sewing): Busy, I suppose.

Mrs Clegg: 'E's always busy. I don't believe men are 'alf so busy as they make out they are. Besides I know 'Enry. I 'aven't 'ad the motherin' of 'im for nothink. 'E don't kill 'imself with work, 'Enry don't.

But, before the final curtain, audiences were aware that there was more to be said for 'Enry, with his slovenly shuffle, his beer-swilling, and his partiality for "fancy women", than had seemed probable. Leslie Faber played 'Enry in London.

"I'm not a bad chap really. I'm just weak. I'd be all right if I had a lot of money and a wife that wasn't better than I am. I ought to have married a woman like myself, or a bit worse. That's what Kittie is. She's worse than I am and that sort of makes me love her. It's different with you. I always feel mean here."

St John Ervine's growing interest in Henry Clegg is the sort of thing that happens as a dramatist works upon his plot. The virtue of *Jane Clegg* is that in spite of the tight hold the author has upon his central theme, natural characters do natural things until Jane Clegg turns out the light in that clean but drab sitting-room and goes upstairs to bed.

Again, how good Norman McKinnel was in *Old English*, an adaptation from Galsworthy's story *The Stoic*. Sylvanus Heythorp was chairman of a shipping company, a king of commerce, such a man as Kipling imagined when he wrote *The Mary Gloster*. Old Heythorp has bamboozled the insurance companies time and again, and now he wants money desperately for the widow and children of an illegitimate son. He determines to buy some worthless ships for his company, and receives a secret commission which will bring in £6,000. But a shady solicitor hears of the transaction and threatens blackmail. Heythorp tells his valet "to remove that hound". Then realizing the game is up, he sits down to dinner and, in lonely solitude, dreams of old-time four-in-hands; of little Robson, the actor; of the singers Mario and Grisi. And in these dreams he dies.

This is how the faculty of play-writing displays itself when a master of the craft is at the stage of invention.

Almost all plays rely to a large extent upon exciting situation, as they all rely in some degree upon character presentation. What varies is the relative importance attaching to one or the other when plot development begins. If the dramatist is less interested in the ingenuities of story-telling and more in the presentation of character, necessarily he will focus attention upon the incidents which develop characters and reveal their interplay.

There is another aspect of character creation, naive, but not without technical interest. At times, a dramatist seeks little more than opportunities for what is known as "a character actor". Ignoring the subtleties of true character creation, the author exercises his ingenuity upon twists and turns of plot which the players can exploit, attention being focused upon the principal character. *The Professor's Love Story*, *Quinney's*, and *Grumpy* are comedies of the type, though a dozen examples come to mind. One of the best was *A Pair of Spectacles*, which Sydney Grundy anglicized from a French original. It has been revived again and again and, when Sir John Hare played Benjamin Goldfinch, seemed a minor classic.

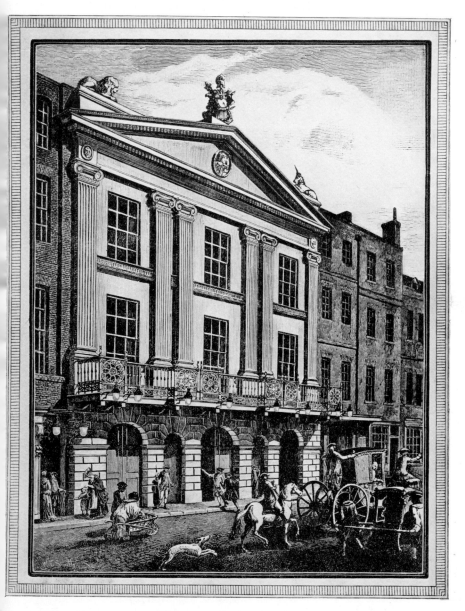

Drury Lane Theatre, as newly fronted by Robert Adam for Garrick (*see page* 27).

Empire Theatre,
Leicester Square,
as it was in 1884.
1. The Foyer;
2. The Audito-
rium; 3.Exterior;
4. The Stairway;
5. The Prome-
nade.

The theme was frankly fantastic. A kindly old optimist puts on his brother's spectacles and his whole outlook upon life changes. No idea could be simpler and, provided audiences accept it, more effective. But epigrams won't help. The author can do no more than "feed" his leading man. Sydney Grundy brought Benjamin Goldfinch to life in his first sentence. He comes down to breakfast, wearing the gold rimmed spectacle, *his own* spectacles.

MR JOHN HARE.
AS Mr BENJAMIN GOLDFINCH

Goldfinch: Good morning, Percy. How do you do, my boy? (*patting him on the back*) Glorious day, isn't it? Sun shining— birds singing—does one's heart good to hear 'em (*rubbing his hands*). What weather for the crops!

Mrs Goldfinch (Kate Rorke): My dear, it's been pouring in torrents.

Goldfinch: Well, all the better for the turnips. We can't have it all ways.

F

John Hare was enjoying himself already and the audience was chuckling. The episodes of the tenants on rent day, beginning with Bartholomew, the boot-maker, with his bill for eighteen pairs. And then, Gregory Goldfinch, from Sheffield, in the dark-framed steel spectacles of ill-omen, is heard off.

Gregory: That's all he'll get. If he wants more, call a policeman.

Characteristically, Gregory has fallen foul of the driver of his "growler", as he is to fall foul of his young son, Percy.

The secret of character creation of this sort is keeping strictly to the job in hand and Sydney Grundy, in *A Pair of Spectacles*, does not deviate a hair's breadth. No nonsense about realism; just enough to establish the theme. For the rest, opportunities for the minutiae of character acting. Above all, slight variants upon the leading idea, Goldfinch's ultra-kindliness, in contrast with the ultra-business qualities of the Man from Sheffield, and, in contrast with both, the generous worldly wisdom of Benjamin's relatively youthful wife, whom Kate Rorke played so charmingly fifty years ago.

Of course, *A Pair of Spectacles* dates; so does *Caste*, but a budding dramatist would not be wasting a morning devoted to an intensive study of Sydney Grundy's technique. Some of the methods of interesting and holding an audience are abiding. Passing from the naive, it is to be remembered that, until the end of the nineteenth century, the story in a play was judged all-important and what the dramatist sought was a dramatic incident, which was not only novel but offered abundant opportunities for acting. But, towards the end of the century, playwrights held strongly to the opinion that a stage character was primarily an individual and not a type, as he or she had been in Restoration comedy. The well-known French critic Sarcey, writing in 1889, laid down that: "a character is a master faculty or passion, which absorbs all the rest. . . To study and paint a character by placing a man in a given number of situations, is to show how this principal motive force in his nature annihilates or directs all those which, if he had been another man, would probably have come into action."

Which brings our inquiry to the problems attaching to subject-matter or theme.

It may be added that, essential as capacity for writing crisp and telling dialogue is, stage-talk is not strictly essential construction. Construction is the equivalent of the foundations and walls which keep storm away from a dwelling, and allow of a happy home arising. About the turn of the century when naturalism was accepted as a cardinal virtue in drama, William Archer, a typical critic of the period, went so far as to claim that the "glorious problem of the modern playwright was to make his characters reveal the inmost workings of their souls without saying or doing anything that they would not say or do in the real world." The reverse is true. Actually, the glorious problem is to carry audiences as far from reality as possible, but this without losing touch. Archer's pet abomination was "the aside". We are more open-minded to-day. In any case, realism is far from being a characteristic of telling dialogue. What stage dialogue sets out to do is to "sow seeds" in the imagination and thus to focus attention upon the stage action. The phrase "sowing seeds" is due to Harley Granville-Barker and he explained what he meant when he added a plea for a touch of magic in dialogue. Mrs Craigie reiterated Granville-Barker's point when she argued, in an essay prefacing *The Ambassador*, that stage dialogue should have more emotional force than the talk of day-to-day existence. Otherwise how could it illuminate character or situation, and possibly both?

CHAPTER 4

THEME IN DRAMA

THEME is a word which obtrudes itself continually when the work of a dramatist is under discussion. It is his first contribution to the coming play. As Ibsen said, "The theme for a play presented itself before the characters and incidents." In connection with novel-writing, the meaning attached to theme is more elastic, but for a dramatist, his theme is essentially a unifier, that is an aid towards assembling the characters who are to tell his story and give the players their acting opportunities. It follows that what will really interest audiences is less the theme itself, than what the author makes of it.

A devouring absorption in children is a theme, and Strindberg worked upon it in *The Father*, the particular angle he chose being the jealousy aroused by it between husband and wife. In order to emphasize the theme Strindberg imagined his characters less as individuals than as types of manhood and womanhood, so that Margaret, the old nurse, became less a personality than a symbol of the horrible fatality which attaches to jealousy when it reaches monstrous proportions. Pondering his theme, Strindberg came to see woman as the bearer of the seed and man as no more than the instrument by which woman renews human life. Thus woman uses a man and, when he has served her turn, she thrusts him aside relentlessly. In *The Father* Laura was such a devourer and her ruthless hunger extended to her man's work and to his children. Laura intercepted his letters and so spoilt her husband's labour for science; she even forced him to doubt the paternity of his daughter. In the end, there was nothing before the Father but insanity and a merciful release by death. The climax came when Laura, in her deadly hate, told her highly strung husband that she could put him into a lunatic asylum and thus be free to bring up her child as she would. "You have fulfilled your function as the unfortunate but necessary father and bread-winner. You are wanted no more. You may go."

Stung by the fiendish taunt, the Father flung a lamp at his wife and the wife received the proof she required of the man's insanity. As the curtain fell his old nurse, Margaret, tricked the Father into a madman's jacket, as once, in boyhood, she tricked him into wearing a coat he was reluctant to wear. As Robert Loraine and Haidée Wright played the scene at the Savoy years ago, it became unforgettable in its pathos.

An example from the plays of the Spaniard, José Echegaray, emphasizes the method in which a theme can dominate an entire play. In Echegaray's *El Gran Galeoto* the idea of thoughtless and cruel gossip dominates the plot so completely that it may be regarded as, virtually, a character in the play. Don Julian, a rich merchant, aged about forty, has married Teodora, a beauty of twenty. She adored him, until Julian adopted a young poet, Ernesto. Ernesto's feelings towards Teodora were brotherly and he loved Julian as a father, but Society chattered. When Ernesto tried to put matters right by leaving home, gossip only increased, until Julian's slight resentment turned to uneasy suspicion. The climax comes when Ernesto chances to hear Teodora insulted in a café and strikes the speaker. A duel is arranged, but Don Julian, far from realizing the nobility of Ernesto's action, determines to fight the duel himself. Teodora, in a last effort to prevent the two men endangering their lives, goes to Ernesto's studio and when Julian is brought in wounded, she hides in Ernesto's bedroom, where she is discovered by her husband's servants. Julian dies cursing his wife. At the end, when they have been cast out of Society, Teodora and Ernesto find love in their great loneliness. Gossip, the unnamed character, is the agency which has brought them together.

The mere choice of a theme does no more than focus attention upon the job in hand. Indeed, face to face with a chosen theme, no artist has more than the vaguest idea whither it will carry him. To take a case which has no direct associations with the theatre. In March, 1829, Mendelssohn made up his mind to have a summer holiday in Scotland. As he told a friend, he was going "with a rake for folk songs, an ear for the lovely, fragrant countryside and a heart for the bare legs of the natives". When August came Mendelssohn wandered for days in happy loneliness, but what finally resulted were the "Hebrides" Overture and the "Scottish" Symphony.

Always a play begins with the author's choice of a theme. This is to say no more than that a decision has been made to get to work upon one play rather than another. Sardou, who was a conscientious worker, had files containing fifty dossiers, each being an unwritten play or rather a possible story and character sketches suited for a play. But Sardou's work did not consist of a vague preference for this theme or that. Rather the work meant grey matter expended upon devising what old-time criticism termed "the fable". The fable differs from both theme and plot, being the story of happenings to selected men and women in a given environment, whom the dramatist expects to exemplify the chosen theme and also to fit into a plot capable of presentation within the three hours' traffic of the stage. The plot which expresses a theme may be, and often is, highly complex, but a theme can be set out in a sentence or two. Practically all Chekhov's plays, for example, are variants upon a single theme —that of escape from what seems a deadening environment.

When Aristophanes devised *The Frogs* he bethought himself of the fun to be derived from guying the musical and dramatic contests in Athens and his theme took the form of the discovery that all the good tragic poets were dead, forcing Dionysus, the god who presided over the dramatic contests, to go to Hades and bring a poet back. The god meant to bring back Euripides but, in fact, brought back Aeschylus! The theme gave rise to such jests as the singing match with the chorus of frogs while Dionysus crossed the fathomless mere in Charon's boat, and the weighing of the poetry in a balance, "like mutton", which decided the return of Aeschylus to life. A modern example is furnished by an entry in The Journal of Arnold Bennett, which runs:

"*Sunday, January 13th, Comarques.*

"I outlined in the bath this morning an idea of a play about a man being offered a title and his wife insisting on his accepting it against his will."

The Title was finished on May 10 following and registered 285 performances at the Royalty in 1918 and 1919. When Arnold Bennett added a story to the theme, we were told of the Culver family, in which Mrs Culver was most desirous to be called "My Lady" whereas her grown-up boy and girl were convinced that the title promised ruin to their careers. In the beginning Mr

Culver said "No", then "Yes", and, finally, the matter determined itself through an alien factor which intruded itself in the last of the three acts. This act occupied Mr Bennett four days. By this time the story of the Culvers was converted into a plot, and the players could take over.

Similarly, when Barrie conceived *The Admirable Crichton* the underlying theme was: "Resolved that there will always be masters and servants, though circumstances rather than merit will often decide which is which." The story of Lord Loam and his butler, Crichton, followed, and when the story took on a form suitable for a four-act play, Barrie's work ended.

The commonest of all themes and the one best assured of success is the "Cinderella" theme. Musical comedy and comic-opera would suffer a speedy demise, wanting the Cinderella theme. It was developed in *Mr Cinders*, by the naive device of making Cinderella a young man and changing the glass slipper of pantomime into the bowler-hat of musical comedy which Bobby Howes displayed so effectively at curtain-fall. Again, Edith Day in *Irene* of pleasant memory was a shy little milliner who became a dazzling beauty. Edith had eight encores a night for the dance which accompanied her "Sweet little Alice-blue gown".

The underlying themes of drama have reality enough to justify careful analysis and this was undertaken for the French stage by François Venillot in his *Les Prédicateurs de la Scène*. Thus the heading "Family" included themes devoted to attacks upon marriage and the defence of marriage, as, for example, by indicting divorce, as Brieux did in *Le Berceau*. Or there is the variant in the divorced couple who are still in love. What the dramatist will make of the theme is another problem, involving plot and a number of characters. Priestley considered the divorced couple who have recovered their old-time affection in his *Ever Since Paradise*, a production of 1947. In working out the theme and telling the story which it involved, Priestley introduced a couple of pianos and a small inner stage. Roger Livesey and Ursula Jeans were the protagonists on the outer stage, but their comments upon happiness in married life were mainly directed to two youngsters who were drifting apart and whose varying clashes were enacted for the benefit of the audience on the inner stage, into which Roger Livesey and Ursula Jeans also strayed occasionally. These novel theatrical devices constituted the play. The theme was no more than the excuse for exploiting them.

Similarly, an aspect of feminism was explored by Brieux in *Les Trois Filles de M. Dupont*. The relations of employers and employed, the abuses of the law (treated by Brieux in *La Robe Rouge*), and the celibacy of the clergy (Lemaitre's *L'Aînée*) are other examples of theme. Elizabeth Robins's *Votes for Women*, with its remarkable Trafalgar Square scene which Granville-Barker stage-managed so effectively, was a "feminist" theme of a very different type to that in Brieux's play, while *Love on the Dole* sufficiently characterizes one aspect of the employer and employee theme, as *The Admirable Crichton* did another.

Developing a Theme

The theme of *A Doll's House* and its working out is particularly well documented. Ibsen, at fifty years of age, chanced to be in Rome. During a walk an idea came to him and taking a used envelope from his pocket, he jotted it down. The envelope can still be seen and bears the words:

"Rome, 19.10.'78. *Notes for the Modern Tragedy.*

"There are two kinds of spiritual law, two kinds of conscience, one in man, another, altogether different, in woman. . . In practical life the woman is judged by man's law, as though she was not a woman but a man." Ibsen's note continued: "The wife in the play ends by having no idea of what is right or wrong. Natural feeling on the one hand and belief in authority on the other have altogether bewildered her. She has committed forgery and she is proud of it; for she did it out of love for her husband, to save his life. But this husband, with his commonplace principles of honour, is on the side of the Law."

There is no better example of the potentialities of a dramatic theme, in the hands of a master. Observe that what Ibsen had in mind was a tragedy, though not a few readers of *A Doll's House* would class it among the comedies, as there is no violent death. But Ibsen's insight told him that the sense of futile struggle with very little guidance as to what constitutes moral order was to be the main source of tragedy in generations ahead. Important as Ibsen's contributions to stagecraft proved, his *real* influence arose from his divination of new potentialities in drama in relation to a machine-made age, utterly different from those which had nourished the classical dramatists of France, Germany, or Britain. Above all, Ibsen saw that woman must have a far more important part in dramatic plots. In the liberation of women, Ibsen looked for the regeneration of society. A revealing passage in *The Pillars of Society* sums up Ibsen's social philosophy.

Bernick: I have learnt this in these days; it is you women who are the pillars of society.

Sona: Then you have learned a poor wisdom, brother-in-law. No, no, the spirits of truth and of freedom—these are the pillars of society.

With no thought for this leading actor or that actress, but with a full assurance that what he wrote would be spoken in a theatre by men and women, Ibsen set to work.

Nora Helmer was the plaything of her father's leisure and is no more than the child-wife of her husband. This is a fundamental arising from Ibsen's thesis. So we are shown the child-wife returning home after the Christmas shopping. The very first words are.

Nora: Hide the Christmas tree carefully, Helmer. Be sure the children do not see it till this evening, when it is dressed. (*To her Porter*) How much?
Porter: Sixpence.
Nora: There is a shilling. No, keep the change.

A perfect beginning. Even the spendthrift, the potential forger, is etched in surely. A moment later Nora has taken a packet of macaroons from her pocket and is eating one. She goes cautiously to her husband's study door and listens.

Helmer: Is that my little lark twittering out there?
Nora: Yes, it is.

When temptation comes, the little lark twittering outside Helmer's study is going to react as a child. But, slowly, Ibsen builds the character until players and playgoers alike could accept the possibility of Nora's regeneration and thus make the closing scene of *A Doll's House* possible. Her husband's dangerous illness seemed to justify the forgery. Krogstad's blackmailing arouses sympathy for the woman, as do the husband's hysterical reproaches when the forgery is detected and his even more unmanly rejoicings when the threat of an open scandal is removed. Now it is the man who is the weakling, while the woman who fibbed so readily in Act I can face up to deep lying truths in Act III. At last, she can see only herself as she really is. Helmer is the thing of nought.

Nora (putting on her cloak): I cannot spend the night in a strange man's room.
Helmer: But can't we live here like brother and sister?
Nora (putting on her hat): You know very well that would not last

long. (*Puts the shawl around her.*) Good-bye, Torvald. I won't
see the little ones. I know they are in better hands than mine.

And then the curtain—the sound at the outer door of Helmer's
flat closing, the slam which so shocked the theatre world in
England in 1889. Yet, strangely enough, Ibsen was to write a
variant upon this perfect close—a happy ending. Here is the
unbelievable thing:

Nora: For us two to live together would not make a marriage.
  Good-bye (*Going.*)
Helmer: Very well, go. (*Seizes her arm*) But first you shall see your
  children for the last time.
Nora: Let me go. I won't see them again. I can't.
Helmer (*drawing her towards the door on the left*)*:* You *shall* see them.
  (*He opens the door and adds softly*) Look! There they sleep, so
  care-free and calm. To-morrow, when they wake and call for
  mother, they will be motherless.
Nora (*swaying*)*:* Motherless!
Helmer: Even as you were.
Nora: Motherless! (*After an inward fight, she drops her travelling
  bag.*) Oh, I am sinning against myself, but I *cannot* leave them.
  (*She half falls against the door.*)
Helmer (*delighted, but softly*)*:* Nora!
                    (*The Curtain Falls*)

The second version was written by Ibsen as early as March
1880, and was made at the request of a German actress. Ibsen, of
course, was fully aware that the happy ending weakened *A Doll's
House*. But to return to Ibsen's beginnings, *A Doll's House* in embryo. The child-wife gets her name and after that the husband.
Week by week, characters are added and characters grow. To
the macaroons are added Nora's fibbings, the amorous tricks she
plays upon Dr Rank and the Italian costumier, and the Tarantilla
which lead up to the connubial love passages between the half-
drunk Helmer and his frightened wife and, at last, the retort of
retorts:

Helmer: But no man would sacrifice his honour for the one he
  loves.
Nora: Hundreds of thousands of women have done this.

C. E. Montague wrote. "Scarcely one of these things can be found, even in germ, in the first draft of *A Doll's House*. The thing grew like a piece of encrusted architecture. First a bare frame; then the precious stones, the gold, and the mosaics were fastened upon it, as they were built on to the frame of St Mark's at Venice until, by degrees, the thickened walls glowed into full expressiveness." I do not accept C. E. Montague's imagery. The real process is one of growth. My faith is that the Nora whom Janet Achurch, Madge Titheradge, and the Duse brought to life was conceived on an October day in Rome, 1878, and the rest was a process of natural growth, though this does not forbid second thoughts. A second thought of high significance in *A Doll's House* is to be found near the end. As Ibsen drafted the letter scene it ran:

Helmer: You are saved, Nora, you are saved.
Nora: How saved?
Helmer: Look here. He sends you back the promissory note.

In the revised and infinitely more moving version, the dialogue ran:

Helmer: I am saved, Nora, I am saved.
Nora: And I?
Helmer: You, too, of course.

These second thoughts were what Ibsen had in mind when he wrote that, after completing the rough draft, comes the elaboration, the more energetic individualization of the persons and their modes of expression. "Hundreds of thousands of women have done so" was such a second thought.

The ever-present war between the sexes which displays itself so often in the intimacies of married life is a fundamental theme in modern drama. It may be that masculine victory is the solution; on the contrary, the dramatist may have feminine prejudices; lastly, there is the possibility of a stalemate.

Feminine victory was the underlying theme in *Grounds for Divorce*, which reached the London stage in 1925. It was an adaptation from the Hungarian of Ernest Vadja and provided Madge Titheradge with a telling part. She was wedded to a lawyer who specialized in divorce practice and was so interested

in his fair clients that he neglected his wife. Enraged, the wife
burst into her husband's study and flung a pot of black ink at him.
The aim was poor and the inkpot landed upon the wall, but, in
passage, did some damage to the husband's white waistcoat. As
the husband was played by Owen Nares, beloved of matinée girls
in the 'twenties, there was a big laugh in the auditorium, though,
on the stage, the result was a divorce. The husband prepared to
marry again, but Miss Titheradge had other ideas. In the next
act she consulted her husband in his professional capacity and so
interested him that the second wife, in her turn, flung a pot of ink,
this time red and not black. Victory thus remained with Miss
Titheradge.

A more subtle variant illustrating the influence of the underlying theme upon play-making associates itself with *Reunion in
Vienna*, one of the Lunt triumphs. Robert Sherwood, the dramatist, sums up his theme thus, "Wonder is among the indestructibles." A statement to this effect by Carlyle in *Sartor Resartus*
moved Sherwood to write a romantic comedy of Viennese life
dealing with the tendency of human beings to escape from time
to time into lost realms of wonder or romance. It should be
added that *Reunion in Vienna* dates from the years of disillusion-
ment we associate with the Economic Blight of 1931, and that
psychiatry was in the air, doubtless because it was one of numerous possible escapes from an overplus of uncomfortable reality.
Reunion in Vienna begins with Kathie, a middle-aged servant in the
house of Doctor Anton Krug, turning off the wireless, "lest it
should disturb the Herr Doctor". To Kathie, comes Krug's wife
Elena, in the early thirties, but still a prepossessing and self-
possessed woman. How could it be otherwise, when Elena is
played by Lynn Fontanne? The Herr Doctor is forty-five and
unexpectedly tall and handsome. How could he be otherwise, for
the part is in the safe keeping of Alfred Lunt? Now what can
Robert Sherwood have up his sleeve? He tells us that the Herr
Doctor is not only a psycho-analyst but a man with a mission in
post-war Vienna, a Vienna whence the Hapsburgs have been
banished, together with all that once stood for romance. Moreover, the Herr Doctor is bent upon banishing from the world all
false fear of God, so that man may know Him only as "a measur-
able force in cosmic technology". We are coming to grips with

Robert Sherwood's theme, "Wonder is among the indestructibles," when Elena makes this comment: "Well, that *does* cover about everything, doesn't it? And when you have absorbed all the knowledge there is, what will you do with it?"

Mr Sherwood's intentions became plainer still when one of the Herr Doctor's students tells how she was kissed by a taxi-driver, who proves to be none other than the Archduke Rudolf Maximilian von Hapsburg. Which brings to light the intriguing fact that Elena and Rudolf are old acquaintances—indeed so friendly that the old Emperor Franz Josef once caught the couple posing on the fountain at Schönbrunn, naked as the day they were born.

A pretty problem is developing for the Herr Doctor if the taxi-driver from Nice should materialize once more in Vienna. By the end of the act, it is plain that this is precisely what is going to happen. It is the hundredth anniversary of the birth of the Emperor Franz Joseph, and what remains of Viennese aristocracy has determined to celebrate the occasion. Rather unwillingly, but almost forced by her husband, Elena faces a return to the romance of old-time Vienna, to the strains of *The Dollar Princess* waltz.

Anton: Now come, my dear, dress yourself up and try to persuade your old friends that you are still one of them. Sing, dance, flirt, relax! Let yourself go completely!
Elena: Let myself go?
Anton: And see what happens.
Elena: Is that the prescription?

In Act II Elena meets her old flame and she finds that the Hapsburg spirit has not been broken. The Archduke is as possessive as ever, still a sufferer from "Elephantiasis of the Ego" and the disease characterizes the delightful love scene with which Act II culminates. Rudolf picks up Elena and holding her in his arms, waltzes into the archducal bedroom, while what remains of Old Vienna raises champagne glasses and toasts the couple behind the closed door.

Sophia: Happiness and love!
Poffy: May the night last for ever.
Sophia: It is the same Vienna—the same exquisite Vienna.

No, you are wrong. This is not a bedroom comedy but a study in psychological reactions. Elena does not spend the night in the archducal arms. She escapes by way of the bathroom and we meet her again in the Herr Doctor's flat, flustered and breathless and minus her ball-dress, but innocent. Still, what Sherwood's third act promises is the psycho-analysing of Rudolf and the Herr Doctor's reaction to his strange patient. The archduke is a man who lives on sensations. They are meat and drink and the breath of life to him. At the moment he is desperately in need of nourishment—nourishment for his self-esteem. The possession of Elena for a single night would suffice. Well, the cure does not take that form, or did it? In any case, the archduke departs with the words: "I call your roof tree blessed, for beneath it a Hapsburg has been entertained and has been granted into the bargain a superb demonstration of applied psychology."

But, if you have not seen *Reunion in Vienna*, do so, and, in it, the Lunts. If you cannot, read the play. And, by the way, how good Cecil Parker was as the Herr Doctor in the Lyric Theatre production in 1934!

The Money and Love Theme

The conflict between money and love has been the theme of successful plays, comic and tragic, times without number. M. Bernstein, a Parisian of Jewish parentage, treated the theme more than once, doubtless because he found opportunities for highly emotional acting which were his chief aim in play-making. When Bernstein wrote his *Samson* in 1907, he treated the problem from the standpoint of the money-maker and his wife. We were shown the money-making husband not only avenging the attack upon his personal honour by a successful Stock Exchange coup which ruined his adversary, but in the process, regaining his wife's regard and affection.

In *Après Moi* (1911), M. Bernstein pictured an apparently prosperous sugar refiner, Bourgade by name, magnificently played by Le Bargy. Unknown to Bourgade, his wife is indulging in an ugly intrigue with a young friend of the family. M. Bernstein, however, had no intention of repeating himself. Whereas in *Samson* the money was an actuality, in *Après Moi* the supposed millionaire is not only a bankrupt but a swindler, in danger of instant arrest. Indeed, his only chance of financial salvation is that the young lover whom he has defrauded may not prosecute. Loving his wife, the unhappy man determines to commit suicide. We see him taking the revolver from its case, he puts it to his temple and at that moment there is the sound of a door opening and closing in the corridor. The hand with the revolver drops, the man rushes out to find Irene, the wife, in night attire, for she has just left her young lover. Irene refuses to reveal the name of the man and her husband has no suspicion that it might be his young ward. Yet, as she makes her confession, Irene notices her husband's condition and extracts a confession in turn from him. He is a thief, in danger of prison. But now there is no more thought of suicide. Bourgade has something to live for—to discover who is his wife's lover, the wife for whom he had intended to make a supreme sacrifice.

M. Bernstein has still one of his three acts to fill and emotion is piled on emotion when the young lover reveals his part in the intrigue by regarding the loss of his personal fortune as negligible in comparison with the possible loss of Irene. Instead, he demands the right to console the wife who is wasting her youth and beauty upon a ruined man. The climax comes when Bourgade understands that without Irene life will be insupportable and he faces suicide a second time. But now Irene cannot bear the thought of sending a man to death. Bourgade, the husband, needs her more than her lover. As the curtain falls upon *Après Moi*, the wife faces the torture of a loveless existence which will continue until death.

It will be noticed that in *Après Moi* the unhappy wife was faced with the dilemma that life with her lover was only possible over her husband's dead body. Rather than face this, Irene chose lasting unhappiness. What if she had accepted her husband's suicide and thus asserted her right to happiness? This dilemma was akin to that propounded in Keith Winter's *The Shining Hour*, a production at the St James's in 1934, which gave Gladys Cooper and Raymond Massey telling parts. The characters in Mr Winter's play belonged to the Linden family and the story was particularly concerned with Mariella's love for her brother-in-law, David. The third character in the story was David's

G

young wife, Judy, admirably played by Adrianne Allen. Realizing that, without her husband's love, life has nothing to offer, Judy throws herself into a blazing barn. The climax of *The Shining Hour* comes when Mariella has to persuade David that his young wife's sacrifice would have been in vain unless he felt free to marry again.

Dodie Smith's interest in the theatre developed when she became an actress in early womanhood. This was also the time when she wrote her only unsuccessful play. Realizing her disabilities as an actress, Dodie Smith turned to business and became buyer for a London furnishing firm. Her work took her to the Leipzig Fair and when it ended she took a holiday in the Tyrol. Here she imagined a Manchester working girl falling in love with a Tyrolese innkeeper, not knowing he was a married man. Returning home, Dodie Smith spent two or three hours each evening writing a play around the imagined girl and the young innkeeper. When it was finished she spent three months typing a fair copy. *Autumn Crocus* proved a sensational success, largely because Franz Lederer, a Czech actor, who knew no English when he came to London to play the part of the young innkeeper, supported Fay Compton in the prettiest love story of 1931.

In Dodie Smith's *Dear Octopus* the theme was the dominating influence of family life, that is, the theme which was explored from another angle in *Theatre Royal*. Dodie Smith's play took its name from the toast which Nicholas Randolph (John Gielgud) proposed in the final act: "Here's to the Family—that dear octopus from whose tentacles we are never quite able to escape, nor, in our inmost hearts, do we wish to do so."

The Randolph family have gathered to celebrate a golden wedding and the action of the play is thus confined to a week-end. It might be said that there is no plot in *Dear Octopus*. Almost the only thing that happens is that Nicholas, the middle-aged bachelor, finds that for many a long year he has loved the self-sacrificing Fanny (Angela Baddeley) and did not know it. Again, Dame Marie Tempest, the grandmother in both *Dear Octopus* and *Theatre Royal*, sings an old-time song which sends her prodigal daughter, home after seven years in Paris, weeping from the room. But, plot or no plot, Dodie Smith introduced us to a number of pleasant and essentially real people, including the inhabitants of a nursery, with characters played by Muriel Pavlow, Pat Sylvester, and Sylvia Hammond. Add Valerie Taylor as the prodigal daughter and Leon Quartermaine and Kate Cutler in other rôles, and every playgoer admitted full satisfaction.

Dodie Smith's gift is that of making something which will furnish excellent acting opportunities out of relatively little. When she has decided upon her theme, she gets to work upon a suitable environment and a set of characters with actable things to do. In *Call It a Day* (the Court, 1933) Owen Nares was a respectable accountant, comfortably married to Fay Compton, with a couple of daughters and a son approaching the dangerous age. All five came face to face with temptation in the course of a day which began in Owen Nares's bedroom, with the accountant occupying one bed and Miss Compton in another nearby, as his wife, Dorothy. The day ended with the two in bed at midnight. Most of the first act was occupied with the struggles of the Hilton family for possession of the two bathrooms of their suburban house; but, what matter, every one had been amused and pleased.

But a theme may be far removed from the day-to-day matters which interest Dodie Smith and which she treats with such insight and ingenuity. Lord Dunsany, of all people, once decided to write a play based upon the Voronoff glandular treatment which its discoverer claimed would postpone old-age. He called it *Lord Adrian* and it was played at the Gate Theatre. The particular angle he selected was an aged duke anxious to deprive a grandson of the family estates. The scheme succeeds inasmuch as a son is born to the aged duke. Now for the Dunsany touch. Fourteen years have gone by and the son and heir is adolescent. But the monkey-gland has not worked altogether to plan. The boy develops an astonishing love and understanding of animal-bird life, and with this goes a contempt for the human race. There is no animal on the ducal estates which is not there for man's pleasure. This the boy decides must end. As the power to create fire alone gives the man superiority over the beasts the boy decides to give them this knowledge and with it power to control the earth. Lord Dunsany's fantasy succeeded because, though the fundamental idea was utterly unacceptable to the reason, the details were precise. Read *Lord Adrian* and see.

The Invasion Theme

An imaginary invasion of Britain by the Germans was the theme of two well-known plays, Guy du Maurier's *An English-man's Home* and Noel Coward's *Peace in Our Time*. The comparison is interesting because *An Englishman's Home* was the work of an amateur and Noel Coward's play that of a man of the theatre, with all the devices for arousing and sustaining interest at his fingers' tips. Nothing could have been simpler and more direct than the treatment of the invasion of Britain theme in *An Englishman's Home*. We are introduced to Myrtle Villa in the Essex village of Wickham. Geoff Smith twits Paul Robinson for wasting hard-earned leisure as a volunteer. "A mug's game", is Geoff Smith's phrase. Mr Brown, the typical John Bull of the play, is inclined to think that the volunteer movement is tending to convert the English people to militarism. Mr Brown suffers a quick change of mind and mood in the second act, when the German invasion is in full progress and Paul Robinson, who at least "tried to do something", is found wandering idly about because "no one has ever told him what should be done." In the end, Mr Brown dies defending his home.

When he wrote *Peace in Our Time*, Noel Coward worked on a canvas of bigger proportions and used a much larger variety of colours. Dating his play, the Spring of 1940, he showed a typical "pub" in the West End, the sort of place where Londoners of all types might resort and whence a resistance movement might be organized and launched. Plainly the background in itself gives promise of difficulties. Coward has allied a theme with heroic potentialities with a background which not a few playgoers may well regard as ignoble. But the dramatist is the Coward who wrote *Cavalcade* and he has "theatre" in the marrow of his bones. Note how he introduces his theme. "The Shy Gazelle" lies somewhere between Knightsbridge and Sloane Square. Drinks are being served; a lorry-driver or two drop in; there is the editor of a weekly who betrays a tendency to Left-Wing sympathies. Just an ordinary "pub" bar, entertaining a cross-section of our people. Then comes the moment for the nine o'clock news. The wireless is turned on. Big Ben strikes.

Publican's Wife: It's funny to think that that can *still* be heard all over the world.

The word *still* comes with the crack of a pistol shot, as Coward knew it would. Why the word *still?* A moment later, we know. The wireless tells us that Adolf Hitler and Goering are to parade the Mall on the morrow. London is in the hands of the Germans. Thanks to Coward's ingenuity, audiences accept his amazing thesis, and are ready to follow the dramatist's imaginings. As for those in charge of "The Shy Gazelle", regardless of the invasion, they get on with their job, serving drinks to Germans and Britons alike. When the publican's wife urges flight to the country, this man of the bulldog breed avers that he will go on serving drinks until a little British army is ready once more for its rounds. His boy is reported killed, but he carries on. When he is alone, he pours himself a drink and lifts his glass: "Here's to you, son!"

I am not concerned to answer the question whether Coward, in fact, met all the difficulties inherent in his choice of such a background for such a theme. In the end an allied army musters in France and this time the news comes to the Knightsbridge pub from the secret radio. There follows the National Anthem and the time for curtain-fall. When *Peace in Our Time* was produced at the Lyric in 1947, London had a chance to see a very different treatment of the same theme in a play by Sartre, in which France was the invaded country. For *Men Without Shadows* Sartre chose as his background a school-house in the hills near Grenoble. We see an attic in which three members of the Resistance movement, a boy of sixteen and an unhappy girl, are awaiting torture by the Gestapo. The schoolroom below, with its rows of children's desks, is the torture room. One by one the victims are taken below for the knouting, the finger-nail tearing, and other fiendish devices. Will any of the five reveal the name or whereabouts of the French resistance leader? The three men are sure of themselves, so is the girl; but the boy of sixteen?

John Steinbeck's *The Moon is Down*, which had a run at the

Whitehall Theatre in 1943, reached imaginative heights which *An Englishman's Home* and Mr Coward's invasion play neither attempted nor achieved. It turned upon precisely the same theme, the invasion of the homeland by an invader, and the reason it was a better play is that, directly Steinbeck got to grips with his theme—assuming a conquered country was his theme—he found a secondary theme. This was that the one impossible thing in the world, the one thing that can't be done, is "to break man's spirit permanently".

Steinbeck's scene was laid in a small mining town, anywhere, and quickly it was plain that what interested Steinbeck was what people like Mr Brown or Fred Shattock, Noel Coward's publican, will do to preserve their freedom. Slowly the victors find that their nerves are strained to breaking-point consequent upon the hatred they have created. The German colonel knows that the repressive orders he has to carry out are cruel and futile, but, for a German, orders from a superior are orders and he obeys. Opposed to the German is the old mayor who is the chief instrument in persuading the German that shootings will not break the spirit of a freedom-loving people. The close of *The Moon is Down* shows the mayor going to his death, but assured that the warfare will go on. As the mayor said, "They can't arrest the Mayor. The Mayor is an idea conceived by free men. It will escape arrest." But the complementary truth was that the enemy, too, realized defeat. They were being defeated by the white faces behind the curtains listening. As one of the Germans said: "We have beaten them; we have won everywhere, and they wait and obey and they wait."

When Denis Johnston sat down to write *The Moon in the Yellow River* his theme was the evils of a machine age. The title was doubtless an afterthought due to a Chinese poem about a man who attempted to embrace the moon which he saw reflected in the Yellow River and which seemed a symbol of the evil that machinery could do to things of beauty and imagination in Ireland if Tausch's power station was allowed to arise in Eire. Consequently Blake, the Irish reactionary, and his friends decided to blow up the power station, informing Herr Tausch of their intention beforehand.

"I might be like you, Herr Tausch, if I chose, and this country might be like yours if you had your way. But I don't choose and you won't have your way, because we intend to keep our small corner of the globe safe for humanity."

From another angle *The Moon in the Yellow River* is a symbol of the crazy logic of the reactionary Irishmen, which drives Herr Tausch, the clear-headed scientist, to his final outburst. "This is no country. It's a damned debating society."

When Shaw wrote *Widowers' Houses*, in which the theme was the responsibilities of those who owned slum properties, he did not fall into the error of harping continually upon the suffering involved, as the writer of a blue-book would have done. On the contrary, his first scene was laid in the garden of a Rhenish hotel and was concerned with the heroine's efforts to secure a chaste kiss from her nervous lover, Trench. This was the memorable salute the report of which "reverberated down the Rhine". Thus half an act was exhausted and it was not until curtain-fall, when the prospectus regarding the young lady had been fully discussed, that Shaw introduced the ominous word, mortgage. The moral of *Widowers' Houses* only begins to unfold with the entry of Lickcheese (Jimmy Welch's first great part), when Shaw's underlying purpose is disclosed. Lickcheese does the dirty work for Sartorius, the owner of the slum properties. What really mattered was said when Lickcheese turned furiously upon the bridegroom who-was-to-be with the devastating: "Which of us is the worse, I should like to know? Me that wrings the money out to keep a house over my children, or you that spend it and try to shove the blame on to me?"

But the word "theme" can have connotations and craft consequences apart from the working out of a line of thought. It may focus attention upon a character; indeed, that is one of its primary functions. Thus the theme in Shaw's *The Doctor's Dilemma* was what type of person had the best right to have a chance of life—the genius or the useful citizen. Plainly, the choice of the theme forced attention upon the genius and Shaw has told us that he constructed the role of Dudebat from three elements— the sexual exploits of Aveling, Wagner's "End of a Musician in Paris", and the letters of a lady who deifies her dead husband as Jennifer deifies the dead Dudebat.

It is no easy thing to suggest genius on the stage. Shaw did it successfully in *The Doctor's Dilemma*. So did Gordon Daviot in *The Laughing Woman*, which was based upon the life-story of that unfortunate sculptor, Henri Gaudier, and his companion Sophia Brzeska. The play was more mature than Gordon Daviot's successful *Richard of Bordeaux* and deserved better than it got from London playgoers. Stephen Haggard as René Latour was the bohemian genius, bent upon creating beauty in a chaotic world. Equally good was the Ingrid of Veronica Turleigh.

Whereas plots and characterizations are infinite in number and variety, themes are limited. Thus, the thesis "love is stronger than death" may be the theme of a play. It was in *The Sacred Flame* which Somerset Maugham wrote for Gladys Cooper, when she was managing the Playhouse in 1929. The particular aspect Maugham discussed was whether death was better than the shattering of a man's faith in the reality of his wife's love. When he came to add a plot to the underlying theme Maugham conceived a mother who gave an overdose of a sleeping draught to her son, lest he should discover that a well-loved wife was about to have a child by his own brother. As a further complication, the son had been maimed in an aeroplane disaster six years earlier.

Naturally, the puzzle "Who killed Maurice Tabret?" was presented to playgoers, but the real issue, the thing that players cannot forget, proved to be the motives which moved the mother of the stricken man to kill him, not in spite of, but because of her all-wise, all-embracing love. Mary Jerrold played the mother and Gladys Cooper the wife. To them was added Clare Eames as the nurse, whose affection for the man she had tended for so many months was akin to idolatry, the idolatry a starved soul can feel for the thing which gives her some release from sex repressions. The character of the nurse in *The Sacred Flame* is an example of the complex weaving of character and theme which comes to a master dramatist if he has what Maugham calls the "knack".

As has been said, for Somerset Maugham the "knack" means telling a story with economy of means and the fullest possible unification. "My preposessions in the arts are on the side of law and order. I like the story that fits . . . I like a story to have a beginning, a middle and an end. I have a weakness for a point." In other words, Maugham was the greatest exponent of the well-made play in his day and generation, though he had a hold upon the human realities which the dramatists of the 'eighties and the 'nineties of the last century ignored because of their obsession with Act Three and its exciting situation. In *The Casuarina Tree*, Maugham said of the "reality approach" to story telling, "actual characters are much too shadowy to serve as characters in a work of imagination. We see real people only in the flat, but for the purposes of fiction they must be seen in the round. To make a living personage, it is necessary to combine suggestions from a dozen sources." But this analysis would mislead if another dictum of Maugham were not added. It comes from the Preface to *Don Fernando*. "A writer constructs characters by observation, but he only gives them life if they are himself." Which means that a vital character in play or novel is not a mosaic but a fresh creation.

CHAPTER 5

PLOTS AND PLOT-MAKING

W HEN a theme has been chosen and the dramatist is assured that no more than three hours' traffic of the stage will suffice for its development, a new task presents itself—the preparation of a plot. The progress from theme to plot can be illustrated from Paul Hervieu's *L'Enigme*, a play which masqueraded in London under the title *Caesar's Wife*. Its theme was the question whether a husband had the right to kill his wife or his wife's lover if he finds she has been unfaithful. For his plot Paul Hervieu imagined two brothers in their country house with their two wives. There are also two guests, one of them young M. de Vivace, whom the brothers surprise on the stairs. Has Vivace come from the bed of Giselle or Leonore? Both women deny any guilt, until Vivace shoots himself to save the reputation of the unknown. She proves to be Leonore, who breaks down and confesses everything.

Old-time critics used to call a plot of this type "the fable", but before its construction is entered upon yet another decision must be made. Is the play to depend for its success upon an exciting situation or upon varied incident, giving ample scope for character-acting? Sardou was a dramatist who relied markedly upon exciting situations. So did the majority of British playwrights trained in the Victorian and Edwardian tradition. Remember that the younger Dumas, a master in the construction of situation, said that "the art of the theatre is the art of preparation." Elsewhere Dumas wrote, "Before every situation that a dramatist creates he should ask himself three questions. In this situation what I should do? What would other people do? What ought to be done?" No more useful hints have been given to budding dramatists. Every really thrilling scene in drama has called for careful preparation and even over-preparation. The third act of Pinero's *The Gay Lord Quex* is thrilling in a high degree, but how tortuous was the preparation! Nevertheless, recalling the playing of John Hare and Irene Vanbrugh, the tortuous preparation was easily forgiven.

Sophy Fullgarney is a successful West End manicurist; indeed, she is the owner of an establishment at No. 185 New Bond Street, devoted to manicuring and the dispensing of articles for the toilet. Just the place where a marquis and his cronies might foregather as a preliminary to a meeting at Fauncey Court, Richmond, in the following act. Even Act I of *Quex* did not suffice for the foundations. Act II takes place in the Italian Garden, Fauncey Court, as Sophy Fullgarney now has to spend the night in close proximity to an errant Duchess, once on very friendly terms with the gay Lord. Sophy is to sleep at Fauncey Court, instead of driving back with her plebeian lover, the Bond Street palmist, in the cool of the evening, as had been arranged. The novelty of the scene in the manicurist's establishment, with Miss Moon, Miss Huddle, and the rest at work, and the luxurious charm of the Richmond garden with the quaint little fountain from the Villa Marchotti, almost justify the lengthy preparation. Nevertheless, it is the *dénouement* that matters, and, at midnight, in the Duchess of Strood's boudoir and bedroom, Pinero springs his surprise. As has been said, the Duchess is an old flame of the gay Lord and she calls for a parting which befits "the numb despair of a piteous climax". The parting is to take the form of drinking the self-same champagne which associated itself with a colourful evening in Stockholm years earlier. Quex comes. The Duchess disrobes discreetly; the champagne, Felix Poubelle, Carte d'Or, is uncorked; the cigarettes, Argyropulos, are lit, when a sound is heard in the maid's room adjoining the boudoir. It is Sophy at the keyhole, bent upon saving her foster-sister from the gay Lord.

From that moment Pinero is on sure ground. The gay Lord realizes that "he is done for," but he determines to save the reputation of the Duchess. He sends her away and lures Sophy into the bedroom. Perhaps she can be bribed. No, then she can be frightened. She is defiant. But what will be the plebeian lover's reaction to the news that Sophy has spent a long night with the gay Lord, for the bedroom door has been locked? Yes, that is an idea. Sophy storms, pleads, and weeps, and, at last, is persuaded to write a compromising letter to be used if she "splits". It is no sooner written than Sophy realizes that this is "selling" her foster-sister to the wickedest man in London.

"Why, it's like selling Muriel. Just to get myself out of this I'm simply handing her over to you. I won't do it! I won't!"

Seizing the bell-rope, Sophy pulls it and alarms the household. But it is now the turn of Quex to relent. He sees Sophy now as "a fine plucked 'un". When the household comes, the manicurist opens the door a few inches, makes some excuse for ringing the bell and, as the gay Lord turns down the lights and creeps from the Duchess's bedroom, Sophy returns to her own room.

On that memorable first night at the Globe, Irene Vanbrugh was recalled again and again. In the part, she was a player of the front rank. John Hare's Lord Quex was no less accomplished, but then London audiences had known Hare's gifts for a quarter of a century. Irene Vanbrugh's acting had been a revelation. She had written a page in theatrical history on that April evening in 1899.

The Gay Lord Quex of Pinero was a comedy of situation. Everything worked up to the highly theatrical but wholly effective third act. Frederick Lonsdale wrote another comedy of situation with a very similar third act when he penned *The Last of Mrs Cheyney*. This was the play through which Gerald du Maurier lost a small fortune because he went to sleep while the author was reading the script aloud. Gladys Cooper, who kept awake, bought the rights for £5,000 and made £50,000. Mrs Cheyney, whom Miss Cooper played herself, was a shop girl when she was discovered by a gentleman crook (Ronald Squire), lately of Eton College, and was persuaded that she was meant for better things, better things meaning prettier dresses, jewels, and more certain and richer food. All that was asked was that the shop girl should become a pupil of the old Etonian and prey upon the better-to-do. In particular, Ronald Squire, masquerading as a butler, was bent upon stealing a famous rope of pearls. They were to be abstracted from the bedroom of the owner by Mrs Cheyney. Unfortunately, in the bedroom the ex-shop girl was faced by Lord Dilling (Du Maurier) who had £30,000 a year and no occupation and was no better morally than Pinero's Lord Quex. Naturally enough, the situation developed on lines similar to those in which Sophy Fullgarney met her gay Lord. At the end of the bedroom scene Mrs Cheyney also rang the bell and alarmed the household, sacrificing the pearls, but with the shreds of her honour intact, at any rate in the eyes of Lord Dilling.

Another variant upon the situation which Pinero exploited in *Quex* is to be found in *Potiphar's Wife*. Edgar Middleton wrote the play for the Globe Theatre in 1927, with Jeanne de Casalis in the title rôle. The husband was an Earl, aged sixty, and the Joseph of the story was the Earl's handsome young chauffeur, whom Lady Potiphar lured to her bedroom at midnight on the pretext that an electric fan needed mending. When Miss de Casalis was in pyjamas and the chauffeur still remained unresponsive, Lady Potiphar staged a *Quex* scene in reverse. Locking the door, she roused the household and complained of an assault, with the result that the chauffeur was arrested and had to stand his trial for illegal assault. However, the lady broke down under cross-examination and all was well.

What the younger Dumas meant by "preparation is everything" can be illustrated equally aptly from Anthony Armstrong's excellent thriller *Ten Minute Alibi*. In this play, the preparation took the form of a "dream crime", in which the criminal saw enacted the "perfect" crime he was to commit in the following act. Very cleverly, the dramatist saw that excellent "theatre" would arise from the audience comparing the dream version with the actual thing and, incidentally, he gave the players a chance for some subtle effects, when they added a thought more energy to the real murder than was called for in the dream version. There were also slight changes in the action which kept the attention alert.

Apart from this clever "preparation" for the actual murder, Anthony Armstrong's plot could claim some originality in treating a familiar device (tampering with the hands of a clock). The trick sufficed to deceive the detectives but (clever touch), it did not deceive the girl who had loved the murdered man but, who in the end, came to see that the man she really loved was the murderer. The closing lines of the play were:

Colin: May I see you again—after this?
Betty: I don't know, Colin. Not just yet. Wait a little.

Just enough to send audiences away with the comforting conviction that the murderer-hero would not be punished too severely. Remember, Armstrong had to justify a rather callous murder and, to this end, had to emphasize the very ugly nature of the dead man. For the rest, there was ample action, rapid alternations of fortune and no waste of stage time. As for the tampering with the clock, what would take a lot of explanation on paper was very easily understandable when played at the Embassy and the Haymarket, with the actual clock well in view and the moving of the hands done in full sight of the audience. Just enough suspicion attached to the murderer-hero to make his examination by the two detectives in the third act highly exciting. An excellent cast headed by Celia Johnson, Robert Douglas, and Anthony Ireland helped the dramatist to a signal success. Maisie Darrell, of happy though short-lived memory, was the first Betty and was fully as charming as Celia Johnson who took up the part later.

In this matter of story-telling for the stage J. B. Priestley's beginning as a dramatist is instructive. He was an established man of letters. Desirous of finding out whether he *could* write a play, he got to work upon *Dangerous Corner*. He chose as his theme, "What might have happened if a single sentence had remained unspoken?" In order that the test he was applying to himself should be complete, it seemed important that the story should not be too simple. Accordingly, he made his curtain rise upon a family party, which was listening to a broadcast play, entitled *The Sleeping Dog*. It dealt with a husband searching for secrets which would be the better if unrevealed. *The Sleeping Dog* should have served as a warning to Robert Caplan, but it did not. His untimely questions recalled to his family an unrevealed mystery, how their brother Martin had died. Quickly, Priestley made it plain that the dead brother was the skeleton in the Caplan cupboard. The catastrophe was reached when one of the party, played by Flora Robson, recognized a certain musical cigarette box. The exchange of gossip led to vague suspicion, suspicion to recrimination, and recrimination to definite accusation, and all because Robert Caplan had not kept his mouth shut. Had he done so, he would never have blown out his brains in the closing act and the "dangerous corner" of Priestley's title would have been avoided.

But let us come to closer grips with Mr Priestley's two-fold problem, to tell a good story in terms of the theatre and at the same time to provide a body of players with varied opportunities for the display of their talents. Having stated his theme, the writer lost no time. Quickly, it is found that two of the party, Freda, Robert's wife, and Olwen Peel saw Martin Caplan on the afternoon of his death and yet had said nothing of the meetings. It seems £500 had been stolen and both Freda and Olwen had wanted to clear Martin from the accusation of theft. In fact, the family conclave quickly discovers that the £500 was stolen by Charles Stanton, who is ready enough to acknowledge the theft now that Martin's suicide so plainly burdens Martin's memory with the theft. Nevertheless, Stanton's confession, while clearing Martin of theft, only serves to make his suicide more mysterious. Pressed, Stanton explains that Martin's life was in a tangle because Freda, Robert's wife, was in love with her brother-in-law. Indeed Freda admits that she had lived with Martin for a few days, though she knew only too well Martin had no real love for herself.

It was at this point in the family conclave that Olwen Peel came prominently into the dramatic picture. Priestley's second act ends with her cry, "Martin didn't shoot himself," while Act III opens with her confession, "I shot him." It was not murder, but an accident. Olwen went to Martin's cottage to inquire about the missing £500 and found him under the influence of drugs. In a mood of devilish gaiety, he had taunted Olwen with her spinster repressions and had tried to stir her to passion by showing her some horrible obscene drawings. Then Martin had locked the door of his room and threatened her with a revolver, until in a struggle to maintain her maidenhood, the revolver went off and Martin was killed. Flora Robson played Olwen Peel and the enforced confession and the description of the death struggle lost nothing in Miss Robson's telling.

There only remained the youthful Betty, who had not been present during the greater part of the family conclave. She, at any rate, was without taint. But wait, Stanton, the thief, had not been alone on the evening of Martin's death and when Olwen left the cottage it was to Stanton she went for help and guidance. When she reached Stanton's room, she found him with Betty and had

crept away. Indeed, it was now plain to Olwen that it was for
Betty that Stanton had stolen the £500. The revelation was more
than Robert Caplan could stand. Betty, whom he respected and
loved more than his own wife, was no more than "a greedy little
cat on the tiles". Finding life was utterly valueless, Robert shot
himself.

Priestley's last surprise was a three-seconds fade out to a black-
out, then another revolver shot, a woman's scream and a
woman's sobbing. We are back where we began. When the
black-out ends, the opening scene is re-enacted to the point where
Robert Caplan refrains from pursuing his awkward questions
regarding Martin's musical box. Instead, some one turns on the
wireless again and a tune comes up. The curtain falls upon the
party dancing to it. The dangerous corner has been passed.

But if, instead of J. B. Priestley, it had been Lord Dunsany—
the lover of fantasy rather than the realistic investigator of social
relations? Lord Dunsany has also written a play treating what
might have happened, though in Lord Dunsany's case it was the
undone deed rather than the unspoken word which was in
question. J. B. Priestley might well have called *Dangerous Corner*
"If", this being the title Lord Dunsany gave his play. What
would have happened if, instead of catching the 8.15 ten years
earlier, one had missed it and travelled by the 8.35? John Beal in
If has an opportunity to find out. On the 8.35 he meets a
woman, pretty and attractive but, plainly, in trouble. The
effort to help her carries John Beal far from the suburb where he
seemed anchored for life. Soon John Beal is in Al Shaldomir, a
Ruritanian kingdom in the Middle East. Nevertheless, there are
drawbacks and Dunsany fastens upon them. One's expectation
of life no longer bears any relation to the statistical tables upon
which British insurance companies rely. Beal has wealth and
power in Al Shaldomir, but perhaps the peace and quietude
which followed upon the journey by the 8.15 was preferable.

Lord Dunsany's *If* makes considerable demands upon the
critical faculty of his audiences, as all writers of fantasy must, but
audiences are generous in this respect. Francisque Sarcey, the
famous dramatic critic of *Le Temps*, was insistent that audiences
would accept any postulate which a dramatist put forward, providing the happening took place before curtain-rise. What was

Henry Irving as Mathias in the Dream Scene from *The Bells*, Lyceum Theatre (1871) (*see page 288*).

The Predecessor of "The Old Vic", Waterloo Road. The Royal Victoria Hall and People's Coffee Tavern in 1880 (*see page* 39).

all-important in Sarcey's judgement was that consequences arising from an unusual event should be plausible and entertaining.
In other words, the public will swallow a camel in times past,
but will strain at a gnat in times present. What are never acceptable are improbable premises reaching impossible conclusions.
Given a suitable setting and a competent cast, the strangest of
coincidences can justify themselves on the stage, as scores of
Mayfair melodramas of the 'nineties show. *Captain Swift*, the play
by Haddon Chambers, which gave currency to the phrase "the
long arm of coincidence", is a case in point.

A retired bushranger able and willing to settle down as a
country gentleman in England after a career of crime was far
from easy of acceptance, particularly when the place had so
many associations with Captain Swift's boyhood. Nevertheless,
Tree's stage setting of a Victorian house carried full conviction;
so did the acting of the principal players. Curiously enough
Captain Swift had small success when it was played by Charles
Warner in Australia. Good actor as he was, Warner could not
persuade Australians to accept the dramatist's postulates. They
knew too much about bushrangers. But English playgoers
flocked to *Captain Swift*.

Here is Haddon Chambers's story, replete with "the long arm
of coincidence" which played so large a part in the play. As a
nameless child, Wilding, alias Captain Swift, was shipped to
Australia to save his mother's reputation and became a bushranger and bank thief. Tiring of these excitements, Swift took
the name of Wilding and returned to England, where he chanced
to come to the very house where his unknown mother was living.
Here Wilding's gay dare-devilry and ready tongue won the love
of Stella Darbisher, the part played by Mrs Tree. In the house,
too, was Wilding's foster-brother, the butler Marshall, who not
only makes a shrewd guess at Wilding's past but hates him and
puts the detective Ryan on Wilding's track. Tree's assumption
of jaunty assurance and outburst of angry fury helped to make
Captain Swift a telling character, though Lady Monckton's
emotional acting as the erring mother and Mrs Tree's playing
of the love scenes with Wilding were other factors in the play's
success. Stella Darbisher's farewell to the man she knew could
never become her husband was a thing of real beauty and, indeed

H

the whole scene, as played by Mr and Mrs Tree, was pathetic in a high degree.

And Tree? Knowing the game is up, he makes desperate efforts to maintain his self-control but fails; then, with trembling fingers, he clutches at the glass with the poison and dies. The hunted Wilding has found life insupportable and he passes to the Never, Never Land.

Undue expense and wastage of time over scene-setting make numerous changes of scenery undesirable under modern conditions, while undue length may make a play practically unactable. Swinburne's *Bothwell* is about four times as long as *Hamlet*. No one has decided how many words are needed to bring a character to life. Shakespeare utilised 1,870 lines for Hamlet's dialogue. Sometimes a line of dialogue suffices and there are even examples of memorable characters saying nothing at all, or even failing to put in a stage appearance at all, the boy Edward, in *Edward, My Son*, being an example. A writer who cannot make a living creature from twenty lines of dialogue ought not to be a dramatist at all. As a piece of practical knowledge, a quarto sheet of double-spaced typewritten paper plays for approximately one minute, so 120 of them make up a three-act play for a modern theatre, while a short play, such as Galsworthy's *The Silver Box* occupies about seventy-five typewritten pages.

Several factors operate when a decision must be made as to the number of acts required for a given plot and the rises and falls of tension the dramatist has in mind. The Greeks were content with a single act, though there was a certain connection between the three or four plays which were acted on a given day. In *Getting Married* (what an excellent cast it had!) Bernard Shaw reverted to the Greek method of a unity of time and place. His play was about the same length as *The Doctor's Dilemma*, with its five acts and five changes of background, but it has only a single scene. Shaw explained that, when a drama reaches a certain point of poetic and intellectual evolution, the Greek form is inevitable. He added that its adoption in *Getting Married* was not a mere display of virtuosity, but the spontaneous falling of a play of ideas into the form most suitable to it.

It may be added that commercial managements demand two tolerably lengthy intervals, the final one permitting a last drink before excise regulations necessitate the closing of the bar. Our study, however, can disregard these mundane considerations.

Pinero's *The Benefit of the Doubt*, which followed *The Second Mrs Tanqueray* and *The Notorious Mrs Ebbsmith*, is blessed with one of the best openings in "well-made" drama. The action begins with the rise of the curtain and the fate threatening the protagonists is at once suggested. The theme is an indiscreet but wholly innocent wife who, following her husband's action for a divorce, is accorded "the benefit of the doubt". The story begins in the drawing-room of Mrs Emtage, the empty-headed mother of Theophila Fraser, the respondent in the suit of Allingham versus Allingham, Fraser intervening. A friend brings the latest news from the Court. "Everything is going swimmingly." The Emtages are in black, but it now seems that, after all, there was no need to have "dressed funereally", as though "they had deliberately prepared for all emergencies." Then comes the announcement of the verdict, but not from any one who was actually in Court, for Theo asked all her friends to leave the Court; only herself and her husband are to hear the verdict. The Emtages are told that Theo has been righted. Mrs Emtage hopes the Judge has had the grace to apologize. But all the while, Pinero has been at pains to emphasize the evidence against Theo., i.e. Jack Allingham's visit to Theo Fraser's rooms after midnight. We are led to the very verge of the full story of the trial when Theophila comes.

Theophila: Yes, Mrs Allingham's petition was dismissed. But Sir John Clarkson and Mr Martyn, my other Counsel, all my friends, in fact—were a little too sanguine.

Mrs Emtage: Too sanguine?

Theophila: Oh much too sanguine. The judge was rather rough on me.

Mrs Emtage: What on earth do you—

Theophila: Rather down on me, severe. My behaviour, my conduct, had been careless, indiscreet, he says—

Mrs Emtage (under her breath): Indiscreet?

Theophila: Hardly characteristic of a woman who is properly watchful of her own and her husband's reputation—honour.

Justina (the sister): Theo!

Theophila (disjointedly): But at the same time he said Mrs Allingham had scarcely succeeded in establishing conclusively in his mind . . . Oh! . . . and he thought that even the petitioner herself on further reflection would be desirous I should receive the—benefit of the doubt . . . and—and something about costs.

Could a theme be put before an audience more neatly and concretely? We were ready for Theo's first meeting with her dour husband. There followed naturally her flight to Allingham, which led, in turn, to the situation in the second act, in which Theo wildly asks Jack to take her away and, by the very deed, persuades Mrs Allingham, who has overheard the scene, of Theo's essential innocence. The play was too "dry" to become a favourite of a large public, but as telling "theatre" it stands high.

"*Oh, and something about costs.*" There was a similar crack of the whip in the opening of *John Bull's Other Island*, the line which brought Thomas Broadbent to life, and, with him, Shaw's play.

Broadbent (calling): Hodson.
Hodson (in the bedroom): Yes, sir.
Broadbent: Don't unpack. Just take out the things I've worn and put in new things.
Hodson (at the door): Yes, sir.
Broadbent: And look here. Do you remember where I put my revolver?
Hodson: Revolver, sir. Yes, sir. Mr Doyle uses it as a paperweight, sir, when he is drawing.
Broadbent: Well, I want it packed. There's a packet of cartridges somewhere, I think. Find it and pack it as well.
Hodson: Yes, sir.
Broadbent: By the way, pack your own traps, too. I shall take you with me this time.
Hodson (hesitant): Is it a dangerous part you're going to, sir? Shall I be expected to carry a revolver, sir?
Broadbent: Perhaps it might be as well. *I'm going to Ireland.*

The opening of *The Case of Rebellious Susan*, a Henry Arthur Jones comedy, was no less masterly.

A footman in Mr Harabin's house shows in Lady Darby.

Lady Darby: Where is Lady Susan?

Footman: Upstairs in her new sitting room, my Lady.

Lady Darby: Where is Mr Harabin?

Footman: Downstairs in the library, my Lady.

Lady Darby: Tell Lady Susan I wish to see her at once.

> (*Inez is shown in by a second footman.*)

Lady Darby (*affectionately*): My dear Mrs Quesnal, you know?

Inez: She wrote me a short note saying that she had discovered that Mr Harabin had—and that she had made up her.mind to leave him.

Lady Darby: Yes, that's what she wrote to me. Now, my dear, you're her oldest friend. You'll help me to persuade her to—to look over it and hush it up.

Inez: Oh, certainly, it's the advice everybody gives in such cases, so I suppose it must be right.

Lady Darby: I don't know, but with a man like Mr Harabin, a gentleman in every sense of the word—it can't be a very bad case.

> (*Enter Lady Susan.*)

Consider what we know already after seventeen lines of typescript. That this is a well-to-do establishment—two footmen. That Lady Susan and Harabin have fallen out. That their circle know of the trouble. We have also more than a hint of the problem which Henry Arthur Jones has in mind for his play. And Lady Darby is already alive theatrically; a competent actress would already feel at home in the part. So when Lady Susan appears, we are interested and want to know what is going to happen. And all in seventeen masterly lines.

In the development of plot the question how much an audience should be told is always with the dramatist. That those in front of the curtain should be on tenterhooks for the unknown is proper, but audiences usually want to know much more than the characters in a given scene if full understanding and enjoyment are to arise. In the first place audiences are flattered by revelations which are denied to those on the stage. Sheridan faced the problem boldly in the Screen Scene in *The School for Scandal* and without doubt he made the right decision when he told his audiences quite clearly that Lady Teazle was behind the screen.

Sir Peter the husband and Charles Surface, of course, were without the knowledge, but the effectiveness of the scene depended not upon the fact of the revelation—that was certain from the beginning—but upon the how. Sheridan could doubtless have contrived a disguise for Lady Teazle so that she looked like "the little French milliner", whom audiences would then have believed to be behind the screen. When the screen was thrown down, a surprise would have been there surely enough, but with what a sacrifice of dramatic effect! The imagination would have been denied the pleasure of watching Sir Peter and Charles Surface alike entangled in a catastrophe they cannot possibly foresee. How cunningly Sheridan complicates the issue. Sir Peter tells Joseph of his generous intentions towards Lady Teazle and we picture the increasing humiliation of the woman as she slowly realizes how she has misjudged her husband. Then Sir Peter's talk with Charles which lets him into the secret of Joseph's lapse from grace.

But there are variants upon the situation in the Screen Scene. What if Sheridan had decided that Lady Teazle must get away unseen, as Lady Windermere escaped in the second act of Wilde's play? One of the most ingenious solutions of the escape problem can be found in *Journeys End in Lovers' Meeting*, a proverb in one act, which was written by George Moore and "John Oliver Hobbes" and played by Forbes-Robertson, William Terriss, and Ellen Terry, surely the cast-perfect.

The playlet opened in the West End flat of Lady Soupise. It is one a.m., as a striking clock tells us. Her ladyship comes in from a dance, wearing a dress which Victorians would have described as "a dream". Lady Soupise is in contemplative mood and does not hurry to her bedroom. Instead, she recalls the dancing floor, the music and, last but not least, the pleasant compliments of Captain Maramour. They were more intriguing because Sir Philip Soupise had been somewhat neglectful of late. Should she have been a little more severe with the gallant Captain?

"Heigho, well it's difficult to look angry when one is only— startled."

Imagine, Ellen Terry's tiny chuckle as she hesitated and then found, "startled". But a moment later what had been no more than an idea became an astonishing actuality. Who should come in but the Captain himself. He had found the hall porter dozing, and, seeing that Lady Soupise's flat door was ajar, dared to hope that the open door was not entirely accidental. Maramour (Terriss was one of the world's perfect lovers) is aflame and offers adoration, nay worship, and Venice! To which Ellen replied: "A week with you in Venice and you will worship me for ever! Your week would be more amusing than my eternity."

So Maramour is dismissed, but before he can retreat, the outer door slams and a footstep is heard outside. Before he quite understands what is happening, the Captain finds himself in the lady's bedroom, while the husband takes on the task of love-making in his place. Sir Philip feels he has been neglectful. There was a time when he read Tennyson and Swinburne to his bride and he recalls that she preferred Tennyson. (Remember that Forbes-Robertson is playing the husband.) But when Sir Philip suggests getting the Tennyson from the bookcase in the boudoir, Lady Soupise's anxiety mounts to terror. She bars the way to the boudoir. The book is not there. To which the husband replies he is certain he is right: "I could find my way to the book blind-folded!"

On the instant, the Lady sees this is her chance. Trembling she binds his eyes with her handkerchief, throws open the door, and, laughing, the baronet gropes his way in as the Captain steals to the street door, and with a bow of admiration for the wifely guile, disappears into the night. With a sob of relief the wife accepts the Tennyson, but when she removes the bandage, the man asks: "What is the matter?"

"Nothing, only I'm so glad you didn't find—the wrong book."

Trifling, maybe, but memorable when acted by players of the standing of Ellen Terry, William Terriss, and Forbes-Robertson.

Akin and also a classic of its kind is the French playlet *Le Dit de Plicon*. A wife, in her bedroom with her lover, is surprised by the unexpected arrival of the husband. There is just time to hide the gallant in a cupboard and the gay lady is in a quandary as to how the lover is to escape. The talk between wife and husband turns into a light raillery as to what would happen if the husband, in fact, had discovered a man in his wife's room.

"What would you do?" asked the wife.

"I would have chopped his head off."

"Bah. You wouldn't have been able to see. I should have thrown this shift over your head. (She does so and during the momentary eclipse of sight and hearing the lover escapes from the cupboard and through the open door.)

The Wife: You see, just like that (*continuing the deception*). Run after him, he's gone.

The Husband (*laughing and brushing back his tousled hair*)*:* You will have your little bit of fun.

A situation very similar to that in Sheridan's play arose in *Lady Windermere's Fan* and Oscar Wilde was faced with a technical problem similar to that in the Screen Scene. When *Lady Windermere* was produced, the audience had no hint at the end of the first act that Mrs Erlynne was, in fact, Lady Windermere's mother. Wilde chose to leave the first night audience guessing why Lord Windermere was so insistent that Mrs Erlynne should be invited to the birthday party. A few nights later Wilde added this snatch of dialogue to Lord Windermere's part: "My God! What shall I do? I dare not tell her who this woman really is. The shame would kill her."

George Alexander, with his wide knowledge of the theatre, had urged this change long before. Wilde took his manager's advice late, but not too late.

And the end of a play? Trollope once wrote of his own art, the novel, that its end should be like that of a well-conducted children's party, "made up of sweetmeats and sugarplums". There is something to be said for the "sweetmeats and sugarplums" theory being applied to the theatre and the alternative endings which experienced dramatists have given to certain plays is evidence thereof. Indeed, a happy or a tragic ending is a problem which has beset playwrights from time immemorial. The Greeks only faced the problem at second-hand as their plots arose from accepted mythology or tribal history. Moreover, there was the god or goddess "in the car" to give a consolatory twist to the plot and thus send spectators to their homes satisfied. In any case, the rite had been duly accomplished. The avenging Aphrodite opens the Hippolytus, but the Voice from the Cloud at the close is Artemis, who, though she "brings but anguish, not relief", is yet a consoling agency and not only for those in the vast auditorium but for the stricken Hippolytus and his sorely troubled father.

With the romantic Elizabethans the character of the final scene was determined by the classification of the play: by death, if it was tragedy, and by a happy ending if it was in the class, comedy. In the seventeenth- and eighteenth-century theatre, a general custom was to leave the closing words to the speaker of an epilogue, an amusing evasion which passed on the task of sending an audience away happy to the leading actor or actress.

During the past hundred years, when realistic drama became common, the problem of the happy or tragic ending became more urgent. It can scarcely be doubted that audiences prefer to be sent home happy, but the happy ending often seemed to the dramatist in conflict with truth and probability.

Alternative endings, one happy and the other tragic, are more common than one would expect. Ibsen's *A Doll's House* is a case in point, and has been cited. So were Charles Reade's version of *The Lyons Mail* and Pinero's *The Profligate*. This was Pinero's problem. Dunstan Renshaw had sown his wild oats and reaped a harvest of miserable regrets, when he married an innocent schoolgirl, Leslie Brudenell, beautifully played by Kate Rorke in days gone by. Coming upon evidence of her husband's misconduct, the girl could only cry piteously, "Deny it! Deny it!" Dunstan Renshaw could not deny it and, towards the end of the play, he faced suicide, feeling he could not hope for Leslie's pardon.

Now the husband's sin had been committed before marriage. There was no real reason why he should be driven to such utter despair. Yet Pinero's original ending was the tragic one in which Leslie, with the cry "Husband, Husband!", caught at the body of the man who had died unforgiven. John Hare, however, persuaded Pinero that the human and right end was the happy one. Instead of drinking the poison, Renshaw threw the glass to the ground and put up a prayer that strength should be given to live on. Thus, when Leslie came in, she was able to bow her head in thankfulness, with the words, "O, my husband!" On the first night, the tragic close was enacted but, later, in response to many appeals, Pinero wrote his new ending. After seeing Forbes-Robertson in the part I was glad Dunstan Renshaw did not take the poison and, curiously enough, William Archer, ardent Ibsenite though he was, shared the same opinion.

A more interesting variant upon the happy or tragic ending to a play is to be found in Maurice Donnay's *La Douloureuse*, where the audience is tricked into a misjudgement, so that the plot actually ranges around the possibility or impossibility of a happy marriage at curtain-fall. The play was concerned with the love affairs of a sculptor and a married woman, whose husband commits suicide in the first act. Contrary to accepted custom, the dramatist seems to be removing an obstacle to the union of the lovers, rather than creating one. Even in the second act, when Hélène is enjoying her year of widowhood, there seems no obstacle to the union. Indeed, this is only hinted at when M. Donnay tells his audience that Hélène's bosom friend, Gotte des Trembles, is also in love with Philippe and the man knows of her passion. Only in the third act does the real obstacle to the marriage disclose itself. It is not Philippe but Hélène who is the cause. Georges, her boy, is not the child of the dead husband, but came to Hélène by an earlier lover and Gotte alone knows the truth. Her revelation suffices, and M. Donnay closes his play with a quiet curtain which adds poignancy to the tragi-comedy he has created for Philippe and Hélène. Both have exhausted their unhappy recriminations. Nothing more can be said.

Hélène: What o'clock is it?
Philippe: Nearly seven.
Hélène: I must be going. (*She dries her eyes, smoothes her hair.*) Help me on with my cloak. (*He holds the mantle and tucks in the puffed sleeves of the gown. Then taking up the lamp, Philippe lights her to the door and out of his flat. Curtain.*)

Very different, but nevertheless, an illuminating example of theatrical finesse, was the conclusion to Shaw's *Man and Superman*, which so delightfully summed up the reaction of audiences to so much of what had gone before.

Ann (with fond pride): Never mind her, dear. Go on talking.
Tanner: Talking! (*Universal laughter.*)

The Small Cast

The number of characters needed to tell a story necessarily depends upon theme, background, and plot, but this may be said: needless complications are to be avoided and the requirements of unification alone suggest that the fewer the characters the better, assuming, of course, that spectacle in a large theatre need not be taken into account. Some outstanding stage successes have been achieved with markedly small casts, which not only allow of inexpensive productions but may offer a few outstanding players special opportunities for the display of their talents. The dramatic sketches of Ruth Draper and Joyce Grenfell exhibit the delights of the small cast when a maximum of economy is practised.

Rejecting the recital as not strictly a stage production, the dramatist who is content to tell a story with two, three, or four characters may be doing a frugal management a substantial service, as well as affording keen playgoers amusing opportunities for comparison and comment. The very cutting of the characters in a play to a minimum places a premium upon the ingenuity of the playwright, and appreciation of the ingenuity involved is one pleasure which instructed playgoers derive from such plays. *Close Quarters* by W. O. Somin, which was cleverly adapted for the English stage by Gilbert Lennox, is a case in point. The craft-skill and the intricate devices called into being to maintain interest and give variety were remarkable.

Close Quarters was first given at the Haymarket Theatre in 1935, when Flora Robson and Oscar Homolka played the two characters. When it was revived at the Apollo in 1941, the players were Beatrix Lehmann and Karel Stepanek. As the curtain rises a woman in a working-class flat comes home somewhat flustered, possibly because she is only just in time to prepare her husband's evening meal. When he arrives, he is in a frolicsome mood, having plainly had a drink or two more than was customary. He is closely associated with a revolutionary Communist organization and has been promised promotion. During supper, Gustav Bergmann tells of his recent doings, boasting of a speech he made at party headquarters. One is puzzled because the wife shows more and more anxiety as the meal proceeds, her only sign of satisfaction coming when the man points out that promotion will enable them to move to a better flat.

What is afoot? The first hint comes when the wireless is turned on and the audience learn that the Minister of the Interior has been murdered. The husband has always hated the minister; he had threatened him in the course of his speech that very evening. Moreover, coming home, he had passed through the very wood in which the body of the dead minister was found. Is there a chance he may be suspected of the murder? Oh, impossible. There is a knock at the door. No, it is not the police! Only a telegram. The man breathes freely once more.

But the wife? What of her manifest fears? She gets her husband off to bed and directly she is alone thrusts a blood-stained pocket handkerchief between the bars of the grate and watches it burn.

A day later the couple are in the new flat, but the husband has not shed his fears. The revolutionaries with whom he has been working are now only too anxious to rid themselves of any possible association with the murder. He has been told to disappear. Meanwhile neither husband nor wife can keep away from the topic. Bloodhounds, they learn, have been loosed; a man has been arrested. At the end of the act, the man rushes from the house in a frenzy of misery and terror.

Still we are not at the heart of Mr Somin's story. This is revealed in the third act. The husband has spent the night tramping the streets and comes back to find his wife in a troubled sleep. When she wakes it is to talk afresh of the murder. Now we hear of a missing glove and, later, that the police have just such a clue in the case of the murdered Minister—a man's glove. Moreover one of Gustav Bergmann's gloves is missing. Yet, how can this be the one in the hands of the police, inasmuch as he was never near the dead man, and, indeed, he was not wearing his gloves on the evening of the crime? In fear and anger, he threatens his wife with a revolver and her reply is to beg him to use "the second bullet". There follows the confession that the wife herself had used the first bullet. The murdered minister had trapped her into becoming his mistress. Moreover, she had also been revealing the secrets of the revolutionary committee to which Gustav Bergmann was attached. At last, there seemed only one way to keep the intrigue from her husband. That was the way the wife had taken. She had fired the shot at close range into the minister's back, using her husband's revolver and gloves, that there might be no finger-prints. As the confession proceeds, the misery of the man grows but his anger now is not against the wife but against the dead man, for he has retained the woman's love.

All this time the unhappy couple are shut off from the outer world. In that lies the significance of the play's title. A world hungry for their destruction is momentarily shut away from the Bergmanns' flat. They are alone with their fate. The wireless tells that the arrest of the murderer is imminent and when a second knock at the outer door again suggests the coming of the police, husband and wife steal off together to an inner room and two revolver shots tell of their end.

But the dramatist has a final stroke of tragic irony for us. Through the letter-box the voice of the charwoman tells that she has found Gustav's missing glove amid the debris in the old flat and she pushes it through the letter-box. And, climax upon climax, the wireless announces that the police no longer attach importance to the clue.

The outstanding part is that of the tempest-tossed woman, generally in control of her fears and passions but from time to time driven to hysteria. Well suited as Beatrix Lehmann was to the part, Flora Robson found in Leisa Bergmann the rôle of a lifetime.

Louis Verneuil's *Monsieur Lambertier* (*Jealousy*), brilliantly played in London at the Little Theatre by Mary Newcomb and John Nyse, is another two-part play of merit. Again, husband and wife are the protagonists and what is at issue is who murdered Monsieur Lambertier, the wife's guardian? *Jealousy* has not the integrity of *Close Quarters*. The stresses depend too much upon the emotional disturbances of a neurotic.

A large measure of economy was achieved when Charles Wyndham produced *The Mollusc* by Hubert H. Davies at the Criterion in a production which was to have a run of more than 300 performances in 1907 and at least three revivals. There were only four characters and all wore their own clothes, while the single set was already in the Criterion properties room. Even Mr Davies practised the strictest economy as he took the fundamental idea of his play from a rival dramatist, Haddon Chambers, who had shown what was required and how it could be done when he wrote the *Tyranny of Tears* for Wyndham and Mary Moore, the very players who were to serve Mr Davies in *The Mollusc*.

In latter-day play-making John van Druten is among the dramatists who have experimented bravely with small casts. There were only four characters in *There's Always Juliet* and three in *The Voice of the Turtle*, which reached London in 1947, after very long runs in America. Van Druten was helped by ingenious scenery, as the curtain rose upon a bedroom, a sitting room, and a kitchen in a single set, just the sort of place where one could conveniently watch a couple of people spending a week-end, with occasional interruptions from a third.

The gay little story—it can hardly be called a plot—was of the Palais Royal type and concerned itself with a pretty little sentimentalist, toying with sexual temptation, Sally, by name, who found herself in temporary charge of a young soldier. He was the boy-friend of the owner of the little New York apartment flat, who had herself gone off for a pleasure-trip with another man friend. Needless to say, Sally, obviously puzzled by what is an unfamiliar predicament, pairs off with the boy who has been left so unceremoniously upon her hands. When night comes at the end of the second act, the puzzled little lady has made the big decision. "One small candle shall serve for them both."

And next morning, what of that? Now Sally's one desire is to pretend to herself and to her lover that the surrender was not love at all, just up-to-date sophistication.

Noel Coward's *Private Lives* with four characters and a bittock in the shape of a maid-servant and Lonsdale's *On Approval* are other examples of small casts used with ingenuity.

Dual and Triple Rôles

A dual rôle is a popular theatrical device and calls for considerable ingenuity, alike from dramatist and player. *The Lyons Mail* in which Henry Irving and his son, H. B., were both effective is the classic double-part play, which Charles Reade adapted from the French. The melodrama had a foundation of fact. In 1769, a highly respectable French merchant named Lesurques was charged with highway robbery and murder and guillotined. In fact, as was discovered later, the crime was committed by a besotted cut-throat, Dubosc, who planned the robbery in the hope that his likeness to the merchant, not only in face but figure, would lead the law to the very error which was committed. So circumstantial was the evidence against Lesurques that his father was deceived and bade his son commit suicide in order to avoid open shame.

In France, the custom was to end *The Lyons Mail* one night on the reprieve of Lesurques, while, on the next night, the innocent man was guillotined. Charles Reade spared audiences the final shock and both Henry Irving and H. B. Irving preferred the ending in which justice triumphed, and Dubosc met his due reward. Emphasizing the difference between the hero and the villain, Irving, as Dubosc, entered chewing a long straw. Later, in the robbery scene in which Dubosc killed the guard in cold blood, the robber callously hummed a few notes of the Marseillaise. Martin-Harvey tells that, even more daringly, Irving substituted some bars from the hymn "Nearer my God to Thee". A shiver of horror went through the theatre.

In *The Corsican Brothers*, which Charles Kean, Henry Irving, and Martin-Harvey all played with great effect, the dual rôle resulted from twin brothers. The story was by Alexandre Dumas and told how one brother, Lucien, a student in Paris, was killed in a duel. Lucien and his twin brother Fabien had sworn an oath that nothing should separate them "not even death", and, surely enough, the dead Lucien appeared in vision in Corsica as he fell. At once Fabien travelled post-haste to Paris to avenge a loved brother. The duel in the forest fought between Henry Irving as Fabien, and William Terriss as Château-Renaud was one of the longest and most exciting in dramatic history. Towards the close, the sword of Château-Renaud breaks. That all may be equal, Fabien breaks his weapon and kills his man with the broken blade. The opening scene in the family home in Corsica was equally good "theatre". So was the scene in Montgiron's flat, in which Emile de Lesparre confronts Château-Renaud and persuades Fabien to shoulder her quarrel. Wilde drew upon the scene when he planned the second act of *Lady Windermere's Fan*.

Plainly, such rôles offer exceptional opportunities to an actor or actress, and "stars" have eagerly accepted a chance to appear in the relatively few plays in which dual parts can be made plausible. Richard Mansfield, in Stevenson's *Dr Jekyll and Mr Hyde*, was only less effective than Henry Irving had been in *The Lyons Mail*. Excellent, too, was Tree's double rôle in *A Man's Shadow*, in which the actor differentiated the spy Luversan from the hero, Laroque, by a sinister cough.

Among the dual rôles for women that played by Margaret Rawlings in *Black Limelight* stands out. One part was that of a wife whose husband was suspected of murdering his mistress in a lonely bungalow on the south coast, while, by means of a flash-back in the second act, Miss Rawlings also played the highly contrasted part of the murdered girl.

When the curtain rose Mary Charrington was approaching nervous exhaustion due to her husband's long absence. The police were watching her house; Scotland Yard had examined her in the hope that the whereabouts of the supposed murderer might be revealed; and the receipt of anonymous letters and the continuous inquiries of journalists all made her life a living hell. Then the husband contrives to break through the cordon of police and journalists and Mary Charrington persuades him to reconstruct the events leading up to the crime. Quickly she sees that her husband is innocent. The real murderer is the Dorset Killer, but how can Scotland Yard be convinced of the fact? The Killer's earlier crimes have been committed at the time of full moon. After watching the murder of the unhappy prostitute in the second act, we are prepared for a final act in which the wife faces the Killer and confronts him with her accusation. She is nearly murdered too, but the police come just in time to save her and establish the husband's innocence.

Nor must the numerous Amphitryons escape mention. When Jean Giraudoux and S. N. Behrman gave us the best-known version, *Amphitryon 38*, the plot had been used again and again and Alfred Lunt scored a triumph as Jupiter who was sometimes the Father of the Olympian gods and sometimes the mortal Amphitryon, at least to Amphitryon's wife, Alkmena. Needless to say Alfred Lunt's triumph was shared to the full by Lynn Fontanne as it was the teamwork of the two which made Giraudoux's play so memorable.

Laurence Olivier in *King Richard the Third*, Old Vic Company, New Theatre (1944) (*see page* 40).

Laurence Olivier and Chorus in *Oedipus Rex*, Old Vic Company, New Theatre (1947) (*see page* 40).

Looking down from Olympus, Jupiter chances to see Alkmena, and, as her charms of face and figure are comparable with her reputation as the most perfect of wives, the god determines to possess her while Amphitryon is at the wars. The ungodly scheme is only too successful, though on the following morning Jupiter is disconcerted to find that Alkmena detected no difference between her experiences with a deity and those with her mortal husband. One of the most comic scenes in drama, ancient or modern, showed Alkmena swatting flies and at the same time intimating to the disguised Jupiter that the night was over and it was time to get up. When Jupiter does come in to breakfast, he tucks a napkin under his chin and observes.

Jupiter: What a divine night.

Alkmena: Your adjectives this morning, darling, are somewhat feeble.

Jupiter: I said divine.

Alkmena: You could say a cut of beef was divine or a meal was divine, but for last night you might find something better.

Jupiter: What could there possibly be better?

Alkmena: Almost any adjective except divine. It's such a worn-out word. Perfect! You could have said it was a perfect night. Charming! There's always Charming! Best of all, you might have said it was a pleasant night! That conveys so many agreeable sensations. *"What a pleasant night!"*

Jupiter: Yes, but don't you think that this night, of all our nights, was the pleasantest, by far?

Alkmena: Well, that depends.

Jupiter: On what does it depend?

Alkmena: Have you forgotten, my own husband, the night we married?

The adjective which Alkmena finally accepted was "connubial". "There was a sense of security about it which gladdened me." Needless to say "connubial" gave Jupiter no satisfaction at all.

An interesting play by a German author, Bruno Franck, *Nina*, was given at the Criterion some years ago. This treated the dual rôle from a third standpoint. Nina was a film star, so famous in the Hollywood world that her autograph (signed by her secretary as habit is) was reputed to have the value of three "Mae

I

Wests". Now Nina was married to an Englishman and he persuaded her to end her career and allow her "double" to take her place. The physical resemblance is all there, but, for the rest, nothing could be less promising as material for stardom. But the very difficulty of the task puts Nina's producer on his mettle. He succeeds so well that the trick played upon the public is never found out and Nina is left happy in her retirement. Her one-time secretary goes on producing the autographs as before. Lucie Mannheim played the two parts brilliantly. The transitions to the vulgar Americanized gold-digger who had once been Trude Melitz was excellent "theatre".

In reverse, the double and triple rôle technique may take the form of two or three players enacting a single personality. In Donald Ogden Stewart's *How I Wonder*, the principal character, Professor Stevenson, was played in America by Raymond Massey in his outward physical form, by Everett Sloane representing the Professor's mind, while a woman, Meg Mundy, appeared as the Professor's conscience. Akin was the problem which the author set himself in the multiple personality play *I Said to Myself*, which had a run in London in 1947. In this drama a wife was played by two actresses and an actor, the purpose of the playwright being to display aspects of character arising from the psychological conflicts possible within a single personality.

Reference has been made to the necessity cast upon dramatist, producer, and players alike for establishing a vital relation between stage and auditorium if what Theodor Lipps described as "feeling into" a stage situation is to arise. On the side of the dramatist, experiments towards establishing still greater intimacy between stage and auditorium were carried further in Bridget Boland's deeply moving *Cockpit*. It was given by the London Mask Theatre at the Playhouse in 1948, with Michael Macowan as producer, and deserved more success than it achieved. Miss Boland had been a writer of documentary films and the origin of *Cockpit* was a series of sketches based upon war experiences, some of which had been given in dramatic form and played to British troops overseas. In the course of writing the sketches Miss Boland had visited several deserted theatres in the war areas of Germany and one of them furnished the locale of her play.

When the safety curtain of the Playhouse went up we faced a tattered theatre curtain, disfigured with such embellishments as a rudely-painted swastika. Already, we were expecting it to rise in its turn and disclose a deserted stage in some provincial town in mid-Germany, pathetic evidence of the ruin which had come upon a world at war. In fact the tattered curtain rose to disclose a party of slumbering refugees—Germans, Czechs, Poles, Jugo-slavs, Russians, and the like—awaiting deportation to their homelands, if any. One of them steals quietly across the stage and takes a saucepan from under a sleeping Jewess. The theft is detected and, at once, the stage is in a riot, quelled with difficulty by a young English captain, who is in charge of the clearing station and only too anxious to get on with a thankless job.

But this is not all. Soon we see that not only the stage of the German theatre is occupied with refugees. The dress-circle and the gallery are also filled with men, women and children awaiting deportation, east or west as the case may be. From time to time a man or a woman comes down and reaches the stage by way of the stalls or leaves the stage to take food to the imagined refugees in circle or gallery. A dramatist is on dangerous ground when he makes his characters scamper about his theatre but Miss Boland and her stage managers do not falter. In an upper box a man is dying and a certain Polish professor is sent upstairs to see what can be done, while the English captain and his long-suffering *non-com* get on with their job of sorting out the refugees.

It might be thought that the audience of *Cockpit* would be quite unable to preserve a due sense of theatre but, in fact, Miss Boland's judgement was not at fault. Thanks to brilliant stage-management we accepted the new convention easily and the story developed in spite of the squabbles, shouting, and impromptu fights which continue until the Professor returns from the upper box. He is not a practising doctor but in his judgement the dying man is stricken with no ordinary ailment, but the plague. The plague! Racial animosities and private strife are forgotten, lost in the common terror. The technique devised by Miss Boland was intended to create an illusion similar to that attaching to a documentary film. The audience in the Playhouse had to be persuaded that, in imagination, it actually was in that mid-German refugee camp witnessing the hate of the centuries still at its ugly work. But *Cockpit* was more than stark realism. There was the stuff of real drama in the story Miss Boland had to unfold: if the deadening fear of the refugees was to be lightened, something had to be done to take their thoughts from the obsession with death. Could any one in the imagined theatre tell a story or recite or dance? Could any one sing? Was there by any chance an actor or actress? At the word actress, a woman in the corner of the stage moved restlessly. She had not said a word since curtain-rise but awoke at the word "actress".

"Are you an actress?" asked the English *non-com*.

"I am an opera-singer."

"Then you can sing!" The woman shook her head, but is over-persuaded. Yes, she will try. The fussy little German stage-manager, sole survivor of the theatre staff, is·there to help. Give him six men as stage hands and he will have a setting for *La Traviata* in a twinkling. A section of scenery representing a balcony descends; behind is a stretch of painted sky, a stage engine is turned and is found to be the steps from the balcony by which the heroine is to reach the stage as her song ends. The stage-hands gather in the wings as the singer enters. A stage dress suited for "the misguided one" has been found. A piano gives her the opening chords. For a few moments the voice falters, then, in spite of hunger and weariness, the training of a trouper asserts itself. The singer is La Traviata in very truth. Forgetful of her strange audience, she is in a real theatre once more. The notes are fuller and richer. Passion comes once more to gestures and movement. Singing, the player comes to the centre of the stage and every movement and sound in the strange theatre ceases. Slowly, still singing, the actress comes down the steps and ends in a tumult of applause, while the impromptu stage-hands gather round and raise her shoulder-high, as they bear her triumphantly off the stage. Surely, at this moment, *Cockpit* justified itself as moving theatre and, incidentally, justified an imaginative effort towards securing the all-important intimacy between the stage players and the spectators beyond the footlights, a problem which has obsessed playwrights from the times of Thespis onwards to our own day.

Noel Langley, in *The Burning Bush*, a translation from a Hungarian original which was concerned with the trial of six

Jews accused of the ritual murder of a Christian girl, utilized a similar technique. The tiny Lindsey Theatre seemed momentarily to be converted into a Hungarian law-court when the auditorium was plunged into darkness and what appeared to be a body of roughs rushed into the stalls, climbed over the footlights and broke up the Court.

In writing an historical or biographical play or such a documentary record as *Cockpit* there are two methods of approach open to the dramatist. One is that of the chronicler, in which a close hold upon facts determines the run of the plot. The other is that of the creative critic. When Miss Rawlings and Wyndham Goldie played in *Parnell*, they were working upon material with a basis of realism. Very different was the approach of Lennox Robinson, when he sat down to write *The Lost Leader*, another play written around the Parnell legend. A hypnotist doctor is staying with a friend in an out-of-the-way fishing village in Ireland, run by the capable Mary Lenihan. With Mary lives the aged Lucius Lenihan, tall, white-bearded, but bent and feeble. The doctor quickly senses a mystery and when he finds that old Lucius talks in his sleep, he decides to hypnotize the man. Thus the dreams of twenty years ago are revealed—"a coffin", "a woman", "false friends", and the like and, at last, the revelation "My name, sir, is Charles Stewart Parnell." The justification lay in the success which followed Lennox Robinson's gamble. The dramatist was wily enough not to answer the obvious question: "Is this Parnell really alive and miraculously recreated to meet the needs of his beloved Ireland?" It suffices that we watch members of the various Irish parties come to the supposed Parnell for advice and support. He has the authority of a leader of men. Plainly a strictly realistic approach would have made it difficult to persuade audiences to accept the theme at all. There had to be a note of mystery and Lennox Robinson gave it life.

A masterpiece of biography in the strictly realistic mood was the story of *Pasteur*, which Sacha Guitry wrote for his father, Lucien.

The play was founded upon Valery-Radot's biography of the scientist and every episode had actuality, even if the aggregation of episodes necessarily failed to achieve dramatic unity, as an earlier school of French dramatists would have understood the words. Sacha, however, knew precisely what he could look for from his father. This truly great actor merged his personality so completely in that of the man described by Valery-Radot that an entire era of scientific research was illuminated. Sacha Guitry chose to omit women from his cast. He made his play from Pasteur, his pupils, his fellows in the medical and scientific world, and the Presidents of the Academy of Medicine and the République Française. This did not entail any failure to reveal Pasteur as parent and husband, but it emphasized that everything that really mattered had been done in a world of men. The first scene, early in Pasteur's career, was laid in his class-room. The year being 1870, the declaration of the Franco-Prussian War provided a stirring curtain. Ten years later Pasteur was addressing the Academy of Medicine and the violent interruptions of his critics gave Lucien an opportunity for an unforgettable display of indignant protest and scornful denunciation. A beautiful scene followed. Pasteur was awaiting a fitting opportunity to put his theories to a test. The chance came when a boy of nine was savagely bitten by a mad dog. We see the terrified boy and his despairing grandfather in the presence of the scientist. Dare Pasteur risk the very life of a mere child? A doctor friend helps him to the decision and the boy is taken into a nearby room for the inoculation. As the curtain falls we see Pasteur preparing for the long and anxious vigil he must face before he knows what he may expect from his life of research.

The full truth is only revealed three years later, when Pasteur is a dying man, and is told that he must stop all work. But despair is turned to joy when the boy who owes his life to Pasteur returns and Lucien Guitry had a chance to show once more the deep and tender humanity of the aged scientist. The closing scene depicted the reception given by the President of the French Republic in honour of Pasteur at which the noteworthies of France were present. Those who were privileged to see the first night production of *Pasteur* in London, however, may well have thought the fitting climax to the evening was the appearance of Lucien Guitry, arm in arm with his son, coming before the curtain to receive the plaudits of a crowded audience. *Pasteur* was an outstanding example of author and players in full understanding with one another, an understanding which is seldom perfect unless the author is himself an actor and thus, in truth, a man of the theatre.

Karel Čapek treated a theme comparable with *Pasteur* in his play which told of the little slum doctor who discovered a cure for a new form of leprosy which was devastating central Europe. Čapek, however, was only concerned with what he conceived to be effective drama. The little doctor makes a bargain with society. He will heal only the poor and the weak until the rich and the strong consent to abolish war. The politicians, the armament-makers, and, at last, the totalitarian dictator himself, watch their homes being invaded by the plague and their lives threatened. Karel Čapek does not load the theatrical dice unfairly against the wealthy and the powerful, but the point to be noted is that in his play there is none of the grip upon actuality which was the strength of *Pasteur*. In the final scene, the little doctor is killed by a mob while on his way to save the dictator. The theatrical as opposed to the strictly natural approach of Čapek's play was emphasized by the fact that Oscar Homolka played both doctor and dictator. It was a brilliant performance, the two rôles being poles apart.

The documentary and biographical play of to-day is akin to the chronicle play of times past, which has a history going back to pre-Shakespearean times. There was a *King John* in morality form and University wits such as Peele and Marlowe enjoyed the form, owing to the movement, the colour and the play upon patriotic emotion which it allowed. It is also an attraction to the dramatist because half the characterization is already done. The real problem is to find a plot with the necessary unification. In Bulwer-Lytton's correspondence with Macready there is an interesting reference to a possible play to be written around Richelieu. As Lytton said, his "wit, lightness, address, churchman's pride, relentless vindictiveness and sublime passion for the glory of France" promised a new addition to the historical portraits of the stage. But Lytton added: "I have no suitable plot and until I find the story the play must stand over." The dramatist added: "Depend on it, I don't cease racking my brains and something must come at last."

A further development of the chronicle play is the historical episode interpreted in the light of latter-day experience. Shaw's *Caesar and Cleopatra* and Masefield's *Pompey the Great* are examples.

CHAPTER 6

THE DRAMA OF INCIDENT

Thus far, we have been considering the problems of play-making primarily from the standpoint of the dramatist in his study, free to range wherever his imagination chose to roam. But already it has become plain that, in numerous cases, the question of this actor or that actress could not be ignored, even in the early stages. From an infinity of happenings and ideas a few had selected themselves as offering promise and, by degrees, the words which expressed the underlying idea had taken lyrical, dramatic, descriptive, or reflective form, as the case might be. As the process of selection continued, emotional reactions or knowledge of dramatic technique emphasized the formal pattern. Thus, rhythm and pace were added.

Consider a few outstanding bits of "theatre" and the imaginative embroidery that went to their making, so that words, the unfolding of plot, and the personality of players alike moved in unison. In Pinero's *The Cabinet Minister*, Lady Twombley, played by Mrs John Wood, was face to face with her boy Brooke. Both had been spending freely.

Lady Twombley: Well, have you got it?
Brooke: My—er—?
Lady Twombley: Your skeddle. (*Brooke hands schedule to his mother.*) There's a dear boy. (*She turns over the leaves and gradually her face assumes a look of horror.*) "Total, three thousand!" (*She folds the schedule, puts it in her pocket, faces Brooke fiercely with hands clenched.*) You imp. (*She boxes his right ear soundly.*)
Brooke: Mater!
Lady Twombley: You villain! (*She boxes his left ear.*)
Brooke: Don't, Mater!
Lady Twombley: Three thousand pounds! Three thousand times I wish you had never been born. I—I— (*She breaks down and*

puts her arm around Brooke's neck.) Oh, Brooke, my dear. Forgive your poor mother.

Again Rudolf Besier, in *The Barretts of Wimpole Street*, conceived Edward Moulton-Barrett as a man of violent passions, precariously controlled by religious principles. The man was so tormented by self-repressions that he sought to impose upon his children similar mortifications of the flesh. Thus he became a lonely figure of tragedy rather than the heavy Victorian father of comedy which he might easily have become. Besier's crowning achievement was the use he made of Elizabeth Barrett's famous dog, Flush.

Less subtle, but displaying all a theatre-man's skill in fitting words and action to a player's capacity was Ivor Novello's creation of the worthless little chorus girl in *Enter Kiki*. The problem Ivor Novello set himself was to suggest every device of possessive womanhood, short of actual surrender. When Kiki (Gladys Cooper) found herself in her manager's flat, apparently as his mistress, though actually she slept on a shakedown in the passage, all sorts of physical wiles were tested, including a disrobing scene, a wrestling bout with a man servant, and sitting cross-legged in white silk pyjamas, until Kiki's tantalized chief bore her bodily from his room. Not even when he threatened to rid himself of the minx by handing her over to a wealthy patron of the theatre did Kiki surrender. Instead she fainted, calling for still further physical intimacies.

The climax came when the triumphant Kiki assured the conquered man that "really, she was a good girl," a statement which Ivor Novello not unnaturally received with a measure of incredulity.

"However did you manage it?" he asked.

Kiki (*snuggling into his arms*): I was keeping myself for you.

But for Ivor Novello, as dramatist, this was altogether too sentimental. Her man accepted the statements, to Kiki's delight, but as the curtain fell, the truth was revealed in the exclamation, "I've got him."

A dramatist himself, Ivor Novello must have had a particular player in mind almost from the beginning, and not a few plays to-day are brought into being on what may be called the "casting" system. The American Clyde Fitch had a note about all the players he had seen and, with this aid, cast his plays according to type. Indeed, every line was expressly written to be spoken by a known actor or actress.

What is involved in fitting a player with a fitting part is happily illustrated by half a score of rôles associated with Marion Lorne. In private life, this pleasant comedienne was the wife of Walter Hackett. Hackett was a big, genial creature who lived in and for the theatre, but, primarily, to provide Marion Lorne with material suited for her marked but strictly limited talent. Born in California in 1876, Hackett was in his late thirties when he came to England in 1914 and entered upon what was to be his contribution to the British stage. Just as R. C. Carton knew precisely what comedy his wife, Miss Compton, could put across, so Walter Hackett, time and again, found just the sort of stories which would allow the talents of Marion Lorne to effervesce. Gauging his wife's capacity to a nicety, Walter Hackett's self-imposed task was, firstly, to introduce Miss Lorne into a bit of trouble and, secondly, to extricate her from these worries. Always, Miss Lorne moved through the excitements of a Hackett plot, flustered certainly, vague in the extreme, but maintaining some sort of poise. It might be that Mr Hackett required no more than that Marion Lorne should evade payment for an expensive cocktail when she had not a penny in her purse. It might be that she had to evade arrest for murder or suspected treason. Always we were assured that innocence would triumph before curtain-fall, though not very long before.

In *The Way to Treat a Woman* the dramatist assumed that one of the British delegates to a disarmament conference was abducted and has been found desperately wounded. Four detectives are called in to track down the would-be murderer, and they decide that a certain girl holds the key to the mystery. The German detective is a bully, and his idea is to force her to tell the truth. The French detective decides to make love to her. Says the American, "Buy her something," while the British detective appeals to "her sporting instinct". A hair-raising series of adventures ensue as the girl finds that she has incriminated the wrong man. In the last act all the detectives decide that the lover of the diplomatist's wife shot the diplomatist. They are about to arrest him when the telephone bell rings. The girl answers it, and announces that the diplomatist has recovered consciousness and has accused his wife. As the wife confesses, and the lover is freed from suspicion, the plot would seem to be completely unravelled. But Mr Hackett has a concluding surprise. The English detective picks up the telephone receiver, and is surprised to hear the question, "Do you still want tickets for Sunday afternoon?" "But, surely, you are Charing Cross Hospital," says the detective. "Not a bit," murmurs the voice at the other end of the wire, "we are the Zoo!" The girl has tricked the diplomatist's wife into her confession.

Observe that the necessity for plenty of action almost forced Walter Hackett to the "thriller" type of play, as Marion Lorne's talents forced him to prefer a comic note to the tragic element which Wallace exploited in a "thriller" designed, say, for Charles Laughton. A characteristic Hackett invention was the revolver which the murderer slipped under a cushion in Monte Carlo and which Marion Lorne was fated to find. Gazing at the weapon with ill-concealed fear and characteristic bewilderment, Miss Lorne was mistaken for a ruined gambler contemplating suicide. What could the management do but refund the lady's losses, expecting, of course, that the money would be spent upon a return ticket back to London? What Marion *does* do is to return to the tables, lose the money once more, and try the bewilderment trick yet again upon the Monte Carlo management. This time, however, she finds herself facing a crook, in straits so desperate that he is ready for anything, including murder. Marion's escape involved the feminine fainting attack, which, happily, left Mr Hackett's heroine alive for his third act.

It may be added that a considerable variety of background and ample action were called for if the butterfly intelligence which Miss Lorne exploited so amusingly was not to wear thin before curtain-fall. And, by the way, do not think that anything less than a first-rate theatrical intelligence is required if the doings of a flutter-brain are to be made acceptable over a considerable period of stage time.

James Bridie is a Scotsman; so is Alastair Sim. When he sat down to write *Dr Angelus* Bridie plainly had Alastair Sim in mind for the principal character. Just as Marion Lorne's sense of comedy was the biggest factor in fashioning one of her husband's plays, so the acting capabilities of a fellow Scotsman were dominant in the making of *Dr Angelus*. He had to be an amusing person, in spite of a predilection for poisoning unwanted relations. Bridie solved his complicated problem by inventing a secondary theme which allowed of sly digs at his fellow professionals and thus enabled Angelus to murder amusingly, indeed so amusingly that Bridie may well have overdone the laughter and made his play too nearly akin to the thriller farce, *Arsenic and Old Lace*. Be this as it may, the theme which set Bridie's imagination going was of the comedy type. He asked himself what situations were likely to arise if a young and inexperienced doctor saw a respected colleague poisoning his wife? Could professional etiquette be stretched so far that a young doctor would refrain from calling in the police? Bridie remembered that a certain Dr Pritchard was publicly hanged on Glasgow Green in 1865 for poisoning his wife and mother-in-law, and the evidence showed that a colleague was actually aware of the poisonings but said nothing because he feared that disclosure would be regarded as "unprofessional conduct".

When Bridie took down his writing pad his first decision was to advance the plot from 1865 to 1919 and, with Alastair Sim always in mind as the poisoner, he began to work upon the young doctor. Plainly, it would be convenient if he was a partner of Dr Angelus, and, sure enough, in the opening scene, we see the inexperienced young man in the joint consulting room, dealing with a far from strait-laced young wife late in the evening. The lady is quickly in her under-clothes and ends by embracing the embarrassed medico at the moment when his chief's wife is entering the surgery.

Then comes the first poisoning, and, though the young doctor has no suspicion of murder, he is troubled when his chief asks him to sign the death certificate. Suspicions of poisoning only begin when the unhappy wife of Dr Angelus sickens. Bridie has a telling scene in which the miserable woman steals into the consulting room and takes a book upon poisons from her husband's shelves. Dr Angelus finds her, and, with a display of loving tenderness, allays her suspicions and sends her back to bed, with the promise of a sleeping draught.

Dr Angelus: But me no buts! Run away to bye-byes and I'll bring you your nice medicine—medicine. And I promise you won't require very much of it.

The departure of the smiling and happy wife to what audiences know must be her death proved thrilling "theatre". But by now the young doctor is really suspicious and his fears are confirmed when he examines the contents of the wife's medicine glass under a microscope. However, Angelus is too clever. Soon, the young doctor is drinking with his chief and thus passes into a drunken dream in which he sees himself on trial as an accessory to the murder of two women. When he wakes he finds Mrs Angelus has died, and, this time, he refuses to sign the death certificate. But James Bridie has not forgotten the indiscreet kiss of the opening scene. Its recollection puts further pressure upon the young doctor. Moreover, an eminent consultant is called in and supports Dr Angelus. It almost seems that the poisoner may get away with the second murder, when his nerve breaks down. In a long and dramatic speech which rose to maniacal hysteria, Angelus tried to justify the murders to his young partner. Even when the darbies were on his wrists, he could not acknowledge guilt, so fixed was his belief that the death of the women was essential for the growth of his own personality.

Mordaunt Shairp gave a similar twist to the straightforward murder story and incidentally hit upon a bit of genuine "theatre" when he conceived *The Crime at Blossoms*. Instead of being a thriller, the play became a skit upon the public interest in crime, as displayed in the popular press. A young wife rents a cottage associated with a sensational murder and decides to convert it into a show place. Clad in purple and standing in the doorway of the room where the crime was committed, she tells the story to crowds of expectant holiday-makers. *The Crime at Blossoms* probably suffered because Mordaunt Shairp did not have the personality of his leading lady continually in mind while writing the play. His task would have been simplified if he had used personal idiosyncrasies to strengthen the part of the young wife.

When discussing rôles which Sardou contrived for Sarah Bernhardt, passing reference was made to the special problems

facing a playwright who has to construct a play for a particular
actor or actress. The problems may take many forms. At times a
leading player with a marked personality may be in question. In
other cases, it may be no more than furnishing a minor member of
a company with an opportunity to display a limited talent. In
musical comedy, no man of the theatre would have offered
Ellaline Terriss a song suited for Ethel Levey. The skill of Adrian
Ross, Basil Hood, Paul Rubens, and their fellow-lyricists had
continually to be checked against the special charms or talents of
an actor or actress in the sort of plays in which they appeared and
the particular theatres where they were starred. Lovers of vaudeville in the late 'nineties remembered the pleasure Ellaline
Terriss had given when she sang "A little bit of string" and, like
Oliver, they consciously or unconsciously asked for more. Consequently, when "The things you never learnt at school" passed
into the "book" of *The Beauty of Bath* it was assured of a welcome.
Similarly, Letty Lind looked for a song and dance of the "Mon-
key on a stick" type in *The Geisha*, and George Edwardes saw she
had it. The Letty Lind song and dance number had established
itself in the days of Gaiety burlesque. The Rutland Barrington
topical songs, such as "The Rajah of Bhong", the Connie Ediss's
social satires, such as "Class! Class!" and the Louis Bradfield
quick-fire patter songs were other easily recognizable types and
all called for a close association between author and player
during the invention stage.

Moreover, in Edwardian musical comedy the producer was
often required to add his quota of charm. A few songs need
nothing but good singing, but when Ellaline Terriss in *The
Beauty of Bath* was accompanied by a chorus of Bath Buns, suit-
ably attired, the effect was enhanced one-hundredfold. Something which might only have filled in an odd five minutes became
a feature of the whole show.

It would be a mistake to exaggerate the talent required for
putting over ditties of "The things you never learnt at school"
order. The truth is that success of this kind is generally due to a
team effort. Certainly such efforts call for some acting ability:
when Ellaline Terriss put over this apparently artless ditty she
was not herself, but her stage self, a very different thing. But
Ellaline Terriss's Phoebe Throstle and her Young Duke were on a

higher plane, and these were due to Ellen Terry, who was responsible for ending the profitable but uninspiring contract which Miss Terriss had with George Edwardes at the Gaiety. Dame Ellen said: "Ella, my child, this form of entertainment, when you have achieved all you can (as you have), only means standing on the top of a ladder, with a hundred young women pulling at your pretty petticoats. Make an end of it!" Ellaline made an end of it.

The Climax

Even if an author has not a particular player in mind, his craft is continually determined by the necessity for finding opportunities for actors or actresses. Henry Arthur Jones, when writing *The Lie*, took as his theme a conflict between two sisters for the love of a man, a conflict in which evil triumphed. The all-important scene was to be in the third act, when the elder discovered her sister's perfidy.

Here is the plot Henry Arthur Jones chose to illuminate his theme. Lucy Shale, daughter of an impoverished baronet, is seduced by a young heir to a title and a large fortune, but he dies and Lucy is left with the unborn child. She confesses her shame to Elinor, an elder sister, who promises to help and hide the ugly truth from family and friends. The plan would have been fully successful, if the doctor had not guessed the facts and passed them on casually, as an interesting story, so that they came to the knowledge of Gerald Forster, who is about to be engaged to Elinor. But Forster does not gather the real facts. He believes that Elinor was the shameless one and Lucy the self-sacrificing sister. When he seeks confirmation from Lucy, she unblushingly agrees and Gerald goes back to his work in Africa, with his love untold. And, worse, when Lucy meets the man again, she sets out to capture the man's love and marries him. The final wrong comes when Lucy takes her boy from Elinor. When the older woman lets herself go, Henry Arthur Jones has his great scene, and as played by Sybil Thorndike, it was fine "theatre". She flew at the liar's throat, crying "Judas sister! Judas sister!", while Mary Merrall, as Lucy Shale, cowered in terror at Dame Sybil's feet, vainly pleading for forgiveness.

Channing Pollock devised a similar play of incident when he wrote *The Sign on the Door* for the Playhouse in 1921, the star being Gladys Cooper. The play was frankly melodramatic but was replete with acting opportunities. A successful professional man, who has not lost his good looks and is not destitute of attraction, invites a young girl, Ann Hunniwell, to dine with him at a hotel of questionable reputation. Only a police raid saves Ann from ruin. Years pass, Ann marries and finds herself with a stepdaughter who is threatened with just the sort of tragedy Ann herself missed, years earlier. In agony, she follows the girl to the lover's rendezvous but, instead, is forced to hide in an inner room as her husband appears and he it is who kills his girl's lover. In order to ensure his own escape, the husband locks the outer door and adds a notice for the chamber maid that "the occupant is not to be disturbed." Consequently, when his wife tries to leave the room, she cannot get out and determines to shoulder the charge of murder herself. She overturns a table, disarranges her dress, and, at last, arouses the hotel staff by firing a couple of revolver shots. Then, when the police arrive, she confesses she has killed the man. The return of the husband and the wilful daughter offered other incidents, which Gladys Cooper, Leslie Faber, and George Tully transmuted into excellent "theatre" just because Channing Pollock kept his attention firmly fixed upon the all-important acting opportunities which loom so large in any play of incident.

Another example of a play of incident is Somerset Maugham's *The Letter*, based upon his short story *The Casuarina Tree*. This was also a Gladys Cooper venture and again there were revolver shots and evidence that Miss Cooper had killed a man. The Malay servants run in and messages are sent to the heroine's friends, before the curtain falls upon one of the shortest opening scenes in all drama. When the curtain rises, the heroine has explained that the dead man had made an attack upon her wifely honour and she claims she shot him in self-defence.

Husband and friends alike accept the explanation but the wife is forced to stand her trial. It is then that her counsel begins to make discoveries. He comes upon a letter showing that the wife herself asked the dead man to visit her, and other damaging facts. However, the woman is acquitted, though, in her hour of triumph, she is forced to confess her guilt. The dead man was her lover, and she shot him because he was leaving her for a native woman. In the last scene, the truth could not even be concealed from the injured husband, as his savings were required to silence native blackmailers. Miss Gladys Cooper's somewhat hard but well-calculated art was excellently suited to the principal part, which also gained much from Sir Gerald du Maurier's production. No English actor of his time had a surer sense of dramatic effect. It is said that Edgar Wallace was so impressed by the improvements which Sir Gerald du Maurier introduced into his crook drama, *The Ringer*, that he spontaneously offered Du Maurier one-third of his author's fees.

Henry Bernstein's *The Thief*, in which George Alexander and Irene Vanbrugh starred at the St James's thirty years ago, is an example of a play written for and around a situation, as was Henry Arthur Jones's *Mrs Dane's Defence* or Pinero's *The Gay Lord Quex*. In the first act of Bernstein's play, young Henry Leyton is accused of theft and the curtain in the second act rises upon the bedroom of the Chelfords, man and wife. Chelford, the husband, is troubled about young Leyton and in an effort to penetrate the mystery he prises open his wife's desk with his penknife. In a drawer are notes to the value of £250 and Chelford realizes that this can only mean that his wife is the thief and that young Leyton may well be her lover. In fact, Marise (Irene Vanbrugh) is in love with her husband and she stole in order to buy the pretty dresses which would please him.

Melodrama: its Appeal

Jean Jacques Rousseau first used the word melodrama to signify a play with musical accompaniment, and, in England, the word was spelt "melo-drama" and applied to Holcroft's *Tale of Mystery*. This was a free translation from the first genuine French melodrama *Coeline; ou l'enfant du mystère* by Pixérécourt. It was produced by Kemble at Covent Garden, November 13 1802, and owed a good deal to the popularity of the romances of Ann Radcliffe, with their background of scowling adventurers and ruined castles. Apart from a prevailing atmosphere of gloom

K

and impending death, melodrama generally involves numerous and rapidly changing scenes, and this means that the story is developed with little or no insistence upon motives which call for detailed analysis. Passion and sentiment there must be in melodrama, but the main ingredients are action and surprise. In fact, melodrama is the play of incident *par excellence*.

Pixérécourt lived during the Terror and worked through the opening years of the nineteenth century. It was a time when the theatre was changing its character and relying less upon the support of the cultured few than the uncultured many, so much so that Pixérécourt boasted that his 120 plays were written for those who could not read. Just because a new stratum of theatregoers was being opened up early in the nineteenth century, melodrama speedily proved as popular in England as it was in France. Very soon, apart from one or two theatres given over to burlesque and Shakespearean performances by accepted stars, melodrama provided the staple dramatic fare in Britain and its popularity persisted for at least half a century.

So far as present-day playgoers are concerned, melodrama flourished in its purest form under the Melville Brothers after Henry Irving abandoned the Lyceum. The melodramatic dynasty was founded by George Melville, a touring actor-manager, who died in 1898. Andrew, his eldest son, specialized in melodrama and left six children, two of whom, Walter and Frederick, not only acted in and produced melodrama, but wrote melodramas, if "wrote" is the proper word. More accurately, they tinkered with the acting versions used by the old-time touring companies, which themselves had been so fully rewritten that any vested interest in the copyright had long been forgotten. After all, the youthful Shakespeare and other Elizabethans had done much the same thing with the plays they found in the Burbage and Alleyn coffers.

By the turn of the century Walter and Frederick Melville were in charge of the Standard, Shoreditch, and here they produced *The Worst Woman in London* in 1899. The lady practised arson on a large scale and finally set fire to a house, so that the heroine only saved her life by escaping to a neighbouring telegraph pole, after using the wires as an improvised tight-rope. *The Ugliest Woman on Earth* followed in 1904 and before the craze for Melville melodrama ended twenty-five companies were in rehearsal at the Standard at one time. Theatre-goers who supported the Melville dynasty easily outnumbered those who swore by George Edwardes or Sir George Dance. The end came with Frederick Melville's *The Bad Girl of the Family* in 1909, after which romance recovered its appeal for the masses.

To-day, the demand is for Grand Guignol thrills, in which a considerable element of the sadistic is plain to view. Grand Guignol is sophisticated melodrama. As the name suggests, it is of French extraction, and about 1908 there was a tiny theatre of the name on the heights of Montmartre which specialized in the gruesome. The cheapest seats cost the equivalent of 3s. 9d. and a crowded house meant about 250 spectators. There was a Gothic atmosphere about the auditorium owing to the whim of an earlier tenant of the building who introduced pointed windows of medieval pattern, carved woodwork, and a raftered roof. Following upon some experiments in the gruesome by M. Antoine at the Théâtre Libre, a certain Max Maurey opened the Grand Guignol as a forcing-house for the macabre in drama and gathered a band of writers who quickly made the place famous alike for the audacities of its farce and the horrors of its tragedy. A typical play lasted no more than twenty minutes and there were six in an evening.

In *En Plongée*, playgoers were shown the interior of a submarine and a shocking scene of fearful panic which was the prelude to the end. The curtain fell, to rise upon the funeral of the dead men, with the Minister of Marine reading a speech telling of the quiet, steadfast courage with which the crew met death. The sting of the satire lay in the contrast between the reality of Scene I and the mock pathos of Scene II.

The irony in which Grand Guignol drama specializes was also seen in *Une Consultation*. Here a famous physician comes for a consultation with a provincial doctor, in a case of supreme difficulty. But the local doctor proves to be an old friend of the famous physician and they talk over old times. Not a thought of the patient. From time to time the wife breaks in. Cannot they tell her something? Not yet. And when the great man rises, stretches for his hat, and prepares for departure, it is only to ask, "How much ought I to charge?" and on this grim irony the curtain falls. In 1921, Grand Guignol drama established itself at the Little Theatre in the Adelphi. Sybil Thorndike headed the company and in two years she established herself at the head of her profession by virtue of the acting opportunities the little essays in the macabre gave her.

In *The Medium* a young sculptor was troubled by certain strange happenings in his studio and through the agency of a model who was susceptible to hypnotic influences, a gruesome murder was disclosed. In her trance the medium describes how the murderer has concealed his victim in a plaster of Paris slab and, sure enough, when the frenzied sculptor breaks down the casing the head of a dead woman is disclosed. In this case Sybil Thorndike's artistry showed itself in a complete absence of "ham". As the medium she did no more than express the natural horror of a woman witnessing a horrible happening. *The Nutcracker Suite* told of a faithless wife (Sybil Thorndike) who was lured with her lover to a lonely inn. Here the husband prepared his revenge, based upon Edgar Allan Poe's *The Pit and the Pendulum*. The ceiling began to fall, slowly, slowly, until at curtain-fall, the lovers were about to be crushed to death. Earlier, the husband, played by Franklin Dyall, had appeared at the window and twitted the lovers about their temporary imprisonment in a room which gained its name from the wife's delight in Tchaikovsky's music. Eliot Crawshay-Williams was the author.

St John Ervine's *Progress* was another effective item in Grand Guignol. It told of a brother and sister, played by Lewis Casson and Sybil Thorndike. She was a war widow and had also lost a son in the first World War. Obsessed with the horrors of fighting, the sister found that her brother was devising an engine which would add still more to world suffering. The inventor preaches a broad view of such problems as war and weapons of destruction. The woman can only recall her dead husband and son. She begs the brother to destroy his paper. He answers, "There are no papers. It is all in my head." "Then forget what you know." And when the inventor refused, the stricken woman killed him.

A thieves' kitchen, with a black-market bully who throttled an unfaithful wife! Plainly, exciting! But one after another, week after week; and not only in the theatre, but on the films and on the wireless! As we had a surfeit of bedroom comedy after the first World War, so theatre-goers have been offered an overplus of horrors in the years following the second World War. There was no more intelligent and attractive actress in post-war London than Ellen Pollock. Shaw's Eliza Doolittle and the understanding Candida were within her range; but so were the horrors of Grand Guignol, as she showed at the Granville Theatre in 1947. In a single evening Miss Pollock was a vulgarian who left her husband on her wedding night; the companion of an unfaithful husband, who murdered his mistress with blood-curdling animalism; and a crystal-hard woman, who played with the loves of two men, only to bring about the deaths of all three. As actress, no one would grudge Ellen Pollock an opportunity to show her powers in the macabre, as Sybil Thorndike had done at the Little Theatre years earlier, but not too often and not for too long.

Grand Guignol is a method of polishing the technique not only of dramatists but of players, for it discourages under-acting and stresses the need for developing the all-important element of tension in play-production.

Tension, in the aesthetics of the theatre, means a stretching of the imaginative effort and thus brings about a mental strain in the onlooker which is only relieved when the stress due to dramatist or player is released. In other words, it is an aggravation of attention, as well as an aggravation of the normal emotion with which a playgoer follows a story in the playhouse. A violin string is in tension when it is attuned; so is an audience. Among British playwrights, Patrick Hamilton is a master in the development of tension, as he showed in *Rope* and *Gaslight*. No less deft was his *Money with Menaces*, originally conceived as wireless drama, and, therefore, able to use the device of telephone conversations with propriety and effect. The theme was the punishment of a bully. Half a lifetime had passed since the man at one end of the telephone suffered the indignities which had poisoned his boyhood and made him determined upon vengeance—whatever the lapse of time. The bully was now a successful newspaper proprietor, wealthy beyond the dreams of avarice and accustomed to have his way in everything. To him comes the unknown blackmailer. He learns that a well-loved daughter has been kidnapped and fear comes upon him. Money no longer talks and the discovery reveals the craven spirit of the one-time bully.

Cruelty was the underlying motif in *Rope* and *Gaslight*, two crisply written melodramas which play up to that ugly trait in human nature which takes its name from the notorious Marquis de Sade, who explored the forms of sexual perversion character-ized by obsession with cruelty. How deep-rooted this human frailty is may be judged from all recorded history down to the annals of the concentration camps. Torture, mental and physical, can be very moving upon the stage and can bring un-suspected acting opportunities into being, as Patrick Hamilton showed in *Rope*, when Brian Aherne played Wyndham Brandon, the criminal, Anthony Ireland, Granillo, and Ernest Milton, Rupert Cadell, the lame poet who brought the murderers to a belated justice.

Brandon and Granillo are Oxford undergraduates who lure a fellow undergraduate to a London flat and strangle him. They hope to stage the perfect crime—a passionless, motiveless, fault-less, and clueless murder. No one has seen the young man come to the flat and no one has any idea that he was expected. In the event the over-weening vanity of the first murderer is his undoing. He invites a party of friends to supper and arranges that the meal shall be served on the lid of the chest in which the dead man is concealed and which crashed so ominously in the darkness of curtain-rise. Among the guests are the father and sister of the victim, so that the party will give the final touch of *macabre* to the crime. As the tension grows, Granillo, the second murderer, shows the first traces of fear. He is already losing his nerve when a theatre ticket is found on the floor. It belonged to the dead man.

Brandon: We could hang on that!

The door bell rings, and Granillo hastily slips the Coliseum ticket into his waistcoat pocket. Sabot, the valet, lays a cloth over the top of the chest, cocktails are served and the party begins. The dramatist is careful that each guest is sharply characterized, Raglan, Brandon's one-time fag, Leila Arden, the sister, and Sir Johnstone Kentley, the elderly bibliophile. And, in particular, Rupert Cadell, with his foppish dress and his affected speech and carriage. Anything less like the typical stage detective could not be imagined, and Ernest Milton was the man to the life.

There is no need to recall the plot of *Rope* in detail. Someone asks for news of the dead man. The Coliseum is mentioned and Rupert notices the blue ticket in Granillo's vest pocket, and secures it. "Odd." Granillo had averred he was never in the Coliseum; he did not even know where it was; thought it was in the Haymarket. The first curtain falls upon the lines:

Rupert: I have just thought of something rather queer.
Brandon: Something queer. What's that?
Rupert: All this talk about rotting bones in chests.

Mr Hamilton's second act followed without a break in the action, and incident after incident focuses attention upon the chest, and, towards the end of Act II, a telephone message tells that the dead man had not come home. The party breaks up and Rupert goes with the rest, but only to return for his cigarette case. He has guessed what is in the chest.

Rupert: I'll tell you what. I'll stay and see you off to Oxford.

The last scene again follows on without a break. Indeed, the preservation of the traditional "unities" is one of numerous craft problems which Patrick Hamilton solves so neatly in *Rope*. In the climax Rupert pins the blue Coliseum ticket on the outside lapel of his coat and faces the murderers.

Brandon: Hullo, what's your button-hole?
Granillo (hysterically): He's got it. He's got it.
Brandon (shouting): Hold your tongue. Hold your filthy tongue.

As the last curtain is reached, Rupert opens the chest and forces a confession from the murderers. The play ends with:

Rupert: You are going to hang, you swine. Hang, both of you! Hang! (*He hobbles to the window, throws it open and sends three piercing whistles into the night.*)

Tension, the sense of suspense, is so considerable a factor in all drama that no writer who is interested in the craft of writing for the theatre will grudge the time given to an intensive study of *Rope*. It is a masterpiece in its class. Every trick of the trade is utilized. The play of light and darkness, telephone calls, gramophone records playing "off", each scene played for what it is worth and no more and, always something for competent actors to do.

From the acting standpoint, the possibilities of sadism were never exploited better than by Michael Redgrave in *Uncle Harry* and by Peter Ustinov in his translation *Frenzy* from a Swedish original by Ingmar Bergman. The latter was played at the St Martin's Theatre in 1948. Ustinov not only translated *Frenzy* but played the principal character, a schoolmaster, whose perversions veered between the torments he inflicted upon his pupils and the fears he imposed upon an unhappy adolescent, played by Joan Greenwood. In ecstasy and despair Peter Ustinov maintained the all-important tension, neither over-playing nor under-playing. The weakness of *Frenzy* as a play was that the principal player carried too heavy a burden. The supporting characters were not differentiated with the skill Patrick Hamilton displayed so startlingly in *Rope*.

CHAPTER 7

THE FACULTY OF LAUGHTER

MORE than one philosopher has propounded the question, "What is common to the clown, the punster, the low and the high comedian?" In general, the answers have insisted too strongly upon some supposed utilitarian quality in the risible arts. Plainly, Dr McDougall was right in describing laughter as an antidote against many depressing influences. Nevertheless, all such antidotes are not laughable. Sweetmeats, for example, or tobacco. Similarly, laughter operates as a social nexus, encouraging sympathies which link individual with individual and class with class. But this is not to characterize laughter. Suffering arouses social sympathies, but not so surely.

Again, Dryden detected an element of malice at the root of man's pleasure in the laughable. Cicero, following Aristotle, held a somewhat similar opinion when he laid it down that the province of the ludicrous "lies in a certain baseness or deformity". So did Hobbes when, in answer to the question "What makes us laugh?" he instanced awkwardness, deformity, or those imperfections which heighten our own self-esteem. Admittedly, laughter enters into satire as an expression of contempt or an instrument of punishment, but, surely, to laugh with Juvenal is to feel more of bitter malignity than of gaiety. Professor Tyrrell said truly: "Juvenal is always in a rage and a laugh appears to sit strangely on his lips."

Doctor Johnson (who laughed like a rhinoceros) called attention to the curious fact that the major satirists—Jonathan Swift and Alexander Pope, for example—never laughed. Nor should it be forgotten that a morality-loving people such as the Jews or the Puritans after them were not given to laughter. What we read of is the derisive laughter of his wife when David danced before the Ark, and the scornful laughter of Sara, when told she was to have a child. Indeed, the sense of social propriety can go so far that the capacity to laugh vanishes entirely. The great Lord Chesterfield once congratulated himself upon the fact that, since he had the full use of his reason, he had never been heard to laugh. To Chesterfield, laughter was evidence of ill-breeding, which reminds one of a dictum of Vico, the philosopher, that neither animals nor wise men laugh; only uninstructed man, who stands half-way between the brute and the sage.

The very search for the final significance of laughter may, in itself, be a jest for Momus, the mocker godling who traditionally presides over the faculty. In pinning a fluttering jest to the cork of a definition we rob it of vitality, just as we deprive the butterfly of half its colour when we pop a pin through its thorax and add it to the sunless camphor cabinet. However, this is relatively unimportant, as our real theme is not laughter in itself, but laughter as we find it in a playhouse.

Incongruity and the Social Code

Any violation of the pattern of the universe entails an element of incongruity and, therefore, may offer material to the dramatist, but it does not follow that every incongruity is dramatic. It is the alliance between situation and personality which is dramatic. The disturbance of the rhythm of life only becomes funny when the incongruity between situation and character obtrudes itself. A grave-digger in a Scottish church-yard is far from being a figure of fun. Nor is an inquisitive visitor from over the Border, but the conjunction may be amusing.

Affable Englishman: I suppose things are quiet here?
Dour Gravedigger: Not so quiet as them there.
A.E.: Yes, indeed, but I suppose people do not die often here?
D.G.: Only once, sir.
A.E.: No doubt. I suppose you have spent all your life here?
D.G.: Not yet, sir.
   (*Affable Englishman retires discomfited.*)

And recognizing the underlying incongruity and its expression in terms of character, we have been amused.

Amused! Scientists assure us that the first smile of a baby may come about the forty-fifth day after birth, though some observers date this smile of smiles even earlier, associating it with the happy sense of repletion, following liquid food. At three months, Baby echoes his mother's laugh and a little later responds to parental tickling. At half a year arises the chuckle which accompanies mere repetition, such as bobbing from behind the hood of the babe's perambulator. By eighteen months a real sense of fun is recognizable and then the humorous possibilities of children develop apace. A child laughs at a Jack-in-the-Box or a Punch and Judy show, or over the tricks of a circus clown. In other words, it has entered upon its career as a playgoer.

But note the value of preparation and repetition if real laughter is to arise. The policeman whom Punch knocks down is up and about again as though he was made of rubber, and every knock-down blow increases the laughter. "Do it again, Daddy," is one of the earliest rewards a parent wins from his laughter-raising tricks. Incidentally, the laughter of children is almost invariably associated with a marked absence of sympathy for the sufferer. As men and women grow up, their humour tends to become more kindly, though always there remains a considerable admixture of the childlike, and therefore of the unkindly. With adolescence comes conscious art, both in the artist creator and his or her audience and it is the laughter which arises from conscious art which interests us, not merely the physical laughter which follows upon, say, tickling.

Tickling induces purely physical reactions, but there are symbolic implications in the word which bring it closer to the theatre. The phrase "tickled to death" is far removed from the physical act. When Harry Lauder put over his song, "Stop your tickling, Jock" the relationship with the physical was fairly close, but it had vanished and symbolism was dominant when Connie Ediss, in *The Sunshine Girl*, sang:

"Oh, I went to the Durbar! Didn't we have a spree:
They say I tickled the Rajahs, but I know they tickled me."

We laughed with Connie Ediss because the nursery sense of the incongruous was still with us. Which reminds us that variants upon nursery rhymes, so dear to the gagging comedian, offer telling examples of the virtue which underlies familiar raw material. We laugh when the familiar "Mary had a little lamb" unexpectedly proceeds:

> But that was long ago;
> And now she has two little calves,
> Which she is proud to show.

A host of funnyosities spring to mind which associate themselves with the introduction of short skirts in the inter-war years. One of them ran thus:

> Mary had a little lamb
> With fleece as black as soot,
> Who in her little porringer
> Once put its sooty foot.
> But Mary, as a pious child,
> Her wrath had learned to smother,
> So merely said a little word
> Which, to the lamb, meant mother.

The nonsensical variants upon Kipling's *Gunga Din*, which "Almost a gentleman" Billy Bennett exploited so continually, are a theatrical equivalent.

In the same way and for similar reasons the schoolboy "howler" offers excellent raw material to the theatre.

The laughter due to a schoolboy's "howler" depends primarily upon two factors: (1) that the many should be familiar with the proper answer; (2) that the mental picture aroused should quickly reveal the incongruity. Because of its familiarity the Bible is a fruitful source of howlers. It was the story of the Widow of Nain which produced the delightful commentary, "It was a glorious funeral. It took four men to carry the beer." Both the incongruity and the mental picture were there, following the rule that the really telling howler is much more than a verbal error. A small girl was writing an essay based upon the widow who cast her two mites into the offertory box, in Herod's Temple. Her comment ran: "People were really generous in those days. We should not, in 1947, find any poor woman throwing her two small children into the Treasury."

Like the Bible, the history lesson is a prolific source of howlers.

The subject matter is relatively familiar and there is a big possibility that any out-scale error will result in an equally monstrous incongruity. Dean Inge is fond of the classical lapses, among them "Socrates died from an over-dose of wedlock." My own classical favourite is the story of the Whitechapel shopkeeper who was somewhat envious of the Latin motto above the doorway of a rival tradesman. This read: *Mens conscia recti*. The jealous trader capped this with the variant: *Men's and Women's conscia recti*.

In its dramatic form, the schoolboy "howler" jest resulted in *1066 and All That* and the song and sketch impersonations of George Robey, Malcolm Scott, and Douglas Byng. The mere enumeration of outstanding stage examples would fill a chapter. What distinguishes the theatrical variants from the errors of ignorance is the element of conscious artistry, whether in the elaboration of the jest or in the imagination of the beholder which itself creates the all-important sense of incongruity.

Is failure to hit a golf ball funny? Of course not. But it can become funny when Sid Field associates it with the song "Little Ball's gone Ta-Ta" and his cockneyisms. Nor is a beating funny *sui generis*. Nevertheless, when, in *The Frogs*, Aeacus whips the god Dionysus together with his servant Xanthias, in order to ascertain which of them is the immortal, laughter worthy of Teufelsdröckh was kindled in Athens, and it will be remembered that this laugh was "not of the face and diaphragm only, but of the whole mass, from head to heel". Which emphasizes the truth that nothing is laughable in itself. The quality of laughter arises from the people associated with the laugh.

Consider such an elaborate and established jest department as Ted Kavanagh's ITMA. This emphasized the added value which a verbal jest gains by association with recognizable personalities, the more because, in broadcast drama, the character is not present in person, as he or she is on the stage. When Ted Kavanagh required Signor So-So, the foreigner who tripped so easily into the pitfalls presented by the English language, to plead "Come to my arms and let me embarrass you," we could not but smile because that was the sort of thing Signor So-So would say, and when he added "You are a divan woman," we smiled again over the double image of the encouched pair.

Similarly, when Tommy Handley innocently remarked upon the undesirability of "dressing shabbily", the Colonel's interjection, "Chablis, sir? A glorious wine—I don't mind if I do," made us smile, because we had met the Colonel before and that was the sort of thing he would say. Poppy Poopah and the stern Miss Hotchkiss, Ali Oop, the pedlar, and the rest were slowly brought to life by Tommy Handley and his company and then, and only then, did Ted Kavanagh's verbal felicities have their full chance. In other words, audiences had to be educated before ITMA was possible.

Assurance becomes doubly sure when the authority of Emanuel Kant is added to that of the creator of ITMA. Kant said, "a jest's prosperity lies in the ear of him that hears it more than in the tongue of him that makes it."

To revert to Sid Field and his golf ball, failure to reach a given goal is certainly an element in many jests, practical and otherwise, but the fun does not arise from the failure; otherwise the failure of a cricketer to play a fast ball would be funny. What is funny is some unexpected interference with the customary rhythm of life. Incidentally, it is because the ceremonial side of social life is easily disrupted that it includes a latent comic element, and that is why one cannot but smile at the whisper of the small boy to his mother towards the end of a first-rate party: "Mummy, carry me home, but don't bend me."

The momentary vision of a tiny belly, tight as a drum, has just that mixture of the comic and tragic which low comedians have exploited for generations. The same elements can be traced in Pinero's picture of the Dean of St Marvell's, in *Dandy Dick*, mixing the bolus for a racehorse.

What may be described as the professional career of jest or anecdote from its early assumption of art form to its climax as material for the theatre is happily illustrated by the history of Spoonerisms and Spoonerizing. Attention has already been called to the comic transposition of a letter or a word in a familiar phrase. Arthur Roberts used to ask "Can a swim duck?" and announce solemnly "Flime ties," and, to this day, Lupino Lane guarantees to tickle an audience by substituting "animated picture of Queen Anne" for "ammoniated tincture of quinine". But this hoary form of jest only reached full manhood when a respected, but short-sighted, Oxford Don misquoted a familiar hymn as "Kingering kongs their titles take." Quickly, undergraduate invention was spurred to supreme efforts and Dr Spooner, the Warden of New College, was credited with "Have you, my brethren, ever nurtured in your breast half-warmed fishes?" whereas he was really interested in half-formed wishes.

In time, Dr Spooner had a world-wide reputation for slips of the tongue, very few of which he would accept as authentic. For example, Dr Spooner resolutely denied that he ever told a porter that he had lost a bug and a rook, or called at an Oxford College and inquired of the butler at the door, "If the Bean was dizzy?" Still less had Dr Spooner ever rebuked the undergraduates of New College with "Gentlemen, you have hissed your mystery lessons and tasted a whole worm." Admittedly, Dr Spooner's attention wandered upon occasion; an example being a lecture upon the Greek historians, which concluded with, "Of course, you will understand that, in this lecture, whenever I said St Paul, I meant Herodotus." The explanation was that an hour earlier, Dr Spooner's theme had been the Greek Testament.

What happened, of course, was the creation of a long series of real or invented anecdotes by association with a memorable personality. The jests redoubled their potency when associated with the snow-white hair, rosy cheeks, and kindly eye of the courtly old Warden of New College. Similarly, a theatrical gag, hoary with age, may be fully effective when put over by a popular comedian, whereas a player with less personality would do well to ignore it.

Dialect and Stage Laughter

One other well-defined source of laughter calls for mention, the Irish "bull", and this because it owes so much to dialect, for the "bull" is quite without humour for Irishmen in Ireland. The humour in the typical "bull" or mixed metaphor depends upon a telescoping of conflicting ideas. As "A.E." very wittily said, "a cat with the body of a dog would be a bull." The most complex of all mixed metaphors is to the credit of Sir Boyle Roche, addressing the House of Commons—"Gentlemen," he exclaimed, "I smell a rat. I see it brewing in the distance. By the grace of God I shall nip it in the bud."

Truly, a very pregnant "bull" and as a mere quotation, good fun, but it must have gained immensely from Sir Boyle's rich brogue. Moreover, the fun is immensely increased if a visual element is added, as it is in the theatre. Here a comic picture is added to the comic play of words and both picture and phrase associate themselves with a recognizable character. The very word "Irish" or Ireland in connection with an anecdote quickens the imagination, as the adjective "Aberdonian" serves the same purpose in connection with a host of familiar stories. Again, there is the classic story of the Cockney, who had the good fortune to secure a place in the front row at a big fire. He later described what happened in these terms: " 'Jump, yer silly fool,' I cried. 'We've got a sheet.' And, blimey, 'e did jump. But there weren't no sheet and he broke 'is bloomin' neck. Larf, I thought I should 'av died."

In this case the jest derived almost all its quality from the dialect. Many an actor or actress has achieved fame because a gift for dialogue has added a much needed authenticity to a moth-eaten gag.

The thrills arising from the sadistic are seldom laughter-creating. As Aristotle pointed out, the comic must not be too painful or too destructive. If deformities, physical or mental, are there they should be toned down. Which brings up the special problems due to farce.

The distinction between light comedy and farce is not absolute. It lies in the handling of material common to both forms of drama. It was undeniably funny when Sydney Howard, as a puzzled and nervous butler, in *Night of the Garter*, watched the grandfather's clock walk from the room in the "haunted house". But that the effect was farcical and not raw material for comedy had been apparent from the moment playgoers noted the title of the evening's entertainment, *Night of the Garter*! No comedy could live and flourish under such a title. Moreover, Sydney Howard's stage name was Bodger.

Coleridge defined a farce thus: "A proper farce is distinguished from a comedy by the licence allowed and even required in the fable in order to produce strange and laughable situations. The story need not be probable; it is enough that it is possible." *Arsenic and Old Lace* might have been a melodramatic thriller,

Jean Cadell, Mary Jerrold, and Edith Evans in *The Old Ladies* by Rodney Ackland and Hugh Walpole, New Theatre (1935) (*see page* 59).

Robert Morley and
Patricia Hicks
in *Edward my Son*,
His Majesty's
Theatre.

and, indeed, was written with that intention. Thanks to its treatment by the first company of players, it won success as a farce and holds the long-run record for any American play ever staged in London. In London and on tour *Arsenic and Old Lace* played to upwards of three million people, and plainly they found it beyond belief as a thriller, but very funny. Not a few play-

NIOBE

MISS BEATRICE LAMB

goers thought it the funniest play they had ever seen. Personally, I did not find it anything like as funny as all that, though Dame Lilian Braithwaite and Mary Jerrold did not miss a point and the Strand box-office could boast "We were up £2" on the night the V1 bomb fell beside the theatre.

Arthur Wing Pinero wrote a number of farces which were produced by a brilliant company at the Court Theatre early in his career. *Dandy Dick* was the best of them, Dandy Dick being the name of a racehorse which came into the temporary posses-

L

sion of the Very Rev. Augustin Jedd, D.D., Dean of St Marvell's. The Dean was unfortunate in having a widowed sister with a passion for horse-racing. As the sister was played by Mrs John Wood and the dignified and decorous dean by Mr John Clayton, *Dandy Dick* might easily have been a comedy. In fact Pinero chose to add a large admixture of farcical sentiment in the shape of Salome and Sheba, the Dean's daughters, and their Hussar lovers, Tarver and Darbey. Add the comic policeman, Noah Topping, and Pinero, in honesty, could only call his play a farce.

The first farce I ever saw was *Niobe, All Smiles*, a Willie Edouin production at the Old Strand, in the 'nineties of the last century. Here is an extract from the programme, which is generous enough to enable an expert to reconstruct the greater part of the play.

Peter Dunn	*In Life Assurance*	Harry Paulton
Cornelius Griffin	*In Love With Himself*	Forbes Dawson
Philip Innings	*In Corney's Hands*	Herbert Ross
Hamilton Tompkins	*In the Clouds—An Art Enthusiast*	George Hawtrey
Caroline Dunn	*Indispensable*	Miss Goldsmith
Helen Griffin	*In Authority*	Miss Charlotta Zerbina
Hattie Griffin	*In Open Rebellion*	Miss Georgie Esmond
Mary	*In Service*	Miss Cynthia Brooke
Madeline Mifton	*In the Way—The New Nursery Governess*	Miss Helen Ferrers
Niobe	*In the Flesh—Widow of Amphion, King of Thebes*	Miss Beatrice Lamb

Act I.	In Dunn's Drawing Room. 7.15 p.m. In the Absence of the Family.
Act II.	In Dunn's Drawing Room. The next morning—in the Presence of the Family.
Act III.	In Dunn's Drawing Room. Afternoon of the same day.

It is already plain that *Niobe, All Smiles* is a variant upon the Pygmalion and Galatea theme. A statue of Queen Niobe of Thebes has been insured for big money with the company which

Peter Amos Dunn serves as secretary. As a precaution Peter brings the statue home. Now, in the spring of 1892, electricity had unfathomed possibilities. When an electric-light fitter unwittingly wound certain wires about the feet of the statue, and the widow of Amphion came to life in Dunn's drawing-room, audiences accepted the phenomenon without allowing an eyelid to flicker. Not so Peter Amos Dunn. Overwhelmed by the potentialities of his situation, Dunn decked Niobe in the clothes of the family governess. Only when the real governess arrived did the full consequences of deceit descend upon him.

Like Galatea, Niobe persists in regarding the unhappy man who gave her life as her lord and master, but, under Mrs Dunn's rigorous examination as to her fitness for the post of governess, Niobe breaks down. She refers everything to events which took place a couple of thousand years ago, when she ruled with Amphion in Thebes.

Plainly, some of the smiles associated with the nineteenth-century Niobe were traceable to the statue's incongruous appearance in a typical middle-class Victorian household, when the mistress was away for the evening and her eminently respectable spouse had settled down to a quiet smoke. There was promise of the comic frustration which Max Eastman has professed to detect in every stage joke, and it began directly Peter Amos reflected upon the certainty of Mrs Dunn's return. Long before Harry Paulton had recited his fears, audiences at the Strand were revelling in a fellow mortal's distress and congratulating themselves that they would have shown more acumen and enterprise than the unhappy Peter Amos.

It may be that a similar sense of incongruity followed by comic frustration is at the root of all successful farces and comedies. Certainly, what is laughable is not the good-hap but the ill-hap of our friends. We laugh over the pains and penalties which others suffer. Why should we weep for them, when we have so many pains and penalties of our own? An incongruity arises when one notes the difference between what things are and what they ought to be. The unexpected absence of the *ought* constitutes the comic situation. Peter Amos Dunn, when embraced by the grateful Niobe, was in just the sort of incongruous predicament that elderly business men would find amusing, if they were spectators and not victims of the imbroglio. The elderly business men see very plainly the differences between what things are and what they ought to be, and the sense of the distinction is essentially laugh-worthy. Add to this incongruous predicament the surprise and tension of a well-constructed plot, and the laughter which *Niobe, all Smiles* aroused is explained. It should be added that the curious suitability of Beatrice Lamb for the rôle of a Greek statue, turned from Parian marble into pulsing flesh, was a considerable factor in the success of the play. Miss

MP HARRY PAULTON

Lamb, who was well skilled in dramatic and melodramatic parts, was substantial but nevertheless charming, and she moved in her classic garments with full grace.

A classical farce of the later nineteenth century was *La Boule* of Meilhac and Halévy. The theme was that misunderstanding over trifles is apt to break marriages, and in working it out the authors imagined M. Paturel consulting his lawyer with a view to a judicial separation from Madame Paturel. The head and front of her offending was that the good lady had introduced a hot-water bottle into their double-bed and M. Paturel hated hot-water bottles. The first chuckles came over M. Paturel's indignation when he learnt that Madame was consulting *her* lawyer, with view to a judicial separation and, egoist as he was, M. Paturel, for the life of him, could not conceive that his wife could possibly have a grievance. Meilhac and Halévy had great fun with the trial scene, upon which witnesses and judge alike found it difficult to concentrate. But then, with Mlle Lavallière as Mariette and Max Dearly as the Judge, the plot of *La Boule* could wear thin in places and still amuse.

In farce, too, the idea is unimportant compared with the opportunities for incident and situation which an idea promises. Wilde constructed *The Importance of Being Earnest* from the notion, "Bunburying". The imaginary Bunbury was a permanent invalid whose occasional breakdowns in health gave Mr Algernon Moncrieff excuses for escaping into the country when the criticism of his family promised to be annoying. As farcical ideas go, Bunburying was well above the average; most farce writers are content with much less worthy excuses for getting their action going. Farce and light comedy writers are continually on the look-out for themes of this sort. In Reginald Berkeley's *French Leave*, a successful play of the first World War, the theme was the visit of a young wife to her husband while he was in rest billets. Not a very easy happening to make plausible. However, Reginald Berkeley had Renée Kelly to play the newly-married English girl and he made her pose as a Parisian actress visiting her "mother", this being the landlady of the billet in which the captain was resting in between turns in the trenches. Once the major problem of getting the young wife near the front trenches was solved, Berkeley's troubles were largely over. Characterization which was sufficiently realistic and a careful avoidance of cheap laughs and over-sentimentality helped the play to a marked success. Every one was quickly in love with Renée Kelly and in addition to her charms there was the ripe humour of Arthur Riscoe as the mess waiter.

The division between light comedy and farce is not to be determined with precision. Is Noel Coward's *Present Laughter* comedy or farce? The author does not tell us. And what of the lighter plays of Frederick Lonsdale? Plainly, *The Last of Mrs Cheyney* is comedy, but what of *Spring Cleaning* or *Canaries Sometimes Sing*? In light comedy the dramatist is often tempted to incidents which are amusing but strictly belong rather to farce than comedy.

Lonsdale, who specialized in the more frivolous aspects of life in High Society, was very prone to this temptation. In *The High Road*, his theme was that of a youthful aristocrat desirous of marrying a lady of the musical-comedy stage. In the first act the ducal family assemble to discuss the scheming girl of the stage, who has entangled the future duke. To their astonishment, they discover that there is another aspect of the matter. What if the young heir is not good enough for the actress? This point of view is developed by the girl's father. His daughter can earn £10,000 a year; can the aristocrat do that? She can bring joy into the lives of people after a trying day's work. The father convinces himself, and the audience, that the actress would sacrifice herself if she wedded a nincompoop, and, before the curtain falls, the actress comes to the same conclusion. She not only throws over the young heir, but refuses the duke himself, who has been won over by her beauty and cheerfulness. Lonsdale's actress, in fact, does precisely what the young mill-hand does in *Hindle Wakes*, so we grant Mr Lonsdale the benefit of the doubt and pronounce his work "comedy".

In *Spring Cleaning* the temptation to arouse laughter by easier means was continually present. Lonsdale's theme is a wife contemplating an elopement with an obviously reluctant lover. Quickly, audiences seize upon the fact and realize that reconcilement with the husband is the obvious alternative. Yes, but how will this be brought about? Lonsdale's answer was, not through anything done by wife or husband, but by the reluctant lover. The last act of *Spring Cleaning* was devoted to the lover engineering the reconciliation of the married folk and thus extricating himself from what was plainly an awkward situation. The delicious impudence of Ronald Squire was the making of *Spring Cleaning* and fully justified the description "comedy".

In light comedies of the Lonsdale type and in all farces there are usually two easily distinguishable phases, the one creating a confusion and the other extricating the protagonists from their worries. Thus Tom Walls thought that a haunted house would furnish the needed confusion and his author, Ben Travers, began by inventing a grim title, *Thark*. Travers is a believer in telling titles. Given the theme, the next factor in a successful farce is a motive for the happenings which will allow the situations to arise naturally. It is all-important that the characters of farce should be recognized as ordinary human beings. Lastly, there is the dialogue, which must be carefully timed. Ben Travers acts the dialogue as he works upon it, striding up and down his study to assure himself that it can be spoken by the players he has in mind, perhaps Alfred Drayton, perhaps Tom Walls, perhaps Robertson Hare. What the comic dramatist contributes is, primarily, the logic which combines the opposing halves into an acceptable whole, though the ingenuity which allows the confusion to occupy two or three hours of time acceptably is no mean factor. The fun in farce must not peter out, rather it must have opportunities to burgeon. The underlying incongruity in farce is the equivalent of the theme in more serious drama. In both cases the best service an idea can render an author is that it should keep him sufficiently amused during the tiresome process of elaboration which alone gives acting opportunities.

Which calls to mind that the theme of a farce may be no more than a player with marked physical characteristics. One of the natural comics of all time was Edward Garratt, as the one-year-old baby in Michael Morton's farce, *The Little Stranger*. Garratt was fifteen years old when it was produced and had no previous theatrical experience. In his white muslin frock, with the large pale blue silk sash, he was a "scream". The knowing wink to his grandfather which accompanied "I'm going to have a brandy and soda" has only to be remembered to arouse a chuckle. Here was one of the stock farcical situations, exploited to the nth.

From time to time a surfeit of bedroom farces oppresses the English stage, as from time to time an overplus of bathing beauties encumbers the daily and weekly illustrated newspapers. The attacks come and go like the measles or chicken-pox. During the first World War there was such a surfeit of bedroom comedies. *Up in Mabel's Room*, *The Naughty Wife*, and *Very Good, Eddie* were some of the titles. Thus in *Very Good, Eddie*, at the Palace, Nelson Keys whispered "Honey, Honey," outside the keyhole of a lady's bedroom, bringing forth the retort that hers was "a bedroom, not a beehive". *Up in Mabel's Room* was a Hawtrey venture and ran a month. The incidents arose from Hawtrey's desiring to recover

Mabel's "chemise", euphemistically described as Mabel's "whereabout" when the lady was enjoying her bath. Naturally, Charles hid under Mabel's bed, and, equally naturally, Mabel displayed some bewitching pyjamas. Even remembering the dicta of Socrates in the *Republic*, quoted in an earlier chapter, one is puzzled as to who really enjoyed these bedroom plays. They can scarcely amuse the sophisticated male. One can only believe that they have significance for the youth of the opposite sex. It is generally accepted in theatrical circles that women have little liking for knockabout farce, which men enjoy. The jests women enjoy are those which display masculine stupidity. The very phrase "I am a married man" will arouse laughter if there are enough women present to seize upon the joke. Can it be that the patrons of *Up in Mabel's Room* and *Very Good, Eddie* were women enjoying a stolen laugh at the expense of their male friends who paid for their tickets?

CHAPTER 8

THE FACULTY OF TEARS

EMPHASIS has been laid upon the faculty of laughter, as evidence of successful "theatre". What of its concomitant, the faculty of tears? If the incongruities of social life arouse laughter, other disturbances of the social round gives rise to a contrary emotion, indicated by strained attention, the tightening of the muscles of hand and throat and, in the last resort, tears akin to those drawn from the more emotional players in moments of extreme tension.

No one will ever determine how much is due to dramatist and how much to player in creating such emotional strain. When Robert Loraine and Haidee Wright came together in the closing scene of *The Father*, Strindberg had created an opportunity. The plot had been operating through three acts to this end. Every preparation had been made, and this by a master dramatist. But the art of actor and actress embodied the final beauty which compelled the tears, as the old nurse, recalling a trick which had served years earlier to tempt an unwilling youngster into his coat, used the same device to put the grown man into the strait jacket of a lunatic.

The terror of the small boy in Sacha Guitry's *Pasteur* is another instance. What brought the catch in the throat to even hard-boiled playgoers was much more than a youngster's fear of the unknown which an operation under an anaesthetic aroused. To this the dramatist had added the tension of Pasteur's own anxiety. It was a test case for him and of such crucial importance that he was risking the boy's death, and this in so shocking a form as hydrophobia. Or again, the poignant bedroom scene in *The Unknown Warrior* in which the soldier and the girl spend the night together and an added pathos arises from the fact that, though the woman knows her man is going to death, she cannot feel as he feels. What she gives is so much less than she would wish to give.

Then there is the aged mother in Synge's *Riders to the Sea*, who has given so much to the hungry ocean and now finds her last boy taken from her. It seemed an echo of the agony of the aged Hecuba when the Herald took her baby grandson Astyanax, Hector's boy, that he might be thrown from the walls of fallen Troy. Again, there is Rose's parting from Sam in *Street Scene* and the moment when Emily comes back from the grave in Thornton Wilder's *Our Town* to find that there is no longer a place for her in the world she had loved so well and in which she was so loved.

In each case what arouses intense emotion has a two-fold origin, the beauty of the dramatist's imagination and the beauty of the players' craft, both so entwined that they have become one. Years pass, but the emotion has not spent itself. It is remembered and, with the memory, once more the tell-tale tears.

That the tribute of tears rather than that of laughter is now to be the test of successful theatrical illusion suggests that we have moved into new ground. The plays we shall next consider have less of the traditional in their make-up and the methods by which they are thrust upon audiences differ considerably from the plays of incident we have considered hitherto. There will be more of wonder and of magic, and the beauty which arises from wonder and magic must be evoked by means other than those which sufficed upon the plane of day-to-day reality.

Fundamentally, what is happening upon any stage is the embodied will of man in conflict with the mysterious powers of the natural world which continually check and belittle human endeavour. To these must be added the conflicts between man and man and between man and society. In these conflicts lie the seeds alike of comedy, tragedy, and farce. But the personality of the dramatist and, indeed, his passing moods will dictate the special approach, for at one time a writer will be inclined to farce or comedy and at another to tragedy. Given integrity, all express something timeless in the experience of humanity, but particularly tragedy.

In human life nothing strikes the imagination more forcibly than its fleeting nature. So much so that the recollection of coming death is not wholly to be forgotten even in moments of joy and, indeed, as Keats has said, may give that joy its special savour. Tragedy is latent in the idea of life, coupled as life is with the relative littleness of man's stay on earth. What remains of time is too short to be wasted upon sin and suffering. Some such thought lies behind every tragic theme. A hero can only maintain his dignity by facing the time-wasting evils with fortitude; thereby he will establish an inner harmony, even if outer harmony is denied. Thus Job suffered; thus Oedipus suffered.

In the Middle Ages, the spiritual escape was of a different kind. Boethius, faced with imprisonment and death by torture, found peace in his faith that a gracious Providence would grant present release and future happiness, if only passing passions were subdued to the dictates of reason. Similarly, Shakespeare taught that those who violated the moral laws of Providence would assuredly expiate their offences by suffering or death. Thus, the way to happiness was avoidance of temptation. When, in the eighteenth century, the leaders of thought conceived an ordered universe, in charge of a deity who could make all things good for the well-to-do, tragedy passed for a while from the theatre. It was reborn from the modern conception of pigmy man, struggling with a relentless destiny, now taking the form of crushing poverty, now of uncrossable class distinctions, and now of a sense that the harmony between man and nature which had existed in some golden age had been lost, and, perhaps, lost for ever. In this sense of futile struggle the modern dramatist finds his surest origin for the emotion which creates tears. Modern man finds himself in what appears to be a disordered universe and he refuses to be comforted because he cannot understand. This may be why the imaginings of Maeterlinck always moved in the misty hinterland from which the dark cruelties of our waking experience seem to arise so naturally. Maeterlinck found not a little of his dramatic material in fears which were the more troubling because they seemed to have no tangible cause. But note that if the background was nebulous, the men, women, and children who moved in the limbo of lunary souls which Maeterlinck inherited from Poe's *Ulalume* were far from having the substance of dreams. It was Maeterlinck's strength that he gave his human creations a curious vitality and this in spite of presentations which involved many repetitions and placed a heavy burden of symbolism upon his human puppets.

"Half-waking, half-dreaming." This is how James Bridie characterized the approach of Thornton Wilder to play composition. The phrase happily suggests the approach which not only dramatists but theatre-goers should cultivate in relation to poetical plays seeking to break new ground. An excellent example of a play which was written and should be watched with the critical faculty only half-awake is *Our Town*. Thornton Wilder's body of thought was not without originality, but what characterizes *Our Town* was the determination to dispense with scenery altogether and, moreover, to present his characters on a stage almost bare of ornament.

Our Town proved to be of historical importance, not because numerous plays lend themselves to such treatment, but because of the evidence that, if the imagination of theatre audiences is excited, scenery and realistic properties matter very little. When the curtain rose on Wilder's play, his audience faced a bare stage and the manager stepped forward to announce that this was the town of Grover Corners, New Hampshire. Plainly, it might equally have been any other small town, anywhere else, as was to be shown in the first half-hour's traffic of the stage. A milkman appears to deliver the milk, while Mrs Gibbs prepares an imaginary breakfast in an imagined kitchen at one side of the stage, as, indeed, Mrs Webb is doing at the other side. Breakfasts over, the children go off to school and the ladies Webb and Gibbs exchange gossip over potato-peeling and pea-shelling preparatory to the mid-day meal.

Before a couple of acts have been played Thornton has brought Grover Corners to life, in spite of what might well be regarded as heavy theatrical disabilities. We watch Emily Webb, nervously clutching Mr Webb's arm, as she moves to join George Gibbs at an imaginary altar, to the music of Mendelssohn's "Wedding March". Many familiar faces are in the congregation or the choir, but a few are absent. We come upon them again in Act III of *Our Town*. They are the dead and they sit in chairs on one side of the stage. George's mother; Emily's younger brother. It is raining. A funeral procession is coming. It is Emily's funeral. She has died in childbirth, but Mrs Gibbs is there with words of comfort, and when Emily is allowed to return to life for a single day, it is enough. She returns contentedly to the world of the dead, and George, the widowed husband, sobbingly throws himself across her grave. If *Our Town*, when competently acted, had not been accepted as moving drama, something would have been amisss in the modern theatre. In fact, *Our Town* was accepted as a contribution to drama of acknowledged worth by all who could make the imaginative effort and could abandon a critical approach engendered on a very different plane of reality.

In the nineteen-twenties a school of philosophy flourished which professed to find in the doctrine of a meaningless universe an instrument of liberation, promising release from certain sex inhibitions and, incidentally, proffering some small justification for annexing the property of what was known as "the classes". The consequence of regarding God's universe as meaningless proved to be anarchic and led to social, political, and economic chaos, but, incidentally, gave some tragic themes to drama. To-day, the philosophy of the meaningless having lost its appeal, our more advanced thinkers are pinning their faith to existentialism, the doctrine of the immediate present. We shall see what existentialism offers to playwrights and players.

The plays which present themselves for analysis in this chapter differ widely from what were called "problem plays" when I was a young man. Those dealt with current social problems, but were chosen mainly because they promised striking situations and characters in dramatic conflict. Amusement was still a primary aim. Bernard Shaw established a different approach to the theatre. He wanted the theatre to persuade Society to revalue its ideas and ideals, though he never grudged audiences any amusement they might enjoy as a by-product of the enforced dose of social propaganda. Shaw's justification was that towards the end of the nineteenth century Western Europeans were in urgent need of enlightenment. The old dispensation was passing and man was far from sure where he stood in relation to the new dispensation. Family ties were weakening. The relations between husband and wife, father and son, mother and daughter, master and servant were changing and theatregoers wanted to know how and why.

Bernard Shaw and Galsworthy in their time, and J. B.
Priestley and Eugene O'Neill in our own day, naturally accepted
such a challenge and the tasks they set themselves disclosed new
theatrical possibilities and brought new factors into prominence.
But still the drama was moving on the plane of reality. What
Shaw and Galsworthy offered were plays of ideas, illustrating
some aspect of social conduct. M. Hervieu, who specialized in
such things, was once asked how these plays emerge into an
author's consciousness. Replying, Hervieu indicated that he regarded himself as "an organizer of conflicts of ideas, feelings, and
passions". Thus, in Hervieu's *Le Dédale* the plot was built around
the idea that a woman, whether divorced or not, re-married or
not, always feels she belongs to the man who first made her a
mother. Plainly this mental approach is quite different from that
of the dramatist who imagines a dramatic situation and then sets
to work to find the characters and plot which will create the
situation which acting may make exciting. But this approach is
equally removed from the mood of poetry, with the background
of magic and wonder in which poetry arises.

Perhaps the plays grouped under the heading "The Modern
Morality" are best characterized by an injunction of Bernard
Shaw concerning his own *Androcles*, which is on the border-line
where the realms of realism and wonder meet. Shaw said: "Be
very careful not to start public opinion on the notion that
Androcles is one of my larks. It will fail unless it is presented as a
great religious drama—with leonine relief."

Most of the plays which follow are not bereft of "relief",
leonine and otherwise, but what must be stressed is their essentially religious nature. When Clifford Odets wrote *Waiting for
Lefty* he was plainly writing left-wing propaganda, but it was
more than party propaganda, for Odets felt he had a mission and
it is the missionary element which gives his plays their distinctive
character and lifts them to the plane of poetry. There was a
similar note of poetry mingled with a sense of missionary enterprise in Clifford Odets's *Awake and Sing*, with its dream of a brave
new world, in which the misfits of a Jewish family in a New
York slum would share.

The Poetical Play

In the twentieth century what used to be called "poetry" has almost vanished from the theatre. Browning's *Strafford*, Byron's *Manfred*, Tennyson's *The Cup* and *Becket* come to mind as typical nineteenth-century plays. The movement culminated in the plays of Stephen Phillips, *Paolo and Francesca*, *Herod*, and *Nero*, though it is doubtful if it was the poetry or Tree's spectacular productions which gave Stephen Phillips his vogue. Lady Tree did not exaggerate when she described the setting of *Herod* as "prodigious, triumphant, a wonder, a mirage", and it is significant that when Phillips was reading the play the actor-manager only woke up when "trumpets were heard in the distance." As Stephen Phillips said afterwards to William Archer, rather wistfully, "Tree divined it all at that one touch."

Binyon's *Attila* and Flecker's *Hassan* (with the music of Delius) were other poetical plays which justified production, and, it may be added, reproduction. *Hassan* was a rich experience. Hardy's *The Dynasts*, when given by Granville-Barker at the Kingsway Theatre in 1913, achieved a *succès d'estime*, though it did not recreate the poetic drama in Britain. Instead, the production gave dramatists a measure of assurance that the chorus and the soliloquy were still serviceable and poet-dramatists have profited by the lesson since.

Israel Zangwill, in his symbolic play *The War God*, also made some early experiments in the use of blank verse, which purposely avoided any suggestion of the poetic diction we associate with Elizabethan drama. Thus Zangwill was able to utilize even slang without obvious incongruity, yet retained the rhetorical quality arising from a strict poetical measure. Zangwill purposely obliterated every element of lyricism from *The War God*, so that the intellectual quality in the satire should have full play.

Perhaps the earliest poetical play in the twentieth-century manner and one which can also be described as a modern morality was Imra Madach's *Tragedy of Man*, though it dates from mid-Victorian times. Madach died when he was forty-three and only *The Tragedy of Man* keeps his memory alive, but the play has been given hundreds of times at the Hungarian National Theatre. Like the *Book of Job*, the opening scene is laid in Heaven, where the rebel Lucifer criticizes God's creation, while the Angel Host is loud in praise of the divine work. For this, Lucifer is driven from Heaven. Two trees in the Garden of Eden, however, are placed in his charge and they suffice for the ruin of humanity. "A corner's all I need; enough to afford a foothold for Negation, whereon to raise what will destroy the world."

To Adam and Eve in Eden, Lucifer appears in the guise of the Serpent, promising knowledge and immortality if they will but eat the forbidden fruit. Adam chooses knowledge and is vouchsafed a series of dreams. Now Lucifer appears as an Egyptian Pharaoh or the Athenian Miltiades; now he is Tancred the Crusader, Kepler the Astronomer, or Danton the French revolutionary. What Adam sees of man's future almost drives him to suicide, but, before he can act, Eve conceives her firstborn child. The close of the play is God's voice from Heaven, urging that life is still worth while, if only man will strive and trust.

With Marc Connelly's negro play, *Green Pastures*, we come nearer to a modern morality. It was first produced at the Mansfield Theatre, New York. Censored in Britain, it has become familiar through the Hollywood film version. The play opens in a New Orleans Sunday school, where a preacher is recalling the story of the Old Testament. Marc Connelly bears his audience to Heaven and his story proceeds as though the world was peopled by negroes, so beset by sin that De Lawd has, perforce, to descend the golden stairs to punish humanity. He comes to an argumentative little preacher, Noah by name, and tells him to build an Ark for the salvation of the race of man. De Lawd similarly visits Moses, the gentle shepherd, and always as the benign frock-coated negro pastor, who is at once kindly towards erring humanity and yet a god of wrath when wrongs have to be righted. Here is a typical bit of dialogue.

De Lawd (to his principal lieutenant, the archangel Gabriel): You going past the pits, Gab?
Gabriel: Can if ya want me to, Lawd.
De Lawd: Then look in and tell Satan, why does he think he is fighting a guy as big as I am.
Gabriel: Okay, Lawd. I'll spit right in his eye.

MAN
AND
SUPER
-MAN·
=

ALL THE WORLD's A STAGE-SOCIETY.

Design for a Statue of "John Bull's Other Playwright" after certain hints by
"G. B. S." (*see page* 194).

William Archer.

Clement Scott.

Dramatic
Cricket
of the times.

FOUR PROMINENT VICTORIAN CRITICS

Above left: William Archer (*see page* 188).   *Above right*: Clement Scott (*see page* 187).

Below left: Bernard Shaw (*see page* 189).   *Below right*: A. B. Walkley (*see page* 189).

Marc Connelly has said that *Green Pastures* is an attempt to present certain aspects of a living religion in the terms of its believers. With terrific spiritual hunger, and the greatest humility, these untutored black Christians have adapted the contents of the Bible to the conditions of their everyday life.

The Modern Morality

So far as Britain is concerned the vogue of the modern morality may be dated from William Poel's moving resurrection of the mediaeval morality, *Everyman*, in the grounds of the London Charterhouse in 1901. A production at the Imperial Theatre followed a year later, with Edith Wynne Matthison in the title part, and Reinhardt's remarkable spectacle, *Everyman*, later still.

The modern morality, however, really established itself when *The Miracle* was staged by Charles Cochran, first at Olympia in 1912 and later at the Lyceum in 1932. Cochran had seen Reinhardt's *Oedipus Rex* at the Circus Schumann in Berlin and he found himself obsessed with the possibility of converting the barn-like hall at Olympia into the semblance of a mediaeval cathedral. Together with Frederick Payne, Cochran collected £32,000 and persuaded Reinhardt to co-operate. £12,500 was spent upon costumes and £8,000 upon scenery. Which suggests that Payne's work in charge of the finances was only less important than that of Cochran as producer, Reinhardt as inventor, and Karl Vollmoeller as author. In later productions, such as that at the Lyceum in 1932, the acting opportunities were increased and such performances as the Madonna of Diana Manners, the Spielmann of Leonide Massine, and the Nun of Tilly Losch are still remembered.

Less of a pageant and nearer to a theatrical performance was Ronald Duncan's morality *This Way to the Tomb*, given at the Mercury in 1945. This had the form of a masque and anti-masque and the music of Benjamin Britten ranged from Latin hymnology to modern jazz, a choir off-stage being another addition to the machinery of the masque. Whereas the masque treated the temptations of St Antony on the island of Zante, the anti-masque was laid in our own day and treated the monkish

M

legend as it survived into the twentieth century. Robert Speaight as the fasting Antony held the stage throughout the first act, but in the anti-masque Ronald Duncan's fancies had full play. It was the birthday of the Saint, and the Astral Group, with microphones and a television set fitted for a world transmission, had assembled to see if any miracle, in fact, associated itself with the Saint's burial place. The message of the morality was that the doubters missed the miracle which the simple islanders of Zante, by virtue of their very faith, could witness.

T. S. Eliot's *Murder in the Cathedral*, which has the death of Thomas à Becket as its theme, is another play in the morality manner, though it is also akin to the chronicle play. It was written in an abbreviated form for performance in the Chapter House of Canterbury, a significant feature, as it emphasizes a ritual element which links Eliot's play with earlier moralities. Comparable with the anti-masque in *This Way to the Tomb* was the episode of The Four Tempters. It is to be regarded as giving voice to the deep-rooted workings of the Saint's conscience—his old-time love of gay living, his lust of power, and the rest.

Similarly, the justification for the murder which the knights addressed to the audience after the death of Thomas was a calculated departure from the realism of a chronicle play, in favour of the symbolic appeal of a morality. The chatty modernity of the Knights' speech, curiously enough, seemed to emphasize the calculated departure from realism, though, at first thought, one would have expected the reverse.

Mr Eliot's handling of the chorus is also worthy of close study in connection with the place of poetry in modern drama and, indeed, with the wider problem of establishing relations between stage and auditorium which Theodor Lipps described as "feeling into" a play. As we have seen, in the eighteenth and nineteenth centuries a play was little more than a story enacted on the far side of the footlights. Ronald Duncan and T. S. Eliot had very different aims when they wrote their modern moralities.

Mr Eliot has also experimented in what he called "an ecclesiastical revue" (*The Rock*) and the fateful *Family Reunion*. The latter is best correlated with Eugene O'Neill's *Mourning Becomes Electra*. Both are to be regarded as modern tragedies in the ancient Greek manner, the underlying theme in each case being Orestes pursued by the Furies. T. S. Eliot spent most of his thought upon an experiment in language—he was seeking a form of dialogue which would link a modern plot with a discussion of the abiding values which underlie religious belief in the twentieth century. Eugene O'Neill, on the contrary, was more concerned with the formal problem of bringing Greek drama up to date. Watching *Mourning Becomes Electra* one feels the movement and pulsing throb of Greek ritual drama as a recurring pattern designed to give unity to a story of our own time. O'Neill's task was harder than that of Aeschylus whom he was directly following just because the religious mood had to be created in a modern audience, whereas the Greek came to the theatre in a mood more akin to that of taking an active part in a religious rite.

Outward Bound had some of the qualities of a morality play. The opening scene was on ship-board with what seemed a normal company of passengers. A possible exception was a young couple who apparently had entered upon a suicide pact. No sooner does the ship leave its mooring than strange things begin to happen. One of the passengers notices that none of the party has any idea whither the ship is bound. Moreover, the vessel carries no lights, nor is there any sign of a crew. Only an elderly steward appears, and it is the steward who reveals the dread secret. Every one aboard the vessel is dead! They are all voyaging towards the Great Unknown, where their fates will be determined. Memories of mis-spent lives fill all with dire forebodings. However, the Examiner (Lyall Swete) proves an old gentleman with a kindly voice and the gentlest of methods and, one by one, the passengers learn their fates. The boy and girl of the suicide pact prove to be only half-dead. They recover consciousness and are given another chance of life on earth.

James Bridie's *Mr Bolfry* was less a morality than an opportunity for a dour debate upon the nature of good and evil, with the Devil predominant. Bridie is a Scotsman. The home of a minister of the Free Kirk (McCrimmon, by name, and played by Alastair Sim) is invaded by a number of youngsters. They rebel against the boredom arising from McCrimmon's grim Calvinism, and indulge in a bit of necromancy. This, literally, raises the Devil, in the form of Mr Bolfry (played by Raymond Lovell) and Mr Bridie's debate is in being. Bridie is primarily a realist, but his thoughts move on the plane of poetry.

Passing from moralities with a Bible background, *The Adding Machine* of Elmer Rice presents a very different type of modern morality. Here, the principal characters are denoted by numerals. There were Mr and Mrs Zero, Mr and Mrs One and Two and so on, indications of what may be expected when Hilaire Belloc's Servile State is in full operation. Throughout the first act, Mr Zero lay in bed, a victim to his wife's night-long nagging: "Twenty-five years in the same job! Seven years since you got a raise!"

In the next scene it is Zero's turn. He is at the office, but Elmer Rice is still exploiting the monologue which tells of repressions welling up from the unconscious. " 'Boss,' I'll say, 'I want to have a talk with you. I been on this job twenty-five years now and, and if I'm gonna stay, I gotta see a future ahead of me.' 'Zero,' he'll say, 'I'm glad you came in, I've had my eye on you, Zero. Nothin' gets by me.' 'Oh, I know that, Boss,' I'll say. That'll hand him a good laugh, that will. 'You're a valuable man, Zero,' he'll say, 'and I want you right up here with me in the front office.' "

In fact, Zero is sacked. The Boss has installed an adding machine, causing Zero to add murder to his burdens, and Elmer Rice allows us to look into his soul during the trial. At the end we watch the Little Man undergoing cleansing in a sort of cosmic laundry, preparatory to another entry into the everlasting round of creation and destruction.

What has happened is that not a few dramatists no longer see a human being as a clear-cut entity, which is born, lives and dies, and fits neatly into the three or four acts of the old-time well-made play. Men and women are conceived as a congeries of memories, emotions, and ideas, any of which may dominate action in any given crisis and all of which must be present in the imagination of those who are following the play, if real understanding is to arise.

Elmer Rice's "Street Scene"

Characteristic of much play-writing in our time is Elmer Rice's *Street Scene*. It had only one scene but numerous parts, each of which was carefully selected because it represented a typical New Yorker, living in a walk-up apartment house in a mean quarter of the town. Casting to type seemed so important that Elmer Rice chose a number of players with no previous experience of the stage when he selected the sixty men, women, and children who made up the cast. Produced by William Brady at the Playhouse, New York City, in 1929, *Street Scene* came to London with an American cast which included Mary Servoes and Erin O'Brien Moore, the Anna Maurrant and the Rose Maurrant of the original production. At first sight, the murder of a love-starved wife and her lover by a jealous husband in a low quarter of New York cannot have seemed promising material, but Elmer Rice knew better. What he was seeking to put on the stage was the chaos of thought and feeling, desires and passions, which characterize so much of modern life, and these not only in a few chosen characters but in a typical New York suburb.

Having determined that the street scene itself should be the principal character in his play, the dramatist had to discover how his story and the characters who were to tell it might best be presented. His choice was the symphonic form, in which not a lone voice or a lone instrumentalist but a company of players would be responsible for the final effect. Moreover, the presentation was not to have the relative simplicity of a concerto, the point-counter-point, let us say, of a piano and orchestra or a violin and orchestra, but the fullest extension of symphonic form, as this shows itself when a theme and its related aspects are inter-related by the whole gamut of instruments in a full orchestra—strings and wood-wind, brass and percussion. This symphonic quality is very noticeable in the best of twentieth-century drama. Whereas in the well-made plays of fifty years ago two or three strands and two or three passions were inter-connected and blended into a harmony, to-day a score of dramatic strands call for unification, such as Elmer Rice attempted in *Street Scene*.

Noting this quality in Elmer Rice's play, it is, perhaps, not surprising that his plot proved first-rate material for musical treatment. In 1947, *Street Scene* was produced as "a dramatic musical" by the Metropolitan Opera Company, on Broadway. The musician was Kurt Weill and he said "As soon as I began to think about the music for *Street Scene* I discovered that the play lent itself to a great variety of music, just as the streets of New York themselves embrace the music of many lands and many peoples."

Kurt Weill went on: "I had an opportunity to use different forms of musical expression, from popular songs to operatic *ensembles*, music of mood and dramatic music, music of young love, music of passion and death, and, over all, the music of a hot summer evening in New York."

In play and dramatic musical, the curtain rises to disclose the exterior of the walk-up apartment house. It is of ugly brown stone and was built in the 'nineties. Against one door-way is the sign, "Flat to Let, 6 Rooms—Steam Heat". On a scaffolding nearby is the ominous notice, "Manhattan House-wrecking Corp". At a ground-floor window, a middle-aged Jew is reading a Yiddish newspaper. From another window a stout Italian is leaning and fanning herself with a paper fan. The heat has registered ninety-four degrees, "the hottest 15 June in forty-one years", as the papers announce.

Mrs Jones: Good evenin', Mrs F. Well, I hope it's hot enough for you?
Mrs Fiorentino: Ain't it joost awful? When I was through with the dishes, you could take my clothes and joost wring them out.
Mrs Jones: Me, too, I ain't got a dry stitch on me.

Throughout, against an undertone of the noises of a great city, "L" trains, automobile sirens, the whistle of river-boats, radio sets, and human voices, Elmer Rice stresses the heat. Willie Maurrant wants a dime for an ice-cone. An Italian wheels in a cart and breaks up a block of ice. Filippo Fiorentino, the jolly Italian music teacher, comes in with his violin, and five ice-cream cones which he distributes to the gossips about the doorway. Kurt Weill did not have far to look for expressive music. And when notes of deeper passion seemed called for if the symphony of life in a mean street was to arise, Elmer Rice was to hand with his mother in child-birth. The lovers are talking, timidly, secretively:

Rose: Oh, just listen to her!
Sam: Oh Rose!
Rose: The poor thing. She must be having terrible pains.
Sam: That's all there is in life—nothing but pain. From before
we're born until we die.

And on a lower and uglier plane of emotion.

A girl appears at the left, glancing apprehensively over her shoulder at a man who is walking down the street behind her. They cross the stage and go off at the right.

For this mood, Kurt Weill finds material in popular New York "low down", "moon-faced and starry-eyed", sung and danced by a woman of the street and her drunken boy friend, or the sardonic "Lullaby" which is sung by two nursemaids, anxious to see the scene of the murder of poor Mrs Maurrant, which provides the climax of *Street Scene*.

The gossips about the doorway prepare for the final tragedy. The woman comes from her rooms. They watch Mrs Maurrant in dead silence, as she is out of earshot. Then the storm breaks.
Mrs Jones (rising excitedly): Didja get that.
Mrs Fiorentino: Its joost terrible.
Jones: You think she's just goin' out lookin' for this guy Sankey?
Mrs Jones: Ain't men the limit?

Willie, Mrs Maurrant's small boy, comes in chanting:

> Fat, Fat, the water rat
> Fifty bullets in his hat.

and in the "dramatic musical" Mrs Maurrant expresses her maternal affection by singing "A Boy Like You". Rose, the daughter, a poorly-paid typist in a real estate office, is half in love with the Jew boy, Sam. In the play Sam recites; in the dramatic musical he sings:

When lilacs last in the door-yard bloom'd
And the great star dropp'd in the western sky in the night
I mourn'd and yet shall mourn with ever-returning spring.

Rose: No, not that part . . . I mean the part about the farmhouse.

Sing it for me, Sam.

And, at last, the killing. Frank Maurrant, not altogether bad but ill-tempered, self-opinionated, and callous, has been drinking. He comes home unexpectedly and finds his wife—innocent enough, Heaven knows—with her lover Steve Sankey. Two shots are heard. Sankey appears at the window of the Maurrants' flat, his face deformed by terror. There is another shot and Maurrant comes into the street, revolver in hand. The Chair, that is his fate. And Rose, with her dreams! What of her? And Sam. It may be that they escape from Mean Street.

Rose: No, not that part, I mean the part about the farmhouse. *She sits at his feet.*

Sam. In the door-yard, fronting an old farmhouse near the white-washed palings, stands the lilac bush, tall-growing, with heart-shaped leaves of rich green, with many a pointed blossom rising delicate, with the perfume strong I love.

Rose: Yes, that's it! That's just what I felt like doing—breaking off a little bunch of flowers. But then, I thought, may be a policeman or somebody would see me and then I'd get into trouble.

A similar symphonic construction is to be noted in *The Counsellor-at-Law*, another Elmer Rice play. George Simon is a New York lawyer and a Jew, wedded to an ice-cold American aristocrat. Years before the play began Simon had connived at perjury to save a mere boy from a life sentence, following his fourth offence as a petty thief. A rival lawyer, a Christian, discovers the early lapse and attempts to disbar Simon, and thus ruin him. Simon retaliates. Hunting in the dark cupboards of his rival's married life, he discovers a discreditable affair with a widow in far-away New York.

The entire action takes place in Simon's office and most of it in the outer office, where the telephone operator is at work and the clients of the firm are waiting for their talks with the principals. At any moment the action of the play seemed chaotic, but at curtain-fall all was clear and the story told, and told, moreover, against the background of a Counsellor-at-Law. If Elmer Rice had relied upon traditional dramatic methods he might well have come upon a telling plot, but the breathless movement of events which gave the play its character would have escaped us. In the London production Hugh Miller was memorable as Simon, as was Elspeth Duxbury, the tongue-tied secretary who saves Simon from suicide.

Flaubert once said "the conception of every work of art carries within itself its own rule and method, which the artist himself must discover before the work of art can be achieved." Nevertheless, there is a restraining influence; very early a body of tradition established itself in relation to each of the recognized art forms, and the nature of the true work of art is to remain within the tradition, though there must be a continual effort to extend traditional boundaries. While the assertion of individual personality is one factor in artistic expression, the primal chaos will reassert itself when craft tradition is not there to check extravagance. For the greater part of a career, and during much of the time any play is in the making, a dramatist will recall what earlier masters of his craft have done, but he will not thereby abandon the bursts of freedom which stamp a man's work with personality; on the contrary, he will seek every opportunity of winning freedom, for originality within a tradition is the way of freedom. This was the impulse which gave rise to the plays which are usually described as "expressionistic".

J. B. Priestley's nearest approach to a modern morality was *Johnson Over Jordan*. Johnson is the English Everyman at the moment of his funeral. When the curtain rises, Jill, the wife, with her nice-looking boy and her daughter, is coming downstairs. The coffin of her husband is passing from the house. At this point Priestley drives to the root of his problem—the real Johnson, the four-dimensional Johnson, as he lived in a Time which is inextricably mingled with Space. Priestley tells us that Johnson is not in the oak box which the undertaker's men are bearing to the hearse. He is on the stage in this very theatre. The delirium of fever has not entirely passed and the tangle of events associated with the last illness is still unsorted. But Johnson is waking up to the fact that, whatever has really happened, he is not on the earthly side of Jordan. Memories of the office, Bolt, Cross, and Clayton, East India Merchants; memories of home, with Jill, with Richard and with his girl, Freda; and, inextricably mingled

with the memories, regrets for things done and things left undone; opportunities not welcomed; opportunities rejected; opportunities taken, but not pushed through to a definite end. A
bit of sharp practice, too; nothing criminal; perhaps not really
wrong as business men judge right and wrong; but a bit more
ugly on the farther side of Jordan than it seemed a week earlier
in the relative security of the counting office of Bolt, Cross, and
Clayton.

We are not concerned with Priestley's reactions to Johnson,
alive or dead. We are concerned with theatrical methods. What
interests us is that Priestley was driven to describe Johnson's
life by means of a series of cameos, in which the time element in
experience is practically ignored. Memories of boyhood, memories of his early life with Jill, memories of friends who made a
mess of their lives. Some of them are actually before our eyes on
the other side of Jordan, and undergoing the same haunting
examination by a supernaturally tender conscience as that of
Johnson himself.

Yet another device used by Priestley (he got it from the stage
of ancient Greece) was the mask. The invention of Expressionism did not really enlarge the boundaries of the dramatic. What
happened was that the ever-growing demands of the dramatist
called for the resuscitation of old-time methods and in this fact
lies the justification for Expressionism. In this sense only did the
exponents of Expressionism enlarge the boundaries of drama.
Their lasting service may well be the proof given that no human
experience is outside the possibility of dramatic treatment. With
this proof went evidence that no worthy play, worthily presented,
need fail for want of a public. The men and women interested in
the modern theatre are numerous enough, and theatres vary so
much in size and type, that, somewhere, an audience can be
found for any play which has integrity.

Even more apposite is the case of Pirandello, who interested
himself in that branch of metaphysics which is concerned with
the nature of Reality. Pirandello lived in an age which was beginning to distrust the evidence of the senses. Accordingly, he
chose continually to tilt at reason, and at ideas which seemed to
derive their validity from reasoning processes. For these he
substituted experiences and symbols drawn from dream imagery.

Reason suggested that the individual was a self-contained unity, but Pirandello chose to regard any man or woman, as he or she moved through the world of men, as a multiplicity of individuals. It followed in Pirandello's logic that characters invented by a novelist or dramatist, because they had imaginative unity, might well have greater reality, in the philosophical meaning of the word, than creatures actually moving on earth, such as the players who acted parts in a Pirandello drama. As Pirandello saw the matter, the invented characters *were* the more believable.

Beset with these ideas Pirandello wrote *Six Characters in Search of an Author*, first played in London in 1922 and revived at the Westminster by Tyrone Guthrie in 1932. The curious criss-cross lighting effects devised by Guthrie to suggest the emptiness of an empty stage alone were interesting. Picture a stock company opening rehearsals on a dark and empty stage. The author is not present and the leading-man, the leading lady, the *ingenue*, the juvenile lead, and the rest show no special desire for his aid in puzzling out the details of the production. But, on a sudden, the perfunctory rehearsal is interrupted. The six characters invented by the dramatist themselves put in an appearance. They are dressed in black but their faces are whitened with chalk, symbolizing their relationship with the dead. Their complaint is that they have been forbidden an opportunity to fulfil their destiny. There is an elderly man (the Father), his unhappy wife, their young son and a showy and impudent step-daughter, with whom are two children. The Father was played in London by Franklin Dyall. As the stock company is unable to cope with the difficulties presented by the grim story, it calls upon the Six Characters to reincarnate the episodes. It seems that the Father has gone to a *bagnio* and there met his step-daughter, while the Father's wife has eloped with his secretary, taking with her a young son. Needless to say, the Characters re-enact the plot with an intensity of emotion such as no body of players relying upon the manuscript of a dramatist could emulate, though they remain dissatisfied with the dramatist's effort to the end.

As the Father complains, "How can we ever hope to understand one another if to the words I speak I set the value and the sense of things as they appear within me, while the listener gives them the sense and value that are within him?"

In his play *Naked*, Pirandello gave yet another turn to his belief that imagined people in a play or novel are more real rather than less real than those who pass from birth to death through the material world. In *Naked*, a novelist named Ludovico Nota brings a destitute girl to his room and proposes to use her unhappy life-history as material for his next book. Ersilia Drei, the young woman, is at first pleased at the idea, until she finds that Nota is more interested in the tale of her adventures than in herself. However, she is persuaded to accept the situation. After all, it is better to be a heroine in a novel than not to exist at all. A second difficulty comes when Ersilia finds that Nota has imagined a totally different heroine from herself, though he has annexed her life story. Thus Ersilia finds she is faced with the problem, "Have I ever been anybody?" Throughout the play Ersilia desperately wants to be somebody, but the other characters in the play go on stripping fiction after fiction from her creature-self, until nothing remains but a naked soul.

"We all of us want to make a good impression. The worse we are, the uglier we are, the more anxious we are to appear good and beautiful . . . I was naked. I had nothing beautiful to put on, yet I wanted a goodness which would serve as a shroud to die in."

What Ersilia Drei really wanted was "the most beautiful dress in the world; the one I had dreamed of; a wedding-dress; the dress of a bride; the dress of a wife"; and she only wanted it as a decent shroud. A few tears of sympathy, that was all. "But no, no, not even that I have been allowed to keep. I must die, discovered, despised, humiliated, found out; go tell them all that I am dead, yes, and that I died naked." (*Curtain.*)

Make no mistake. All the amusing juggling with philosophical notions would have served Pirandello ill if he had not been endowed with an instinct for dramatic writing. He could gauge to a nicety how curious and complicated ideas should be shaped if they were to tell in a theatre.

Like Pirandello, O'Neill is profoundly interested in the subliminal experiences and is often driven to distortions of surface fact and surface truth, so that he may reach the deeper truths which relate to "behind-life". In *Strange Interlude*, O'Neill not only revived the asides and soliloquies of pre-Ibsen drama but utilized them on a grand scale in order to reveal the behind-life of his characters. Indeed, the device was used so continuously in *Strange Interlude* that it can scarcely be regarded as a revival, but rather as fresh invention, allowing Eugene O'Neill's audiences to share the inmost thoughts and experiences of his creations. In *Strange Interlude* three men lust after Nina and for a few moments the woman sits and gloats over the discovery.

Nina: My three men . . . I feel their desire converge in me to form one complete beautiful male desire which I absorb . . . I am pregnant with the three . . . husband! lover! father! and the fourth man, little man, little Gordon. He is mine too . . . that makes it perfect. Why, I should be the happiest woman in the world.

Evan (the three turn to her): Nina? What's the matter?

Ibsen would have rejected such a soliloquy in his social dramas as utterly destructive of the illusion of reality. Eugene O'Neill, working in a different psychological atmosphere, showed us that the soliloquy could be in a high degree revealing.

One more example, out of scores which come to mind—*Miracle at Verdun*, as it was played at the Embassy in 1932, when Edward Crankshaw translated Hans Chlumberg's fine play. The first scene was laid in a small military cemetery in the Argonne. A party of tourists were going the round of the graves. One of them was aggrieved because, in Flanders, she saw 20,000 graves of unknown German soldiers for 200 Belgian francs, including a couple of meals, whereas she was being charged 200 French francs to see a couple of thousand graves in the Argonne. "That's the French all over." Still we have only a hint of Chlumberg's objective. It becomes clearer when we are taken to the Arc de Triomphe and hear the French Premier delivering an Armistice Day address. France is prepared as never before. Every soldier has a machine-gun; there are aeroplanes in plenty; and poison gas, enough to hide the mountains of the earth! "Are the mighty dead listening?" asks the orator. "If, by some miracle, they could return to life, would not they say, 'Well done!'?"

It is then that Hans Chlumberg reveals his secret. The miracle takes place. We are in the cemetery at Verdun. The graves open; the dead soldiers come to life and each tells us his name and whence he comes. "From the common grave!" The general who asks the question recoils. "Angels and ministers of grace, defend us!"

The satire goes on its way. The French Prime Minister receives tidings of the miracle in a bedroom he is sharing with a prostitute. The English Prime Minister, happily, is a bachelor. In any case he is not interested in the miracle. "It is purely a continental affair." Even the people of Verdun cannot credit that the miracle for which they have prayed has actually happened.

Perhaps the theme of *Miracle at Verdun* was beyond the skill of any dramatist and any cast. We are shown the news spreading through France. Newsboys cry it in the streets. Priests preach the gospel of resurrection triumphantly from their pulpits. But the dead men find they can make no real contact with their lost lives. Wives have remarried; there is no work for the risen dead. In the end, there is nothing left except a return to the "common grave".

Hans Chlumberg's theme was not to be presented against the single background of the Greek open-air theatre or the open stage of Elizabethan fashion. Still less would the four or five acts of Victorian usage, with a sensation scene two-thirds of the way to curtain-fall, have sufficed. New methods were essential. The wonder is that the production on the tiny stage at the Embassy enabled so much of *Miracle at Verdun* to get over the footlights and make contact with the imaginations of onlookers.

Sean O'Casey's *The Silver Tassie* is an Anglo-Irish example of Expressionism. Doubtless this is why the directors of the Abbey Theatre in Dublin turned down the play, in spite of the fact that O'Casey already had *Juno and the Paycock* to his credit. In the original production Charles Laughton played the hero, Harry Heegan, a football player of note who has won the D.C.M. in the War and is now on leave. The tassie is the cup which Harry enables his club to win and the first toast drunk is to his bride: "Here she is now. Ready for anything. Stripped to the skin."

Thus the silver cup becomes the emblem of youthful strength and animal exaltation. It is all too plain that the women are ready to take any risk, even that of forfeiting their claim to happiness hereafter. "The men that are defending us have leave to bow down in the House of Rimmon, for the men that go with the guns are going with God."

On this display of youthful energy and joy, O'Casey drops the curtain on his first act. In the second, we see nothing but desolation. Augustus John painted a grim figure of Death squatting upon a dug-out, to drive home the ugly moral to be drawn from a world at war.

> "Cold and wet and tired
> Wet and tired and cold."

The choral chanting of the massed soldiery and the formalized background against which they moved sustained the mood of emotional instability which Sean O'Casey needed to link his fable with the heart-sickness he found in a world at war.

The massed soldiery are awaiting the attack which will mean death for so many, or even worse, maiming, which will be no better than a living death. In O'Casey's third act we see Harry Heegan a cripple and barely able to maintain his hold upon a useless life. The closing act is laid in the dance hall of the football club. Harry is in his cripple's chair and knows that neither Jessie nor Susie, the woman he wooed and the woman he jilted, love him any more. Maddened by jealousy and indignant at the harsh deal he has had from fate, Harry finds the dancers demanding a song. As the champion football player he used to sing negro spirituals to the music of the ukelele. The closing lines of *The Silver Tassie* were Mrs Foran's. "It's a terrible pity Harry was too weak to stay, an' sing his song, for there's nothing I love more than the ukelele's tinkle, tinkle in the night-time."

Charles Laughton was at his best as Harry Heegan, D.C.M. and he inspired a large cast to a memorable performance.

If there was an element of the symbolic in *The Silver Tassie*, symbolism dictated the whole layout of O'Casey's *Within the Gates*, dating from the eve of the second Great War. There is characterization but this is not a play of character and certainly has nothing resembling a connected plot of the cause-effect type. O'Casey is seeking to write about being alive; how it feels to live in a world in which the beautiful and the ugly, goodness and sin, are so strangely mingled. He had noted the variety of human types to be found in a public park and, to this insight, he added his broodings upon the human hunger for some abiding faith in a world of conflict. The four scenes were entitled: "On a Spring Morning; On a Summer Noon; On an Autumn Evening; On a Winter's Night."

When the curtain rose upon the first of the park scenes the outstanding object was a War Memorial, showing a steel-helmeted infantryman. Against this background a masque-like dance of the spring flowers suggested a Dreamer's musings upon life and immortality.

To the Dreamer come a bishop, an atheist, a gardener, two park chair attendants and Jannice, a young whore, who has been educated in a nunnery and bears the fear of God and fear of Hell in the marrow of her being. A chorus of down-and-outs and some nursemaids form the realistic element in Sean O'Casey's dramatic plan. In the third act the bishop comes to see that in Jannice there is a soul to be saved, and the girl dies in the last act, making the sign of the Cross. Here is the climax of *Within the Gates*.

Young Whore (almost in a whisper): I die, Dreamer. I die, and my soul is heavy with a great fear.

Dreamer (standing over her, gently): Fear nothing: God will find room for one scarlet blossom among His thousand white lilies. (*The Bishop rises from his knees and goes over to where she is lying. He kneels again, and takes one of her hands in his.*)

Young Whore (staring at the Bishop): Guide the hand you hold into making the sign of the cross, that I may whisper my trust in the golden mercy of God.

To them comes the chorus of down-and-outs, with its dreary and hopeless dirge. But the dreamer has a richer philosophy and demands a passage for the strong and the fearless.

"Life that is stirr'd with the fear of its life, let it die;
  Let it sink down, let it die, and pass from our vision
    for ever;
  Sorrow and pain we shall have, and struggle unending;
  Way for the strong and the swift and the fearless."

In *The Star Turns Red* Sean O'Casey pleaded the cause of the underling and demanded an equal chance for all, wasteful beggary being replaced by fruitful labour. If these things are not given, he urged, they would be taken, and then a Star would turn red and shine the wide world over. In the play, the Red Priest is opposed to Red Jim, but there is also a Brown Priest, representing the spirit of compromise. In the beginning a Fascist shoots a

Scene from John Van Druten's *The Distaff Side*, Apollo Theatre (1933). Dorothy Holmes-Gore, Dora Barton, Margaret Carter, Sybil Thorndyke, Haidee Wright, Clifford Evans and Alexander Archdale (*see page* 55).

On the Spot by Edgar Wallace, Wyndham's (1930). Gladys Frazin as Maria Pouli
Charles Laughton as Tony Perelli, and Ben Welden as Con O'Hara (*see page* 211)

Worker, whose Communist daughter is to be whipped by order of the Red Priest. Later a Worker beats up half a dozen corrupt Trade Union leaders, and, in the third act, the halt, the maimed, and the blind gather about the dead Communist's coffin. In the last act the military police besiege the workers, while the Star turns red.

It may be that Sean O'Casey would have written a better play if he had not sacrificed so much of artistry to his interest in the cause of Communism. O'Casey's imagination does not move easily in the arena of the mysterious, and his stylized characters in *The Star Turns Red* suggest that the dramatist was less than sure of his power to put his real thought before his audience. Where the methods of Expressionism are essential to put across a difficult or complex body of thought, they are justified; and the same may be said of the simplifications necessary if the type is to be dominant over the individual. In *The Star Turns Red*, too much of the machinery of the drama is far removed from poetry, just because propaganda was forced from the background of the play into the forefront. There was an element of propaganda in the *Trojan Women* of Euripides, but Euripides did not allow his thought upon the terror of Melos and the dread weaknesses of the Athenian jury to diminish the clarity of his portrait of Hecuba or the poetry of the great choruses.

It may be added that Sean O'Casey is the only living dramatist in Britain with the vocabulary needed if modern moralities are to reach the plane of poetry. The rhythms of the Bible are coupled in his plays with those of the vernacular of his native Ireland. The result is a speech which is fully individual and yet can be used for comic and tragic ends. *Red Roses for Me* was first given at the Embassy, Swiss Cottage, in 1946, and was concerned with a strike leader who sacrificed his life to gain an extra shilling a week for a body of strikers. As the woman who loved him said, "Maybe he saw the shilling in the shape of a new world."

The most striking scene in *Red Roses for Me* had as its background a Dublin quay. A dozen young loafers are seen lounging about in the semi-darkness when the strike leader comes to them with his theories and his hopes for a regenerated society. The light changes and the Nelson Pillar which identifies the place with a symbolic Dublin is charged with a new beauty, while the

N

flower women on the stage dance to the music of a fiddler, a
markedly interesting mixture of the realism of harsh fact and the
symbolism of healing poetry.

There have been times in dramatic history when the description "beautiful" and the fact that pleasure arose sufficed to determine successful craft. Beauty was defined as that which gives
pleasure, and it was assumed that the pleasure fully explained the
part which beauty plays in art and production. To entertain and
create a sense of the beautiful was the avowed aim of the dramatist, as it was the aim of painters, sculptors, and other artists. The
Greek idea was that beauty was given to perception, in the form
of the graceful and the dignified, and, when Greek aesthetic was
fully developed, Plotinus taught that beauty was the revelation of
reason in sensuous form, and that the entire world of sense, being
a symbol of the divine intelligence, must of necessity be graceful
to the eye that could see it in its relation to the divine Creator.
Following a similar line of thought the sense of beauty had an
outstanding influence upon Renaissance art and consequently
upon what there was of poetic drama in Victorian times, when
artists in general were guided by the aesthetics of Greece and
Renaissance Italy.

The tests of beauty and pleasure are no longer accepted as all-
important, at any rate in modern drama. Indeed, by many
theatre-goers, the avowedly beautiful is regarded as suspect.
Ideal beauty, as the Greeks understood it, based upon the idea of
a possible or potential perfect state of nature, served as a working
hypothesis in aesthetics just as long as man accepted the evidence
of eye, hand, ear, or touch as giving all the experience an artist
was able to handle. Idealization is less acceptable to-day, when a
social state has arisen which interests itself in aspects of experience
which are often the reverse of beautiful and, indeed, range from
"rose-pink to dirty drab", as George Meredith put it when he
treated this very problem of idealization in the opening passages
of *Diana of the Crossways*.

To-day, if it is to retain any useful function in the aesthetics of
drama, beauty calls for careful definition in relation, not to a
part, but to the whole of human experience. That things of beauty
give pleasure is still true, but the mere fact of pleasure does not
enable us to identify the dramatically beautiful. Whatever Plo-

tinus may have thought, the modern view is that nature itself is neither beautiful nor ugly. We have come to see that often material ugliness may be redeemed by a quality which arises from some latent idea. An instance is an Indian idol, in which a conception of deity may be seeking expression in company with a material form which troubles the Western mind. Thus beauty of subject-matter balances the apparent ugliness of material form, as, in the alternative, charm on the material side may balance or eclipse any troubling "ugliness" in subject matter. Indeed, it is at this point that the modern playgoer comes up against beauty and the beautiful. Subject-matter which is plainly ugly continually presents itself for treatment on the stage.

Not a few modern dramatists are welcomed as though they were prophets engaged in preaching social revolutions, or, to lower the plane, as advertising managers putting some political nostrum over upon the public. I am not objecting to this. On the contrary, the effort has given the modern stage some of its biggest thrills, as well as its distinctive character. Capek's *R.U.R.* and Elmer Rice's *The Adding Machine*, such a play as *Now Barabbas*, in which William Douglas Home described the last fourteen days of horror endured by a murderer awaiting execution, and a score of similar plays come to mind. If this passion for exploring the highways and by-ways of misery and sadism has justification, the excuse lies in the maladjustments which so many individuals face under the tangled circumstances of latter-day life. Too many men and women seem unable to come to terms with existence and the results are self-hatred and resentment against society at large. A philosophy known as Existentialism ran riot in Paris in the years immediately following the second World War. It presupposes a set of fore-ordained circumstances which leaves man in fetters. There remains in the unknown future a possibility of salvation, but, here and now, man reacts upon his fellows and they upon him until both they and he die. Existence, in fact, is the only reason for existing. It follows that those who accept Existentialism live for the moment. Passing experience is everything. Beauty, it is a meaningless concept. History, it has nothing behind it. History merely yields raw material for the present.

It is an unhappy philosophy, this of Jean-Paul Sartre. Violence is the essence of Sartre's reaction to life and its justification as an element in dramatic construction lies in the fact that it preaches the doctrine that full responsibility for living at all belongs to the man or woman and to them alone. It thus focuses attention upon individual character. Most people according to Sartre refuse to take full responsibility for their existence and evade life, it may be through drugs, drink, sex, or petty crime. If the pessimism of Sartre can be evaded it is by the few who achieve freedom, even if this be only the freedom to do nothing at all.

As Jean-Paul Sartre and his followers conceive drama it is written for a theatre in which the analysis of character is everything and situations are only important because their creation may put characters in a fuller light and relief. And yet this is not Sartre's meaning. He believes that the dramatist's task is to present a coward, a liar, a man or woman in the throes of passion or frustration, and yet what is presented is not a man or woman in love, whose character has been moulded by heredity or environment. The will which lies at the core of any passion is the real man or woman. Thus the cards are in his hand. He can play them as he pleases and by his actions the man or the woman is to be judged.

Jean-Paul Sartre's *Men Without Shadows* was given at the Lyric, Hammersmith, in 1947 and showed half-a-dozen hand-cuffed prisoners awaiting torture and death. The immediate problem is, Will any of them disclose the name of their leader to the Gestapo-trained militia of Vichy? All are obsessed, not by fear of torture, but the fear that, under torture, the name of the leader will be disclosed. One of the prisoners, a girl, murders her young brother, in fear that he may speak. The end is the firing squad.

Sartre is a Jew and seems to suffer from the fact that he faces life problems as one who cannot be fully assimilated into any community. Indeed, the absence of any spiritual home devised by man is the only justification for the pessimism of Sartre's philosophy. Perhaps this absence of a spiritual home is the root trouble in the modern outlook. All of us are too far from our God.

The subject matter of this chapter might well have occupied a book. With this apology, I pass it on rather as a stimulant to memory and further analysis than as a satisfying statement of the part the poet-dramatist has in the theatre of to-day. What is interesting is that there are sufficient playgoers in the big cities of our time to justify such productions and thus persuade playwrights that tears may be as rewarding as laughter. The word "rewarding" has connotations other than those of the box-office and it is good that the commercial theatre should have evidence that poetry does not necessarily spell disaster. The Irish Players for a generation added things of worth to the London stage and their distinguishing characteristic was a fuller use of symbolism than was common. Symbolism, and the sense of weaving actuality with the supernatural which it creates, will never be acceptable to all theatre-goers. Happily, the world of the theatre is big enough to-day to ensure a place for every worth-while talent. This is a discovery of recent years and it is comforting.

CHAPTER 9

THE FUNCTION OF CRITICISM

Criticism, damn criticism! Give me applause—Charles Mathews

I N stage circles it has long been an accepted myth that the dramatic critic is a foreign body. Useful, it may be, to the advertising department, and invaluable when a house has to be papered on a first night, but a disturbing element in the theatrical ensemble. This is wrong. The triumphs of players, producers and dramatists would be short-lived if it were not for the corpus of criticism which not only carries the news of production far and wide, but leaves it on record for the attention of future generations.

It cannot be denied that, at times, criticism is death-dealing. Few of those who helped in its presentation can have welcomed Charles Brookfield's description of a costume play, "It's about the Wars of the Roses, and it's twice as long and twice as bloody." In lighter vein, a critic of a Broadway revue opened his notice thus: "I have seen this show under the worst possible conditions, having a seat from which I could see and hear everything distinctly." The writer closed, "I see that I have knocked everything except the chorus girls' knees and there God has forestalled me."

What is the function of a theatrical review? It should state the theme of the play, give a hint of the plot, add some analysis of the contribution made by the players and not omit a judgement upon the reactions of the audience. In fact it should serve as the judgement of an ideal spectator. If the play has a philosophy, the public will want to know what it is. Lastly, if there is real creation (a rare thing), it is the due of the dramatist that this should be put on record and the critic, with his wide experience, is the man to do so. It is more debatable whether it is the task of the critic to instruct the public as to what it should like, though in recent years there has been a growing tendency in this direction.

It is not the function of the dramatic critic to appraise the social opinions of the dramatist, as opposed to their presentation in dramatic form. William Archer, *qua* dramatic critic, was less than just to his "esteemed and religiously studied colleague and old, intimate and valued friend" when he described Bernard Shaw as "a paradoxist, a sort of Devil's Advocate, who goes about picking holes in every well-known fact". Or again, when he wrote of *The Philanderer* "the whole play is steeped in an atmosphere of bloodless erotics that is indescribably distressing."

The judgements may or may not have been true. What is certain is that the critic will be fully occupied during the three hours he spends in a theatre in estimating the play as a vehicle for acting. After stating the dramatist's standpoint he can properly leave the ethics to politicians or social historians. The old-time thesis play or the problem play (which we have to-day in the form of tendentious moralities or symbolic dramas) come to the dramatic critic for judgement as things to be acted in a playhouse, not for moral disquisitions. The arts may well be moral teachers of high import, but they have a right to judgement as pictures, sculptures, operas, or plays. There was abiding wisdom in John Morley's caustic comment, that drama will not become a great moral force "by imitating that colossal type of histrionic failure, the church pulpit", and it is not the job of the critic to launch the theatre on so perilous a path.

The Theatrical Reporter

When I was a young man the doyen of the London dramatic critics was Clement Scott, of the *Daily Telegraph*. His standing in the profession was comparable with that of Françisque Sarcey in Paris. There is no one in London to-day with a comparable influence, though the late James Agate could advance a claim in his later years. Whereas all the other critics of his day were content with a stall on a first night, Clement Scott expected a box. And, believe me, a Clement Scott notice was good value. Theatre managers heaved a sigh of relief when they saw the *Daily Telegraph*'s critic removing his fur coat, adjusting his pince-nez and settling down to study his programme. No less happy were the members of the cast, for mention in a Clement Scott notice might mean real recognition. On one occasion he went down to Colchester to see a Ben Greet production of *The Hunchback*. A dark-eyed, dark-haired, willowy-figured lady was playing Helena. Clement Scott's report resulted in Mrs Patrick Campbell coming to the Adelphi to play the feminine lead in George R. Sims's melodramas and thus to Paula Tanqueray and fame.

In the 'nineties of the last century an important first-night, say a new Gilbert and Sullivan opera or a Pinero play, was "news" and a report might run to 3,000 words. As a theatrical reporter, Clement Scott claimed that the journalist who could not write at top speed should not represent a morning newspaper. When a play ended at 11.15 p.m. he was back in Peterborough Court and in his shirt-sleeves; a quarter of an hour later, the compositor's boys were pounding up and down the corridors, as the critic filled sheet after sheet of copy. Nor did Clement Scott's influence end with *The Telegraph*. There was an entertaining column in the *Illustrated London News*, and, as likely as not, a contribution to *The Theatre*, not to mention articles overseas and an occasional book.

William Archer, dramatic critic of *The World*, was a very different type. He was deeply interested in drama. I am less sure whether he had a genuine love for the theatre, a rather different thing. Though a Scotsman, I regarded Archer as a fellow country-man, his father being Agent General for the State of Queensland and a friend of my father, in virtue of their common association with Australia. What one missed in talking "theatre" with Archer was the traffic in reminiscence which H. M. Walbrook of the *Pall Mall* conducted so happily. Recalling Irving's Mathias in *The Bells*, when he saw it in the 'eighties, Walbrook described how, in the first act, when the two villagers were chatting before the fire in the inn-parlour, while Madame Mathias was knitting, on a sudden there was a crash and Madame hurried out. It was only a maid breaking a china plate. "Yet", said Walbrook, "it made me jump at least an inch from my seat, and after that, I was ready for anything."

One gets the same satisfaction when drawing upon the reminiscences stored in S. R. Littlewood's fifty years of theatrical criticism. It is an unhappy but unescapable fact that the great mass of theatrical entertainment has no abiding value. Pleasant reminiscence of this or that bit of acting, this or that scenic effect, is all that most dramatic criticism can recover.

Sydney Carroll, who preceded James Agate on the *Sunday*

Times, has described himself as, "a confirmed theatromaniac". I like that approach to things theatrical. Beginning as an actor, and later establishing the Open Air Theatre in Regent's Park, Carroll brought wider sympathies to his dramatic criticism than the writers who regard a play as primarily drama. The criticisms of Malcolm Watson, who followed Clement Scott on the *Daily Telegraph*, indicated a similar approach to the theatre. So do those of W. A. Darlington, who followed Malcolm Watson. Both were dramatists, and, therefore, impressed with the importance of pit and gallery in the world of the theatre. Darlington's pet crusade is for audibility in the theatre, and what crusade could be more justifiable? A. E. Wilson, of *The Star*, with his jolly interest in pantomime, and Willson Disher, telling of the old music-halls, are others whom lovers of the drama can consult with profit because they are primarily concerned with the theatre as entertainment They are, in fact, ideal spectators.

William Archer wrote the first critique of Ibsen's *A Doll's House* in *The Theatre* as early as April, 1884. That was the foundation of his life's work. The range of his reading was remarkable, and his memory capacious, while the integrity of his approach to the problems of dramatic criticism was crystal-clear. If knowledge were the only guide to a judicious commentary, Archer, in the 'nineties, was the man for your money. The larger public belonged to Clement Scott, and when his influence waned, to Bernard Shaw and A. B. Walkley, both of whom graduated on *The Star*, then a halfpenny evening newspaper, edited by T. P. O'Connor.

Seen in the perspective of history, Bernard Shaw was the most influential critic of his time, wrong-headed as he could be and only too often was. The evidence is enshrined in three volumes of reprints from his *Saturday Review* articles. They not only tell the story of some important transitional years in English theatrical history, but established not a few principles of criticism which had long been ignored. Similarly, Walkley's interest in the French and Italian theatres, enshrined in his work for *The Times*, helped to establish a new standard not only in comedy acting but comedy writing in England. With William Archer, Bernard Shaw and A. B. Walkley, dramatic criticism was exercising a direct influence upon drama and the art of acting.

Belonging to an older school of thought than Shaw and

Walkley was Joseph Knight, of *The Athenaeum*. He lived on until 1907, when he died, aged seventy-eight. He is best remembered by a volume of dramatic criticism covering the London stage in the 'seventies and doing the service for that decade which the *Essays in Dramatic Criticism* by Mowbray Morris, of *The Times*, do for the theatrical 'eighties. The judgements of both men were markedly unlike those of Clement Scott and serve as a useful reminder that the more emotional outpourings from Peterborough Court called for an antidote even before the coming of Bernard Shaw and A. B. Walkley. The articles in *The Athenaeum* were only a part of Joseph Knight's influence. Supplementing his theatrical notices was his table talk. A big man, with a big bass voice and a head and beard which suggested Olympian Zeus, he could hold a select audience into the wee sma' hours, fortified by tumblers of spirits and soda. Max Beerbohm has left a thumbnail sketch of himself and another in the remark, "Knight had a thousand drinks and I but one."

Joseph Knight worked for a weekly paper. James Agate, seated in the Café Royal, now pouring out reminiscences, now fixing a canon of criticism for the benefit of the young, had a similar advantage over rivals who represented morning papers and therefore had to hurry back to Fleet Street and write for dear life. Walkley, on the *Star*, could avoid the worst consequences of the rushed review. Indeed, after he was promoted to Printing House Square and was required to serve up his "excellently light omelettes" to the readers of *The Times*, theatre-lovers rated his weekly contributions to *The Times Literary Supplement* considerably higher than the supper dishes prepared for the morning paper.

Dramatic critics often attend a dress rehearsal and some dramatists (Pinero was one) have offered a printed copy of the play, but the rushed story of an important first-night remains a problem inextricably associated with the function of criticism. The curtain rising at seven and falling at ten p.m. has made things easier, but is not a final solution, the more because the newspapers themselves go to press at earlier and ever earlier hours.

The truth is that theatrical reviewing for a morning paper under modern conditions cannot be more than cultivated reporting. The space and the time allowed permit of little else. It was pleasant to see T. C. Worsley getting away with close upon two thousand words when writing a eulogy of Dame Edith Evans in Bridie's *Daphne Laureola*. All honour to the far-sighted editor of *The New Statesman*. Is this the solution?

When William Archer wrote of Pinero's *The Notorious Mrs Ebbsmith* in 1895 he had something like 4,500 words at his disposal in *The World*. Bernard Shaw, in the *Saturday Review*, could demand 2,500 words for a similar notice, whereas Charles Morgan in *The Times* had to be content with 700, 600 or 500 words. Even C. E. Montague, writing in the *Manchester Guardian* at the turn of the century, could cull a full column of close print from his editor for a notice of Frank Benson's *King Richard the Second*. Those spacious days have gone, as surely as those in which Steele drew upon the pages of *The Tatler*, Addison upon *The Spectator*, Goldsmith upon *The Bee*, Hazlitt upon *The Examiner* or the *London Magazine*, and George Henry Lewes upon *The Leader*.

I first met Agate in 1921, when I was doing some work for the *Saturday Review*, in a period when it was being edited by Filson Young. Looking in each week for a possible book for review or with an idea for a "middle", I came upon James Agate, fresh from Lancashire. I quickly acquired the habit of pondering his theatrical notices, a habit I did not lose until his death in 1947. In the *Manchester Guardian* and the *Saturday Review*, on the wireless, and from 1924 to 1947 in the *Sunday Times*, James Agate has left a continuous record of contemporary criticism covering forty years. It is the more valuable because so much is preserved between the covers of books, and not merely in what Kipling called, "the all-recording, all-effacing files". The Agate reviews display the gusto of the man, Moreover, they are supported by a fund of genuine knowledge and experience, based upon an exceptional capacity for hard work and a fixed determination to leave his mark upon the letters of his age.

I have put in a disclaimer against dramatic criticism as an excuse for ethical debate. But this does not mean that the theatre should not provide texts for public discussion. On the contrary, the theatre is only really alive when it is a forum for contemporary thought and therefore furnishing ideas which burgeon long after curtain-fall. Among the dramatic critics of our time, Charles Morgan has been most interested in ideas. For Morgan, "ideas

live and are reborn and nothing else does live." His search is for
the human values which enrich life. Because "values" cannot
adequately be explored and discussed in half a column of a morning paper, Morgan suffered more than the majority of his fellow
critics. His experience suggests the need for longer criticisms,
comparable with those of the eighteenth and nineteenth centuries. How else is the critic fully to justify his calling? A weekly
page in *The Times Literary Supplement* would be very welcome, if
only as a record for generations of playgoers yet to be. In present
usage guidance from a single writer will never suffice. The real
lover of the theatre reads, not one criticism, but half a dozen, and
from the multiplicity of counsellors he makes a shrewd guess at
what is worth while, *for himself*. The puff direct, the puff col-
lateral and the puff oblique—these can safely be left to the business manager or his press representative. They will provide
clichés in plenty—"the hand of a master", "mine of invention",
"Attic Salt", and the rest—which Charles Mathews's approach
to criticism required.

For the lover of the theatre, the function of criticism is very
different. He seeks guidance regarding new productions and a
source whence the past history of the stage can be reconstructed.
To those who endure not a few hours of boredom while furnishing
this guidance, the playgoer is in continual debt, although the
keen critic is among the lucky few who are paid for what they
want to do. May the rewarding hours in the playhouse more than
balance those of little worth. For my own part I am convinced
that they do.

CHAPTER 10

"ONLY ACTING". ENTER THE PLAYERS

Only acting! Only acting! Great heavens, woman! To act is to create the perfect union between body, mind, and spirit.—James Bridie, *The King of Nowhere*

AND after the play, the players. For a quarter of a century the aesthetics of the English theatre have suffered from a too ready acceptance of theories which under-rate the contribution of actors and actresses. This has been largely due to George Bernard Shaw, whose ideas won acceptance mainly through the wit with which the Irishman enforced a corpus of criticism comparable with any in dramatic history. Always the Shavian body of aesthetics has suffered from a lurking antipathy towards the actor or the actress, which revealed itself in the splenetic attacks upon Henry Irving, and, fundamentally, was due to professional jealousy. As Shaw confessed, "The very originality and genius of the performers conflict with the originality and genius of the author."

I am in no way denying that a reaction in favour of the dramatist as student of life and contributor to the ideology of his time was over-due in the early 'nineties. But, to-day, we should call a halt to such influences. Our own plea is for an approach which allows the art of the actor the fullest recognition. We need to be reminded that it is the job of the dramatist to fit his theme and its presentation so that the acting talent at his disposal may have the fullest scope. In the theatre, the actor's art dominates that of the dramatist.

When Granville-Barker wrote that the laws of dramatic art are the natural laws of the medium in which the play exists he put his finger upon a fundamental fact. It is the player's craft, coupled with a successful production and a pulsing auditorium, which finally determines dramatic form. Henry James put the argument thus, in a letter to F. Anstey, years ago, when plays began much later than they do to-day:

"The author who seriously attempts that most difficult and elusive art of expressing his impressions of life in dramatic form— be that form tragedy, comedy, melodrama or what you will— every dramatist, then, as he sits at his desk to evolve his conceptions, must first visualize, or have before his mental eye, the proscenium of a theatre. And above that proscenium an immense clock, its hands indicating the hour of eight-thirty. Those hands will move inexorably on till they reach eleven, and that deplorably insufficient space of time is all that is allowed him in which to make the actions and motives, however intricate, of his dramatis personae intelligible to an audience which he dare not count upon as possessing more than an average degree of intelligence."

Not words then, but two hours of busy acting apart from intervals are at the dramatist's disposal. And the same must be said of the producer. Actors and their actions are their raw material, playing against a background of stage scenery, costumes and lighting. The dialogue and *décor* of a play have no right to being apart from the things which actors and actresses can do within the two and a half or three hours' traffic of the stage, including the substantial intervals. Finally, all three—dramatist, producer and actor—must realize that, in the last resort, the eyes, ears and emotions of an audience are the raw material of their art. The reaction from well-filled stalls and crowded pit and gallery is the final evidence of successful play-writing and play-production. Perhaps one-third of an average audience asks little more than entertainment after a day's work. Another third seeks imaginative release from actual or potential depression. The remaining third—the real theatre-lovers—enjoy the glow of the footlights, the thrill of an unfolding story, and above all, the skill with which a team of players gives unity to the thought of a practised dramatist.

Remembering Bernard Shaw's tremendous capacity and authority, it is to be regretted that, in the days when he practised theatrical criticism, he never pretended that he was anything else than a critic desirous of becoming a successful dramatist, and establishing a new school of drama. He was, therefore, not over-scrupulous as to how he reached his objective. In so far as he was a critic-dramatist, he gloried in his "critical inhumanity", citing as justification a pleasant story in which Lessing reproached Heine, "for not only cutting off his victims' heads but holding them up afterwards to show that there were no brains in them". Lack of brains was Shaw's chief complaint, not only against rival dramatists, but against the body of actors and actresses which was to lift him to fame a few years later. Here are a few sentences from a diatribe directed against Tree's *Henry IV, Part I*, "as good work as our stage can do", as Shaw admitted, though he went on to write:

"In this column I have prated again and again of the mission of the theatre, the art of the actor, of his labor, his skill, his knowledge, his importance as a civilizing agent, his function as a spiritual doctor. Surely I have been in this the most ridiculous of all dupes. . . . However, I am cured now. It is all a delusion, there is no profession, no art, no skill about the business at all. We have no actors. We have only authors and not many of them. . . . We authors find that the actors have only one note, or perhaps, if they are very clever, half a dozen."

This sort of thing was the more maddening because Shaw could be so maddeningly right, as when he wrote, "On the highest plane one does not act, one is." Why, then, did the same pen write of Irving's Corporal Brewster, in *A Story of Waterloo*, "The call-boy could do it," when all who were not blind to the effect the actor was creating were convinced that Henry Irving was not acting the old Waterloo veteran but *was* the very man.

However, this all happened many years ago, and, as he has been fully rewarded, the mellowed Shaw might well admit that the time has come for a re-alignment of functions in a theatre so that actors and actresses may once more claim the attention of critics.

The aesthetics of drama are for the study, but the aesthetics of acting are for the theatre. Indeed, their character becomes plainer when something less than the greatest in drama presents itself for criticism. Acting is not fully to be understood in the light of genius; its implications become much clearer when one recalls Marie Lloyd, thrusting her personality upon a crowded house— making every male momentarily a lover and every woman jealous of those enticing wiles. "Oh", you say, "Marie Lloyd was just herself!" Don't believe this for a moment. From the second the curtain parts, she is thrusting an imagined self upon her audience, forcing it to accept Marie Lloyd at her own valuation and not at something less. Always a player must impersonate somebody, even if that somebody is only his or her imagined self. On the stage there is no such possibility as "being one's self". The safety curtain, the framework of the proscenium, the footlights— all forbid this. This coming on of a pretty girl or a well set-up man is not acting. It is only a stage appearance. Which is why good looks in a player are just as likely to be a handicap as an asset. After facing an audience, Marie Tempest once returned to the wings with tears in her blue eyes: "I'm an ugly little devil," she whispered to a friend, "but they like me."

The player who makes stage history is the one who fashions an unexpected thing out of the raw material given by the stage circumstances, whether they be the plot of the dramatist, the setting, or a particular conjunction of characters. An actor or actress is a weaver, charged with making the best possible from given raw material, and his or her contribution may vary in quality from homespun to the rarest tapestry.

The Good Trouper

In connection with acting which satisfies dramatists of worth and delights audiences year after year the phrase "a good trouper" is common. What does it imply? Louis Calvert said, "Write me down as an actor who puts himself personally immeasurably below his beloved art." Now Louis Calvert came of sound theatrical stock. His father was an actor-manager and his mother (Mrs Charles Calvert) had played with Charles Kean when she was six years old and I saw her playing Mrs Malaprop at the Haymarket sixty years later. All the Calverts were good troupers.

So was Dame Marie Tempest. If the curtain went up at 8.30 Marie Tempest was in her dressing-room by 7. And she was not tired, for she had had a sleep—a real sleep—in the late afternoon. The tiny periwinkle-blue eyes were rested. By 7.5 the actress was in a dressing-gown and playing patience. "It is very calming," explained Dame Marie. Making-up began at 7.30 and was completed by 8. Thus, by 8.25 everything was ready, Dame Marie taking care never to sit down after she had put on her stage dress.

Dame Lilian Braithwaite was a good trouper. So is Jean Cadell. So was Dame May Whitty, who died at the age of eighty-two, after serving the public of two continents for sixty-seven years. Experienced theatre-goers come to recognize the trouper from the non-trouper by instinct. Their experience is that the trouper never lets the play down, as Beerbohm Tree did continually, as Mrs Patrick Campbell did often (bless her burnished wit), and as all who are less than "troupers" do from time to time. Tree went so far as to say that "acting was not an art at all. It is purely a matter of the imagination." Speaking to W. L. Courtney, he added, "I have not got technique. It is a dull thing. It enslaves the imagination." True, on their own nights, the non-troupers may reach heights which the troupers rarely achieve, but day in and day out—matinées as well as evening shows—how much we owe to the troupers who rank their personal likes and dislikes immeasurably below their beloved craft.

The team spirit which has so large a part in the make-up of the good trouper is partly a matter of temperament, but it can be inculcated. That is why it is often associated with a theatrical family. Handing on the torch from one generation to another, members of a theatrical family tend to pass on the all-important lesson that not one member of a cast constitutes a worth-while play, but an ensemble. The Grossmiths, the Lupinos, the Terrys, the Robertsons, the Hammonds (Miss Kay Hammond has ancestors in the profession dating back to the eighteenth century); their fathers and mothers, their brothers, cousins and sisters, were born into the purple. Consequently, they were not only caught young, but caught fit for high office. A history of modern drama in the last hundred and fifty years could be written around the Websters, the Emerys, the Rignolds, the Batemans, the Bishops, the Broughs, the Calverts, the Comptons, the Fairbrothers, the Farrens, and the rest, and largely, because they learnt the lesson of "the team spirit" early and never forgot it.

Coquelin was a trouper of outstanding merit though he was not born in a theatrical family. He was the son of a small baker in Boulogne and as a boy he worked in the family kitchen, making tarts. And as he worked he recited French verse. There were no stage associations in the family history, but already young

o

Coquelin meant to be a classic actor. He left the bakery when he was eighteen, and a year later won a prize which ensured his entry into the Comédie Française. Success came when he first played Figaro. In twenty-two years he had mastered forty-four rôles. If Coquelin played a character after twenty years it was still the same clear-cut, sharply-etched portrayal, the same harmonious union of mind and body.

Coquelin was once asked how many rôles he could play at a moment's notice. He took a piece of paper, wrote for a while and then said "Fifty-three!" His hearers expressed doubt. "The plays are all in the library. Get them from the shelves and try me. Choose any cue you like and give it to me." The party made tests in sixteen plays and Coquelin was not once at fault. Banville wrote *Gringoire* for him when Coquelin was twenty-five. Later Banville said:

"When the good God was very busy finishing a batch of mortals, He realized that He had not included an actor. He set to work and quickly copied the face of Molière. He made the same deep-set eyes, lively, inquisitive and observant, the same queer eyebrows, the same thick but delighted and mobile lips, the same wide nostrils made wide to sniff up thoughts of all kinds—and when He had finished He named His actor, Coquelin."

The Nature of Theatrical Illusion

This ideal actor or actress, "the good trouper", raises the questions every player must face when creating a new part. What can he put across; how can it be put across; and, lastly, what do we mean by "put across"?

The normal in experience is familiar enough. Something has happened and the evidence comes through eye and ear in the form of what we call "reality". Reality is behind stage happenings too. Nature sets the scene, as Shakespeare told us when he wrote of plays and players holding the mirror up to nature. It is from things done between dawn and dusk, between dusk and dawn, that dramas are fashioned. The theatre, like all other arts, is rooted in the day-to-day life of men and women.

When, however, these natural happenings are put on the stage, factors which are markedly unnatural begin to operate. On the stage the player is a man or woman, but he or she has to project voice and appearance out of the frame formed by the proscenium arch, so that an imagined person in an imagined situation may seem alive, not only for those in the stalls, but at the back of the gallery. The voice must not be too loud for those in the stalls, or too low for those at the back of the gallery. Similarly, with play of features, costume, gestures and bodily movements. Make-up must not be so marked that it troubles those in the stalls, or so weak that it does not have its effect upon the gallery; and this is equally true of gesture, dress, and movement. A few moments consideration surely shows that being natural is an impossibility on the stage, if something is to be "put across" which an average audience will accept as "the real thing". Herbert Tree, as a stage executant, may not have been a final judge of what constituted the greatest in acting, but he was a good showman. He stated the underlying canon governing all theatrical art with full accuracy when he said, "Illusion is the first and last word of the stage; all that aids illusion is good; all that destroys illusion is bad." The securing of convincing illusion is what we mean by the words "put across".

It is at this point that the ideal spectator claims to be heard. Though the dramatist's appeal is to the individual as a member of a crowd, mass applause can furnish no final test of illusion. The individual spectator alone decides whether the maker of "theatre" has achieved successful expression. A play, a character creation, a stage setting or what not, has just as many meanings as there are understanding spectators, for beauty and truth attach, not to any given play or acting opportunity, but to its semblance in the mind of a spectator. The only judge of such values is the spectator who can yield himself so that he is thrown into emotional disturbance, laughter or tears as the case may be. Nor can any final decision be delegated to a licensed theatre-taster, though guidance from those familiar with the methods of the theatre may help greatly towards a right judgement. Not every one who reads a play or pays for a seat in the pit will come to a useful decision as to the place of a given work in the hierarchy of the theatre. Nevertheless, it is for the individual play-goer to say, "I like this. It is beautiful."

Consider a few examples of illusion, which every playgoer who came under the particular thrill will acknowledge to be as complete as human effort allows. What better than the third act of *Mrs Dane's Defence*, in which the constructive skill of Henry Arthur Jones and Charles Wyndham's immense experience as a producer were so entwined with Lena Ashwell's emotional presentation of the frightened and distracted woman who was under cross-examination. Only later analysis made it plain that what mattered most and what was rarest was Miss Ashwell's display of nervous tension, which was so authentic that it was in itself exciting. Even as a young and inexperienced amateur Miss Ashwell had the promise of this power. She could imagine a situation so vividly that the words of the dramatist had a quite unexpected vitality. Ellen Terry has left us this impression of Lena Ashwell reciting a speech from Shakespeare's *Richard the Second*.

"A pathetic face; a passionate voice; a brain, I thought to myself. It must have been at this point that the girl flung away the book and began to act, in an undisciplined way, of course, but with such true emotion, such intensity, that the tears came into my eyes. The tears came into her eyes too. We both wept and then we embraced and then we wept again."

Leave out of account the emotion due to an experienced actress sensing unusual talent and that of a young girl realizing that she was impressing an actress of Ellen Terry's reputation. Forget this, and it must have been evident that, if and when Lena Ashwell gained full voice control and the skill in timing which betokens the finished actress, there were triumphs ahead.

Playing the name part in *Irene Wycherley*, a grim tragedy by Anthony P. Wharton, Miss Ashwell was married to a veritable devil. After four years the wife found him indulging in a vulgar intrigue. Being a Catholic, Irene was unable to divorce her husband, so she left him, and only returned when he was blinded by a gun accident. Hideously scarred, but cruel as ever, the husband sought to force his ugly passion upon the wife who still hated him. When the husband drew the shuddering woman to his knees, playing upon her sense of pity, the dazed submission of Lena Ashwell and the agonized disgust with which she broke from the blind man, leaving him raving like a wild beast, proved thrilling "theatre". Norman McKinnel as Philip Wycherley shared

Lena Ashwell's triumph, as Charles Wyndham did in *Mrs Dane's Defence*, but the woman's command of nervous tension furnished the fundamental thrill.

Nervous Tension

In this connection, Meggie Albanesi's career, short as it was, calls for recollection. Petite, pale-faced and dark-eyed, she was the daughter of Carlo Albanesi, a musician. Her mother was a novelist, so Meggie came of artistic stock. She studied at the Royal Academy of Dramatic Art under Helen Haye and worked hard, cultivating clear enunciation and the range of her speaking voice, until it had an astonishing emotional power for one so young and inexperienced. When she was seventeen, Meggie won the Bancroft Gold Medal for a performance of Lady Teazle in a production of *The School for Scandal*, a success which led to an engagement to play in a revival of *A Pair of Spectacles*. From Jill Hillcrist in Galsworthy's *The Skin Game* Meggie passed to the love-sick school girl in *The Charm School* and then to the triumph in *A Bill of Divorcement*.

Margaret (Lilian Braithwaite) had married Hilary (Malcolm Keen) soon after the outbreak of war in 1914 and her daughter Sydney was seventeen years old when the play opened on Christmas Day, 1933. Clemence Dane placed the action twelve years ahead of time in order to allow of a possible change in the divorce laws. The scene was laid in a room in a small country house. To Margaret comes her shell-shocked husband, who had been confined as a lunatic practically ever since his daughter's birth. He had escaped from the asylum and seemed to have recovered his reason, loving Margaret as of old. But Margaret had been granted a divorce on the ground of Hilary's lunacy and was on the eve of marriage to a new lover, so the return was very unwelcome. Meggie Albanesi's chance came in the closing scene. Only seventeen, engaged to Kit, and looking forward to "heaps of kids", Sydney put aside all thought of marriage and sacrificed herself upon what she regarded as the altar of daughterly duty. Meggie's great moment as Sydney Fairfield was her last despairing cry: "Father, don't believe her. I am not hard."

Before every performance Meggie shut herself in her dressing-

room and would see no one. She was re-creating in imagination
the spiritual agony, not only of the daughter but of the unhappy
father. The effort was more than the girl should have made. The
play was partly rehearsed in Meggie's bedroom and she went
from bed to the last rehearsal and her doctor and a nurse went
with her to the theatre on that memorable first night. The reward,
if reward it was, came at curtain-fall, when there were general
cries of "Meggie! We want Meggie!"

Meggie Albanesi died in December, 1923. She was only
twenty-four.

Different in type, but similar in the underlying principle that a
highly dramatic situation had been prepared by a dramatist of
parts, able to draw upon acting ability of outstanding quality, was
a scene in *The Likes of Her,* which a cast headed by Hermione
Baddeley and Mary Clare made so memorable. Charles McEvoy
was the author and he was a leader in what was then known as the
Manchester School. The characters were London Cockneys and
the background an alley, a coffee-house, and a garret-bedroom in
an East End slum during the first World War. No devisings were
omitted which could add verisimilitude. We saw Barbara Gott
with arms akimbo in the opening scene embodying a blowsy ter-
magant, whom the plot required as a contrast to the heroine,
Sally. Sally is a waitress in a coffee-house, but her spare hours are
spent at Waterloo Station, hoping against hope for the return of
her soldier lover, Alf Cope. The folk who live in Sally's alley
know only too well what has happened. The disengaged males,
to a man, have proposed marriage; others in the alley have invented all sorts of reasons for Alf's absence. In truth, Alf Cope has
been so cruelly disfigured in battle that he fears to face Sally.

When, at last, Alf overcame his fears, he found Sally's garret in
the possession of a little slattern, Florrie Small, the unhappy
daughter of the virago of the opening scene, whom Sally had res-
cued from misery. But the child was both thief and liar. In Sally's
phrase, "It would give you the hiccups to tell the truth." True to
her type, Florrie lied to Alf and he left the garret in deep distress,
convinced that Sally was lost to him. McEvoy's first surprise
came when Sally grasped the situation and, in place of punishment, set to work to convince Florrie Small of her viciousness.
Hermione Baddeley was only seventeen at the time, but she

brought the little slattern, used to nothing but the discipline of belt and buckle, fully to life. McEvoy's solution for the psychological problem was the memorable scene in which the maddened girl broke up the garret home, while Sally encouraged the orgy of breakage, until Florrie burst into a flood of remorseful tears, in which wonderment and regret were so strangely mingled.

Jean Forbes-Robertson is another actress of rare sensitivity and able to call upon rich stores of emotional power. Her gifts displayed their highest potency in that curious Jewish drama, *The Dybbuk*. The dybbuk is a demonic force which can take possession of a human being. In the play the demon took possession of Leah on the day of her marriage. It would not be exorcized until the girl's death made it possible for her spirit to be united with that of the poor scholar, Channon, for all eternity. It is the dead Channon's spirit which has entered Leah's body and the aged Rabbi Azrael calls a Rabinnical Court and from it obtains leave to cast out the invading spirit. While Ernest Milton gave Channon the suggestion of passionate ecstasy which the part required, the mingling of terror and spiritual exaltation of Jean Forbes-Robertson's Leah displayed a beauty which must haunt the memory of all who saw the play. The close of *The Dybbuk* was masterly. The Rabbi Azrael, after the exorcism, comes in to take Leah to her earthly bridegroom and finds her room in darkness. The old nurse who was to have guarded the girl is asleep.

What is "Ham"?

Opposed to the strongly emotional approach of such players as Lena Ashwell and Meggie Albanesi are the methods of the exponents of "reserved force". Of one such player, it is told that an elderly playgoer (a lady) was once chaperoning a party of schoolgirls. She was restless as the first act came to its end, and then said gently: "Come, my dears, we had better come again another day, when the actors know their parts."

Which brings up the very debatable problem of "ham" and its place in the theatre of to-day. The truth is that "ham" may equally well be over-acting or playing a part for all it is worth. Of "ham" Noel Coward once said that all acting worth the name is "ham", and Marie Tempest added, "Cover up the 'ham' but don't take it away." Even when a play offers less than worthy material, "ham" has value as it teaches an actor to play a truly dramatic part for all it is worth when it does come along. It is noteworthy that players who have never appeared in pantomime

Sarah Bernhardt teaching *the Young Idea how to Act*

or melodrama tend to lack the power required to dominate large audiences. If one used the word "ham" to describe the example of classical acting which follows, would the adjective be derogatory? Joseph Knight, a critic of mark, is describing Sarah Bernhardt in the second act of *Phèdre* in the year 1879, when she was at the height of her power, old enough to use all the wiles of an actress and still young enough to seem what she wanted to be. Of the tortured Phèdre, Joseph Knight wrote: "Her supple form writhed beneath the influence of mental agony and restless desire and her posture seemed chosen with admirable art for the purpose of blending the greatest possible amount of seduction with the utmost possible parade of penitence." If this be "ham", then the more of it we have the better.

The capacity to mobilize nervous energy, that is to say, the power of sudden and intense emotional excitation is invaluable.

"Striking twelve, all at once" was the way some one summed up the gift. Charles Warner had the capacity in a high degree and it accounted for his success in such a melodrama as *Drink*, or in that telling bit of Grand Guignol drama, *At the Telephone*. Willard also had the power; so has Olivier among present day actors. Henry Arthur Jones, discussing this, recalled that Fechter displayed the gift when he gave "O, what a rogue and peasant slave am I" speech and lashed himself into depths of galling self-contempt, until this spent itself in the phrase, "a scullion; fie upon it".

Without the capacity for mobilizing nervous energy it is difficult to see how many well-tested theatrical effects could be secured. Not a few playgoers will recall Mlle Polaire in *Le Visiteur*, a music-hall sketch at the Palace Theatre twenty years or more ago. Polaire, with her wasp-like waist and her curious mop of jet-black hair, had the part of an actress who had been discussing with her lover the question of fear. "I shall not be frightened," she tells him, when he threatens to visit her rooms that very night, disguised as a burglar. His answer was "We shall see."

When the curtain rises again, the actress comes into her bedroom. A few moments later, there is an ominous sound at the window and "The Visitor" climbs in. Too late the actress realizes that the brute in the cap and tight-fitting trousers is not her lover, but a desperado of the worst type, bent upon securing the pearl necklace she is wearing. Moreover, she learns that he has murdered her lover.

How shall she be revenged? She asks the man to stay. She smokes with him, for she is going to kill him with his own knife! To this end the woman pretends that the murder of her lover was really a blessing in disguise. She had come to hate the man. In gratitude, she will dance for the Apache, and she enters upon the *Danse des Faubourgs*, a sensuous whirl which she has been giving in the theatre that very night, and which the Apache has often seen from the gallery.

Enthralled, the man drops his knife and the actress secures it. Amid growing excitement, the Apache joins in the mad dance, until the man who murdered her lover is within her embrace. She seems to yield herself to him. Then, working her arms over his shoulder, she plunges the weapon into the Apache's back.

The two fall to the ground. Then the woman rises slowly, shakes herself free from the body, and continues the dance to its grim end.

A very characteristic bit of "theatre" and redeemed from melodramatic vulgarity by the relatively rare conjunction of a Polaire with the acting opportunity.

A Player's Personality

The personality of a player may allow of numerous impersonations, but each actor and actress has limitations. Marie Wilton (Lady Bancroft) was a born actress and this story is told of her deep-set grey eyes, with their long dark lashes, which were to endear her to a couple of generations of theatre-goers in the 'seventies, 'eighties, and 'nineties. As a child Marie Wilton was playing the boy Fleance to the Macbeth of Macready. It was the actor's farewell performance, and when the curtain fell, Macready sent for his Fleance and thanked "him". "I'm going to play Lady Macbeth when I grow up," whispered Marie shyly. Said Macready: "You will have to change those curious eyes before you play *Macbeth* or you will make your audience laugh instead of cry. But I see genius through those little grey windows."

Pliable as was the imagination of the great Duse, and ample as was her technical proficiency, there were marked limitations to the rôles she could fill and there were times when she essayed the impossible. Nora, in Ibsen's *A Doll's House*, was too confined a part for so tremendous a personality. Even Paula Tanqueray did not display Duse's sense of the beautiful and the true to the full. But in *Magda* and in *La Gioconda* her talent could move freely. Eleonora Duse did not assume the character suggested by a dramatist. What she did was to merge her own personality into the image adumbrated by the playwright, so that a new thing arose, Eleonora Duse as the imagined creature. And in the merging of the self with the imagined thing, none of the beauty of body, mind, or spirit, which was Eleanora Duse's natural endowment as a player, was lost.

Max Beerbohm put it this way. "Irving's voice, face, figure, port were not transformable; but he was multi-radiant." Always there was Henry Irving, as there was Eleonora Duse or Sarah

Bernhardt, but it was not always the same Irving. The player's imagination sufficed for many memorable rôles. Laurence Olivier, on the contrary, has a different approach. His purpose is to adapt his physical qualities and mental equipment to the character given by the playwright. His voice, face, figure and port were as transformable to Puff in *The Critic*, to Justice Shallow in *Henry the Fourth*, as they were to Oedipus. He is not an actor of the multi-radiant type, wide as is his range.

Receiving a manuscript from his producer, an actor first seeks a general perception of the plot and its relation to the character he will be impersonating. That is, he should do so, though some actors and actresses of fame have been blind to the duty. Mr Chance Newton, in *Cues and Curtain Calls*, tells an amusing story of Henry Irving when he found that William Terriss, his Bassanio, had never read *The Merchant of Venice*. "Breezy Bill" had good looks and a voice of rich beauty, but Irving could not forgive this disrespect for the Bard. "Yonder he stands, up stage, Will Terriss. I pay him eighty pounds a week and in many respects he is well worth it, but he will not read this marvellous dramatist."

When Chance Newton, at Irving's request, put the matter before "Breezy Bill", Terriss replied: "The dear old Chief, God bless him, has engaged me to play Bassanio in this play. I have learned the part. I shall give a rattling good performance. Very well. Why worry me to read this damned Shakespeare play?"

In fact, William Terriss was a player with amazing assurance which enabled him to thrust his personality upon any audience and put across any dialogue without arousing a smile. In Adelphi melodrama he was accepted as authentic hero from the front row of the stalls to the back row of the gallery. But he lacked the sensibility necessary for the higher flights of drama. No one, however, would have denied to Terriss the description "good trouper" and he was a "born actor". Accordingly he left to his "Dear Old Chief" the job of fitting his Bassanio into the production as a whole.

Assuming a somewhat more pliant attitude towards the play as a final unity, the job of actor or actress is to discipline voice, gestures, movements and silences so that the character has its best chance of coming to life. To use an image of Sir Cedric Hardwicke, a good actor is an open canvas. He begins by reading the script in order to know what sort of character he is going to paint, knowing there will be a process of gradual growth, though the final conception of the complete character may well come in a flash. Thus when Dame Madge Kendal read *The Second Mrs Tanqueray*, her reaction to Paula was very different from that of Mrs Patrick Campbell, under Pinero's direct guidance, or, indeed, from that of the Duse. Mrs Kendal's imagination fixed upon Paula's wild desire for the love of Tanqueray's daughter, fresh from her convent school and untainted by the world. "Oh, if I could be like you." This mad yearning was what Mrs Kendal was experiencing when she took up the mirror in the fourth act. It was not the passing of Paula's beauty but the knowledge that her sin for ever made it impossible that the girl could love her which brought tears to Dame Madge's eyes and inspired her rendering of the rôle. *The Second Mrs Tanqueray* was not a Kendal success; nor, for that matter, did Eleanora Duse shine in the part, though her playing of the mirror scene was deeply moving. Indeed, I would put it among the richest experience of my sixty years of playgoing. The play as a whole was not tragic enough for the Duse's genius. Her command of emotion was too deep for the earlier situations which came so perfectly within the scope of Mrs Patrick Campbell.

Another interesting example of varying interpretations, and again Dame Madge Kendal was one of the protagonists, is concerned with Gilbert's *Pygmalion and Galatea*. Galatea was a Madge Robertson creation in 1871 and was one of her early triumphs, but Mary Anderson played the part in America and also during a famous revival at the Lyceum in 1883. The beauty of Mary Anderson as the statue was haunting, but critics, remembering Madge Robertson, asked if Gilbert really meant Galatea to be so chilly and statuesque when she descended from her pedestal and became one of the mortals. In fact, Madge Kendal gave Mr Gilbert his Galatea and Mary Anderson gave Lyceum audiences her own. Gilbert, who produced both performances, could only say that though the American's playing was artistically the more beautiful, it was dramatically less effective. The climax of Madge Robertson's was her deeply pathetic cry, "Pygmalion", as she felt the love and life fading away and the icy cold marble taking her to itself once more. Mary Anderson's cry was a ghostly "Pygmalion", as of a woman entering a tomb. Remember, too, this is not the first "Pygmalion!" At the beginning of the play there was a very different use of the cry.

Galatea (*behind the curtain*): Pygmalion!
Pygmalion: Who called?
  (*Pygmalion tears away the curtain and discovers that Galatea, the statue, has come to life.*)
Pygmalion: Ye gods! It lives!
Galatea: Pygmalion!
Pygmalion: It speaks!

No small part of the thrill arising from the farewell cry was due to overtones which lingered in the memory of Dame Madge Kendal's hearers from the earlier scene. It is the player's task to create such overtones.

Acting as Re-creation

Acting is the physical representation of Cedric Hardwicke's imagined picture, and players must work upon some such "open canvas" if they are to be worthy members of a troupe. Movement and non-movement, diction and silences, must be woven into a cunning whole, appearing as spontaneous as nature itself; and yet, not nature, for, on the stage, everything must not only be natural, but also highly coloured. As Dame Madge Kendal said, "Acting is Nature, with the rouge on it." The end of study comes when the player is an integral part of that greater whole, the play, and does not appear to be acting at all. Certainly more is needful than "carving out, cutting and stitching at one's own skin" if pulsing characterization is to arise.

All of which implies that, when an actor begins to work upon a part, he brings to the task much more than impressions derived from the dramatist's text. The player's insight will be coloured by many other associations, some conscious but many sub-conscious, though all of them will help to create the final picture which will determine his performance on the opening night. Nor is the mental and emotional approach the only one. Acting of worth, if it is to be exciting, individual and picturesque, must also concern itself with the voice, bodily form and capacity for gesture at the player's command. Henry James, speaking as a novelist, compared the act of composition to "a cauldron simmering over a hot fire", into which were thrown "real experiences, characters, emotions, incidents", and in such a way that all became saturated with the essential stuff of the author's mind and thus were in a very real sense "re-created".

The re-creation accomplished by an actor is similar. Reading his author's script, recollections of men and women seen in the flesh or on the stage help towards character-creation; so do ideas regarding dress or bodily movements or recollections of the re-action of real men or women to emotional crises akin to those in the play which is being studied. Apropos of the aid to be derived from such general experience, Ernest Thesiger was once cast for Captain Hook, the "pirate-king" of *Peter Pan*, and asked Barrie's advice as to the characterization. "Remember", said Barrie, "that Hook was a Balliol man." When Charles Laughton played Captain Hook, he omitted the Balliol touch. Barrie's comment was that he feared the children who saw this Captain Hook would be frightened.

Apart from this continual drawing upon earlier experience, the player's final picture will be governed by the imaginative vision of the actor or actress, imagination being the faculty which he or she shares with dramatist and audiences alike, and which, indeed, is the only sure link between the three main theatrical factors. How is a player to impress his or her heroic character upon those on the other side of the footlights, if the imagination has not these heroic qualities firmly fixed. In this connection it is told that Edith Evans once gave this advice to a young actress at the Old Vic. "My dear, always try to think you are the most wonderful creature that ever lived when you are on the stage, and the audience will believe it too."

Esmond Knight, recalling the incident, said that Miss Evans was playing in Pinero's *Trelawny of the Wells* at the time. A minute or two later, with head held high, "she glided on to the stage, her irregular features illuminated by a sort of ethereal radiance. Huddled together in the O.P. corner, we watched her move about the stage—surely she was the most beautiful woman in the theatre."

To be compared with the advice of Edith Evans is that Maisie

Gay gave to Jessie Matthews. I tell the story in a later chapter.

Consider the amazing fertility of imagination of a Charles Laughton or an Edith Evans, which enabled them to create such a vast variety of characters. And this without losing contact with their own personalities, which are all-important in "stardom". Tyrone Guthrie once described Charles Laughton as an inspired amateur because he does not translate a rôle into a carefully measured pattern of gestures, inflections and movements, as Coquelin did, as Madge Kendal did, as Marie Tempest, John Hare and other troupers of happy memory did. What Guthrie meant was that Laughton seemed to be moved by emotions generated when he was well into the skin of a part and he recalled that, when he was spending the day rehearsing *Macbeth* at the Old Vic, Laughton was incapable of doing justice to the Rev. Canon Chasuble, in Wilde's *The Importance of Being Earnest*. Even Laughton's vivid imagination could not make the transition from one character to the other when the re-creation of a third stage personality was occupying so much of his thought. Tree evolved his Fagin, his Svengali and the rest by emotional efforts akin to those of Charles Laughton. He, too, was an inspired amateur, which incidentally explains why Tree was so uneven an actor. A playgoer was lucky if he saw Tree at his best one time in three.

Imaginative Identification With a Rôle

There are stage stories innumerable illustrating the curious effects of imaginative identification with the supposed character. Lionel Brough used to tell how he played Squeers to the Nicholas Nickleby of Fred Leslie, Nellie Farren being the Smike of the play. Lionel Brough was aware from the first that he was in danger from a Nicholas who might be carried away by simulated passion in the school scene. He suggested Squeers' beating should be with a stuffed stick, but Fred Leslie pointed out that Dickens had written "cane" and the Gaiety audience would expect a cane. The rehearsals were rather painful but on the production night Leslie "saw red". He flew upon the unhappy Squeers, grinding his teeth and lashed the schoolmaster with might and main. Lionel Brough's cries were all too natural for he was writhing in agony. When he got back to his dressing-room and showed Leslie the weals, Fred was very distressed. He had not the least idea of his frenzy.

When Richard Bird played the Babe in Harry Wall's *Havoc*, he was a very young man. He was the second lieutenant of that West Front mess, consoling himself with picture-postcards of Phyllis Dare and Gladys Cooper, though conscious the while that the semblance was not quite as satisfying as a girl all one's very own. Youth did not explain Richard Bird's success, but imaginative identification with the part, which perhaps only extreme youth could achieve. The happy grin of boyhood was still at Richard Bird's command, not yet swamped by the sophistications of manhood.

Akin are the stories which illustrate the effects which the identification of player and character have upon audiences. Years ago, when Lewis Waller was playing d'Artagnan in *The Three Musketeers*, an excited priest in the stalls suddenly rose from his seat crying exultantly, "Got him!" Lewis Waller had pinked the last of his foes. Again, there was an elderly gentleman who had been listening entranced to *Caste*, as it was played by the Bancrofts. When the news came that Esther's husband was still alive, the old man started forward excitedly with the words, "Tell her quickly; oh, tell her quickly." And in the same play, John Hare, as Old Eccles, was filling his pipe. He searched one pocket after another in vain, and finally emptied a little tobacco dust from a waistcoat pocket. It is on record that on one occasion an elderly occupant of the gallery was so troubled that he threw his pouch on to the stage for Hare's benefit.

And the relation between imagined character and its players. What of that? At the Maudsley Hospital Mr Frederick Mott and Dr Golla once tested the physical reactions of a number of actresses by means of a psycho-galvanometer. The most "soulstirring" recitations did not influence the mirror of the galvanometer a hairsbreadth, whereas fear due to a crashing plate or other noise aroused all the expected galvanic responses—the tears, the quickened pulse and quickened breathing, the shudder of the spine, and the pallor or blushing of the cheeks. Mr Mott and Dr Golla drew the conclusion that the great actor by modulations of voice and variety of gesture arouses physical distur-

Somerset Maugham, from *The Jester* by Sir Gerald Kelly (*see page* 290).

David Garrick as Richard the Third, from the painting by Hogarth (*see page* 302

bances in audiences, but does not experience them himself.

Following the same line of thought, Dr Charles Myers, another student of psychology, reached the conclusion that players should not completely identify themselves with a character or situation, but maintain a middle position. They should feel the part but not lose sight of the fact that they are artists imposing certain ideas and emotions upon expectant audiences. Dame Edith Evans supported Professor Myers when she said, "in acting I, in a sense, forget myself, but it is almost a case of dual personality. There are two people all the time—the character created and the technical self, who is a spectator cool and unstirred, while the tears roll down one's cheeks, and one's hand gesticulates passionately, who is always on the watch and must never be permitted to be lost in the actual individual impersonated." Miss Evans likened the relationship of these two selves to a rider and his horse. The talent is comparable to the swiftness of the horse and his skill in jumping. But always the rider is on the alert, calm and collected, directing and controlling whenever necessary.

It by no means follows, however, that tears and even hysterical sobbing are necessarily evidence that the player has not had full control during scenes calling for the fullest emotional expression. The last act of Rostand's *L'Aiglon* was one of Sarah Bernhardt's most exhausting efforts. Alfred Sutro tells that Madame once invited him to her dressing-room at curtain-fall. To his amazement the actress came in sobbing. Motioning the dramatist to a seat, she said, "Now, let us talk business."

"But, Madame, let us wait."

"No, no", replied Sarah, between her sobs. "This is nothing, it is purely mechanical. I cannot stop and it will go on for some time."

And when the business talk ended, Madame was still weeping, though the sobs had subsided.

In the same connection Flora Robson has told us that, early in her career, she used frequently to continue weeping when she left the stage, if she had been playing a strongly emotional part. But, in time, she learnt to master her emotions, until she could weep or even enact madness on the stage and yet smile and joke directly she reached the wings.

P

Diderot's Paradox

From what has been said it will be plain that there are two main types of players, those who rely mainly upon intelligence and training and those whose approach is markedly emotional. Criticism has long debated the relative importance of the two factors. In particular, the actor's reliance upon intelligence as opposed to emotion was examined in detail by Diderot, and the French philosopher decided against emotion and over-sensibility. In his view the accomplished actor studies every gesture, vocal inflection and nuance of facial or bodily expression, so that, automatically, he can move audiences to tragic emotion or comic laughter. Only players of lesser talent rely upon emotion, said Diderot, and this is why their performances are usually so uneven. Illustrating his point of view, Diderot said that, in Paris, Garrick once put his head through the doorway of a drawing-room, and in the space of a few seconds, his face ran the gamut of emotions from wild joy to tragic suffering and back again.

Nevertheless, many actors and actresses do not subscribe to Diderot's "Paradox". Mounet-Sully was one, though he agreed that this entailed uneven performances. "To-night the god will not come," was his phrase.

Coquelin, on the contrary, agreed wholly with Diderot. As he said, "I am convinced that one can only be a great actor on condition of complete self-mastery and ability to express feelings which are not experienced." Or again, "Genius is displayed far better by a complete and enduring self-mastery than by intermittent flashes—sublime, if you will, but incoherent and incomprehensible. To my way of thinking, nothing is more likely to produce inspiration than good hard preparatory work, the fertilizing of the brain by meditation and constant rehearsing of the rôle."

It would seem that actors or actresses of the highest capacity may best be described as possessing a double consciousness. The one allows the emotions the fullest play; the other keeps a close check upon the details of craft. Only the player who is at once alive with passion and yet has a full mastery over the resources of his art is fully equipped. Whereas Diderot may have been right when he argued that extreme sensibility makes for middling actors, and middling sensibility makes the ruck of bad actors, he was wrong when he went on to say that "in the complete absence of sensibility is the possibility of a sublime actor." The actor Talma was nearer the truth in his view that sensibility is the very source of imagination and "to form a great actor the union of sensibility and intelligence is required."

The actor, Got, had a rather different belief. His view was that the actor feels his rôle, but the reasoning faculty is still alert, criticizing, changing and improving the rendering of the rôle. No doubt, the truth lies somewhere between the extremes propounded by Diderot's Paradox; emotion, if it is to have its full effect, must be controlled by the player's intelligence.

Of the two faculties, there can surely be no doubt that the more fundamental is the subconscious working of the mind, which may best be described as imaginative. Grace and beauty, a magnetic personality, a voice of considerable compass all help, but, as Laurette Taylor has said, the imagination builds the picture which the audience across the footlights accepts if success has been won. And the interesting thing is that this law applies to drama in all its forms, from the humble anecdote to the fully-fledged tragedy. Illusion only arises when the listener's imagination is aroused, so that the veiled situation can be pictured, and the imagined picture is due to the artistry of the narrator, be he dramatist or player.

Perhaps, there is no better witness on the problems suggested by the Diderot paradox than Fanny Kemble, an actress who could also put her thoughts into telling phrases. She wrote, "The curious part of acting to me is a sort of double process which the mind carries on at once, the combined operation of one's faculties, so to speak, in diametrically opposite directions; for instance, in that very last scene of *Mrs Beverley*, while I was half dead with crying, in the midst of the *real* grief created by an entirely *unreal* cause, I perceived that my tears were falling like rain all over my silk dress and spoiling it, and I calculated and measured most accurately the space that my father would require to fall in and moved myself and my train accordingly in the midst of the anguish I was to feign and absolutely did endure. In short, while the whole person appears merely to be following the mind in producing the effect and illusion upon the spectator, both the intellect and the senses are constantly engrossed in guarding against the smallest accident that might militate against it."

Beerbohm Tree's implicit reliance upon an active imagination would scarcely achieve what Fanny Kemble judged all-important, though, lacking imagination, there would be much less than complete absorption in the part.

The Character Actor

Mention has been made of comedies of character in connection with the art and craft of the dramatist. It will be remembered that they differed from comedies of situation, mainly because the writer was content with a theme allowing an infiltration of quaint fun and happy sentiment, if only his players had opportunities for amusing acting. Horace Annesley Vachell's *Quinney's* is typical and provided Cyril Maude with a first-rate opportunity for displaying his gifts. Quinney was a Yorkshireman by birth, and an antique dealer in Soho Square by trade. Vachell's main point was that Quinney too often allowed his pride in his profession to disturb his judgement as a father. Good-hearted fellow as he was, Quinney easily persuaded himself that his Chippendale chairs were the real thing, whereas every one else saw they were plainly fakes. On the contrary, when his daughter Posy fell in love with his foreman, Quinney was obsessed by the belief that the young man was, humanly speaking, "a fake" and not the real man whom Posy deserved. As a story-teller, it was Vachell's job to describe how the old antique dealer learnt wisdom and he was fully successful. It was Cyril Maude's job to bring Vachell's fancy to life on the Haymarket stage.

John Hare in *A Pair of Spectacles*, as has been said, and Willard and H. B. Irving in *The Professor's Love Story*, were set similar tasks by their authors and were equally successful. So was Horace Hodges, as Andrew Bullivant, in *Grumpy*. The third example is the more interesting because Horace Hodges was part-author of the play and knew precisely what episodes and business were required to bring Grumpy to life on the stage. Cyril Maude's Grumpy is mentioned later. Even when a play cannot properly be described as a comedy of character, it almost invariably includes character actors. Apart from Grumpy, Horace

Hodges, as that genial toper Lightnin' Bill Jones, and as the Doctor in *White Cargo*, showed himself an outstanding exponent of character acting. You recall the twitch of the kindly old doctor's cheeks when the incoming mail brought him no letter. Cedric Hardwicke as Churdles Ash, the sharp-tongued mysogynist in *The Farmer's Wife*, with his "women be wanted for the next generation; they ain't no manner of use to our own," was another masterpiece of character acting, comparable with the creations of Sir John Hare a generation earlier. Eden Phillpotts has a gift for writing comedies of character and his primary endowment is his rich knowledge of out-of-the-way types, which bear the impress of reality in spite of their quaintness. If a comedy of character is in the making, avoid an elaborate theme and overemotional incident. These may be virtues in another type of play but they will distract attention from the actor or actress who, by hypothesis, is being fed with opportunities. Similarly, an author is wise to avoid over-accentuating character in plays of sentiment or emotion. Success, in itself, would only mean that the character actor "ran away with" the play.

The elements of critical appraisal in the acting art may be divided into these rough categories, remembering that none is fully exclusive. The players whose names are attached are, of course, merely illustrations.

Integrity: Eleanora Duse.

Beauty: Ellen Terry and Johnston Forbes-Robertson.

Power: Salvini in *Othello* and Sarah Bernhardt in *Tosca*.

Craft-Skill (use of voice, gesture, etc.): Coquelin in Molière's *Tartuffe*; Dame Madge Kendal in almost any rôle; and Dame Edith Evans who could play both Millamant and the raddled Lady Wishfort.

Emotional Sensibility: Lena Ashwell, Meggie Albanesi and Jean Forbes-Robertson.

Imaginative insight: Henry Irving, Edith Evans or Charles Laughton in very varied parts.

Alertness in detecting acting opportunities: Noel Coward and Sacha Guitry in their own comedies.

The Trouper: Dame Marie Tempest, Dame Lilian Braithwaite, and a score of good supporting players—Sydney Valentine in times past or Felix Aylmer to-day.

CHAPTER II

PRODUCTION AND THE PRODUCER

THREE factors must be recognized if the theatre is to flourish in any given community. They are, firstly a psychological climate which will furnish the dramatist with material fitting for expression on the stage, and the term "fitting" implies a public willing to pay for its entertainment. The second factor is a sufficient supply of trained actors and actresses. The third is a management capable of assembling plays and players and putting them before the paying public. The keeping of expenditure within due limits alone calls for prescience which is far from common. Of the famous French manager, George Pitoëff, John Palmer said, "He has produced more plays for less money than any manager who has ever lived."

If a fourth factor must be added, it is the producer. On the modern stage, he is the unifier and is best regarded as a factor rather than an individual, for he may well be either a dramatist, a leading player or a theatrical manager.

The English tongue has no single word for the harmony which arises from a properly rehearsed play. What modern production implies can best be judged when what the Germans call the *inscenierung* is finally embodied in the Prompt Book, whence it may pass into the history of the stage. Photographs of the players, scenery, costumes and properties, notes of make-up, off-stage effects and lighting, all may figure in a modern prompt book, and in the majority of cases, the producer is finally responsible. It is the producer's task to conceive the *inscenierung*, and having done so to discover and instruct the human agents needed to put it on the stage by the first night. Some plays, especially those of Shakespeare, permit of a dozen *inscenierungs*. If it is *Hamlet*, the producer can regard it as as Elizabethan play given from an apron stage; again he may experiment with ample scenery in the Beerbohm Tree manner; or he may be content with no scenery at all and put the players into modern dress.

But the producer's task does not end with such decisions. When energy flags, he, like the actor-manager of old, is there to whip up interest. He rehearses the various surprises, suspenses and climaxes until the right *tempo* is achieved, and *tempo* applies not only to a particular scene but to the whole play. Of *tempo*, Henry Irving once said, "Every play has its rhythm; every scene has its rhythm; and every part should be played in that rhythm." Perhaps the producer's most important task is to engineer, maintain, suspend, heighten and resolve the various tensions suggested by the dramatist's script.

Apropos of the consummate construction of Sophocles' *Oedipus Rex*, John Martin-Harvey, in his *Autobiography*, has drawn attention to what he called "the strain curve". Speaking with the authority of one who had played Oedipus, he described the curve as a perfect and unbroken sweep up to the moment when the children were brought in. It then declined from an almost unbearable horror to the pathos of the close. If the dramatist has not defined the strain curve sufficiently, the producer must do so. In any case, no single player can be trusted with the task. It applies to the play as a whole, not a single part, though this may also have its strain curve.

Seventy-five years ago the problem of production was simpler. Fixed methods of expression were associated with certain dramatic situations and these methods were perpetuated the more readily because the types of plays were strictly limited. Because of the wider scope of modern drama and the larger audiences which must be interested, the calls upon the talents of a producer are infinitely more numerous than they were. So important does production seem nowadays that every actor of ambition seeks experience in play-producing, looking forward to a time when he will control his own theatre. It may be that the actor has a leading part in the play, but, equally, he may accept a fee from a business management, as Gerald du Maurier did frequently. He begins with a careful study of the text until its characterization is as clear as it can be, apart from the actors and actresses to whom the management has assigned the several parts. Intensive study of the background, historical and actual, follows. When the producer knows precisely the function of every part of the script, and only then, should rehearsals begin.

Often it will be the producer who reveals the value of individual lines to actor or actress, for he alone, apart from the author, knows the play as an organic whole, and therefore, the relative possibilities of its parts. Kitty Clive said of Garrick at rehearsals, "I have seen you with your magic hammer, endeavouring to beat your ideas into the heads of creatures who had none of their own." This may be regarded as extreme measures, but Dame Madge Kendal was a past-mistress in this department of stagecraft. Her gifts of mimicry were such that, during rehearsals, she would snatch a hat or stick from an actor's hand and come on to the stage playing a male rôle. But that was only the beginning. Players of limited experience had to be encouraged, or, in the alternative, shown their due place in the theatrical arena. In this connection Seymour Hicks used to tell an amusing story of Dame Madge Kendal's methods. He was a young man at the time and the rehearsals were taking place in New York, while the Kendal company were touring. Lunch-time came, and when the rest of the players were dismissed for a much-needed meal, Seymour was "kept in". Mrs Kendal intimated that she proposed to take him alone. A wiser youth would have been grateful for this special attention from a famous star, but Seymour was hungry.

"How can I act without an audience?" he grumbled.

"Go out and get a cup of coffee, Seymour, and be back in a quarter of an hour. Then we will resume."

A quarter of an hour later, Seymour was back on the empty stage, with Mrs Kendal facing him and a bare curtain, separating both from the auditorium.

"Now, Seymour, I understand you want an audience. Quite right. All good actors do. White (the stage manager), ring up the curtain!"

When the curtain rose, Seymour saw that the two front rows of stalls were filled with goggle-eyed urchins, whom Mrs Kendal addressed: "Now, children, you are Mr Hicks's audience, so give him three cheers. Take the cue from me. Hip, Hip, Hurrah!"

By this time Seymour's sense of humour was fully awake and Madge Kendal saw her lesson had been learnt.

"Now, White, lower the curtain and give the children twopence apiece, or whatever that means in American money; it is quite beyond me."

An actor or actress tends to worship a producer as human as the heroine of this story. Here is the salt of the stage and if ever this salt should lose its savour the theatre will be in a sorry plight.

The Chess-Board Method

Outstanding among the producers of our time was Harley Granville-Barker. Writing to *The Times* after his death, John Gielgud paid a high tribute to the man who gave us *Twelfth Night* and *The Winter's Tale* at the Savoy just before the first World War and *King Lear* at the Old Vic in the years between the two wars. Granville-Barker had been studying *Lear* for a life-time, and recognizing this, the Old Vic players placed their talents at his disposal whole-heartedly. John Gielgud, Fay Compton, Stephen Haggard, Cathleen Nesbitt, and Jessica Tandy admitted afterwards that every movement, and almost every intonation, was inspired by Barker's scholarly insight. In Gielgud's phrase, "the actors were spell-bound by his authority." With the book of the words in his hand, Barker occupied an arm-chair on the stage. Then, he would rise and demonstrate a speech. No stage costume, only a red-haired, blue-eyed man in a dark lounge suit, mingling dreamy asceticism with emotional intensity, and yet, in John Gielgud's words, "commanding the stage with a stillness that was chilling in its authority; his voice, still low, full of infinite variation, in spite of a limited range and rather metallic diction; his face alive with thought, emotion, passion; his body relaxed and his gestures few, but dynamic in their breadth and vigour."

Throughout the rehearsals for his own *The Madras House*, Barker, like Dame Madge Kendal, would show precisely what he wanted from an actor or actress, passing from youth to age and young spinster to elderly dame. Barker's methods were precise. The stage was marked into compartments, each a foot square, and the cast had to move this way and that, as though they were pieces on a chess board.

Lillah McCarthy said something of the same sort about Dion Boucicault, who produced so many plays for Charles Frohman, including *Peter Pan*.

"The cast became the pieces on a chessboard. You might be king or queen or bishop, but the moves you made were Dion's. He led each one about the stage, planting it on the proper square. Whilst the moves went on, Boucicault used to make us copy his intonation of the lines which he recited in an unattractive hammering voice. Boucicault knew what he wanted and reduced his cast to a state of automata."

Plainly, this method did not please Miss McCarthy. On the contrary a trouper like Marie Tempest reacted happily to the chess-board technique. "The man who moulded me into an actress", was Dame Marie's description of Dion Boucicault the younger. He was a little man and he relied upon irony for maintaining stage discipline. He never shouted and his patience was boundless. He would expend hours of rehearsal time upon ten minutes of stage action that correct "timing" might be achieved. Dame Marie has described how an actor took out a cigarette; two steps, the cigarette was tapped on the case; a few more words and the match was lit. A few more words and the match was blown out. Dion used the same method if it was the play of a fan, the drinking of a cup of coffee, or taking off a pair of gloves.

Henry Irving had a similar patience, though he was not so insistent upon minor details and in any case players found it easier to accept the minutiae of instruction from "The Chief" than from a lesser leader. At rehearsals Irving would stop any one, from Ellen Terry to a messenger with news of battle, rise and explain what he thought wrong. The line or bit of action would be repeated again and again until all was well. Edwin Booth described Irving as "the perfection of stage patience".

Basil Dean has perhaps had more varied experience as a producer than any man in Britain. Beginning at the Liverpool Repertory Theatre in 1911 he became assistant stage director to Beerbohm Tree at His Majesty's in 1913. Following upon his experiences during the first World War when he organized the plays given by the Navy and Army Canteen Board, he entered into the memorable partnership with Alec L. Rea, known as Reandean Ltd. Galsworthy's *The Skin Game*, Clemence Dane's *A Bill of Divorcement*, Maugham's *East of Suez*, Capek's *R.U.R.* (the Robot play) and Flecker's *Hassan* were a few of Basil Dean's productions in the years immediately succeeding the first World War.

Basil Dean's characteristic as a producer lies in his passion for accuracy in detail. Perhaps because of this absorption in what seems to Mr Dean thorough-going efficiency, his relations with his band of players during rehearsals have sometimes tended to be less than happy. Only a strong-minded actor or actress can contribute what he or she believes to be essential and yet conform to Basil Dean's sense of the pattern to be achieved. Very different was Nigel Playfair's approach to rehearsals during the years he controlled the Lyric, Hammersmith. His method was to ease the anxieties of rehearsals by a constant discharge of small jokes, a method which one of his victims described as production "with more elfishness than authority". I have forgotten who said this, possibly Mr Coward, but it shows that the happy mean between too much and too little discipline in the theatre is hard to come by. Perhaps that is why productions by actor-managers have been so fruitful. They, at any rate, know from personal experience how nerve-racking it is to accept the direction of emotions from any outsider. Moreover, there are many things a highly-gifted player can impart without offence. Of Noel Coward, as producer, Ivy St Helier has said that "he has complete mastery of the effects he is aiming at. He knows what every member of the company should do and can show them exactly how to do it."

Authors as Producers

The part which dramatists take in production varies, Somerset Maugham intervenes very little; only a whisper or two in the stage manager's ear, from time to time. On the contrary Pinero, with considerable experience as an actor, took Mrs Patrick Campbell in hand when *The Second Mrs Tanqueray* was in rehearsal and coached her in every phrase and gesture. Mrs Campbell was in doubt, even after the curtain fell, on that memorable first night. "Have I really made a success?" she asked Cyril Maude, as the two walked up and down the yard outside the stage door of the St James's. J. B. Priestley is an author who enjoys rehearsals and a sixteen-hour day is not unusual when one of his plays is being produced. He has acting ability enough to demonstrate the effects he requires from his company.

Because they were actors as well as playwrights, Noel Coward and Emlyn Williams, like Granville-Barker, developed an uncanny sense of what could be expected from any given cast and how to achieve it. Peter Ustinov has the same concatenation of talents. In *Cavalcade*, Noel Coward's training of his crowds went far towards constituting the play. During rehearsals, he sat in the dress circle and directed operations through loudspeakers placed at each side of the proscenium. Below in the stalls were the 200 supers, all experienced actors and actresses who had either retired from active stage life or were willing to accept relatively small salaries for a Drury Lane run. Each was wearing a numbered breast-plate with a differential colouring and so they were divided into groups, each under its own leader. Noel's method was to indicate their positions on the stage, tell them the atmosphere required and then leave each actor or actress to fill in the stage business as he or she judged right. They had the necessary experience. Trained assistants can be of great use in training a crowd. Louis Calvert took six weeks to rehearse the big crowd at His Majesty's when Tree played *Julius Caesar*. Yet he produced the equally difficult Convention Scene in the last act of Sardou's *Robespierre* in three days. The explanation was the trained assistants who came from His Majesty's to the Lyceum, to help with the Irving production.

In production, as in play-writing, it is all-important to make the underlying theme crystal clear, and, above all, not to establish one theme and then switch over to another, because the material provided by the author seems insufficient. This way lies distraction alike for players and audience. Though this is primarily the dramatist's responsibility, a producer can easily tumble the action of a play from the plane upon which one theme moves to that which really carries what the playwright meant to be of secondary interest. Indeed, the producer's treatment of a play may easily upset the balance against the audience, for a danger facing every production is the elaboration of effects which for a moment seem to excite but, in fact, put the imagination to sleep. Some critics thought that when Basil Dean produced Priestley's *Cornelius*, he paid so much attention to the details of office life that audiences were left in doubt as to what Priestley's play *really* was about.

The Rights of the Dramatist

Certain ultra-modern producers of the classics show a similar tendency to place personal whims above the obvious intentions of the dramatist. Komisarjevsky's production of *Macbeth* at Stratford-on-Avon in 1933 is a case in point. Komisarjevsky chose to see *Macbeth* as an echo of a state of affairs that must arise when any nation, ancient or modern, is facing the tensions of a revolution. In conformity with this idea the three witches were stripped of their supernatural quality and Lady Macbeth, lacking her heroic characteristics, was presented as merely breaking down under the strain of her murderous plot. As for Macbeth, he was a brave soldier, afflicted with nerves. A living dramatist could protest if a producer man-handled his work in such a fashion. The dead must suffer in silence. Perhaps the final word on the subject is that if a dramatist is likely to owe much to a sympathetic producer, emphasis must be laid upon the qualifying adjective, sympathetic.

Apropos of Komisarjevsky's production of *Macbeth*, it will always be a matter for debate how much a producer should alter a play in order to bring it into line with contemporary opinion or events. After all, it is always possible to commission a new play. On the other hand, certain changes may give fresh life to a masterpiece, and that suits dramatists, players and audiences. In a sense every change in cast entails some change in production, so the passage of time entails even more drastic alterations if the play is to make its due appeal. When Granville-Barker, dramatist, actor and producer, wrote the first volume of his *Prefaces to Shakespeare* in 1927, he made it plain that the change from the bare platform of Elizabethan times alone made any direct tradition of production valueless. Playing *Hamlet* under the stage conditions which rule to-day entirely changed the methods necessary to secure illusion. In particular, Granville-Barker considered the modern producer was free to experiment in securing that freedom from the limits of time and place which Shakespeare manifestly valued and Elizabethan audiences readily accepted. Michael Macowan, drama director of the Arts Council, set out the position of the modern producer facing *Macbeth*, let us say, when he said of the Elizabethan stage conventions: "The gruff mutterings of Banquo's murderers are still in our ears while we see Macbeth and Lady Macbeth welcoming the guests to the banquet with grace and good fellowship. Interpose a falling curtain, a black-out with music, and the effect is lost."

The Victorian and Edwardian usage was to alternate a full stage scene with a "front cloth", the front cloth scene being one which the actor-manager judged relatively unimportant, and which the audience similarly regarded as mattering little. The publication of *The Prefaces* has done much to put the problem in better perspective. There have been experiments in rearranging the text so that one permanent set covers the whole of a Shakespeare play, or even, as in Michael Benthall's *Taming of the Shrew* at Stratford in 1948, with no scenery at all. The properties, chairs, tables, a bed and the rest, were carried on and off by members of the Company of Strolling Players, who were supposed to be acting for the benefit of Christopher Sly.

A more daring experiment was putting Shakespeare plays into modern dress, the alleged justification being that the plays of a master-dramatist are "timeless". Some of these experiments were very moving. I can recall a *Troilus and Cressida* at the Westminster Theatre about the time of the second World War, which gained a new significance when Priam and his sons were played in khaki, but, too often, these crazy tricks seem no more than jesting over an interesting craft problem. Frankly, I do not want to watch Hamlet masquerading in the costume of the Prince Consort, or, for that matter, Molière's *Tartuffe*, with the characters presented as labelled puppets. Molière was not interested in puppetry, and good manners alone should make a producer of worth give some consideration to the feelings of his authors, dead or alive.

I was spoilt for such trifling when I had seen Coquelin in the part in Paris, years ago. For Tartuffe, Coquelin imagined "a great fish face" to which he added the "movements of a great snail putting out its head and drawing back into its shell". As the hypocrite, Coquelin moved as little as possible. When he was exposed and was about to be marched off to prison, Coquelin turned his back upon the audience and stood motionless with his head bent. Then he turned and moved off, allowing the audience just a glimpse of features convulsed with frustrated passion. The overpowering effect owed everything to the earlier stillness.

Nevertheless, circumstances governing the production of a classic may differ so markedly from accepted tradition that highly novel methods may not only be justified but essential. The performances of Shakespeare in the Open Air Theatre in Regent's Park, which Sydney Carroll inaugurated and Robert Atkins produced so effectively, are a case in point. Of *A Midsummer Night's Dream*, an unnamed writer in *The Times* once said that it is beset with moonlight, but not by the moonlight of the astronomer. Accepting the dictum, the primary task of a producer of *The Dream* is to distil the enchantment which arises from such a sorcerer's moon. Where could the mood be conjured up more happily than on the measureless stage of an open-air theatre, when evening was fading into night? Perfect presentations of *The Dream* were given at Regent's Park.

Passing on from the fairylike *Dream* to the magic of *The Tempest*, the writer in *The Times* recalled how wondrously Shakespeare's spell-bound island could be conjured up in the open air, using the space of not quite natural light which the limes picked out from the darkness:

"The background fades to black through a fantastic green unknown to daylight vegetation, and seems to cover with necromantic night the solution to the mysteries that hover behind the phosphorescent veils of the verse and the enigmatic movements of Ariel, Caliban, and their master—the mystery of the warring of the flesh against the spirit, of the relation of the maker to things made, of the beatific vision of the artist and the penitential price he pays."

Single Set Scenery

Plays of ideas, comedies of character and situation, melodramatic thrillers and romances all present their special problems to a producer, with his attention fixed upon his main jobs, the unfolding of the dramatist's invention and providing the fullest opportunities for players. The time element alone may necessitate considerable invention in scenery if valuable minutes are not to be wasted. Following a method exploited by the Motleys in the scenery used in *Richard of Bordeaux*, Harald

Melvill designed fifteen scenes for John Clements' production of *The Kingmaker* and yet was content to work upon a single basic framework. All the scenes looked different from the auditorium, yet any change could be achieved within two minutes. Ingenuity of this order is an asset of importance in any theatre. In *The Kingmaker* scenery Mr Melvill produced the appearance of stained glass windows by dyeing linen panels which were lit from the back; added lines of black distemper sufficed to suggest the leading. Nigel Playfair's production of *The Beggar's Opera*, with scenery and dresses by Lovat Fraser, affords a similar example. The designer furnished a brilliant series of designs, which were judged acceptable until a fortnight before curtain-rise. Then Nigel Playfair saw they were too elaborate and needed a much larger stage staff than was to hand.

"Lovat," he said, "the whole damn thing has got to be done somehow in one scene and you've got to produce that scene by to-morrow morning."

Lovat's face went white and his voice husky, but he said, "All right," and by morning had produced a basic design which brought little less than a revolution in production methods. Lovat Fraser's scale model can be seen at the Victoria and Albert Museum. The chandelier was an addition made by Gordon Craig.

The single set scenery which John Gielgud, Paul Sheriff and Rodney Ackland devised for the production of Dostoievsky's *Crime and Punishment* was full of interest. Producer, scene-painter and author were faced with a plot which ranged over numerous places and involved many characters. Instead of solving the problem by numerous quick changes of scene, they decided upon a single set. Accordingly, Rodney Ackland concentrated all the action his "fable" involved upon a single locale. Essentially, this locale might be described as a boarding-house where the murderer Raskolnikoff might have lived and where the Marmeladoff family could meet the blows of their miserable fate. But a good deal more was involved and even more was suggested. At the top of the proscenium arch a stretch of cloudy sky was to be seen, and, just below, the rounded and angled roofs of a great city. The locale suggested an integral part of the monstrous St Petersburg where Dostoievsky chose that his tragi-comedy should be enacted.

Tamara Geva and Raymond Massey in Robert Sherwood's *Idiot's Delight* at His Majesty's Theatre (1938) (*see page* 88).

Anton Walbrook,
Diana Wynyard,
and
Rex Harrison
in Noel Coward's
Design for Living
at the Haymarket
Theatre (1939)
(*see page* 276).

The tumbled domes and roofs of the dark cruel city seemed, in some curious way, to echo the squalid hall-way below in which the Marmeladoffs had piled their few remaining family possessions. On the left was Raskolnikoff's bed-sitting room, and on the right an iron stairway leading to an upper storey, as well as an outlet to the street and the porter's store-room, all-important, for here the murderer was to find the axe.

But the set was required to do more than provide a plausible home for the murderer and the Marmeladoffs. Here the police magistrate Porfiri Petrovitch had to torture the unhappy murderer into repentance and confession and Sonia had to practise her healing arts upon the miserable man. Above all, dramatist, producer and scenic designer had to bring on the varied folk who made up the people of St Petersburg—a retired official, a clerk, a socialist student and the like, whom Dostoievsky's crowded canvas demanded if it was to reveal its mingled horrors of madness and death.

The London production at the New Theatre in 1946 was far from perfect, but a just critic must remember the difficulties of timing, so that the colourful movements on a crowded stage did not clash with the displays of individual emotion in the murderer's bedroom or some other individual happening upon the composite set.

John Gielgud faced a similar problem when he produced the three bed-sitting rooms with their connecting stairway, in which the tragi-comedy of Lucy Amerest, May Beringer and Agatha Payne was worked out in the stage version of Hugh Walpole's *The Old Ladies*. The scenic problem was solved by taking out the fourth wall of hall, stairway and the three bed-sitting rooms, as may be done in a doll's house. As house architecture, the device involved absurdities, but for stage purposes the set proved a notable invention. The three Motleys were finally responsible for this most ingenious setting.

The Problem of Revivals

In connection with theatrical revivals—and may they ever be numerous—a nice question arises. How long after production

Q

does a comedy of manners become a period piece? Is recognition as a "period piece" and its stage equivalent, "period production" a necessary stage in the history of any comedy of manners? Was there, for example, a time when producers were in doubt whether *The School for Scandal* should be played with the dresses and scenery of Sheridan's time, or, let us say, without wigs and with the males displaying the strapped trousers of early Victorian fashion? This may be regarded as the equivalent of Allen Aynsworth's production of *The Importance of Being Earnest* when he revived Wilde's farce at the Haymarket in 1923, whereas, when Nigel Playfair revived the play at the Lyric, Hammersmith, in 1930, there was a touch of Aubrey Beardsley in the setting, presumably because Beardsley and Wilde were contemporaries.

To-day, it is an accepted stage tradition that Wilde's "trivial comedy" is a period piece, but is the same thing to be said of Mayfair drama in general? Are all the masterpieces of the 'nineties to survive only as period pieces, to be offered to an amused public with a slight smirk? Lamb's essay *On the Artificial Comedy of the Last Century* is concerned with this very problem. Lamb debates the distinction between a comedy which players and playgoers accept as real, and one in which the characters suffer no translation into real life. When the drawing-room melodrama of Haddon Chambers, Wilde and Pinero flourished, actors and actresses played them for what they were worth as stories. I do not mean the critics of the 'nineties failed to detect excesses of coincidence, but the fun arose from the acceptance of each plot as a human problem. There was no room for guying. Indeed, in the case of Oscar Wilde, the author places quite enough obstacles in the way of his characters being accepted as human beings, without producers adding to the burden of proof.

For these reasons it seems worth while asking whether recent revivals of Mayfair drama have not suffered under a tinge of satire which may be proper in an accepted "period piece" but which, surely, destroys the illusion underlying melodrama, whether this be the Adelphi brand, or that in which Wilde, Pinero and Haddon Chambers specialized in what may be described as Edwardian times.

Let me recall one of those evenings of long ago when Lewis Waller, a newcomer to management, produced *An Ideal Husband*.

It was the third of Wilde's drawing-room melodramas and followed upon *Lady Windermere's Fan* and *A Woman of No Importance*, both of which had enjoyed lucrative runs. *Lady Windermere* had been played 158 times, and *A Woman of No Importance* 113 times, considerable runs in the 'nineties.

On paper, the cast of *An Ideal Husband* seemed much stronger than, in fact, it was. There were Charles Hawtrey, Julia Neilson, Lewis Waller, Charles Brookfield, Fanny Brough, and Maud Millett, not to mention Waller's wife, Florence West, as the naughty Mrs Cheveley. Lewis Waller and Florence West were the weaknesses. Waller was seldom at his best in modern costume, and Florence West lacked the charm, dignity and authority which Marion Terry had displayed in so high a degree in Wilde's earlier plays. Looking back half a century, what comes to mind is, first and foremost, the theatrical craft displayed by Charles Hawtrey as Lord Goring. He had to be a Victorian Horatio to the Hamlet of the unhappy Robert Chiltern. He had also to hold a ricketty plot together and yet fire off such epigrams as "Vulgarity is simply the conduct of other people" or "The only possible society is oneself." The task was not easy.

However, there was the apple-blossom charm of Maude Millett, as delightful as ever she had been, though in no way resembling the Tanagra statuette of Wilde's stage directions, and Fanny Brough did all that was possible with Lady Markby, the part which Irene Vanbrugh played in a very different fashion in Robert Donat's revival at the Westminster Theatre in the middle 'forties. The loveliness of Julia Neilson, however, failed to bring Lady Chiltern to life, and as regards the adventuress rôle, Martita Hunt's Mrs Cheveley, in the Donat revival, clearly showed the earlier shortcomings of Miss West. Indeed, the scene with Roland Culver at the Westminster, in which Mrs Cheveley exchanged the letter which incriminated Robert Chiltern for that which threatened the happiness of Lady Chiltern, when played in the true spirit of Mayfair melodrama, proved fully acceptable.

Perhaps the weaknesses in the plot of *An Ideal Husband* justified the prominence Robert Donat accorded to Rex Whistler's stage settings. I am less kindly disposed towards Cecil Beaton's rococo *décor* at the Haymarket, in the Gielgud revival of *Lady Winder-*

mere's Fan in 1945. A Cecil Beaton *décor* can be amusing, but surely the play is the primary thing; and, moreover, playgoers with the requisite knowledge are entitled to compare their memories of Marion Terry, George Alexander, Winifred Emery, and Nutcombe Gould with the efforts of Isabel Jeans, pretty Dorothy Hyson, and the rest. What happened was that the morning-room setting devised by Cecil Beaton ran away with the show. One resented a green "lime" playing upon the collars of the flunkies in the ball-room scene, for all the world as if Mr Cochran's fancy had been at work upon an interlude for a Pavilion revue.

This note of subdued satire was noticeable in several revivals of Victorian and Edwardian musical comedies in the 'thirties and 'forties, and, if I am right, it robbed them of much of their glamour and all their distinctive style. *The Merry Widow* is not to be played in the manner of *Oklahoma!* or *Annie Get Your Gun*. It belongs to a more leisurely age.

If *Lady Windermere*, why not a revival of *A Woman of No Importance*? In that case, it will suffice if the terrace at Hunstanton has the quiet charm of an English country-house and the drawing-room and picture-gallery are of the period. What will matter much more than a *décor* with advertising value will be a company of players, convinced of the integrity of the play as acting material, a very different thing, by the way, from the integrity of an author as a student of life. Given such players as Beerbohm Tree, Fred Terry, Rose Leclercq, Julia Neilson, and Marion Terry, as she was when she took over Mrs Bernard Beere's rôle when *A Woman of No Importance* was revived at His Majesty's, Wilde's play will prove still to be good "theatre". When Tree first gave the play at the Haymarket it was hailed as the best written, best produced, and best acted Mayfair drama of its year, and believe me, Victorian audiences were fully equipped critics, though the pose of the present generation is to doubt the fact. Fewer Londoners understood the theatre half a century ago because there were fewer playgoers, but the instructed were well aware when an actor or actress was thrusting a character across the footlights.

The Importance of Being Earnest presents a somewhat different problem to a producer. Here we are concerned with farce, but assuredly not with a story which admits of "guying". When Edith Evans took over the part of Lady Bracknell, she showed precisely what was called for when a masterpiece of the 'nineties is revived. She added to stage history by creating a character comparable with Millamant, Magda, or any other of the classic rôles which test the full capacity of a player. Edith Evans made it certain that, in times to come, every comedienne of note will have a hankering to pit her skill against the memory of what Edith Evans achieved. A comedienne henceforward will wish to play Lady Bracknell as an actor of worth cannot but be wishful to play say, Justice Shallow. Recall: "You may kiss me, Cecily." And, when the matter of passionate celibacy was introduced, Miss Evans's devastating: "That is not the destiny I propose for Gwendoline. Algernon, of course, can choose for himself."

George Alexander played John Worthing with a gravity which was far removed from the modern method. A similar gravity marked the love-making of Irene Vanbrugh. And the reason for the gravity was that serious people do not want the triviality of Wilde's play emphasized. The fun underlying Gwendoline's contest with Cecily in the garden at Woolton depends upon the reality, not the unreality, of the conflict, and this in turn makes Cecily's retort momentarily crushing.

Gwendoline: Quite a well-kept garden this is, Miss Cardew.
Cecily: So glad you like it, Miss Fairfax.
Gwendoline: I had no idea there were any flowers in the country.
Cecily: Oh, flowers are as common here, Miss Fairfax, as people are in London.

Judging by the dearth of well-constructed plays in the post-war years, we seem ready for Pinero revivals. The Arts Theatre has shown that *The Thunderbolt* remains excellent "theatre" by virtue of its carefully planned plot and the opportunities vouchsafed to players. *The Benefit of the Doubt*, as it was played by Winifred Emery, too, promises any hard-working actress a chance. So do *Letty*, *The Notorious Mrs Ebbsmith*, and *Iris*, but not if they are produced as "period pieces" by managements which, in the final analysis, distrust their company of players and look to *décor* by a well-advertised scenic artist to fill any gap.

When Gladys Cooper revived *Mrs Tanqueray* at the Playhouse, she did not efface memories of Mrs Patrick Campbell's Paula. On the contrary, she made the memories of past triumphs glow once more. The capricious mischief which Mrs Campbell found in Paula, and which enabled her to add those welcome touches of comedy to the part, largely escaped Miss Cooper, as they escaped Eleanora Duse. Nevertheless, Gladys Cooper's Paula was not only memorable, but unforgettable. It had beauty, and it had power, because it displayed the tragedy of a woman battling for all that seemed to make life bearable. Pinero may not have been a profound social psychologist; he was not; but he knew how to write a moving story in terms of stagecraft, and present a character which an actress of talent could bring to life.

The players for successful revivals can be found, if only they are made to understand that their task is to present men and women "capable in law", to use Lamb's phrase, "of sustaining an injury"—"persons towards whom duties are to be acknowledged". If Wilde, Pinero, Haddon Chambers, and Henry Arthur Jones, in truth, offered the stage nothing but the unbelievable, then revivifying the 'nineties is a vain hope, and rococo stage settings can be left to those who enjoy backgrounds better than the authentic art of acting.

CHAPTER 12

SPECTACLE IN THE THEATRE
DRESS, SCENERY, AND LIGHTING

Wᴇ have treated production from the standpoint of the
producer as the interpreter of the dramatist's script,
and the energizer of the company of players. We have
given him final responsibility for what will pass into the prompt
book and serve as the basis for revivals and the raw material of
stage history. But there is another aspect of production, and it
has special importance in days when the larger theatres are in
active competition with Hollywood. Not a few theatres stage
costly musical shows and the producer is engaged because he is
expert in the elaboration and staging of spectacles.

A simple example of the value of expert direction is the "Tell
me, pretty maiden" number in the musical comedy *Florodora*,
which dates from the turn of the century. The author and composer saw it as a duet, but Sidney Ellison put six chorus men into
grey frock coats and gave them the job of making love to six
pretty maidens. The result was a hit number which largely
accounted for a run of 455 performances.

The intervention of Oscar Asche as the producer of *The Maid
of the Mountains* is another example. When George Edwardes
died in 1915, Daly's Theatre was in a sad plight. Determined to
pay twenty shillings in the pound to the creditors of the Edwardes
estate, Robert Evett decided to risk an all-British production.
Freddie Lonsdale's script dated back to 1905 in its original form,
and had been the round of all the managers, but Evett had a
brain-wave in his choice of a producer. Instead of a prosaic beach
scene, Oscar Asche made the first scene a magnificent mountain
lair, with a cave for the robbers. Add Harold Fraser-Simson's
music and the interpolated songs of James W. Tate, and the success of the venture was assured.

The value attaching to charming production in light musical

shows was first recognized by Madame Vestris and Planché, and the psychological factor which justified their reforms was based upon easily recognizable principles. An analogy comes to mind. The sordid intrigues of Restoration comedy were contrasted with the exquisite in manners and the delightful in rococo costumes and furniture, and this very contrast added point to plot and edge to dialogue. Similarly, in vaudeville, touches of beauty and grace tend to enhance absurdities and even knockabout humour. Prior to James Robinson Planché and the Vestris, grotesqueries and exaggerated parody were regarded as *desiderata* in musical burlesque, but when Planché planned *Olympic Revels* and *Riquet With the Tuft* he decided that ridiculous dresses and make-up weakened the effect of his nonsense, and that pleasant scenery, pretty dresses, pretty faces, and pretty music promised a sounder background to the harsher elements in burlesque.

Gilbert produced his own comic operas with this principle ever in mind. In *Trial by Jury*, a comic wig and a red nose would certainly have labelled his judge as the funny man of the piece, but Gilbert considered that a competent actor could be trusted to put across funny lines, so he left the judge's costume to follow the custom established by the Inns of Court. Experiment proved Gilbert to be dead right. I have never been able to accept the new dresses which Charles Ricketts and others devised for recent revivals of the Savoy operas. There was more magnificence but, to my mind, the costumes which Gilbert himself approved fitted the film better. Happily, Dame Carruthers, singing "The screw may twist, and the rack may turn," was not affected; nor were the Tower Warders. Nanki-Poo, the Three Little Maids, and the Mikado himself suffered.

Following W. S. Gilbert, George Edwardes, who had his early training in management at the Savoy Theatre, based musical comedy upon the self-same device. Probably the charm of Kate Vaughan was a factor in persuading Edwardes to pass from the grotesqueries of burlesque to musical comedy. The underlying difference was young men with pleasant manners, features and figures making love to pretty girls, as opposed to guying the heroes and heroines of history or romance. Charm and sentiment replaced the grotesqueries. If she had had the necessary physique, Kate Vaughan might have been a classical dancer of the Taglioni or Carlotta Grisi type, but she could not stand the training needed for point-dancing. Consequently, when Kate Vaughan found herself in burlesque, she devised a new dancing delight, partly waltz, partly minuet, but wholly lovely. In company with Teddy Royce and fluttering the familiar lace handkerchief, here

Dame Carruthers, The Yeomen of the Guard

was grace incarnate. Thus George Edwardes was persuaded that boisterous fun and buxom chorus girls were by no means all that Gaiety audiences could appreciate. His decision was that the sentimentalities and minor incongruities of contemporary life might well bear exploration, even if this meant abandoning chorus girls in tights, and the rough and tumble antics of his lower comedians.

Hassard Short, Spectacle-Maker

To-day, the demand for bright and varied backgrounds and a considerable element of spectacle have brought about further changes in musical productions. In the larger theatres, spectacle is much more important than the clowning of low comedians or the sentimentalities which constituted old-time musical comedies. The popularity of ballet dancing and the high-speed changes of background popularized by the "talkies" were factors in bringing about the changes. Recall Hassard Short's revue *Stop Press*, staged at the Adelphi Theatre some years ago. What remains in memory is not this comic turn or that sentimental ditty, but "The Mirrors" scene in which hundreds of dancing couples seemed to fill the Adelphi stage, thanks to clever lighting devices combined with some out-size looking-glasses.

Another brilliant effort in *Stop Press* was a reconstruction of an Easter-time parade in Hyde Park in the year 1879, which was linked up with a song sung by Dorothy Dickson. Doris Zinkeisen reconstructed the costumes of 1879 and presented them in varying shades of brown so that the final impression was a sepia drawing, including the entire company and occupying the full stage.

The emphasis upon spectacle has given the chorus a new importance. Greater skill and more intensive training are called for and the earnings of chorus boys and girls have increased proportionately. It was about 1927 that the revolution in the ensemble work of the chorus began in America. Albertina Rasch, who trained some famous troupes, gave the lead. Steps which had hitherto been associated with classical ballet were introduced into musical comedy and revue. The Totem Dance in *Rose Marie* and the Ballet in the first act of *Oklahoma!* are typical. The elaborate chorus effects which accompanied Sonnie Hale's "Dance Little Lady" in Noel Coward's *This Year of Grace*; and Helen Burnell's song "My Heart is Saying" in Jack Hulbert's *The House that Jack Built* showed that London was ready to follow Broadway's example.

When *Wild Violets* was given at Drury Lane in 1932, a party of Albertina Rasch girls opened the show. The background was a Swiss Alpine scene, and in the foreground were shapely youths and maidens in the equivalent of bathing costumes, apparently indulging in gymnastics, but really dancing to the tuneful music of Robert Stolz.

But the real triumph belonged to Hassard Short, who wrote a goodly part of the English book, devised the scenic and lighting effects and staged the entire production. Aided by a revolving stage, Hassard Short was able to pass easily through time, so that sixteen scenes were staged, in which our parents in 1900 mingled readily with the patrons of the "Stone Jug" in 1932. Only a Hollywood "talkie" could have rivalled the ever-changing spectacle and Hassard Short's skill showed itself in the fact that he met the "flicks" on their own ground and was not worsted. There was a skating rink scene, a ballet in the dormitory of a girls' school, with the Rasch dancers singing the "Dashing, flashing nineteen hundred girls"—all the familiar ingredients of Hollywood. Add a well-balanced company with Charlotte Greenwood as laughter-maker, and it was not surprising that with *Wild Violets* Old Drury signalled "a success". Charlotte Greenwood was blessed with an unforgettable presence. The long limbs and angular shoulders and hips alone impressed themselves upon the memory, apart from the American vim and assurance.

Ball at the Savoy, also given at Drury Lane, was a similar chorus piece, but with a highly sophisticated plot, in place of the pleasant sentimentalities of *Wild Violets*. It was the old story of the wife who flirts because the husband has flirted, and accepts "tit for tat" as the rule governing matrimony. The climax was the wife's public confession of her lapse during the ball at the Savoy. When the curtain went up the Marquis and the Marquise were in a gondola in Venice and the moon was rising. All too quickly, the Marquis arranges to meet an earlier "flame" at a masked ball, and, aware of the assignation, the Marquise follows. But the story was also concerned with a certain Mustapha Bey, a portly humorist (played by Oskar Denes), replete with as many wives as his predecessor, the Rajah of Bhong. With Mustapha was an impudent little baggage, Kathi by name, sufficiently characterized by her announcement, "He's a Turk, but I'll cure him of that," together with their combined number, the hilarious "Oh why, oh why, oh why?" Nevertheless, what really mattered in *Ball at the Savoy* was not the story, or even Paul Abraham's music, but the medley of dance and dress and limbs, so successfully ex-

ploited by a highly trained chorus. On one occasion, the girls of
the chorus rode pick-a-back on their men-folk, on another they
were whirled around the shoulders of their partners. It was "Up,
the Chorus" from curtain-rise to curtain-fall when *Ball at the
Savoy* was staged, and, in this case, the all-important factor was the
author-producer Oscar Hammerstein who gave the chorus their
setting and their opportunity.

Another characteristic Oscar Hammerstein production at
Drury Lane was *Three Sisters*. The sisters are the daughters of a
travelling photographer and the eldest, Tiny, mothers the other
two while saving hard that she may marry Police Constable
Titherley, a stalwart baritone. As Tiny, Miss Greenwood was to
lose a lot of money over a big race, so we were shown Epsom
Downs on Derby Day, 1914. Later, came Tiny's wedding day,
with the whole village *en fête*, while a happy end was reached in
Boulter's Lock, on August Bank Holiday, 1922. For the *Three
Sisters* Jerome Kern provided the music, Gladys Calthrop the
décor, and Ralph Reader stage-managed the all-important racing
scene.

Ivor Novello at Drury Lane

The series of Drury Lane record-breakers from America was
broken by Ivor Novello, who produced a series which, if it did not
eclipse the American "musicals" as spectacles, nevertheless
added something which was new enough to be very welcome.
What Ivor Novello aimed at was what Noel Coward had sought
in *Bitter Sweet*, that is to do away with "committee" authorship
and revert to the individual responsibility which had proved so
fruitful when Gilbert worked with Arthur Sullivan. Indeed, Noel
Coward and Ivor Novello in a sense eclipsed the great Gilbert,
inasmuch as they not only wrote their own *libretti* but their own
music. It may even be said that Ivor eclipsed Noel in these Drury
Lane ventures, as he added a personal appearance as singing
hero to his functions as author, composer, and producer.

A beginning was made in 1935 with the all-British *Glamorous
Night*. It had a Ruritanian background, "Glamorous Night" be-
ing the title of an opera, in which Mary Ellis was to appear at the
Opera House, Krasnia, the while she was engaged in a desperate

political adventure, in which Ivor Novello, as an Englishman, quickly became involved. Thanks to Ivor Novello's effort, acting, singing and story-telling were once more given their due place at Drury Lane, though charming scenery was not wanting. The production of the opera "Glamorous Night" was one of them, the skating ballet aboard a liner another; the gipsy wedding was a third, and the nobility of Krasnia doing homage to the Englishman who saved the King's life a fourth, but this time the spectacle and the chorus work did not monopolise interest.

Committee Authorship at the Turn of the Century

Careless Rapture, which followed a year later, was less of a romance and rather more of a comic opera than *Glamorous Night*. The heroine was a musical comedy star, engaged to a middle-aged politician and easily persuaded to indulge in a flirtation with an unknown admirer, Michael, who turned out to be her fiancé's half brother. As Dorothy Dickson was the star and Ivor Novello Michael, and Dorothy was making her final appearance in *The Rose Girl* when she met her new lover, the musical comedy element was plain. Very lovely was the Rose Ballet which formed part of the play, with the ladies of the chorus in dazzling white, indeed as lovely as any stage picture in the long history of Drury Lane.

The musical comedy convention generally demands a second act overseas, so Ivor Novello took us to Fie Chin, in China, where

Dorothy Dickson and Walter Crisham danced *The Manchuko* in appropriate surroundings. An Eastern earthquake, which enabled Dorothy and Ivor to take refuge in an Eastern temple and fall asleep at the foot of the great idol, helped the story to its close, which took the form of yet another all-white scena, "The Bridge of Lovers", in which Michael and Penny became man and wife. Drury Lane audiences recorded their delight by denying the management its customary Christmas pantomime. As the West End "libraries" alone subscribed £100,000 for tickets to *Careless Rapture*, the money argument was unanswerable.

Scale of importance in the production of a modern revue

With *Crest of the Wave* Ivor Novello broke a Drury Lane record by producing a third consecutive success of Gargantuan proportions. That one man should invent, compose, produce and act a leading part in three outsize musical shows was an achievement indeed, and it was astonishing that *Crest of the Wave* did not suggest some falling-off in the author-composer's sense of popular melody, pageantry and romance.

Passing reference has been made to the necessity for experienced management, so that capital and running expenditure may be kept within due bounds. Of Pitoëff, the French manager and producer, it was said that he could suggest a bell-tent in Africa by looping up two thin pieces of silver ribbon against a dark background. Scores of examples could be gathered illustrating the fact that it by no means follows that the greater the expenditure, the greater the effect. The reverse is nearer the truth. No one in the far-away 'nineties spent more generously than Augustus Harris at Drury Lane, but there were candid critics. George Conquest, who produced melodramas at the Surrey Theatre, south of the Thames, was one of them. He said, "Gus Harris buys a steam engine, but I look round for a few tables and paint the tops like wheels."

This matter of capital and current expense has special import-ance in connection with spectacular musicals, designed to com-pete with the spectacular films of Anglo-American commerce. £15,000, £20,000 and more may easily be spent upon a large-scale show. So the service of a producer with a keen sense of value for money may easily make all the difference between a box-office success and a disastrous failure. Moreover, such plays as *Show Boat*, *Rose Marie* or *White Horse Inn* present difficulties which make special calls upon inventive and authoritative pro-ducers. Rarely is a London theatre available for rehearsals. More often one section of the "show" (say the stars) rehearses dialogue in one place and dance numbers and songs perhaps half a mile away, where music and ampler stage space are available. Mean-while, in such a place as the Helvetia Club, rows of chorus girls, in practice-dress, are beating out laboriously the rhythms of elaborate dance numbers. In these early stages only the pro-ducer has any real idea of the effects which are being aimed at and how they are to be interwoven. If final unification is to be secured, he must not only be heard directly a play has been chosen for production, but, daily and hourly, until the first night is safely over.

Indeed, during the process of incubation the final unity does not even exist in the imagination of the authors and composers, that is unless they chance to be a W. S. Gilbert and an Arthur Sullivan. While the average comic opera or musical comedy is in process of production, authors and composers are continually darting off and dashing back with some emendation, which, of course, calls for fresh rehearsal.

High Speed Productions

When Albert de Courville began to produce his spectacular revues at the Hippodrome, an outsize theatre, he worked upon the principle that speed and incessant change were primary essentials. What the producer was always working towards was a spectacular speciality number in which the leading lady or comedian had a place, though what really mattered were the show-girls and chorus who had to plug the signature tune into international popularity. The de Courville methods were followed by George Black at the Palladium, and for similar reasons. Only speed can disguise the inanities of entertainments devised for popular audiences in out-size theatres, and speed alone provides the theatrical time needed for the all-important spectacles. In the search for speed, nothing in an author's script is sacrosanct. All that a producer regards as "dead matter" is cut ruthlessly. It is hard to tell what may have been sacrificed, but things of entertainment value arise and the box-office profits accordingly.

As I write, *Oklahoma!* and *Annie Get Your Gun* have re-established American musicals in a leading place on the London stage, though Ivor Novello productions, and Charles Cochran's *Bless the Bride* by A. P. Herbert and Vivian Ellis show that British productions have not lost their appeal. *Oklahoma!*, regarded as the successor of *Rose Marie* and *Show Boat*, registered its amazing success at Drury Lane in 1947, 1948 and 1949, thanks to exceptional professional competency under the guidance of Reuben Mamoulian, the Hollywood producer. The story was no more than adequate, the music was pleasant and catchy but in no sense outstanding. One of the principals hit off the technical qualities of the play, as it left author, lyricist, and composer, very deftly in her description of her own virtues:

> "I may not be better than other folk are,
> But I am damned if I'm not as good."

On the contrary the singing, dancing, and acting were tip-top, abrim with zest and vim. Aggie Pigtails, with her grasshopper leaps, was an example, and seldom or never has an English chorus acted as that in *Oklahoma!* acted. It may be because the American Equity minimum for a member of a chorus is the equivalent of fifteen pounds a week, compared with the five pounds a week demanded by British Equity. Be this as it may, what is certain is that in *Oklahoma!* team-work triumphed and the consequence was a tonic quality which assured between two and three thousand playgoers at Drury Lane nightly that they were getting value for money, a rare experience when stalls and dress-circle are on the sixteen shilling basis. When the team-work is as good as it was in *Oklahoma!* audiences do not clamour for "stars". Zest in song and dance suffices.

It was also to the credit of *Oklahoma!* that the curtain rose and fell upon a note of optimism, very acceptable in times when every news-sheet was shrieking "Crisis". At the end the cast and chorus were not content to accept the customary plaudits of a delighted house. Instead, after curtain-fall, the players repeated the smash-hit numbers, and with this final gesture the theatre emptied!

> "Oh, what a beautiful mornin',
> Oh, what a beautiful day."

As for its Broadway run, *Oklahoma!* registered 2,202 performances, was seen by 4,500,000 people, and gave the Theatre Guild, its producers, a return of 2,500 per cent upon an original investment of 80,000 dollars. Some success!

Lighting Devices

By the way, some of the working models used by producers and scenic designers are highly ingenious. Michael Northern designed such a one for the Coliseum. It had an acting area of 3 feet 10 inches by 2 feet $3\frac{1}{2}$ inches, as compared with the 92 feet by 35 feet of the Coliseum stage. Controlled by a console, the curtain can be lifted to disclose, say, a scene in the Balkans, the trees, the nearer rocks, the distant mountains and the rest being lifted into view by stage lifts comparable with those actually in the theatre. Flood lamps in the wings can produce the illusion of morning, afternoon or evening light, enabling all sorts of effects to be tried out before rehearsals even begin. The saving of time, money and patience is considerable.

Electronic Console Control and the Delicolor Unit are other

R

developments in stage lighting which should quickly establish themselves in up-to-date theatres. Jack Hulbert was early in the field when he utilised the Delicolor Unit in the revue *Here Come the Boys*. By merely turning a switch this way or that the stage electrician could control the stage lighting, as a conductor does the various instruments of an orchestra. In rehearsal alone, hours of experimentation are saved. No longer will there be any necessity to swarm up ladders to adjust the amber or the green switch. The delicolor knob makes a hundred colours available and this by working upon the three fundamental colours—blue, red and green, with white added as a balance.

An up-to-date lighting system, such as that in the London Hippodrome is installed in the roof. Thus the smallest possible shadow is cast on the stage. In time, maybe, scenery will consist of a permanent white back-cloth and a series of lantern slides, each throwing a new image. The ideas of a dramatist, a player, or a stage designer may be changed or amplified by the lighting devices at the disposal of a modern producer. A Russian designer, Madame Boutkovsky, who worked in Paris, has been markedly successful. By varying her lights she conjured up entirely different scenes on a single backcloth. By switching on a new set of lights she could convert a garden scene into a drawing-room, or a forest into a seashore. With a new light certain of her colours would disappear, thus forming a new colour scheme. Mme Boutkovsky was even able to introduce figures, such as fairies, and make them disappear at will, the whole being a matter of ingenious lighting.

The newer methods are more convenient but not necessarily an improvement upon those open to Irving and Tree. Recall the coming of night over the sea in *Herod*, while the crowd awaits the cry which will tell that Agrippina has been killed. For the Heath Scene in *Macbeth* Tree imagined a stretch of boggy moor, in which the light from the moon was reflected from a few menacing pools.

From a detailed story of the Lyceum when Henry Irving was in charge, a thousand apposite instances might be cited. For example, the small "pin" of steel blue limelight which enabled Lyceum audiences to follow the play of the Chief's features in *The Bells*, or the patch of moonlight on the floor of King Louis's bedroom when the half-mad king was chattering vaguely to the leaden images which lay on the lap of his robes. The moonlight was there to give full significance to the shadow of the murdered Nemours. Irving's gaze concentrated upon the menacing shadow, and he gasped, "Mercy! Mercy!"

Or the opening scene in *Richard the Third*, as I saw it from the Lyceum gallery fifty years and more ago. Irving, the Richard, entered through deep-shadowed arches. The slow tolling of a bell announced the funeral procession of the dead King Henry and the sense of impending tragedy grew as the mourners passed from the semi-darkness of the wings into the patch of light in the centre of the stage. At the last was the frightened yet fascinated victim of Richard's plot, the Lady Anne. Everything in the lighting of the scene followed naturally from opening lines which are as fitting for the drama which was to follow as poet ever devised:

Gloucester: Now is the winter of our discontent.
 Made glorious summer by this sun of York.

Irving said that stage lighting and grouping were of more importance than scenery and he implied that whereas scenery is static, grouping and lighting are dynamic.

Unlike Irving and Tree, Gordon Craig favoured the utmost simplicity in stage setting, believing this would help towards the creation of the all-important unity, and, moreover, reinforce the acting. Believing realistic scenery tended to hamper the free movement of the imagination, he favoured scenic backgrounds calculated to fire the imagination and create a mood. Hence, his columns, curtains and flights of steps were flooded with symbolic light. Influenced by Gordon Craig, when Esmé Percy produced *Hamlet* at the Court, the audience was shown a massive pillar, a terrace walk beyond, with two flights of steps leading to it, one of them straight and the other turning, and broken by a landing. An open oblong in the floor served for the graveyard scene at the Court. Shadows and coloured lights were thrown upon this highly simplified scenery, so that the play-scene and the final duel were silhouetted in dense black in the foreground against the illuminated spectators behind.

American dramatists and producers have exploited the co-ordination of scenic, lighting and acting effects with marked success in recent years. I have not seen Tennessee Williams' *A Streetcar named Desire*, which had a Broadway production in 1947, but New York critics suggest resemblances to Elmer Rice's *Street Scene*, with the spiritual squalor of New York exchanged for an equally unhappy underworld in New Orleans. Two sisters are battling for their souls. Blanche du Bois, beautifully played by Jessica Tandy, has sacrificed the best of her life to her parents, watching youth, love and creature comforts passing her by until she seeks relief in sex and drink, which bring in their train final madness. Stella, the sister, is a simpler-hearted creature, married to a Pole, whose primitive passions mingle shockingly with an equally primitive humour. In one scene Tennessee Williams utilized a backdrop which became transparent and thus showed the open street beyond the walls of the New Orleans home which housed so much misery. Another telling effect was the closing scene in which the unhappy Stella, after a violent quarrel with her Polish husband, hears his call from the foot of a circular iron stairway, leading from the tenement flat. Stella comes slowly down the iron steps, bathed in an intense white light, her head bent and her night-gown trailing behind her. The wife is drained of self-will and obeys some primordial instinct, which forces her to the arms of the man waiting below. The black stairway and the woman in the blaze of white light are inextricably commingled with the acting of the man and the woman.

The Impressionist Producers

Since Gordon Craig initiated the movement fifty years ago, a long series of "isms" have been devised to express variants in scenic presentations. Whereas the word "naturalism" covers the settings approved by Victorian taste, "realistic" indicates the use of scenery, properties and lighting designed to leave the impression that members of the audience actually are in the place represented. On the contrary, the "selectivist" offers the public as bare a stage as possible, thus leaving fuller opportunities to the actor. The "impressionist" endeavour is to intensify the mood and significance of any scene, with a view to the fullest emotional response from the auditorium. Gordon Craig was an Impressionist, though he might also be described as a "formalist", as non-representative steps, platforms and columns played so large a part in his stage designs.

As for "expressionism", this implies an extreme type of formalism amounting to marked distortions which are intended to stress the author's ideas. The staging of the Robot play *R.U.R.* was an example of expressionism. "Constructivism" is a cognate development but is concerned with stage production rather than with play-writing. Here the scenery suggests the naked structural forms of an up-to-date factory. Its first apostle was the Russian Meierhold and the gospel preached was anti-bourgeois philosophy. Varying levels on the stage are features of constructivism. Lastly "theatricalism" involves the use of back-drops of "the penny-plain, tuppence-coloured" order, with furniture painted on the scenery and similar antics guying naturalism and realism. Theatricalism has been used largely in revues and ballets and often affords opportunities for amusing colour effects. In general, though the stage designer expresses his ideas in two-dimensional form, they are finally translated into three dimensions, and moreover, must allow of free movement by cast and chorus. This cannot but be a hampering condition to pictorial composition. Were it not for lighting devices successful stage pictures would be almost impossible of achievement. In fact, no branch of theatrical art is more fully developed.

Costume in the Theatre

There remains stage costume. Dresses which are historically accurate, and naturalistic make-up, are so ingrained in dramatic representation to-day that only with difficulty can we visualize a theatre in which symbolic costume and masks were the rule, and not the exception. In Ancient Greece, the actors usually wore bright coloured robes, suited for a large open-air theatre, but characters in distress wore grey or black costumes. A queen was distinguished by a purple dress, a traveller by his round hat and a huntsman or soldier by his *chlamys*, this being a short cloak suit-

able for riding. Nor was the Elizabethan playgoer less alive to the
significance of symbolic costume. One of Henslowe's inventories
includes a "robe to go invisible in" such as was used by Ariel in
Shakespeare's *The Tempest*. When Oscar Wilde planned his
Salome, he asked that the coloured robes of his players should have
a similar symbolic quality. Thus Herod was to be robed in gold,
the Romans in purple and the Jews in yellow.

Londoners who saw John Gielgud's delightful production of
Richard of Bordeaux in the early 'thirties may remember the *décor*
of the Motleys and the ingenuity with which they made the
King's dress express his changing moods, and the ageing of the
man as he passed from youth to manhood and from manhood
to premature old age. The Motleys, Elizabeth Montgomery,
Audrey Harris and Peggy Harris by name, also designed the
dresses for Gielgud's production of *Hamlet* at the New Theatre.
"Magnificent but cheap", was Gielgud's summing-up of their
achievement.

Colour may be used as a means of symbolic expression, not
only in dress, but in the whole *décor* of a scene. When Leon Bakst
produced D'Annunzio's *La Pisanelle* in Paris, a slave girl was to be
smothered under a mass of roses. Early in the scene a red, verging
towards purple, made itself felt; thus, in the costumes of the
women, red became more intense and more and more purple,
until the executioners brought in flowers of a vivid violet-red
which smothered the unhappy girl.

In the higher flights of drama, players and audiences alike are
well aware of the potentialities of striking colour in a stage dress.
When Ellen Terry was rehearsing in *Macbeth*, she appeared in a
blood-red cloak. "What a wonderful splash of colour", was
Irving's comment. Characteristic of both players was the fact
that Irving wore the cloak on the first night and Ellen appeared
in a heather-coloured wrap, designed at the last moment. However, Miss Terry found compensation in the famous beetle-
wings dress, in which Sargent was to paint her as Lady Macbeth.
Ellen saw Lady Randolph Churchill wearing just such a gown at
a private dinner and Lady Randolph obligingly tore off a morsel
of the material, which Miss Terry passed on to her friend Mrs
Comyns Carr, the clever wife of "Joe" Carr. Mrs Comyns Carr
copied the scraps of material in soft green silk and blue tinsel, and

to this she added real green beetle wings. Over the gown Ellen Terry wore a cloak of shot velvet, upon which great griffins were embroidered in flame-coloured tinsel, while Lady Macbeth's wimple was held in place by a circlet of rubies. Two heavy snake-like plaits of deep-red hair, in-twisted with gold, hung almost to Ellen's knees. It was a triumph in *décor*, suggesting at once the clinging chain armour of an Amazon and the scales of Eden's serpent.

No actress has worn stage costume with greater effect than Ellen Terry. She almost always chose dresses which were rather longer in front than at the back, this in order that she might catch at the front folds, with gestures of infinite variety and grace. Mrs Comyns Carr left a record of the reaction of an audience when Ellen Terry returned to the stage to play Portia under the Bancroft management. "It seemed a revelation of womanly beauty when the curtain rose upon the tall, slender form in a china-blue and white brocaded dress, with one crimson rose at her heart." Memorable too, was the dress Mrs Comyns Carr made for Ellen in *The Amber Heart*. The designer used unstarched muslin "which she boiled in a potato steamer to produce the crinkles". As for the association between dress and characterization when Ellen Terry was the player, those who loved her will recall the cream and gold dress with the sapphire-blue cap which she wore as Viola. And some of them still tell us that there was a subtle difference in the way Ellen carried her boy's costume when she was in the company of men and the way she wore the attire when she was alone with Olivia.

An up-to-date management is no longer content to commission an artist to design a series of colourful costumes, as Percy Anderson, for example, was commissioned to design costumes for a George Edwardes production. What is aimed at now is a series of stage pictures, chiming in with the producer's ideas of the harmony which should arise from a properly devised and rehearsed play. Whereas the producer is responsible for *inscenierung*, the German word *buhnenbild* covers the work of the expert who is required to design fitting scenery and costumes.

As there has been a reaction against realistic scenery, so there has been a reaction against realistic costume in recent years. It began in Russia. Until Diaghileff came to Paris forty or more

years ago, the popular theatres all over Europe were content
with little more than an illusion of reality in respect of costume.
To-day, designers are painter-poets. Braque, Derain, Léger,
Picasso, Dufy and Utrillo were among those who first exploited
the stylized costumes.

Costume and Character

Appropriate and comfortable costume contributes not a little
to successful characterization. One of Maisie Gay's big successes
was the cockney charlady in Coward's *This Year of Grace*. She was
never happy in the rôle unless she was wearing the bonnet old
Fred Emney wore when he played in *A Sister to Assist 'Er*. The
bonnet was fully thirty years old, but Maisie Gay clung to the
Emney bonnet. On the general subject, she said "in all my
character studies, I select the costume first. When the proper
atmosphere has been obtained, I find it easier to adopt the right
voice and mannerisms." And Maisie added, "I always felt fully
in character directly I put on the bonnet which Fred wore in *A
Sister to Assist 'Er*."

Which may explain why leading ladies, and for that matter,
leading men, often require their costumes to be fashioned by
their own dressmakers or tailors, while lesser members of a cast
are perforce content with what a less expensive and less adver-
tised talent supplies. Tactician though he was in such matters,
George Edwardes lost Marie Tempest to musical comedy owing
to a stormy dispute over a pair of knickers. It may be added that,
when Vera Beringer was cast for the name part in *Little Lord
Fauntleroy*, Mrs Kendal, the producer of the play, made her wear
trousers all day. "That she might know where her pockets were",
was the way the producer put it, but what Dame Madge Kendal
really required was that Vera should assume the habits of a little
man rather than remain a small girl.

Equally illustrative of the relation between costume and
characterization is the story of Cicely Courtneidge's discovery
that she was not a soubrette but a natural comic. In Cicely's case
the breeches of a subaltern did the trick. Putting skirts aside gave
her the assurance required if Cicely, comedienne, was to give her
comic gifts full play. Players as different in type as Marie Tempest

and Violet Vanbrugh have testified to the value of an appearance in tights, when a young actress is striving to achieve stage
assurance. And when the assurance is assured, stage dress may
well be the determining factor in creating a proper sense of period
In this connection Athene Seyler, in *The Craft of Comedy*, recalled
that the very steps taken in walking vary in the different periods.
Discussing the consequences upon the art of the actor and actress, Miss Seyler added: "I should say that a woman ought to
dance as she moves in a seventeenth-century dress (with tiny,
even steps under crinoline or bustle) and to stride in the twentieth century."

To this Athene Seyler added the valuable hint that, apart from
costume, players should not forget "what is underneath". The
late Victorian costumes in Wilde's *Ideal Husband* could never
look right over a modern elastic belt, and worn by a lady who
crossed her legs. A boned corset and three full stiff petticoats
are essentials in late Victorian revivals and there should be no
lounging.

After all, this is what we should expect. A player does not act
with voice, features, and hands alone, but with the whole body.
A far-sighted critic once said of Flora Robson, "the very folds of
her dress act," and he recalled that Eleonora Duse had the same
gift for making insentient things sentient. "The Italian could
communicate fatigue to a shawl so that when it dropped from her
shoulders, it fell with infinite weariness to the ground." If the
critic had seen the Duse pass from the sparkle of Goldoni's *La
Locandiera* to the drab pathos of her Santuzza on a summer
afternoon at the Savoy half a century ago, he would have known
how apt was his allusion to the shawl. Indeed, consciously
or unconsciously, Santuzza was doubtless in his mind as he
wrote.

Apposite is the recollection of Sarah Bernhardt's practice
when she played the aged grandmother in *Rome Vaincue*. Sir
George Arthur saw her in the part in the year 1876 and he said
that the folds of the great cloak Sarah wore in the last act suggested the wings of a monster bat. Posthumia's grand-daughter
was a Vestal who had broken her vows of chastity and was condemned to be buried alive, with only a loaf of bread and a jug of
water to prolong the agony. As the old and blind woman, Sarah

unloosed the girl's white robe and ran her fingers over the bare breast, searching for the heart, and as she did so the wings of the monster bat fluttered.

It will suffice to recall without comment some typical stage sensations, based upon costumes, among them that due to the lace pyjamas which Jeanne de Casalis displayed in a bedroom scene in *Potiphar's Wife*. Akin was the delight admirers of Tallulah Bankhead derived from that young lady's undergarments. Women of two continents would wait for hours for a front seat in the pit on a Tallulah first night, attracted partly by the magic of that Christian name, but even more by the frank sex appeal of a vibrant personality, who was so generous in her display of what is more usually hidden. The apotheosis of Tallulah, in other words her release from certain restrictions which attach themselves to normal social life, took place in *Her Cardboard Lover*. The play was translated from the French with aid from P. G. Wodehouse, and Miss Bankhead played a woman divorced from a husband whom she still loved. Tallulah accordingly engaged a secretary, whose task was to arouse the jealousy of the divorced husband. The secretary was only too successful, for the husband was quickly forgotten. The ensuing complications enabled Miss Bankhead to undress three times. After two love scenes, played in underwear, Tallulah donned pyjamas for the last act and ended the play in bed.

The gown which Julie Opp wore in the second act of Pinero's *The Princess and the Butterfly* was a comparable stage effect, though the virginal white worn by Mrs Ware was character-revealing in a very different way from Miss Bankhead's amusing improprieties. Pinero's stage directions described Mrs Ware as a curiously striking woman of problematical age, with large lustrous eyes and luxuriant golden hair, rolled back from a broad white brow. As Julie Opp's beauty created some moments of hushed excitement in the theatre on that memorable first night, so Mrs Ware aroused excitement in Mrs St Roche's smoking room, which was precisely what Pinero had in mind when he clothed Mrs Ware in virginal white.

When Camille Clifford appeared in the white silk dress, cut *en Princesse*, without an ornament of any kind, impersonating the Gibson Girl at the Shaftesbury Theatre, there was a similar hush

of delighted surprise. Miss Clifford's silent passage across the
stage emphasised the thrill, until it seemed to be making theatrical history. The roomy "whites" which Vera Pearce wore in the
gymnasium scene in *Please Teacher* at the Hippodrome, and gave
Bobby Howes a chance to fire off the malicious "Can I see you?",
constitute a special case of the costume which supplements and
enriches comedy. By this time Vera Pearce had established herself as the strong woman of musical comedy, an example being,
her appearance in *No, No, Nanette*, when, with aid from Joe
Coyne and a couple of "wives", she hoisted George Grossmith. A
comedy effect similar to the gymnasium "whites" was Vivien
Leigh's back view, while she was dusting the furniture in
Thornton Wilder's modern morality.

I do not think Mrs Patrick Campbell's dramatic change of
dress in *The Notorious Mrs Ebbsmith* was fully successful. In truth
Mrs Campbell was no more beautiful in the Bardini gown with
"a mere strap for sleeves" than she had been in the dress which
Pinero described as "plain to the verge of coarseness". Playgoers
rather resented the blindness of Lucas Cleeve. However, some
other actress may some day exploit Pinero's situation in a different way and justify what seemed the dramatist's undue insistence
upon the virtue of the Bardini gown. But why chatter? *The
Notorious Mrs Ebbsmith* was a red-letter evening. I was so elated
when I left the Garrick Theatre, that I walked home to Dulwich,
giving the blood time to cool. I saw the play twice afterwards,
and in each case left at the end of the third act. I wonder how the
play has weathered in fifty odd years?

It is not easy to resist these memories, they had so large a part
in our stage enjoyments. Robert Loraine as Mirabell, in the
bright orange coat and green vest which captured the attention
of Millamant at the Lyric, Hammersmith, and lingers so happily
in our memory of that delightful evening, together with the frills
and furbelows in which Edith Evans moved "with the beauty and
grace of a ship under full sail". At the same theatre, too, and
about the same time, the hooped dress of black and white over
yellow-green which Elsie French wore in Sheridan's *The Duenna*.
Sheridan, who invented the costume, thought in terms of the
theatre and that is why we remember the costume. For the same
reason we remember Marie Tempest's cardinal red dress in an

early act of *Theatre Royal*, which was later to contrast so effectively with the white of the death scene.

Perhaps the following memory is not strictly apposite, but it had its place in theatrical gossip in its day. Cyril Maude had been at Charterhouse and was very popular with Old Carthusians. After one Charterhouse reunion, stalls and dress circle were packed with Carthusians, wishing to see their old school fellow in *Toddles*. The big moment came in the second act when Cyril Maude sprang out of bed, clad from neck to toes in pyjamas of the old school colours!

The art of make-up must not detain us. Technical methods, as they apply merely to an actor or actress, are not the concern of the theatre-goer. He is only concerned that the illusion sought should be satisfying. Nevertheless, such a master of make-up as Tree added immensely to the pleasure of audiences by his manifest skill. So did John Hare, Cedric Hardwicke, Cyril Maude and others with their faithful studies of old age. When he was playing Grumpy, Cyril Maude had to appear as a man of eighty-three. Having put on the flesh tint, Maude used to add the shadows. This meant emphasizing the lines and masses of his own face, considering all the while how they would appear if he should attain the years of Grumpy. The hollows of the sunken eyes were emphasized, so was the middle of the upper lip, and the slanting planes from the nose on each side of the mouth, all of which deepen with age. A touch of red on the eye-lids added to the effect. A wig, bushy eyebrows and due emphasis upon the veins in the hands and old Grumpy was ready for the stage, bar the costume. Already, Cyril Maude was feeling elderly. When the call-boy's voice was heard he would be eighty-three.

Another minor triumph in the art of make-up was Miss Stanley's *Queen Victoria* in Laurence Housman's series of short plays. To reproduce Victoria's high forehead Miss Stanley had her hair shaved every evening, and, as the Queen grew older, she added more and more woollen pads to her figure. All Miss Stanley's clothes belonged precisely to the various periods covered by the plays, down to some tiny elastic-sided blue satin boots. In the later scenes Miss Stanley fixed four lumps of red dental wax in her mouth, two at the top and two at the bottom.

They broadened her face and thickened her speech, until the likeness to the old Queen was uncanny.

One other memory, the Napoleon of Henry Irving in *Madame Sans Gêne*. For once, Irving's task was not to emphasise his personality but to submerge it, and the transition involved changing what usually seemed a tall and thin man into a small and stout man. The green coat was buttoned high and the sloping of the front was generous, so that there was a big display of waistcoat, which, in turn, was markedly short. Again, the breeches were cut so that the thighs stood out, thus giving an impression of short and sturdy legs. And this was only the beginning. For his Napoleon Irving had the stage furniture made higher than was usual, the door knobs were raised and the lower panels exaggerated in order to dwarf the figure of the Emperor. As for the supporting actors, they were all tall men. The play had been chosen on Ellen Terry's account and Napoleon's part was relatively unimportant, but having chosen it, nothing was spared to give the rôle verisimilitude. It may be argued, and indeed it was argued, that the part was unworthy of Henry Irving, but it was played for all it was worth, down to the white silk stockings and the black shoes.

How does a player of genius transform, not only his appearance, but his whole personality? Irving's Charles the First was quite unlike his Becket, as his Becket was quite unlike another famous churchman, Cardinal Wolsey, as Irving portrayed him, in lonely state at York House, his lips moving to the rhythm of one of the dances which Edward German wrote for the revival. All were different, yet all were Henry Irving. About the time of Irving's death, Fred Barnard drew a page of impersonations for "Black and White". It is an excellent presentation of one of the abiding puzzles which the Theatre presents to theatre-lovers.

CHAPTER 13

CREATING A STAR
HOW THE PLAYERS MADE GOOD

THUS far, we have regarded the body of players, past and present, as so many actors and actresses, ready to hand when authors, managers or producers called for their services. Like Topsy, they grow, and usually from humble beginnings.

How did they begin? How did they reach their dizzy eminence? It is a fascinating study and what follows can be no more than a cross-section of recent theatrical history. Its ramblings must be forgiven because the territory which might be explored is so various and the temptations to wander from the straight path are so numerous.

Sometimes the gods are kind. They were kind to Noel Coward and Gertrude Lawrence. These had their struggles but the vast majority of players have waged a weary battle for their fame, and always, and overshadowing every triumph, there has been the grim truth which was impressed upon W. H. Berry half a century ago when the genial creature was on the eve of his big success: "You'll find making a name for yourself very like climbing a greasy pole. It's difficult to climb up—more difficult to stay up—but darned easy to slip down."

There have been actors and actresses dowered with the silver spoon of early success. Ellaline Terriss was one, but she was the daughter of one of the best-loved actors on the stage. Florence Kemble, too, played Juliet at her stage début and won an immediate success, but again she came of theatrical stock. Usually, even beautiful women have had to earn experience in a comic opera chorus and men with manifest ability have played in repertory or provincial tours for years before a London success was assured. Gladys Cooper was one of the beauties who graduated in the chorus at Daly's and the Gaiety when George Edwardes was in command, but Miss Cooper had brains and grit. As she has said: "I am by instinct a business woman. I am by nature energetic." At times, Miss Cooper did impulsive and even silly things. In early years she declined an offer to understudy Phyllis Dare in a big West End success *The Catch of the Season*. "Like a little fool", as Miss Cooper said later. But the business capacity asserted itself and she was rewarded by Frank Curzon's generous offer of partnership in the management of the Playhouse, without asking for any financial backing at all. Incidentally, Miss Cooper had a chance to subscribe £400 towards staging Somerset Maugham's *The Letter* and her reward was £40,000.

A score of similar instances could be quoted. In the programme of *Monte Cristo, Junior*, a Gaiety burlesque dating back to 1886, I see "Valentine . . . Miss Birdie Irving", now our Ethel Irving. Constance Collier was another Gaiety beginner. A chance gibe of Beerbohm Tree at Connie's expense—"You're only a Gaiety Girl," helped to change the pretty young lady of musical comedy into the accomplished actress of latter-day experience. Gwen Ffrangcon-Davies began in the chorus of *To-night's the Night*, which was on tour during the first World War. Elsie Randolph was in the chorus at the Gaiety when the leading comedienne and her understudy went ill. Elsie volunteered to take a principal part in *My Girl* and never missed a line or a dance step. The opportunity made her. Examples could be multiplied indefinitely.

Let us examine the beginnings of a few more careers which have ended in stardom. It matters little in what order, or, for that matter, in what country the beginnings were made. Always the emphasis is upon opportunities for hard work, and not infrequently associated with poverty which puts a high premium upon constant effort. Very seldom are there such spectacular jumps into fame as that which attended upon the early efforts of Hermione Baddeley or Vivien Leigh. In any case, Hermione had been on the stage from childhood and Vivien Leigh chanced upon a part which suited her quite exceptional beauty, while not a little of her success belonged to the films rather than the theatre. Both Binnie Hale's parents were in the profession, and the story goes that both ran away from home in their 'teens. At the time of their meeting, Robert Hale was earning thirty shillings a week and sported a monocle. Belle Reynolds first attracted his attention by flicking cherry-stones at the eyeglass. They were duly married, played together in melodrama such as *The Lights o' London* and *Drink* and became the father and mother of Binnie and Sonnie Hale. When Binnie followed her mother's example and ran away from home to begin an acting career, she was already a good mimic, and she was soon to show that she had inherited her father's energy and versatility. As a child she had written numerous pantomimes, usually in rhyme, but they were seldom or never completed.

Lynn Fontanne stands upon a peak in her profession and was never without natural gifts for the stage, but her progress was not sensational. Her father was a Frenchman, and she had the luck to fall in with Ellen Terry. Miss Terry gave the young girl a home until she had a footing in the theatre. Even this introduction yielded no more than a place in the chorus of a Drury Lane pantomime, though later Lynn Fontanne had a part in Knoblock's *My Lady's Dress*. In her diary Ellen wrote: "Must get Lynn more money. It's wicked. She is so intelligent."

If any one brought fame to Lynn it was Laurette Taylor, who took the young actress to America, where she met young Alfred Lunt. As man and wife the Lunts worked for eight years with the Theatre Guild, until there was stardom for both.

So far as I know there was no "theatre" in the family of Edith Evans, and she entered upon a stage career in the most casual fashion. A friend was running an amateur theatrical society at Streatham and had an annual Shakespeare week. William Poel saw Edith Evans at one of these performances and asked her to play Cressida in one of his Elizabethan Society productions. There she was seen by Vedrenne, who gave her a couple of parts in *My Lady's Dress*, a cast which also included Gladys Cooper and Lynn Fontanne. Later, Edith Evans toured with Ellen Terry, playing Mistress Ford in *The Merry Wives* to Ellen Terry's Mistress Page. By 1923, her gifts as a tragic actress were revealed when she played Caroline in *The Three Daughters of Monsieur Dupont*.

From her own experiences Edith Evans places two qualifications for success high. The first is a physique which can withstand the strain of a theatrical career, particularly when touring. The second is good elocution. To these she adds the ability to move

John Gielgud and Pamela Browne in Congreve's *Love for Love* at the Haymarket Theatre (1944) (Problem of Revivals, *see page* 229).

Lewis Waller as the Comte de Candale and Grace Lane as the Comtesse de Candale in *A Marriage of Con-venience*, Imperial Theatre (1904).

(*see page 293*).

gracefully on the stage and wear clothes effectively. All can be taught. What cannot be taught and yet is all-important, is the creation of an illusion of beauty by sheer force of personality.

If ever there was an actress with a natural gift for her art it is Flora Robson. Yet, twice, Miss Robson abandoned the stage as a career, dispirited by what seemed ill-fortune. On one occasion she gave up acting for manual work at the Shredded Wheat factory, Welwyn. She had a small part in *Will Shakespeare* at the St Martin's in 1924, but established herself in Bridie's *The Anatomist*.

Louise Hampton comes of theatrical stock. Her parents were members of an old-time touring company; her father was actually in a Stockport theatre playing *Hamlet* when Louise was born. She had her first part at four and a half, and has been earning her living as an actress ever since. For years she played Irene Vanbrugh parts on tour, her first big part in London being in *The Silver Box* at the Court. Similarly, Haidee Wright began to act when she was three, but she was twenty-seven before she made her first London appearance as the boy martyr, Stephanus, in *The Sign of the Cross* at the Lyric. No one who heard the shriek of terror in the torture scene was likely to forget Haidee Wright. At the first interval playgoers turned to the programmes to register the name, and they did not forget it for half a century and more.

Eva Moore, another trouper with fifty or more years' active participation in things theatrical, began as a teacher of dancing to small boys. An early pupil was Winston Churchill, the naughtiest of his tribe, whom Miss Moore sometimes thought the naughtiest small boy in the world. Her first part was in *Partners* at the Vaudeville, under Tom and Fred Thorne. Then one pound a week, playing in *The Cricket on the Hearth* with Toole, Eva being the "Spirit of Home" and the lovely Kate Phillips the Dot. Eva Moore was Toole's leading lady on tour at three pounds a week, when she was only seventeen, this being about the time when she met Harry Esmond. Three pounds a week meant more in the 'nineties of the last century than it does to-day, while the association with Toole and Willard meant opportunities. So Esmond and his pretty young wife soon made good with *One Summer's Day*, the play which also established Constance Collier in the profession.

s

Constance Collier has been mentioned. She has told us that she would not change the life of an actress for any other in the world. She was born into the profession. Her father and mother were both on the stage, and had some provincial fame. When she was three years old, Connie was dancing in pantomime and soon was appearing in child rôles with Wilson Barrett in *The Silver King*. The dingy lodgings of touring "theatricals" did nothing to deter this veritable daughter of the stage. At fourteen, Connie was a Gaiety Girl in the burlesque *Don Juan*. A small part in *The Shop Girl* followed. A figure which was the reverse of lithe, tousled hair, and hands badly in need of a manicurist, did not suggest a Gaiety "show girl", but George Edwardes had his methods, and dancing, singing, and fencing lessons worked wonders. The Gaiety girls, and Miss Collier among them, were also taught how to wear their frocks. Then came a deserved piece of good fortune, an introduction to Tree and the chance to play in Stephen Phillips's *Ulysses*. Before she left Tree, she had played Cleopatra.

What a lovely thing she was in those days, as Chiara the gipsy in *One Summer's Day*—the first time I noticed her—as Pallas Athene in *Ulysses* and Poppaea in *Nero*! And what an actress she was to become; the Duchess in *Our Betters*, for example.

Nancy Price, as a child, had a similar absorption in the theatre. Her favourite toys were tiny theatres, with doll actors and actresses, who were called upon to play pieces of Nancy's own composition, in the Sheila manner. When she grew up Nancy induced Sir Frank Benson to listen to her recitation of the Duchess Anne's speech from *Richard the Third*. Benson rewarded the girl with a walking-on-part.

Born in 1898, Elizabeth Bergner was a frail and delicate girl. Of middle-class origin, she displayed no marked taste in dress, nor did there seem any promise in her voice. What stood out was an insatiable desire to succeed on the stage. She read books upon the theatre, learnt rôle after rôle, until this very persistence won admission to the Dramatic Academy in Vienna. When she had finished with the Academy, there still seemed little prospect of a career and the Bergner was twenty before she made her first appearance in a minor part in Berlin. It was not until she played Rosalind in a German version of *As You Like It* that playgoers realized the heart of fire that burned within the frail body.

London discovered Elizabeth Bergner in Margaret Kennedy's *Escape Me Never*, as the waif wife of Sebastian Sanger, a family playgoers had already met in *The Constant Nymph*. Her husband is unfaithful and cowardly. Her baby is dead. Yet, having borrowed a shilling to light the gas-fire in the wrecked flat, Gemma quietly takes her husband's broken head in her arms, and with the words, "Shut up!" croons him to sleep. The low sweet tones of the wife's voice, perfectly modulated, were deeply moving, and even the unshapely canvas shorts fitted the stage picture. We shall never know what was the relative importance of the Bergner's playing, Margaret Kennedy's invention, and Komisarjevsky's production. The three in combination made *Escape Me Never* unforgettable.

Lena Ashwell was born on a training ship, the *Wellesley*, where her father, a retired Royal Navy man, was captain. Later, the family moved to Canada. In her teens, Lena wanted to become a singer and studied at the Royal Academy of Music, but her voice broke badly and the legitimate theatre proved the more urgent call. Elocution lessons with Millard (Evelyn Millard's father) helped, but what mattered more was that, already, Miss Ashwell had realized the worth of "concentrated imagination" in acting. Her first stage appearance was as a maidservant at the Grand Theatre, Islington, but, already, there was promise enough to justify an engagement as understudy to Winifred Emery at the Court, where Comyns Carr was in management. Comyns Carr introduced Lena to Ellen Terry. The career commenced in earnest when Irving chose her as Elaine for his production of *King Arthur*.

Sybil Thorndike, like Irene Vanbrugh, was a daughter of the church. Her father was Canon Thorndike of Rochester. He borrowed £100 from his son Russell, and the money was paid to Ben Greet in return for teaching Sybil to act. Ben Greet's school touring companies, frequently out-of-doors productions, were a first-rate training ground in the 'nineties. When Sybil reached stardom she had played no fewer than 108 Shakespearean parts, among them the Fool in *Lear* at the Old Vic in 1918. Her brother Russell had played even more Shakespearean rôles, his tally being 180, sixteen in *Macbeth* alone.

Angela Baddeley, like Hermione, has been on the stage since

childhood, acting child parts at the Old Vic, until she was ready for her fascinating appearances in *The Beggar's Opera* at the Lyric, Hammersmith. She is married to Glen Byam Shaw, which accounts for the fact that they have frequently played together, in particular as Gratiano and Nerissa when John Gielgud revived *The Merchant* at the Queen's in 1937.

Mary Clare, who shared the honours with Hermione Baddeley in *The Likes of Her*, entered a competition organized by The British Empire Shakespeare Society. George Alexander and Irene Vanbrugh were the judges and Mary Clare won the bronze medal, to which Alexander added an engagement for a small part in a coming production. Later Mary borrowed fifty pounds in order to get some stage training under Ben Greet. After five years' absence from the stage, she came back to play Chloe when Basil Dean produced Galsworthy's *The Skin Game*. Sally in *The Likes of Her* followed, and then the memorable Lady Maryon in Noel Coward's *Cavalcade*.

Edna Best, like Mary Clare, came into the profession by a relatively easy path. Her family agreed to a thorough grounding in theatrical work under Miss Kate Rorke and this was expected to take four full years. After the second year, money problems obtruded themselves, but Miss Rorke solved them by offering Edna a post as her secretary, which allowed of time to complete the training. Three provincial tours, the first of them with a *Charley's Aunt* company, followed, with a pay packet of two pounds ten shillings a week and then London and success.

Wendy Hiller, who was born in 1912, began her career as a student at the Manchester Repertory Theatre when she was eighteen years old. For a year she understudied and played small parts until she was made assistant stage-manager in 1934. Some touring and then success in London as Sally in *Love on the Dole*.

Mrs Patrick Campbell was a relatively late beginner, though she was the star of the Anomalies Dramatic Society at Norwood before she became a professional. Dame Lilian Braithwaite, too, acted with the Strolling Players, while yet a girl at the Hampstead High School. Other students were Dorothea Baird and Lady Tree, whose first appearance was as the Maid in Gilbert's *Sweethearts* in Mrs Alec Tweedie's drawing-room. Tall, graceful, and with a pleasant singing voice, Maud Holt had no difficulty in passing to professional status when she married young Beerbohm Tree, a few weeks after her debut at Mrs Tweedie's.

It was in 1926 that Frances Day made her start in the theatre. It was in cabaret. Her first real successes were in *Jill Darling* and *The Fleet's Lit Up*, and when she appeared in *Black and White* at the Hippodrome it was as leading lady. Frances Day's first idea was to become the Sarah Bernhardt of her day and generation. Just as Bea Lillie and Gracie Fields were persuaded that their real gift was for burlesque, so Arthur Riscoe discovered the real gifts of Frances Day. "You're a born comic," he said. This was how Frances Day came to give us the delicious, the delightful, the delectable, the de-luxe nonsense which we associate with her name on a programme. Remember Vivian Ellis's ditty:

> "I'm just a little girl,
> Lost in a fog,
> I had a dog, lost in the fog,
> Me and my dog,
> I'm just wandering in the fog,
> Won't some kind gentleman see us home?"

By the time we are aware that Miss Day's father is on the booze, her mother's on the stage, and her sister's on a cruise, Vivian Ellis's song is akin to tragedy on the one side, even if we are all chuckling with the singer's comic approach. "Underneath the Arches" was another Frances Day number, with a dual twist.

When Dorothy Dickson appeared in *Sally*, she was only known as a dancer, who had appeared with her husband, Carl Hyson. As her stage experience was even less than the volume of her small voice, Jerome Kern expressed grave doubts as to the wisdom of entrusting "Dot" with the name part, but proved to be wrong. Dorothy Dickson scored heavily and the London run made a profit of £40,000.

Violet Loraine might well have been content with her relatively easy successes as a juvenile lead, but she chose to test her capacity as a character actress. Playgoers with memories which go back to the second decade of the present century will remember the beginning of the experiment. The curtain rose on the Hippodrome stage to disclose an elderly Cockney, in charge of a winkle stall, the background being Piccadilly Circus, during a thick fog. A couple of dudes stopped to sample the old woman's "oysters", and she entertained them with "Dear Old Saturday Night", to the music of Herman Darewski. On the evening the sketch was produced sophisticated playgoers slowly penetrated Miss Loraine's disguise, and felt stage history was in the making. It was. There followed an engagement at the Hippodrome and Vi Loraine's appearance in the *Bing Boy* series, in which she displayed a wholly unexpected versatility alike as singer, dancer and actress.

Not infrequently, a player discovers his or her stage personality by accident. Gracie Fields began as a singer of straight songs until chance revealed the value of "guying" her songs. Cicely Courtneidge, in spite of numerous theatrical contacts, was relatively a failure as a soubrette. As has been said, she found her comic gifts when she put on "the bags" of a member of the R.A.F. and appeared at a Colchester music hall, first "making 'em cry" and then "making 'em laugh".

Dolores Gray scored a minor triumph on the first night of *Annie Get Your Gun* in London. The theatre was the Coliseum and the first night chanced to coincide with her birthday. Dolores was just twenty-three and she experienced the thrill of her young life when the huge audience, learning of the birthday in a fall of the curtain speech greeted her by singing "Happy Birthday to You". But if the leap to stardom seemed sudden, there were years of preliminary spade work, going back to school days and early appearances in song and dance before cabaret audiences in San Francisco and Los Angeles. Experience in Broadway musicals followed and then the offer of Ethel Merman's part in *Annie Get Your Gun*. Dolores Gray's youth, high spirits, and sense of fun conquered London in a night.

Jessie Matthews entered a troubled world on a March morning in 1907, and the place was Soho, where Jessie Matthews's people served a stall in Berwick Market. There were eleven children in the family, seven girls and four boys, one of whom became a page boy at the National Sporting Club, and for a few months was feather-weight champion of England. Among the girls, Jessie was number four, a fact of importance as it gave her an elder sister, Rosie, who first detected the odd thing known as "promise" in the dark-eyed, long-legged child who was passing into girl-hood during the first World War.

The theatre was an ever-present romance in Soho, and some of the barrow-folk were even able to pay for dancing-lessons for their children which promised escape into the encircling world of golden lights, which was so near and yet seemed so far from Berwick Market. One of Jessie Matthews's little friends was among the lucky ones. Jessie used to accompany her to the door of the school until one day the dancing mistress noticed thirteen-year-old Jessie tapping her toes on the pavement to the tune of a piano tinkling inside and asked Jessie to come in.

This was what Rosie had worked and prayed for when she took her young sister to an occasional show in the world of golden lights; what Rosie had in mind when she persuaded Mummy Matthews to invest a few shillings in Jessie's first pair of toe-shoes. Imitations came easily to Jessie; shedding Cockneyisms proved more difficult. She entered an elocution competition in which there were five hundred entrants and won a first-class certificate, but not the gold cup Rosie coveted for her young sister. Jessie Matthews has confessed that the biggest hiding she ever got was for saying "loit" when she meant "light". Coming home in the Tube Jessie argued the point, "But I didn't say 'loit'," until the unhappy Rosie decided that a spanking was the only remedy, when the sisters reached home. An advantage of ten years in age gave the requisite authority.

At fifteen Miss Terry of Terry's Juveniles judged that Jessie Matthews was ready for any chorus in London and the Palace Theatre was chosen for the first audition. Charles Cochran was producing *The Music Box Revue*, and, sure enough, Jessie got her engagement. Charles Cochran, who has a professional eye for talent of the kind, says that already Jessie was an interesting child and he gave the little chorus girl a verse all to herself in a song "Down on the Farm". A tiny streak of a voice chanted some lines proper to a chicken coming out of a casserole. *The Music Box Revue* had no success and Jessie Matthews took a chance in an André Charlot revue. This time she reached the understudy stage, her principal being Gertrude Lawrence. During an American tour, Miss Lawrence went ill and Miss Matthews took her place. The news came to Charlot in "Lawrence ill. Matthews in!"

The interesting child with the big eyes and the funny little nose had justified sister Rosie's fondest hopes.

But wait. Jessie Matthews, during her first American tour, was far from being a great success. When she returned Charles Cochran greeted her with, "Well, what a flop you've been!" The grim greeting was managerial in its origin, as Cochran was contemplating offering Jessie a three years' agreement covering revue at the Pavilion, and the salary he proposed did not seem generous to Miss Matthews. However, she did sign on for four shows, £60 a week for the first, £100 for the second, £150 for the third, and £200 for the fourth. As Jessie said, "Not bad, for twenty!" particularly as the shows included *One Dam Thing After Another*, *This Year of Grace*, and *Wake Up and Dream*.

The best piece of stage advice Jessie ever had came from Maisie Gay. She had had some small success by dint of recalling Gertrude Lawrence and imitating her renderings as closely as possible, but Maisie Gay cured Jessie of the fault: "Develop your own personality. Think continually of your own face. Never forget your round face, the straight hair and the fringe. Visualize it all the time while you are working and exploit it for all you are worth."

Charles Cochran knew that Jessie was a potential star when he offered the four parts. He would have been less generous to an imitator.

I am doing the masculine side of the theatre less than justice. Let me conclude with two biographies of troupers, Noel Coward and Gertrude Lawrence. Their careers have commingled in some degree so the story will be the easier to tell. Born at the end of the nineteenth century, on 16 December 1899, to be precise, Noel Coward has lived through the greater part of three national wars and has worked through two of them. Every war means a wastage of young men, and the war which began when Noel was fourteen years old was cruelly wasteful. It is not too much to say that a primary evil to-day is our shortage of leaders, that is of men who began their working life during the testing years of the first World War, and reached maturity during the second World War, experiences which were to give a new bias to almost every value and principle which the Victorian Age judged inviolable.

Apart from war services, Mr Coward was busy at his profession between 1914 and 1918, so he matured early. I will lay no stress upon the song and dance competition for the kiddies on the beach at Bognor in which he chirruped "Bedtime at the Zoo" and was rewarded with a big box of chocolates (three-parts shavings). Heedless of any question of copyright or composer's fee, the budding vaudeville artist stole an attractive number which Gertie Millar had sung in *The Orchid* to the music of Lionel Monckton. In view of the publication of *Present Indicative* a quarter of a century later, one regrets young Noel did not complete his Gaiety raid and replace the saucy sailor suit by a miniature version of the white-knickered costume in which Miss Millar sang "Good night Mr Shepherd". It would have illustrated the autobiography very pleasantly.

Noel Coward's Beginnings

The big box of chocolates and shavings at six years of age indicated precocity. When he entered his 'teens Noel was among the income-earners. The run of *The Goldfish*, his first professional venture, was not spectacular; nor was the salary generous, but the scene of the production was the Court Theatre, soon to witness the early triumphs of Bernard Shaw and Granville-Barker. What really mattered was that Noel's appearance did not escape the eagle-eyes of Messrs Bellew and Stock, Theatrical Agents, and, when Charles Hawtrey wanted a page-boy for a comedy production at the Prince of Wales's, Noel was adjudged just the thing. This time the pay was two pounds a week, from which Messrs Bellew and Stock took 10 per cent. The page boy's task seemed simple. Hawtrey, in his stage character, was playing the piano. In his buttoned suit, Noel had to enter boldly and say: "Stop that noise at once, please. Making such a horrible noise. We're used to good music here."

In *Present Indicative*, that invaluable record of stage life between the two World Wars, Noel tells of the hours of rehearsal at home which preceded his entry upon the stage at the Prince of Wales's. They proved unrewarding. Hawtrey, at the piano, listened to the end and then swung round on the piano-stool with a glare of horror in his eyes (Noel's own description). What he said was: "Tarver, never let me see that boy again."

In fact, Charles Hawtrey was generosity incarnate. When
Noel's over-emphatic diction had been toned down and translated into something approaching Cockney, the lines were
adjudged acceptable and Noel drew his two pounds a week
throughout the run of *The Great Name*. And more; Noel was engaged by Hawtrey off and on for several years, and Mr Coward
has told us that to no one on the stage did he owe more as a young
man.

In an era of outstanding actor-producers, Hawtrey was
equalled by few and eclipsed by none, if generosity, an uncanny
insight into human weaknesses and vast and varied professional
experience are among the tests of capacity. Charles Hawtrey was
not markedly successful in keeping the money he earned, but his
productions ranged from *The Private Secretary* to *A Messenger From
Mars*. Moreover, Hawtrey's experience ranged well beyond the
theatre. At Eton, when he was fourteen, he "made a book" on the
Derby and cleared two pounds ten shillings, thanks to his faith in
an outsider named Doncaster, which won at 45 to 1. He was early
in his twenties when he came upon the German farce which he
converted into *The Private Secretary*, and put on for a London run
with W. S. Penley in the "fool parson" rôle, which Beerbohm
Tree had been playing at the Prince of Wales's Theatre. Transferred to the Globe, with Penley beginning at eight pounds a
week, Hawtrey's farce proved one of the big money-makers in
theatrical history.

This was the man whom Noel was to worship, honour and obey
during the greater part of the formative years. It was Hawtrey
who produced *Where the Rainbow Ends*, the Roger Quilter musical
piece which vied with *Peter Pan* as a Christmas holiday attraction
in the first quarter of the century. Master Noel Coward played
William in the Savoy production, William being a comic page
boy. Noel specialized in such rôles in his early teens, but when he
outgrew the buttons stage, he played The Slacker, a curious mixture of a big boy and a small dragon. The stage costume included
a tail and a make-up in which pronouncedly yellow cheeks vied
with the glittering green sequins on Noel's eyelids. Years later
Noel found the word "macabre" to describe his performance as
The Slacker.

To Charles Hawtrey, as a formative factor, must be added the

ever-present influence of Miss Italia Conti and her sister Mrs
Murray, who collected, trained and dosed with Epsom salts the
flower fairies, dragon-flies, elves, toads, hyenas and dragons who
added so much to the attraction of the Christmas musical. It was
Miss Conti who engineered a three weeks' engagement in Lancashire, with the Liverpool Repertory Company in the Spring of
1913. Basil Dean, then a young man characterized by a rasping
voice and eye-glasses, was producing *Hannele*, a play by Gerhart
Hauptmann, which had had two earlier London runs. The
engagement made theatrical history inasmuch as it meant the
introduction of Noel to the second of our troupers, a vivacious
little minx, wearing a peaked military cap and a black satin coat.
Even at fourteen she carried a handbag and powdered her little
turned-up nose. At their first meeting she said her name was
Gertrude Lawrence, but Noel could call her "Gert". One
gathers Noel has been doing so ever since, though, happily, the
hideous curtailment has not extended to the playgoing public of
two continents.

In *Hannele*, Noel began as an angel in the dream scene, and
later was one of the school children wearing a blue smock. He
did not enjoy his Liverpool and Manchester appearances, though
they did bring Gertrude Lawrence into his life.

The Career in Being

This is not a biography, but a sketch of the background against
which men and women of the theatre developed between the turn
of the century and the ugly post-war years which have followed
the Year of Victory 1945. Little need be said of the dreary hours
in agency waiting-rooms, hidden, to-day, in the foundations of
the career of Noel Coward. None of us are likely to see the
comedies *I'll Leave it To You* or *The Young Idea*, any more than we
will strive to recover memories of Noel as Basil Pyecroft in *The
Light Blues* or Clay Collins in *Polly With a Past*. Suffice it to say
that soon after the first World War ended Mr Coward, as actor,
was on the twenty pound a week level. With *London Calling* (1923)
we come upon the very man.

London Calling was an André Charlot production at the Duke of

York's and Noel had been instructed to share the writing of the libretto with Ronald Jeans and the composing of the music with Philip Braham. Jeans was a good twelve years older than Noel, and had had a big part in founding the Liverpool Repertory Theatre. A succession of plays and revues were to his credit as author or part-author, among them, *Tabs*, *Buzz-Buzz* and *Bran Pie*. Philip Braham, too, had written the epoch-making "Limehouse Blues", not to mention the music in Charlot's very successful *Bubbly*, a 1917 revue at the Comedy. But Noel "stole" the show. He was lucky in being in at the beginnings of *London Calling*. Ned Lathom had financed Charlot's earlier revue *A to Z*, and having heard the songs and sketches Noel had, as it were, up his sleeve, called Charlot to Davos where both Lathom and Noel were convalescing. A series of cigar-laden conferences between the three brought *London Calling* into being. Noel edited his songs and sketches in the morning and submitted them to Lathom and Charlot in the afternoon. In a few days the revue, with its twenty-five Calls, was outlined, and, wonder of wonders, Ronald Jeans was allowed a few sketches and Philip Braham achieved at least a place among the "additional numbers". Moreover, Noel was Number Four in a quartette of comedians which included Maisie Gay, Gertrude Lawrence, and Tubby Edlin. Later A. W. Baskcomb took over the part. Maisie Gay was at the top of her form in *Call Five*, a Ronald Jeans scena, entitled "The Ministering Angel". As the bouncing Nurse Doodah, Maisie made life in a nursing home unendurable alike for patient, patient's wife and patient's doctor. Five calls later the same Maisie was Mrs Parish, an old lady of seventy, "Showing her muddle". Add, "There's Life in the Old Girl yet," with Maisie as a *passée* soubrette, and her Hernia Whittlebot in the Sitwell Family skit, and it will be plain that *London Calling* was a Maisie Gay triumph.

Another bit of luck was making contact with Elsie April, whose name did not appear on the crimson programme, but who transferred Mr Coward's melodies and harmony on to paper with the swiftness of an expert stenographer, as the composer put it. With this aid, Noel's music not only reached theatre audiences but was heard in restaurants. As final evidence that the authentic Noel had arrived in the world of the theatre, the words *Noel Coward* in pink electric light bulbs twinkled as the author-player approached the Duke of York's Theatre from Seven Dials each night. All this meant that Noel Coward had tested his powers as author, composer and creator of "a running order" and was ready for a triumph five years later in the shape of *This Year of Grace*.

Enter Miss Lawrence

As has been said, with *London Calling*, Gertrude Lawrence once more joined forces with the trouper, who, as actor, has been so closely associated with her own rise to stardom.

"I come of modest little show-folk, where each one had to pull his weight in the boat. I can cook, sew and scrub—things you learn of necessity and never forget."

Thus Gertrude Lawrence described her start in life. Her father was a travelling *basso-profondo* in late Victorian music-halls. A few half-pints quickly increased the range and richness of his voice. Before she was three, Gert had learnt to add a few pence to the family exchequer by selling programmes and before she was in her 'teens, there were printed cards: *Little Gertie Lawrence, Child Actress and Danseuse*.

The cards led to Gertie's first pantomime engagement. It took the form of one of the starlings who collected leaves to blanket the little hero and heroine in *The Babes in the Wood*. Six shillings a week! An engagement by Charles Cochran for a part in Reinhardt's *The Miracle* furnished another early opportunity, she being one among fifty girls and fifty boys engaged for that Olympia production. These earnings made possible some valuable lessons from Italia Conti and soon Gertie was able to earn a little by helping Miss Conti to teach even younger children. The extra money was spent upon elocution, singing and dancing lessons during periods of "resting". Nevertheless, it was a long time before Miss Lawrence found her way to London. During the seven long years between fourteen and twenty-one she toured the provinces mostly in fit-up shows. The title *Miss Plaster of Paris* suffices to characterize them, but, in the process, "Little Gertie" became Gertrude. In one such show it fell to her lot to sing the popular "Who were you with last night?" usually regarded as a markedly masculine song. The addition of a mirror which reflected a beam of spotlight upon selected gentlemen in the stalls fitted the song to Gertrude's treatment.

But exotic revues were not all. There was a tour with *The Little Michus*. Lee White and her husband, Clay Smith, chanced to see the show and came back to André Charlot with the news that a promising young girl in the provinces was worthy of his attention. Charlot at once offered a dancing rôle in his revue *Some*, with the reversion of the star part on tour. Then came a bit of bad luck for Bea Lillie, who was playing in *Tabs* at the Vaudeville. Thrown from a horse, she could not play, and Gertrude Lawrence took over her part for two whole months. Little Gertie Lawrence was approaching stardom.

Her first real chance came in the revue *Buzz-Buzz*, which led to a series of engagements as a principal, among them *A to Z*, *Rats* and *London Calling*, in which she shared a handful of honours with Noel himself. "Gertrude Lawrence" was now displayed in letters of neon light, and *not* on one of the side panels, but in the blatant central place, whence it beckoned any doubter into revue, musical show, or comedy, as it might be.

There followed the sensational visit to America with Bea Lillie, which put Gertrude Lawrence into the £750 a week class, so far as the States were concerned. When Gertrude came back to London and appeared without stockings, the powers which controlled fashion accepted "no stockings" without a quaver. Noel had done the same service for coloured pull-overs after the success of *The Vortex* and its fellows in 1925.

This was fame indeed, and Mr Cochran must have congratulated himself that Gertrude Lawrence was to hand to fill the title rôle in *Nymph Errant*. Mr Laver's impudent novel had not only been a best-seller, but a reputation-maker, and when Romney Brent converted the novel into a play, with music by Cole Porter, and scenery and costumes by Doris Zinkeisen, it was plainly destined to be one of the outstanding productions of its year, perhaps *the* production. No expense was spared. The six scenes in Act I ranged from a garden in Oxford, by way of Deauville-sur-Mer, and a French café, to the Palazzo Mantalani, Venice. Act II included the ruins on the Acropolis at Athens, a harem in Turkey, a desert scene and the stage of the "Folies de Paris", ending once more in Aunt Ermyntrude's garden in Oxford.

The opportunities vouchsafed to the heroine were no less varied. They began with a breaking-up party in a girls' school from which Evangeline derived the rooted conviction that the slogan upon which she must base her life was, "Experiment!" As Miss Pratt, the science mistress, sang:

> "If this advice you duly employ
> The future can offer you infinite joy,
> *Experiment*, and you will see."

Thus fortified, the Nymph Errant entered upon adolescence. Before Evangeline had reached Calais, she had fallen in with a famous Parisian revue producer, and experiments gave place to experience. They included some days in a nudist colony in Austria and the Turkish harem aforesaid. A snatch of dialogue will indicate what the Nymph Errant had to face in this phase of her career.

Evangeline: I didn't know if I was to be killed or just subjected to what is erroneously termed "a fate worse than death".

Nymph Errant was a generous show. The best number described King Solomon's matrimonial adventures and was sung by an actress who seemed to be a negress. Another Cole Porter number poked fun at the love affairs of the late George Sand and Alfred de Musset. A third song allowed Miss Lawrence to take the Chief Eunuch of the harem into her confidence regarding the trials of a young girl in love with a young doctor, whose interest in anatomy was purely professional. It will thus be seen that the principals in *Nymph Errant* skated upon the thinnest of thin ice, and narrowly escaped duckings. Happily Gertrude had had the training which made liberties permissible.

The Troupers in Partnership

In partnership, Noel and Gertrude were never better than they were in that glorious burst of happy fortune which attended *Private Lives*, when both were entering the thirties. Noel wrote it expressly for Gertrude Lawrence and himself, and was content with four characters and an unimportant housemaid for the development of his essay on second marriages. Elyot and Amanda had been wedded, and for a few months suffered the woes of passionate attachment. These proved too oppressive and the pair divorced and remarried. There would have been no play if both had not come to Venice with their new partners, and, coincidence of coincidences, selected an hotel with adjoining verandas for their honeymooning. When the four young people moved into the moonlight to enjoy the delights of the Grand Canal a meeting was unavoidable, and soon Amanda and Elyot were once more exchanging reminiscences. Quickly it was plain that memories of times past were more potent than the actualities of times present. As the curtain fell on the first act, the couple stole off to renew Marriage One, leaving the masculine and feminine victims of Marriage Two to make their own decision.

Act II of *Private Lives* showed us Elyot and Amanda house-keeping for a second time. Elyot was comfortable in an attractive dressing-gown, and this snatch of dialogue sufficiently characterizes the opening of the act.

Elyot (at the piano): You are the most thrilling, exciting woman that was ever born.
Amanda (also on the piano stool): Dearest—dearest heart.

But present delights were mingled with old-time memories. Neither man nor maid could banish the past. What, for example, had happened after the parting?

Amanda (gently): You must not be unreasonable. I was only trying to stamp out the memory of you. I expect your affairs well out-numbered mine any how.
Elyot: That is a little different. I am a man.
Amanda: Excuse me a moment while I get a carraway biscuit and change to my crinoline.

From patient disputation to violent quarrel was but a stage, and before the Second Act ended the couple were engaged in bodily conflict and fell from sofa to floor, where they were found by their respective spouses.

Amanda: Marry you again, never, never!
Elyot: Shut up. I wouldn't marry you again if you came crawl-to me on your bended knees.
Amanda: Beast, brute, swine, cat, beast, beast, brute.

Henry Irving in some of his famous rôles: Eugene Aram, Charles the First, Digby Grant (*The Two Roses*), The Vicar of Wakefield, Mephistopheles, Richard the Third, Jeremy Diddler (*Raising the Wind*), Fabian (The Corsican in the duel scene from *The Corsican Brothers*); all different and yet all Henry Irving (*see page* 257).

An Example of Make-up.
Cedric Hardwicke as Sir Toby Belch in *Twelfth Night*, Old Vic Company,
New Theatre (1948) (*see page* 256).

The triple bills of 1936, entitled *To-night at 8.30* (at matinées *This Afternoon at 2.30*) recalled *Private Lives*, inasmuch as the playlets provided acting triumphs for Gertrude Lawrence, as well as evidence of Noel's versatility, as author, actor, and producer. As Noel told us at the time of the Phoenix Theatre production, a short play has one great advantage over a long one, in that it can sustain a mood without technical creaking or overpadding. The chief reason for *To-night at 8.30* was a desire to reinstate the one-act play in its rightful place in the English theatre. Moreover, Noel hoped that playing several rôles each week would keep the company on its toes. He succeeded to the full. The varied fare proved a delight to theatre-goers.

One memory will be forgiven, *Red Peppers*. The red-wigged Lily and George Pepper are music-hall artists, doing a couple of turns at a third-rate provincial Palace of Varieties. We see them first, before the drop curtain, in a jolly song and dance scena, "Has Anybody Seen Our Ship?" Gertrude in bell-bottomed trousers is particularly fetching. Unluckily, the beat of the conductor is fast for the singers and the agitated Lily drops her telescope. She is ticked off by her husband in the dressing-room, so is the leader of the orchestra. Consequently, when the manager appears and fails to restore peace between man and wife, he is moved to some sharp criticism of their stage talents. When the Red Peppers are called upon for their second turn, an appearance as two Men about Town, the conductor has his revenge. The Peppers receive the "raspberry" from an angry pit and gallery and the end is dismissal. The whole provided a caustic criticism of vaudeville as our fathers and grandfathers knew it.

Of herself as trouper, Miss Lawrence has made some icy comments, doubtless expressly designed to persuade the young that stage success is due to much more than good looks and the ability to wear gowns from Molyneux.

"Being a person in the theatre after many years is like slowly building up a terrific sort of general store in which you know your wares from top to bottom. For a thin play you pull out all the tricks you can use, but a good play you cheapen by using devices. The secret lies in not allowing yourself to fall in love with your own tricks, and in knowing when the time has come to put them back on the shelves. Even audiences are not always trust-

T

worthy. If they are too easy or too hard, they may trap you after you have responded by exaggeration or overplaying. Every play has a line and it is your job to follow it. Like a melody, you may vary the tempo slightly from moment to moment, but never essentially. Otherwise it is simply Gertrude Lawrence—not the play."

Miss Lawrence added, "If you have patience and intelligence to criticize you grow." And, by growing, Gertrude meant just this, that after years of constant and intelligent self-criticism, a finished actor or actress can sense the temper of an audience so accurately that, even before the curtain goes up, "I know the mood of the people out front by the noise of the programmes, and the talk and bustle they make." This is the reward which comes to theatre folk for beginning young and learning their trade in a school where sickening failure may follow so closely upon unexpected and often undeserved success.

So far as Mr Coward is concerned, the half has not been told. There remains the triumph of *Bitter Sweet*, the best musical play of our generation, and *Cavalcade*, in which Noel shared the glory with his staunch colleague, Mrs Calthrop. Indeed, if a single lesson had to be extracted from the careers of our two troupers it would be the importance of group effort in the theatre.

Group Effort in the Theatre

In business circles a man generally owes more than he admits to his secretaries, typists, and assistants, but, on the stage, the bond between a successful dramatist or an actor-manager extends well into the private lives of half a dozen men and women. From this standpoint Noel explored some of the emotional reactions of a theatrical manager in *Present Laughter*.

Present Laughter was amusing to watch at the Haymarket; to read, it is not only amusing but informative. Noel played Garry Essendine, an actor of fame. In lemon-coloured pyjamas, red leather slippers, and dressing-gowns of varied hues, Garry moves through his luxury flat, saved from emotional and other disasters by a tactful housekeeper, a very competent secretary, and a wife who knows her man in every aspect and in every guise, and remains forgiving. To Garry Essendine's flat came Joanna Lyppiatt, dressed in a gown of ravishing silkiness, and what the experts described as a long page-boy "bob", and, quickly, it was plain that it is the task of the entourage to save Garry from Joanna. The opening scene is concerned with a less serious affair, though a pretty girl wearing a man's dressing-gown and pyjamas is discovered in Garry's flat when his housekeeper comes in to turn back the curtains some time after daybreak. The housekeeper is not in the least perturbed. She is used to unknown damsels invading the Essendine flat. Nor is Monica Reed the secretary surprised. The only thing that matters in her opinion is that Garry's professional routine shall not be upset by the unavoidable spasms of emotion. When Garry does come in, he has quite forgotten the young lady. It seems she had lost her latch-key and he had put her up in his spare room for the night. Nothing more.

Re-read *Present Indicative* in the light of *Present Laughter* or *Present Laughter* in the light of *Present Indicative*, and not a few current theatrical problems present themselves for analysis. *Introducing the Theatre* will have failed in its purpose if it does not make for the understanding of so typical a man of the theatre as Noel Coward. Coming into the world at the turn of the century, the human material he found to hand was the young men and women who had been herd units between 1914 and 1918, and meant to get a kick out of life when the peace came, the kick which displayed itself in *Dance, Little Lady*, as well as in the later scenes of *Cavalcade*. By the time *Peace in Our Time* was produced in 1947, Noel Coward had immensely extended his range. No longer could it be claimed that his generation was represented by Ritz girls or Savoy youths. Still a relatively young man as dramatists go, he is called upon to present the types and classes who have suffered not one but two world wars. And in the fact lies Mr Coward's significance. He is a leader among the men of the theatre with whom the immediate future rests.

CHAPTER 14

VOICE IN THE THEATRE

Spit out the plumstones, my boy, and let's hear what you've got to say.—
Henry Irving

I F a single factor at the disposal of dramatist and player must be
isolated as of primary importance, it would be, Voice. The
art of the theatre is first and foremost addressed to the ear,
though sight can help hearing immensely. Incidentally, the aid
lip-reading gives to hearing is the reason why barristers and
actors are usually clean-shaven, and why young Arthur Roberts,
early in his career, discarded a neat little black moustache and
imperial. The budding comedian decided that it was needful to
display those pliable lips, if his quick-fire wisecracks were to reach
the gallery-boys. Quality of voice ranks far above beauty of
feature or grace of movement and gesture, and, in voice, variety
and range are more important than mere charm of tone or volume. Given proper enunciation and the capacity to place the
voice, a player can, by subtle changes in timing and stress, attract
and hold the wandering attention of an audience and awaken
hearers to full understanding.

Without training little can be achieved. Coquelin's stage voice
had no special quality at the beginning of his career. Volume,
range, variety, and control were acquired by training, until
Coquelin could play Cyrano, one of the longest and most
trying parts in poetic drama, twice in a day and yet suffer no
vocal fatigue. Coquelin has said: "I never really speak. What I do
is to rap out each syllable, striking it on the head, as it were. The
effect I get is speed, but every word can be heard in the gallery."

And to be heard with ease and to the very back of the gallery
was only one purpose of the training. Coquelin required a big
range of intonation if he was to be the actor he wanted to be. In
this same rôle, Coquelin, in the second act of *Cyrano*, was required
to repeat the word "Oui" twelve or fifteen times, and each time

with a varying expression. He was speaking with Roxane in the eating-house, and she was confessing her love, as to a friend whom she was meeting again after a lapse of years and trusted fully.

Roxane: Listen, I am in love.
Cyrano: Ah!
Roxane: But with one who does not know.
Cyrano: Ah!
Roxane: But one, who if he knows not, soon shall learn.
Cyrano: Ah!
Roxane: A poor youth, who all this time has loved, timidly, from afar, and dare not speak.
Cyrano: Ah!
Roxane: Leave your hand; why, it is fever-hot. But I have seen love trembling on his lips.
Cyrano: Ah!
Roxane (*bandaging Cyrano's wounded hand*)*:* And to think that, by chance . . . Yes, cousin, he is in your regiment.
Cyrano: Ah!
Roxane (*laughing*)*:* Is cadet in your own company!
Cyrano: Ah!

These are the tests which reveal the well-trained actor, but consider the hours of intensive study which led to such craft-skill.

Samuel Phelps, the Shakespearean actor to whom Johnston Forbes-Robertson owed so much, had a weak, reed-like voice at the beginning, but developed organ tones befitting the greatest Shakespearean rôles by dint of continuous breathing and diaphragm exercises. Sarah Bernhardt continued with these exercises until a single inhalation, accompanied by muscular abdominal control, enabled her to declaim four lines of *Phèdre*. It was long and constant training which enabled Sarah to play in a theatre as large as the Coliseum towards the end of her career, and be assured that every whisper would be heard.

Nor was there any sacrifice of quality. On the contrary, Arthur Symons has spoken of the "strangely hypnotic effect" of much of Sarah's stage diction, though, as he said, there were other times when the golden voice had a solemn chant, which seemed to sweep up to a flood of sound, or, on the contrary, break into a swift staccato, recalling the breaking of a wave upon a pebbled beach. And yet, it may be that Rachel was even more accomplished than Sarah herself in the outpourings of words at the high-speed which are all-important in French classical tragedy.

It may well be asked if there can ever have been a more expressive stage voice than that of Yvette Guilbert. In old age, when almost all the beauty of tone had gone, she could still conjure up an immense range of characters and express a vast range of emotion. Now it might be the delight of children watching the miracle of the Mass; now the stilled awe of the Woman of Samaria in the presence of her Lord. The ribald and the heroic (as in the herald-like tones with which the death of the great Marlborough was announced in "Malbrouk s'en va-t'en guerre") all were at Yvette Guilbert's command.

In her *La Chanson de ma Vie*, Yvette Guilbert has told as much as an artist can tell of the methods whereby she thrust home the full significance of a song upon her audiences. Every syllable was duly articulated, not only that it might be heard, but that it might be understood. Regarded as a vocal instrument there was no special beauty, but as an instrument for thrusting home satirical portraiture, everything; and with this endowment went the rarest gifts of impersonation. A woman of the Parisian boulevards in the throes of passion! Yvette Guilbert's sexless body and limbs became strangely feline and snake-like. And as the lust seemed to take possession of the body, the voice changed. Instead of a plaintive murmur, there arose a raucous cry of impassioned revolt. The wretched woman had realized she was being cheated of love by the arch-enemy, Death. As Yvette Guilbert said, her brain aided her voice to colour itself, to enlarge and to create by its rhythm "the spectre of a singer's voice".

Ellen Terry's voice was one of the most charming in the long history of the British stage, though no responsible critic would describe it in terms applicable to the greatest of the French players. Beauty of delivery was what Ellen sought, and this is what she achieved. Few players acquire the capacity to speak verse as Ellen Terry spoke it, making it sound as though it were the proper language of the character in portrayal.

Training Methods

Hard work will not ensure a player the charm of voice which belonged to Ellen and her sister Marion, or the resonance and unsurpassed suggestiveness of Coquelin's diction, but it will do much. Even the modicum required for a successful career is not easy to acquire, and when acquired, only too easy to lose. As in youth Demosthenes practised with pebbles in his mouth on the sea-shore, so Seymour Hicks relied upon the more palatable orange. He has told us that, in his teens, he found *his* voice with the aid of an orange. His tutor said, "Open your mouth wide, round your lips and say 'Orange'." Whereupon he would hold up an actual orange, while the youthful Seymour obeyed the next injunction: "Now open wide enough to get the orange into your mouth."

Again, Elise Craven, the dancer, had not even reached her teens when she was given her first speaking part as the Fairy Queen in *Pinkie and the Fairies*. The theatre was His Majesty's and the girl found it none too easy to "find her voice" on the large stage. Beerbohm Tree's bribe was an outsize box of chocolates. The stronger Elise's voice became, the larger the rewarding chocolates. And the result? After the run of *Pinkie* ended, Elise Craven could earn £100 a week at the Coliseum, and she was still only eleven.

When Violet Vanbrugh was playing the longer Shakespearean parts, such as Queen Katharine in *King Henry the Eighth*, she accepted a hint from Henry Arthur Jones and read Milton aloud for half an hour daily. The music of *Paradise Lost* and *Samson Agonistes* ensured that the vowel sounds should be full and pure, and the consonants crystal-clear.

Johnston Forbes-Robertson was a player, who, like Ellen Terry, relied largely upon sheer beauty of tone. He has told us that, in youth, the historian Brewer took him up and down the scale, until he could speak on the notes of two octaves, as against the five or six notes of the ordinary speaking voice. Brewer used to strike a low note on a piano and required the young actor to speak a line of poetry on the note. Always the instruction was: "Do not sing the words, speak them." Thus Forbes-Robertson passed from note to note until his speaking register had the requisite flexibility and variety of tone. Louis Calvert was another actor of the same generation with a speaking voice ranging over two octaves, while, among the women, a competent critic wrote of Julia Neilson, "She had more notes than any actress I have heard." Some of the gift was due to her early training as a singer, before W. S. Gilbert discovered the actress.

Lena Ashwell, like Julia Neilson, had meant to be a singer before she decided to become an actress. She was still at the Royal Academy of Music when Ellen Terry persuaded Comyns Carr to hear Miss Ashwell, who was then at the close of her 'teens. At the time, she had a light soprano speaking voice, but with help from Comyns Carr and Stanley Hawley, added an octave to the lower register, and this extra octave gave her the instrument required for emotional rôles. As Miss Ashwell intoned a dramatic passage, Hawley played chords on the piano, until the actress began to respond to the harmonies and realize how thin her stage voice really was. The final discovery was that the voice which belonged to her emotional self was fully an octave lower.

The analogy between vocal training for operatic and dramatic work, indeed, almost amounts to identity. George Vandenhoff tells us that training enabled Edmund Kean to deliver Othello's "Farewell" speech night after night, with the same pauses and breaks, the same *fortes* and *pianos*, the same *crescendos* and *diminuendos*, "as if he spoke from a musical score". Realizing the analogy, Bernard Shaw actually annotated the long speeches in *Man and Superman* for Robert Loraine, when the actor was contemplating an American production. The margin of the script which Loraine took with him "twinkled with crochets, crescendos, and minims, with G clefs, F clefs, and pianissimos". In order to force Loraine to avoid any impression of prepared oratory, Shaw turned Tanner's speeches into "grand opera" and, lo and behold, the result was not a sing-song delivery, but what seemed like a series of impromptus.

Indeed, Cedric Hardwicke carried this point of view still further when he said of Bernard Shaw: "Shaw, one fancies, regards a theatrical company as an orchestra, and the individual players as instruments. His dialogue is coloured with the different tones of the individual voices. Each actor and actress must maintain the correct and pleasing harmony of the orchestra, and when the tone of one begins to become tedious, another comes in. . . There are quiet passages as moving as an andante by Haydn or Mozart."

In this connection it may be significant that O'Neill wrote the dialogue of *All God's Chillun* with a metronome ticking in his study. I am also reminded that Alan Dent once compared Gielgud's delivery of the "Queen Mab" speech in *Romeo and Juliet* to a *scherzo*, "the words fluttering from Mercutio's brain as lightly as the elfin vision that they drew".

Beauty of tone in a stage voice is much, but it is not everything. Edmund Kean had command of melody and could express the most tender emotions, but his training allowed of the harsh dissonance of vehement passion and energy, without which many classic rôles would have been beyond his compass, as they were beyond that of, say, Johnston Forbes-Robertson.

Hard work can achieve most things, as the example of Macready shows. He disliked the theatre fully as much as Forbes-Robertson did a generation later, yet Macready was unsparing in his devotion to his art. Writing to his wife, Macready gave this account of a day's work: "I studied *Hamlet* for five hours, recited some poems by Milton for two hours, then back again to *Hamlet* after supper for another three hours." Macready was writing at five o'clock in the morning, and he adds: "I am haunted by this Danish Prince and wonder continually whether I cannot improve my interpretation. Yet alteration is only effective when it is based upon a greater understanding of the character concerned. Finally, I got out of bed and went through the whole play again. And now my letter to you."

As has been said, full command of the lower notes in the speaking register counts for much. Winifred Emery, about the turn of the century, was an actress of persuasive charm and could compel audiences to accept her graces and beauty, as, in very truth, those of the imagined character. No actress ever wore eighteenth-century dress more pleasantly. The poise of her head and her carriage were perfection. But the low-pitched contralto voice, which could make its beauty felt in the largest theatre, was an even more enduring endowment.

Marie Löhr was another actress with a low-toned voice of thrilling quality. So was Margaret Rawlings, as she showed in plays as varied as *Parnell* and *Black Limelight*, the sheer loveliness of tone being combined with that perfect control which suggests passion in which there are reserves of emotion. Remember Margaret Rawlings's "Oh God, oh God, oh God!" as Parnell lay dead in her arms. On the negative side, even the best equipped of players may fail to acquire the variety of elocution necessary for the longest rôles. Those who admire Sybil Thorndike most will admit a certain monotony of delivery, in part due to a trick of lowering the voice in the middle of a phrase and raising it at the end. The absence of full variety was not noticeable in relatively short parts and this accounts for Dame Sybil's marked success as Hecuba in *The Trojan Women*, a success which made one curious over lesser triumphs in the longer Shakespearean parts, such as Lady Macbeth. In Grand Guignol parts, where it was all-important to create a sense of fear, Dame Sybil was unsurpassed. Here her resources of voice and gesture were ample.

Charles Wyndham's voice had not the organ-like beauty of tone which was Willard's, Forbes-Robertson's, Henry Ainley's, Basil Gill's, and Ion Swinley's, but its husky quality was markedly charming and Wyndham could call upon reserves of deeper and higher pitched notes when playing parts such as *David Garrick* which called for a fuller range of emotion. Edith Evans's gift as a speaker of stage dialogue lies in the range of tones of which she is a mistress.

Fred Leslie, of the Old Gaiety

The facts in connection with Fred Leslie at the Old Gaiety are exceptionally interesting and well-documented. By constant practice he acquired a command of his vocal organs which even the initiated regarded as only less than miraculous. Dr Lennox Browne and Dr Emil Behnke, both of whom were vocal experts, explaining the apparent miracle, began by recalling that ordinary vocal tone is produced by the vocal chords meeting a column of air blown from below and setting up two sets of vibrations in the elastic chords. But the tone thus produced is not the whole of the matter, for these primary vocal tones are reinforced by the upper part of the larynx, the upper throat, the mouth, and the nose. Fred Leslie's voice was a light baritone with a compass of a couple of octaves, from G to G but the imitations for which Leslie was famous were almost always produced on the middle A. The differences were due to alterations in larynx, throat, nose, and mouth, which changed the character of each sound.

Not only constant practice but unceasing invention were called for. Before Leslie's time, Farnie's song, "The Language of Love", had been sung by several actors, English and French, but all agreed that Leslie's effort stood in a class of its own. Among the sounds imitated were those of a frog, a bull, a turkey-cock, and a chicken, and Dr Lennox Browne and Mr Behnke studied each. Thus, instead of the customary expiratory breath, the croaking of the frog was imitated by the vocal chords being thrown into action by an inward current of air, taken from without through the mouth.

"The imitation of the bull", continue the experts, "was done by closing the lips and allowing the whole of the sound, which is of the character known as *portamento*, to escape through the nose. The note of the turkey consists of a series of falsetto tones, with an exceedingly rapid trill at the tip of the tongue and lips. A testimony to the excellence of this imitation is afforded by the fact that on one occasion, when Mr Leslie was exercising, he was actually driven by the turkey-cocks from the farmyard, jealous of the attraction which the intruding copyist had for the fair ones of their harem. The cluck of the hen is done by rapid labial movements, but the final tone is effected by raising the back of the tongue and lowering the soft palate, so as to force the laryngeal tone through an extremely narrow aperture.

"The next series of imitations altogether original are those contained in the song written by Mr Leslie concerning the love story of two dolls, in which the sounds of numerous toys, as heard in the Lowther Arcade, are reproduced. They consist of the Punch and Judy, the toy rabbit, the doll which squeaks when pressure is made on its abdomen, and the popgun. With regard to the majority of these there is nothing of novel interest, but the squeak of the doll, which was the prelude to Mr Leslie's imitations of the violin, is really something very marvellous, for it is produced by what is known as the 'small register', a mechanism peculiar to children and women's voices. The note of the squeak is the high soprano A flat, and is perfectly phenomenal, since it is placed more than three octaves above the lowest limit of Mr Leslie's normal singing voice. The noise of the popgun is effected by falsetto *portamento*, followed by a loud explosion which is caused by suction with the tongue.

"Lastly, come the imitations of musical instruments as illustrated by Mr Leslie's newest song, 'Love in the Orchestra'. The musical instruments imitated are the violoncello, the clarinet, the cymbals, and the violin; in this series may be also included another instrument not exactly orchestral, and portrayed by many other artists, but by few so well as the subject of these remarks—namely, the banjo. The effect of the banjo is produced by exceedingly energetic pressure and forcible explosive opening of the lips, the laryngeal tone being the while conveyed entirely through the nostrils. In the 'cello imitation the vocal tone also passes entirely through the nose while the lips are kept firmly closed. This last fact can be demonstrated by the circumstances that a mirror held against the lips is undimmed, however long the imitation is continued, while, held under the nostrils, it is immediately clouded by the moisture of the expired breath. The clarinet tones are imitated by singing in falsetto from the upper part of the scale downwards; the cymbals, by forcing the tone through the closed teeth with labial explosion."

As all the training in the world will not give a singer the velvety tones of a Patti or a Caruso, so training will not give an actor the lovely quality of the voices of Basil Gill, Henry Ainley, or Paul Robeson. Henry Irving's stage voice, telling as it was in a wide range of rôles, never had quality in this sense. In character, it was high and thin, and as Henry Arthur Jones has said, some of the most characteristic utterances were ejaculated from the roof of the mouth through the almost closed teeth and lips, in a hard, super-caustic tone, as bloodless and dry as caked grey pumice. In general, the open vowels were slurred so that the broad "o's" and "a's" became something very like "i's" and "e's". Yet, in certain parts, Irving could command other modes of speech. He would drop into a deep bass better fitted to a nobler and more saintly character, or a momentary generosity in a more complex character. There was such a change of voice in *The Bells*, while Mathias was counting the money put aside for his daughter's dowry. The conscience-stricken Burgomaster came upon the piece of old gold which had belonged to the murdered Jew: "No, no, not for Annette!" In this connection, Jean-Louis Barrault was illuminating when he said of stage speech, "imagine the vowels as the romantic part and the consonants as the disciplined part of language," and added "control the muscles of your mouth and you will control the consonants." The vowel sounds, of course, are controlled by the diaphragm muscles.

One of the pleasures of the theatre is to listen to an actor or actress treating the key phrases which reveal character and carry on a story. Mrs Kendal has recalled what Mrs John Wood made of the words, "Same old gown", in Pinero's *The Magistrate*. Mrs Wood looked the wearer of the gown up and down, from head to feet, from feet to head, not once but twice, and then said the words in accents of pitying commiseration.

This was an actress's effort. For a line which a dramatist devised, knowing he could pass the effect on through a competent player, there is Candida's revealing, "When there is money to give, he gives it; when there is money to refuse, I refuse it."

Ponder a few more memorable lines in the theatre of the past half-century and consider how much hard labour went to their polishing before they achieved the form which made them memorable. For example, Henry Irving as the aged Guardsman in *A Story of Waterloo*: "The Guards want powder, and by God, they shall have it." Or, in a lighter mood, four words spoken by J. H. Roberts as the elderly clergyman-father of the twins in Hastings Turner's *The Lilies of the Field*. A well-loved wife asked him: "John, dear! Husbands do tell their wives everything, don't they?" The reply was, "Yes, my dear, often."

Nor would one willingly forget the "theatre" Tree instilled into a couple of words, when playing the old detective in *The Red Lamp:* "I wonder!"

Ellen Terry said to H. V. Neilson, "the secret of all fine acting is to convey the idea of thinking before you speak." Ellen Terry, Mrs Kendal, Lottie Venne, and Winifred Emery all developed this capacity in a high degree and it is a quality which is sadly lacking to-day and accounts for not a little faulty elocution. The dramatist of worth does not write lines that they may be "thrown away", as the current slang of the stage puts it.

Nor must it be forgotten that not a few of these theatrical coups are shared between dramatist and actor. It was the dramatist who devised the opportunity. Remember Mrs Warren's outburst during her long talk with her daughter in the second act of *Mrs Warren's Profession*. Vivie had been scoring heavily over her all too worldly mother.

Mrs Warren (*querulously*): You're very rough with me, Vivie.
Vivie: Nonsense. What about bed? It's past ten.
Mrs Warren (*passionately*): What's the use of my going to bed? Do you think I could sleep?
Vivie: Why not? I shall.

But ten minutes later, after Mrs Warren has made her rejoinder.

Mrs Warren (*yawning*): Oh dear, I do believe I'm getting sleepy after all. (*She stretches herself lazily.*)
Vivie: I believe it is I who will not sleep now.

Or Somerset Maugham, in his war play, *The Unknown*, when he gave these words to his bereaved mother. "Who is going to forgive God? Not I. Never! Never!" Haidee Wright made the cry an unforgettable thing.

Again, the sex-repressed Eva in Maugham's *For Services Rendered*, when acted by Flora Robson. She had been playing chess with her war-blinded brother and swept the pieces on to the floor with the cry: "Why should I be sacrificed all the time? . . . I'm sick of being a drudge. I'm sorry he's blind. But it's not my fault. I'm not responsible for the war. He ought to go into a home."

Another interesting example comes to mind in connection with that grand trouper, Ellen Terry. The play was Shakespeare's *Cymbeline* and the scene Imogen's bed-chamber in Cymbeline's palace. Iachimo's trunk is in a corner of the room and Imogen is in bed, reading. The stage direction adds that a lady-in-waiting is in attendance.

Ellen Terry knew that audiences at the Lyceum would want a little time to familiarize themselves with the lovely bedroom scene, and that Shakespeare's effect would be wasted if she just put down the book, turned over in bed, and went to sleep, with Iachimo coming at once from the trunk. The scene with the Lady Helen, therefore, could not be hurried. So she called twice, making it plain that Helen had been dozing. Imogen's next question was "What hour is it?" and Ellen Terry asked the question in such a way as to suggest that Helen had been sleeping, but that a kindly mistress had already forgiven the tiny lapse. And Imogen's next speech explains why. Imogen wishes to wake four hours later, and with the gentlest courtesy thus emphasizes her next request,

> If thou canst awake by four o' the clock,
> I prithee, call me. Sleep hath seized me wholly.
>
> (*Exit Lady.*)

Indeed, Shakespeare was equally responsible for this beautiful opening to the bed-chamber scene, but it needed an actress of the richest sensibility to make so gracious a use of the opportunity. Here is the passage:

Imogen: Who's there? my woman Helen?
Lady: Please you, madam.
Imogen: What hour is it?
Lady: Almost midnight, madam.
Imogen: I have read three hours then; mine eyes are weak:
> Fold down the leaf where I have left; to bed:
> Take not away the taper, leave it burning;
> And if thou canst awake by four o' the clock,
> I prithee, call me. Sleep hath seized me wholly.
>
> (*Exit Lady.*)
>
> To your protection I commend me, gods!
> From fairies and the tempters of the night
> Guard me, beseech ye!
>
> (*Sleeps. Iachimo comes from the trunk.*)

There was another equally revealing example in Ellen Terry's study of *Much Ado About Nothing*, when Beatrice cried: "O God, that I were a man! I would eat his heart in the market-place." Dame Ellen made this a sudden passionate sob of suppressed emotion. "O! God, that I were a man! I would—" Then came a prolonged pause, as if the idea was forming, followed by a cry in which anger was mingled with scarcely repressed tears: "I would eat his heart . . ." Or, again, in the Church scene, when Benedick said, "Come, bid me do anything for you." Ellen listened, caught her breath as she realized what the words conveyed and then flashed out, "Kill Claudio!"

And that line from Tennyson's *Becket*, as Irving delivered it: "Men are God's trees and women are God's flowers." But it might be Irving in a score of parts. Of his Hamlet, H. M. Walbrook used to say that, after the words, "when the wind is southerly I know a hawk from a handsaw," Lyceum audience applauded, from pit to gallery. In a very different mood was the leap upon the messenger who brought the news of the moving wood at Birnam. "Liar and slave!" Irving, "a great famished wolf", spat out the words. Or earlier in *Macbeth*, following upon Ellen Terry's scornful, "We fail!", Ellen drew her man aside and in whispers outlined her plot. In wonder and admiration, his eyes flashing and every nerve in his body a-quiver in homage to such a wife, came Macbeth's

> Bring forth men-children only;
> For thy undaunted mettle should compose
> Nothing but males.

And, lastly, as Mathias in *The Bells*, at the climax of the drama, following the dream in which Mathias enacts the murder of the Jew and receives the sentence of death on the gallows. "The rope! The rope! Cut the rope!" Irving fell, clutching at his throat, as though to remove the strangling thing. Then after a pitiful lifting of the eyes, as though seeking some reassurance from wife and daughter, the head fell to the breast and Mathias was dead. The tortures of a haunted conscience do not find expression through carefully remembered movements and intonations alone, however essential preliminary rehearsals may have been. Long pondering, a rich sensitivity, and an ever-moving imagination must all be added.

No less pondering thought and restless imaginings went to Irving's creation of that crafty old ruffian, Louis XI, mumbling his prayers to the little images in his cap, and ending with an evil leer, "If I thought ye knew what was in my mind, I'd burn ye." Or the suggestions of devilish cunning and ugly malice which Irving mingled with the pride and pathos of his Shylock, now cringing, now pawing nervously at his cloak, but, at long last, arousing a deep pity and even indignation because these Christians seemed to be baiting a broken man.

On a lower plane of achievement, similar craft-skill made memorable Lewis Waller's description of D'Artagnan's journey to London in Henry Hamilton's adaptation of *The Three Musketeers*. So rich was Waller's tone and so varied his timing, that every episode stood out in clear outline.

And what is required for a long speech is equally required if relatively unimportant lines are to have their due effect. Ernest Thesiger was often rehearsed by Charles Hawtrey and he tells that, at the close of a long career, Hawtrey would rehearse what seemed a quite unimportant line, testing scores of deliveries, until he struck upon the perfect one; that is to say perfect for Hawtrey. His maxim was, "There is a laugh in every line, if it is delivered properly." Hawtrey's insistence upon detail extended to gesture. Recall the hesitations, a mingling of anxiety and hope, with which, in *A Messenger From Mars*, after giving away the banknotes in the dream passages, Hawtrey took up his overcoat, to find the precious bundle in the pocket. And the reassuring smile when he fingered the notes. Yet Hawtrey was the stage liar of his generation. He could compel a smile just by looking down at his finger nails, when he had been detected in a Hawtrey fib. A pregnant phrase is not a recitation but an interpretation. The player by his timing, his intonation and the emotion he can add to the vowel sounds is carrying the story forward, as an interpreter should.

But it still remains true that supreme art is that which hides art. This is what distinguishes "the cultivated natural voice" from the "acquired artificial one", as Bernard Shaw once put it. The audience should feel that it is following the thought of the character and not the utterance of the actor or actress. When Ada Rehan played Rosalind, she was not reciting Shakespeare's poetry, but revealing a personality whose characteristics were developing in the imaginations of her listeners, under the witchery of the poet. That is why the curtleaxe scene set a crowded house at the Grand, Islington, chuckling. What was heard was the utterance of a full-hearted woman; which was Rosalind or which Ada Rehan, who could tell?

Nor must it be thought that bell-like production is the only

U

voice which gives delight on the stage. Lynn Fontanne's pretty drawl, for example, emphasizing the point of a line; Vesta Tilley's "burr" which accompanied every "R" was no less charming; and who would have deprived the Terry family of the familiar huskiness, a quality which also characterized the stage voices of Martin-Harvey and Madge Titheradge? Cyril Maude could command the low tones which best express emotion, but he invented a falsetto when called upon to characterize Grumpy, and very effective it was when added to a make-up which occupied an hour every evening. Maude's large mouth and pliable lips were recognized assets in a character actor. He could also call upon an attractive drawl, with a touch of the guttural at the end of a sentence. H. B. Irving's voice tended to be hard and metallic —a virtue when he was playing villain parts; the reverse of an asset when he was playing Hamlet.

Ralph Lynn's "half-drawling", half "cold in the head", speech may have had its origin in a weak, lisping voice, but who would have it otherwise?

Nor would any one have wished Adele Astaire's high-pitched "baby" voice to have been other than it was. At the other end of the scale the American musical-comedy star, Ethel Merman, denied any quality of beauty in her singing voice, substituted a full-throated, metallic roar, and, thus aided, she put over upon American audiences George Gershwin's "I Got Rhythm" and Cole Porter's "You're the Top". A long series of Cole Porter triumphs followed including *Dubarry Was a Lady* and *Panama Hattie*. The climax of Ethel Merman's career was her Annie Oakley, the trigger-tease, in *Annie Get Your Gun*.

When Arthur Sinclair, in *Juno and the Paycock*, was playing the slow-witted but cunning Jack Doyle, there was no call for the fiery delivery Lewis Waller used in describing D'Artagnan's ride. Sinclair's delivery had to reveal the workings of a mind which was the reverse of the nimble-witted Gascon. Indeed, there are many variants in voice production, all of which can justly be described as fully successful. Edward Terry's voice was thin and had a short compass; the intonations indeed were so curious at times that he was described as resembling an "animated clarinet". But it served the comedian excellently, not only in full-blooded burlesque at the Old Gaiety but in the pathos which

Pinero required in *Sweet Lavender*. "Last time, Clemmy, my boy."

No more need be said regarding dialect as an aid to character creation, but the sham dialects which players devise as an aid to personal characterization are interesting. The Scottish tongue of Harry Lauder is a case in point, being neither Scottish nor English but a cunning mixture of both. Similarly, there are "Mind my bike" Jack Warner's semi-genteel cockneyisms, which first made their appearance on the Wireless during the second World War. Whereas the Cockney of fact broadened his "ahs" and "aws", Warner flattened them into "e's", while the long "e" became "i". Thus ham became "hem" and bread "brid". The memorable address upon stewed eels accordingly recalled every sort of "ill" which flesh is heir to, curiously emphasizing the propriety of Warner's dictum, "'E didn't ought-er a et it." In the accepted Cockney dialect, girl would have been "gal" and rhymed with pal, but when Private Warner addressed the icy little lady who sold programmes, chocolates, and cigarettes in *Garrison Theatre*, it was as "li'l gel". In general the lips are kept close, so that no broad vowel escapes.

Gordon Harker's cockneyisms were akin to those of Private Warner, both suggesting that the man from Stepney had been rising in the world, and in Mr Lonsdale's phrase, might now be regarded as "every other inch a gentleman".

And, lastly, some of the key lines of drama, noting how directly they associate themselves with the characters who gave them life and to whom they gave life. Mary Clare, as the warm-hearted refreshment-stall keeper in *The Likes of Her*, saying, "There ain't no crocked-up soldiers—not as I sees 'em." or John Gielgud, at the close of *Noah*, asking "Are you satisfied, Lord?" Noah has his axe upon the wood of the Ark and is preparing to build that nice new house for Mrs Noah. A moment and we have God's answer in the form of the rainbow on the back-cloth. The curtain falls on Noah's, "That's fine."

Again, that clever actress, Olga Lindo, was called upon to play in *Tarnish* and had to make the most of a snatch of dialogue which gave the keynote to the play: "They're a poor lot, the men, all of 'em, and dirty too—but the thing is to get one that cleans easy."

A little later, Olga Lindo had an uncomfortable part in Avery Hopwood's *The Best People*. One seemed to look into the ugly little soul of an American chorus girl, when Miss Lindo chuckled, "You know, the purer I dress, the faster I look."

These are tests of craftsmanship. It is on record that Mrs Siddons, in the role of Belvidera, could make an audience mute with the two words, "Remember Twelve," as Rachel could with "Je crois," when she played Pauline. Elizabeth Barry (she died in 1713) played Queen Elizabeth in a forgotten tragedy entitled *The Unhappy Favourite* or *The Girl of Essex* and the dialogue included this commonplace question: "What mean my grieving subjects?" Yet Elizabeth Barry's intonation, accompanied by a gesture of infinite dignity and grace, moved a Jacobean playhouse to a thunder of applause. Mary of Modena who was present was so touched that she gave the actress the wedding dress she had worn when she married James II and the mantle she carried at her coronation, so that afterwards, when Mrs Barry played Elizabeth, it was in the robes of a very Queen.

From Dodie Smith's *Touch Wood* there lingers the memory of Flora Robson as the self-contained spinster, putting embroidery upon some feminine under-garment. A be-monocled ass looks down upon the needlework.

Eric Cowley: Lord knows why girls want to waste so much time on things no one's going to see.
Flora Robson: You seem depressingly sure of that.

More complex, but no less delightful in memory, is Janet Carve's debate with her husband in *The Great Adventure*. The artist had presumably been "buried" in Westminster Abbey, yet the problem of his identity has arisen in acute form. What a wealth of meaning Wish Wynne instilled into:

Janet: But, then, on the other hand, if there is one thing certain in this world it is that you were never married before you married me. That I *will* swear to.

Wish Wynne had a reputation in pantomime and on the "halls", so there was a touch of genius in Granville-Barker's decision that here was the only possible Janet Carve. As she had no theatrical experience, Granville-Barker, as producer, had to coach Wish Wynne in every detail, until she was the artist's good genius to the life, simple, practical, humorous, and understanding. Good as Henry Ainley was as Ilam Carve, playgoers treasure the recollection of Wish Wynne as the authentic Janet, and her "that I *will* swear to" as the *clou* to her characterization. There was the wisdom of two weddings in the five words.

I must not be tempted into a mere recital of the key speeches in drama. It will suffice to recall two or three, as examples of a player's task from a single standpoint. Ralph Richardson, standing in the Inn at the End of the World, as Robert Johnson, in Priestley's *Johnson Over Jordan* was given these words, as troubled but resolute, he moved into the unknown:

I have been a foolish, greedy and ignorant man;
Yet I have had my time beneath the sun and stars;
I have known the returning strength and sweetness of
     the seasons,
Blossom on the branch and the ripening of fruit,
The deep rest of the grass, the salt of the sea,
The frozen ecstasy of mountains.
The earth is nobler than the world we have built upon it;
The earth is long-suffering, solid, fruitful;
The world still shifting, dark, half-evil.
But what have I done that I should have a better world,
Even though there is in me something that will not rest
Until it sees Paradise.
          Farewell, all good things!
          You will not remember me.
          But I shall remember you.

Then there is the prayer which Mrs Doyle put up for her rebel son in *Juno and the Paycock*: "What was the pain I suffered, Johnny, bringin' you into the world to carry you to your cradle, to the pains I'll suffer carryin' you out o' the world to bring you to your grave! Mother o' God, Mother o' God, have pity on us all! Blessed Virgin, where were you when me darlin' son was riddled with bullets. Sacred Heart o' Jesus, take away our hearts o' stone, and give us hearts o' flesh! Take away this murdherin' hate, an' give us Thine own eternal love."

One more example must suffice. This time Emlyn Williams in

Night Must Fall, when, as the boy-murderer Dan, he both wrote the speech, and as actor, gave it perfect expression.

"But everything's slippin' away from underneath our feet. Can't you feel it? Starting slow—and then hundreds of miles an hour. I'm going backwards. And there's a wind in my ears, terrible blowin' wind. Everything going past me. All the things I've ever seen, faster and faster, backwards, back to the day I was born . . . I'm going to die . . . It's getting cold. (*The torch of the detective is seen at the window.*)"

CHAPTER 15

ADD TO VOICE, GESTURE

ESTURE is to be regarded as a non-verbal language, and covers facial and hand movements, as well as gait, any of which in their own time and place may be as character-revealing as speech itself, when an actor or actress of genius is at work. Indeed gesture has one great advantage over speech. It is international in its appeal. Moreover, coming from the sub-conscious, without passing through the cooling chamber of mental criticism, expressive gesture may well have a larger emotional content than the greater part of stage speech, and, in this sense, is to be regarded as the form of speech most nearly akin to what is primitive in human nature. In moments of the highest emotional tension, the passions dictate action, not the mind.

In the Krishna or Rama plays of Malabar (Kathakali), as Uday Shan-kar showed us at the Savoy Theatre some years ago, theatrical miming was so fully developed that stage speech was dispensed with altogether and yet a complicated story could be presented. This miming is still performed in specially-built theatres within the Hindu temple precincts in Malabar. Gesture sequences, facial expressions and traditional postures and move-ments have, in the course of centuries, become a mute language. Twenty-four key *mudras* allow of several hundred combinations, each hand movement coinciding with appropriate facial move-ments. Thus love, hatred, pity, contempt, and similar moods are conjured up and accepted by Hindu audiences, the whole reinforced by appropriate music from drums, a gong and cym-bals. The instruments are well-fitted for an out-of-door art, such as the Kathakali. The actors learn their craft in childhood, the period of training occupying at least twelve years. The make-up of a Kathakali player alone involves high skill.

Here, surely, is justification for a chapter devoted to carriage, gesture, facial expression, and the ingenuities of "business" which relieve and enrich stage speech.

But, first, a few moments upon the nature of seeing, as opposed to listening in the theatre, good seeing being the contribution which audiences make to half of the stage effects open to an actor or actress. The word gesture comes from the Latin *gerere* "to wear" and with the addition of "se" "to display oneself". The derivation alone suggests that a graceful and balanced display of gesture should arise if the training of the player has been adequate. Watching a player may be fully as delightful and revealing as listening to him, and, as the capacity for alert attention is easily exhausted, playgoers are frequently required to choose between the one delight and the other. Among the gestures none are more important than those of the eyes. Among the fundamental rules is "the audience should see both eyes of a player." When in profile, the actor loses a good half of his power to control an audience. While an actor must always be giving the appearance of addressing his fellows on the stage, a well-trained player holds the spectators with his eyes, as he is really looking into the auditorium while he seems to be bestowing full attention upon those acting with him.

A cognate principle is that which Marie Tempest embodied in a remark to one of her supports, "Remember, audiences must see the reactions on *your* face if they are to get the pith of *my* remarks."

Like all stage technique, the trick of gesture must be learnt. Just as Forbes-Robertson and Lena Ashwell followed the notes of a piano when learning to increase the compass of their voices, so Sophie Tucker used a mirror day after day, while learning to gesture gracefully. In *Some of These Days* Miss Tucker tells that, when she sees a fellow entertainer standing in front of the mike, hanging on for dear life, she feels like yelling: "Let go, sister. If you only knew how terrible you look like that, you'd lower the mike, stand clear of it and use your hands as a part of your act, the way an entertainer should."

In connection with this matter of arousing and maintaining attention, an important distinction must be drawn between what the eye, as the tool of vision, sees and what the brain behind the eye perceives and interprets. What we "see" on the stage is not photographic likeness but optical likeness, a very different thing. The consequences of this have been investigated by Dr Lloyd Mills in an interesting paper. Dr Mills recalled that, like the photographic camera, the eye has a focusing lens, a diaphragm, a dark chamber and a film sensitive to light. But whereas the film in the camera is flat and records everything with equal clearness, the retina of the eye is curved and is a hollow hemisphere, with its concavity forward. Thus the lens of the eye brings any object at any given moment to a sharp focus upon the centre of the retina, while the rest of the retina records objects with less intensity. The centre of the retina contains a minute "pit", the fovea, which measures 1/200 of an inch across and is furnished with 4,000 specialized nerve terminals (aones). The lens of the eye brings images to sharp focus only within this tiny area, but this is all-important because upon cone vision depends memory. The fovea is the visual heart. Thus there are two forms of vision at the disposal of the playgoer, central vision and peripheral vision, central vision being concerned with details, accuracy and memory, while peripheral vision is specially sensitive to light effects and general movement. Whereas central vision focuses upon the features of the player who holds the stage at any given moment, peripheral vision is conscious of the other players and the background of scenery.

If the central and peripheral fields of vision were of identical quality, the competition of objects for attention would be highly distracting. And the reason for this is plain. Full perception of an object arises from a rapidly following series of pictures, each of which is a complete optical image, the process being precisely the same as the artificial one on the cinema screen. When we look at an object the central vision registers a series of pictures, each one half of one inch in diameter, until the salient features have been noted. Each fixation lasts 0.2 seconds or longer, the rule being that the greater the detail the longer the time required for fixation.

To remember a face requires sixteen different fixations, that is to say fifteen movements of the fovea, a fact which, incidentally, suggests how seldom a really accurate visual picture in the theatre can be fixed in memory. If any momentary vision fails to interest, the fovea shifts and a new picture presents itself, memory arising when the will to concentrate sets the idle cerebral gears into pur-

poseful activity. As the fovea passes from point to point, only the
concentration at each point can register as a memory. At dis-
tances remote from the fovea objects are no more than blurs of
form, mass or colour, though this does not imply that these are
unimportant. Side vision recognizes light, movement, colour and
form, that is the generalities of the stage, as opposed to the par-
ticulars.

So much for the fundamentals underlying stage gesture in all
its forms. Let us pass in review some of its embodiments, and
as a beginning, who more fitting than David Garrick, as accomplished a player as any in the annals of his art. In person, Garrick
was rather less than medium height but he was delightfully pro-
portioned and he added to a natural grace by constant practice
in fencing and dancing. His full dark eyes and expressive mouth
and cheeks provided additional endowments. Of his facial play,
a critic of his period said, "rage and ridicule, doubt and despair,
transport and tenderness, compassion and contempt, love,
jealousy, fear, fury and simplicity, all took, in turn, possession of
his features." In this connection, a pleasant conversation between
Dr Johnson and Mrs Thrale has come down to us. Mrs Thrale
came to the conclusion that David Garrick was ageing pre-
maturely, because, as she put it, the actor had worn himself out
by being eternally on the rack to give entertainment to others.
Dr Johnson had another and much more plausible explanation.

"David, Madam, looks much older than he is, for his face has
had double the business of any other man's. It is never at rest.
When he speaks, one minute he has quite a different countenance to what he assumes the next. I don't believe he kept the same
look for half an hour together during the whole course of his life;
and such an eternal, restless, fatiguing play of the muscles must
wear out a man's face before its real time."

"Oh, yes," cried Mrs Thrale. "We must certainly make some
allowance for the wear and tear of a man's face."

A sentence from a paper by Francis Gentleman in *The Dramatic Censor* of 1770 will recall what Garrick could achieve. The
writer had seen Garrick's Macbeth many a time, and of his
powers of gesture he says, "who ever saw the immortal actor start
at and trace the imaginary dagger previous to Duncan's murder,
without embodying, by sympathy, insubstantial air into the

alarming shape of such a weapon? Who ever saw the guilty distraction of features he assumes on Banquo's appearance at the feast, without sacrificing reason to real apprehension from a mimic ghost?"

Charles Mayne Young, a well-known tragedian in the early part of the nineteenth century, has left a record of Sarah Siddons in the rôle of Volumnia, in *Coriolanus*. The production was staged by John Kemble and a high-light was the "triumph" after the victory at Corioli. Kemble had no fewer than 240 principals and supers on the stage—victorious soldiers, lictors bearing their fasces, senators, trumpeters, priests, dancing girls, vestal virgins and the rest. And among them Volumnia, the proud mother of the conquering hero.

How did Mrs Siddons handle her opportunity? Charles Mayne Young tells us.

"When it was time for her to come on, sensitive to the throbbings of her haughty mother's heart, with flashing eye and proudest smile, with head erect and hands pressed firmly on her bosom as if to repress by manual force its triumphant swellings, she towered above all around, and rolled and almost reeled across the stage; her very soul as it were dilating and rioting in its exultation; until her action lost all grace and yet became so true to nature, so picturesque and so descriptive, that pit and gallery sprang to their feet, electrified by the transcendent execution of an original conception."

If a lesser actress had made the attempt, this might well have seemed "ham"; with Sarah Siddons as Volumnia it was "playing a part for all it was worth". Leigh Hunt, after seeing Mrs Siddons's Lady Macbeth, paid this tribute: "She has the air of never being the actress; she seems unconscious that there is a motley crowd called a pit waiting to applaud her, or that there are a dozen fiddlers waiting for her exit."

It may be that tragedy of the Sarah Siddons order would not be welcomed in the theatre of to-day. Nevertheless, the great tragic rôles alone give opportunities for the greatest acting and it will be long before tragedies are unacted, even if the dramatists of to-day seldom add to their number and players tend to neglect the training essential for complete success. Genevieve Ward once said "the present-day actresses have not the physique for tragedy.

The work in the old days was so much more strenuous for actresses than it is to-day." Miss Ward might have added that such actresses as Mrs Siddons, and the tragedy queens of the nineteenth century who followed, were careful to cultivate nobility of countenance and dignified movement, neither of which are qualifications likely to recommend them to modern managements, at any rate in the early years of a career. Turn then to an acknowledged masterpiece of acting, in which significant movement, facial play, gesture, dress, and the embroideries of character creation often called "business" all had a part. I mean Charlotte Cushman's first appearance as Nancy Sikes.

Born in Boston in 1816, Charlotte Cushman was taken as a small girl to see Macready as Coriolanus and made up her mind to become an actress. As a stock-actress in New York, an unfriendly manager gave her the part of Nancy, believing it had little importance. Charlotte, however, had other ideas. For weeks she spent her spare time in the slums, studying women of Nancy's type. In the first scene, the stage directions told Nancy to cross the stage and give a sign to the boy Oliver, who was in the hands of the police. It seemed to be a stock entrance and an exit—nothing more. Not a word was to be said, yet Charlotte Cushman discovered an opportunity for a dramatic triumph. Instead of crossing once, she crossed three times and her make-up stirred audiences to hysterical applause. In an old dirty bonnet and shawl, a shabby gown and shoes, she walked stealthily on the outskirts of the crowd, carrying a basket and swinging a key on her finger. Looking with sharp cunning at Oliver Twist, who had been arrested, she attracted his attention, winked an eye and thrust her tongue into her cheek.

Such memories could readily be multiplied for they relate to essentials in great acting. H. M. Walbrook, a life-long lover of the theatre, was taken to see Ristori in *Macbeth* at Drury Lane when a boy. In the scene which opens with Lady Macbeth reading her husband's letter and closes with her excitement over his return as a victorious general, Ristori's closing line was, "Leave all the rest to me." The actress made the words sum up, not only the entire scene, with its shadowing-forth of Duncan's murder, but all that the wife was to contribute to the bloody deed. Moving slowly back towards the door, her eyes fixed steadily upon Macbeth, she paused. Placing a hand first on her heart, then upon her forehead, and lastly, upon her lips, Ristori passed from the stage.

Coming to times nearer the memory of living playgoers, A. B. Walkley left on record his reaction to Kate Rorke's playing of the troubled wife in *A Pair of Spectacles*, in particular, the "merry pout, twinkling glance and slightly raised eyebrows", when her agitated husband (John Hare) brandished his umbrella at her. Miss Rorke managed at once to suggest astonishment and mild amusement, coupled with a wife's determination to overcome a growing vexation. Nor have dramatists been slow to acknowledge the debt they have incurred to the players whose by-play has illumined the spoken words. In *Bitter Sweet* Peggy Wood had been a young woman, a middle-aged woman and an elderly woman in the course of the play, and at its close, she had recalled the whole of this long life, with its triumphs and defeats, its mingled joys and sorrows. Of the final moment of his play, Noel Coward has said:

"To the last crashing chords of 'I'll See You Again', Sari, as an old woman, straightens herself with a gesture of indomitable pride and gallantly walks off the stage. That gesture was entirely Peggy's idea, and the inspired dramatic simplicity of it set her for ever in my memory as a superb actress."

Maugham has paid a similar tribute to Fay Compton, in his play *Caesar's Wife*. Violet, the wife who must be above suspicion, has sent her lover Ronny away. Fay held out her arms to the unhappy man and "the grace, tenderness and beauty" of the gesture were not to be forgotten. Or Dame Madge Kendal's grimace in *The Elder Miss Blossom* when she found her tea was not sugared. Nor would one forget the close of *Night Must Fall*. Reference has been made to the boy's speech on the eve of his arrest. A little later, bravado had replaced fear and the young murderer cried, "I'm going to be hanged but they'll get their money's worth at the trial. You wait!" Dan's smile and the raising of the hand to the hat brim with the old jaunty gesture of farewell were a masterly touch of the dramatist-actor, at once memorable and character-revealing and yet not without a touch of charm.

An outstanding example of speechless drama belongs to John Galsworthy. The scene in Falder's prison cell in *Justice* took no less than thirty-three lines of print to describe. The man in the stockinged feet moves noiselessly. He tries harder and ever harder to hear something. He does a stitch of work, before pacing the cell like an animal at the zoo. Then a tin falls from his hand with a clatter. From darkness, the cell suddenly becomes brightly lighted. The man gasps for breath. A dull beating on thick metal is heard; at first far away, then nearer. It seems to hypnotize young Falder. His hands move with the sound, until he flings himself violently upon the cell door, and beats upon it.

Similar in technique, though less protracted, is the scene in the third act of Pinero's *Iris*, in which the unhappy Iris puts on her hat and cape, and, looking round the room to be sure she has collected her small personal belongings, sees Maldonado's chequebook. It fascinates her, a gradually increasing fear showing itself in her face, until she moves to the table and takes up the book. She is fingering it, uncertain and troubled, when a man-servant returns.

Servant (standing over the bag): Is there anything more, ma'am? (*Iris hesitates helplessly, then, becoming conscious that she is being stared at, advances, drops the cheque-book into the bag and goes out.*)

In Galsworthy's *Justice*, Falder was played by Dennis Eadie; Pinero wrote the part of Iris for Fay Davis.

Reference has been made to the skill with which Yvette Guilbert used her voice. Her command of gesture was no less impressive. Her imagination so fully controlled her muscular reactions that, when singing the familiar sempstress's song, even the biting off of the cotton fitted the rhythm of the action precisely. And, as in small things, so in great; the arms would move instinctively in a gesture which was at once revealing and beautiful, as for example, when the Woman of Samaria recognized her Lord and her God at the well. Yvette Guilbert was often working upon audiences which, as a whole, were ignorant of French. Knowing this, she determined that the co-ordination of voice and gesture should make comprehension the easier, an example of the law that appropriate gesture makes speech far easier to follow in a theatre. So true is this that Sarah Bernhardt attributed not a little inaudibility in the theatre to the player not preparing the audience through the eye for what the ear was shortly to receive. This was what Henry Irving had in mind when he made his gestures slightly precede the words they were intended to illustrate.

Stage gesture in all its forms is to be regarded as akin to stage speech, infinitely valuable in its suggestive power, but on that very account calling for rigid control. There is a story, no doubt apocryphal, that when J. M. Barrie wrote *Quality Street*, he made his hero, Valentine Brown, lose an arm in the Waterloo campaign. It was, as Barrie said, the only way to keep Seymour quiet.

Seymour Hicks died in 1949. Though not of theatrical stock, he began early. At nine, he was playing Buttercup in *H.M.S. Pinafore*, being then at a preparatory school in Bath, where, by a happy chance, elocution was included in the curriculum. Happily, too, Seymour was a thoroughly idle boy, with the result that, in spite of some months with an army crammer, he failed to qualify for entry into his father's profession. As Seymour declined to become a wine merchant's clerk, he was turned out at the age of fifteen without even the proverbial shilling and told to fend for himself. Necessity being a rare educator and remembering Buttercup and other boyish triumphs, Seymour decided to try the stage. In 1887, he was playing with Charles Warner in the melodrama, *In the Ranks*, the theatre being the Grand, Islington. This was a beginning, but Seymour's stroke of real fortune came three years later, when he was engaged to play boys' parts with Mr and Mrs Kendal in America. Dame Madge taught the young man, then nineteen, his trade. His parts included the gipsy in Pinero's *The Squire* and the boy in *A Scrap of Paper*. Dame Madge Kendal could be a merciless critic. "Act! How can you hope to act, my dear Hicks, before you know how to walk the stage?"

Or again, "Why did you move then?"

"I don't know."

"Then for Heaven's sake keep still, unless you have a reason."

The Value of Quietude

When Coquelin sought to express great fear he resorted not to action but inaction. A hand outstretched, not too far from the body, seemed to thrust away the invisible horror, while the fixed stare of the dilated eyes exercised its magic upon an enthralled audience. Of Duse, in *The Flame of Life*, D'Annunzio, the author, wrote:

"Although she was motionless, although she was silent, her well-known accents and her memorable gestures seemed to live about her, vibrating indefinitely ... For no other reason than the motion of a muscle, a sign, a gesture, a line of feature, a tremor of the eyelids, a slight change of colour, an almost imperceptible bend of the brows, a changing play of light and shade, a lightning-like virtue of expression, radiating from that thin, frail body, infinite worlds of undying beauty were continually generated."

Far too many producers fail to recognize the importance of pauses and quietude and seem bent upon maintaining interest by keeping their company on the move, so that the actors and actresses themselves develop an uncomfortable feeling of "being anchored" unless they are passing from chair to sofa, or sofa to chair, every minute and a half. A noteworthy feature in the acting of the Irish Players was their freedom from over-gesticulation. This was, in part, due to the influence of W. B. Yeats, who held strongly that stage speech was infinitely more important than stage movement, so much so that he once propounded a scheme for rehearsing the Irish Players in tubs. "We must get rid of everything that is restless, everything that draws attention from the sound of the voice or from the few moments of intense expression." When the Abbey Company came to London for the first time, playgoers found this quality markedly impressive. Miss May Agate, a pupil of Sarah Bernhardt, has told us that Madame's advice was "never to be afraid of long pauses", adding "Beginners always are, but the public loves stage silence; which speaks better than anything else in the theatre." Diderot did not over-state the case when, in a letter to Voltaire, he wrote: "Silence and pantomime at times have a pathos that all the resources of speech cannot approach." The silence which Irving associated with his Dante, when the poet was asked whence he had come, illustrates Diderot's point. The answer to the question was no more than "From Hell", but what a theatre-goer who heard those two words remembers is the breaking of the long silence. In this connection a passage from Clement Scott comes to mind, apropos of John Hare in Robertson's *Society*. Hare was

Yolande Donlan as Lucrece in *Cage me a Peacock*, by Noel Langley, Strand Theatre (1948). A Noteworthy Modern Production (*see Chapter 11*).

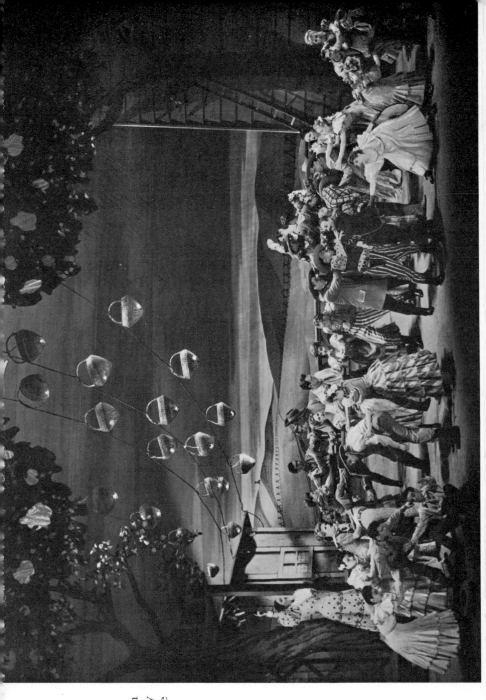

Scene from *Oklahoma!* Drury Lane Theatre *(see page 244)*.

playing Lord Ptarmigan, quite a small part, but he gave it importance, as Forbes-Robertson gave importance to the rôle of Buckingham in *Henry the Eighth*, so that every succeeding revival seemed to require a leading actor in the part. Scott wrote:

"A little delightful old gentleman came upon the stage dressed in a long, delightfully cut frock-coat, bright-eyed and intelligent, with white hair that seemed to grow naturally on the head—no common clumsy wig with a black forehead line—and with a voice so refined, so aristocratic, that it was music in our ears. The part was insignificant. All Hare had to do was to say nothing and go to sleep. But how well he said nothing; how naturally he went to sleep!"

Those bright intelligent eyes of John Hare! You can see them in Hugh Rivière's portrait at the Garrick Club, in which Hare is enacting the fiery Lord Kilclare of *A Quiet Rubber*, another rôle of no great importance, but one which Hare's acting made unforgettable.

Not a few players need to be reminded that expressive listening is in the same order of importance as stage speaking. How can passages of appeal or rebuke have full force if the person or persons addressed do not give the impression of the fullest attention. Robert Speaight in *Acting, Its Idea and Tradition*, recalled what the Italian Ricoboni said of the eighteenth-century actor, Michel Baron: "He always listens to his fellow-actors, a thing to which actors as a rule pay little heed, and his attention is accompanied by such movements of face and body as are required by the nature of the speeches to which he listens."

The law of expression is to avoid exaggeration but never to fear heightening any gesture. Indeed, heightening is the law in all acting. It is the method by which full significance is achieved, it is what we imply in the phrase, "playing a part for all it is worth". Athene Seyler, who is as clever with her pen as she is in mid-stage, has commented upon the variants in flirting behind a fan at the service of an actress. Such by-play may well characterize the ladies of Restoration comedy as opposed to the play of the demure Victorians who may be supposed to have used the fan as a discreet protection from the too ardent gaze of a dancing partner, a consideration which would certainly never have occurred to Millamant. It matters not at all how either Restoration or

v

Victorian ladies in fact used their fans. As Miss Seyler says, what does matter is that the gestures shall inform an audience as to the spirit of the times.

From her own experience Miss Seyler has suggested how a player of talent would solve a particular problem. At the time she penned the advice she was playing a part which called for a display of indignation. In expressing the mood she twisted her hands, palm to palm, as she paced the stage; or, again, she seemed to "lock" the hands back to back. When sitting down she tapped her shoes sharply together, sitting stiff as a ramrod the while, or, perhaps, running an irritated forefinger down the pattern on her dress. Miss Seyler's devices not only produced a comic effect, but emphasized character, and the particular turn of the plot.

The actor or actress is no mere mimic, imitating gestures associated with certain emotional stages in ordinary life. The gestures of a gifted player have been carefully cultivated, so that they not only fit the symbolic images aroused by the dramatist's text, but have a beauty of their own and the added significance which accompanies beauty in the arts. The attitudes, movements, and gestures may seem involuntary, but this is only because they have been rehearsed until they became habitual. As Bernard Shaw wrote, "the power of complying with artistic conditions, without being so pre-occupied by them as to be incapable of thinking of anything else, is hard to acquire and can be perfected only by long practice. Talma estimated his apprenticeship at twenty years."

Mention has been made of the round of applause which followed Irving's treatment of the "hawk and handsaw" passage from *Hamlet*. Such applause in the 'eighties and 'nineties of the last century was commoner than it is to-day. We are more sophisticated, or theatre-goers paid more attention to the minutiae of the stage, perhaps because there were fewer worthwhile plays and those which were to be seen were better known. In connection with that very debatable thing, applause in the middle of an act, there is a story of Henry Neville. He was a first-class Charles Surface. When Neville made his exit towards the end of the Screen Scene in Act IV of *The School for Scandal*, the audience always applauded and sometimes so loudly that a reappearance seemed called for. Neville accordingly made a habit of dropping his handkerchief as he left. When the applause broke, he returned, picked up the handkerchief and bowed to his Lady Teazle, but with such graceful skill that the bow seemed to include both lady and audience. So the performance was free to continue without an uncomfortable break.

May I recall Dame Madge Kendal's Galatea? If the cry "Pygmalion!" in the opening scene gave audiences the clue to the impersonation which was to follow, the play of feature and the gestures which accompanied the cry were no less moving. As the statue came to life on the pedestal, the actress represented the inflowing of life by a slight movement of the eyelids. First she opened the eyes, then fluttered the eyelids, before she fixed her gaze upon the sculptor and stretched hands and arms towards him. The gestures and the slight fluttering of the eyelids were repeated when Galatea said her final "Farewell". This play of the eyelids was no new thing. Mention has been made of Ristori's Lady Macbeth. For the sleep-walking scene Ristori rehearsed until she could play it throughout without the tremor of an eyelid. The wide-open eyes and the fixed stare resulted in something which was at once strange and terrible.

There are exceptions to every rule, and Dorothy Jordan is an exception to the rule that the players who are remembered had to toil for their effects. Of her own methods of study, Mrs Jordan said, "First, I get my words by heart. Then I tell Dame Nature that I'm at her service—that she may do what she pleases with my arms and legs and hands and face. Having become her puppet, I take no more part in the business myself. The audience laugh at me and I at myself. Then they laugh again and so do I." But then, as Hazlitt wrote of Mrs Jordan, "It was not as an actress but as herself that she charmed every one."

Moreover, Dorothy had wit. It is on record that her lover, the Duke of Clarence, allowed her £1,000 a year and the sum was reported to his father, George III. "Too much! Too much! Give her £500!" In turn, the Duke reported the royal command to his mistress. Dorothy Jordan picked up a theatre programme and pointed to the words, "*No money returned after the rising of the curtain.*"

Stage Laughter

The intensive cultivation of gesture may be regarded as including stage laughter, which is a half-way house between speech and gesture. Ellen Terry learnt to laugh from Mrs Charles Kean, who taught her to draw a breath through the tip-tilted nose which was once likened to the petals of a rose. The indrawn breath was the preliminary to the fascinating Ellen Terry chuckle.

The trick of stage laughter came to Ellen Terry early, but it falls to not a few players to create and cultivate a special laugh for some definite special purpose. In such cases the laugh may mean months of experiment and practice. Harry Lauder spent a year in perfecting the laugh in the patter attached to his song, "Tobermory". Similarly, the facial gestures which accompanied "Roamin' in the Gloamin'" called for many weeks of rehearsal, until Lauder was assured that the new song would play upon "the heartstrings of men and women".

Not dissimilar was the inane chuckle with which Vesta Tilley concluded "Algy, the Piccadilly Johnny with the little glass eye". It is scarcely too much to say that the laugh brought not only Algy but the song to life, though the top-hat, the ebony stick, the gardenia, the white spats, the white gloves with the black stripes and the immaculate grey frock-coat and trousers all helped. In the Noel Coward sketch, *Marriage, Past and Present*, Maisie Gay's success depended upon a laugh. Maisie had only four lines to deliver, so it was the right laugh or dire failure. For ten weary weeks, she pondered that laugh and at last it revealed itself and the sketch became an integral part of *This Year of Grace*.

And, lastly, the "Laugh, John, laugh! Watch me and see how easy it is!" which James Barrie put into Maggie's mouth at curtain-close in *What Every Woman Knows*. That called for a good deal of rehearsal before it was made perfect, as did Charles Laughton's nervous laughter when he was accused of his wife's murder in *Payment Deferred*. And the tragic laughter at the end of the opening of *The Unknown Warrior* of Paul Raynal when the woman and the soldier are alone and the spirits of the soldier's comrades have sanctified their unblessed union.

The Woman: Destiny surely cannot see us here, lost in the depths of the night.

The Soldier (gaily): Of course, it can't. Let's laugh at it!

The Woman: Ah! It's you. Just like you used to be!

The Soldier: War will never be declared.

The Woman (nodding wisely): All the same there are some very ugly rumours.

The Soldier: Oh. They're manufactured by the Stock Exchange.

The Woman (playing up to him): But the papers say ...

The Soldier: The days of war are over.

The Woman: Civilization triumphs. You are not the least bit anxious?

The Soldier: I'll bet you anything you like.

The Woman (nodding importantly): On the whole I agree with you.

The Soldier: And besides, even supposing war were to break out.

The Woman: Oh, don't let's think of anything so ridiculous.

(*They burst into peals of laughter.*)

Scientists tell us that, in laughter, the respiratory organs are the first to be affected. When a laugh is in embryo, chest and diaphragm are contracted, and then two sets of muscles in and around the mouth come to the assistance of the coming laugh. The contraction of the muscle attached to the cheek bone causes the mouth to open, so that the muscles in the upper lip draw the corners of the mouth upwards and thus expose the teeth. By this time the laugh is in being and the whole aspect of the face has changed. The cheeks are wrinkled, crow's-feet appear around the eyes and the contraction of the orbicular muscles may bring tears. Meanwhile, lower down, laughter is "holding both its sides", for the contractions of the chest and diaphragm have developed so greatly that the distinction between pain and pleasure is vanishing and a slow return to normality is essential if heart, lungs, and stomach are not to suffer. Incidentally, in laughter, women and children use the vowels "ee" and "eh" and adult men the "ah" and the "oh". As for the smile, at once the precursor and the successor of the laugh, it begins with a slighter lifting of the corners of the mouth. This is accompanied by the formation of wrinkles under one or both of the eyes, having the effect of adding momentary brightness to the eyes and emphasizing the expression of pleasure.

Laughter in the theatre occupies considerably more time than is generally supposed. Ten minutes to the hour is the BBC allowance when an audience is watching a humorous broadcast.

Stage timing, that is the due synchronization of speech, gesture and movement with the ideas of the dramatist, is a subject of abiding interest. A chuckle or a laugh largely depends upon proper timing. So does that catching of the breath and the tightening of the orbicular muscles which are the prelude to tears. The analogy in the realm of physics is illuminating. Any oscillatory body, for example a tuning fork, can be kept in motion by very slight external force, provided this is applied with the same periodic recurrence as the body's own vibrations. The point is that each impulse must reinforce the last at the exact moment when the reinforcement will produce the greatest effect. In other words there must be sympathetic reactions.

The laws regulating the sympathetic reaction between actor and audience or dramatist, actor, and audience have not yet been analysed, but their existence has been fully established. Listen to Noel Coward describing the reception accorded to *Hay Fever* in America and that which the farce won in London and it will be plain that the periodic vibrations were attuned in one city and not in the other. An audience comes to a theatre ready to pick up the vibrations radiating directly from the players and indirectly from the dramatist, and, sometimes, there is no answering thrill; at others the thrill continues in the vaults of memory over a lifetime. Why? The study of centuries gives no satisfactory answer, and it may be that the complexity of the problem forbids a logical explanation. Nevertheless, the fact must be recognized and its implications understood if the aesthetics of the theatre are to be formulated.

Perhaps the analogies which most fully explain the mysteries of stage timing come from Henri Bergson. He has recalled that rhythm in a dance allows the spectator to foresee destined movements, so that the spectator is almost persuaded that he controls them. Thus an actual physical sympathy enters into the conception of grace in a theatre. The spectator finds a superior ease in movements which can be foreseen, whereas no such foreknowledge is possible in relation to a series of jerks, each of which is complete in itself and bears no certain relation to what is to follow. In Bergson's phrase, "the perception of ease in motion passes over into the pleasure of holding the future in the present." It is worthy of notice that rhythm is almost universal in Nature, in the blood stream, in breathing, in sleep, in the rising and setting sun, in the lunar tides, in the seasons, and in the growth and decay of human life itself. Born of the union between organized form and the more generalized sense impression, there arises satisfying pattern or melody such as can be found in a well-devised plot and properly-timed acting.

Under the influence of imagined emotions, gestures correspond with the waves of tension and relaxation associated with the originating images. Herein lies the creative capacity of the mind, as symbolic images, which are the content of imagination, have an originating power far beyond ordinary thought, and particularly when mass suggestion is present. The clanging of gongs or the rhythmic beating of drums in the savage state stirs up mass emotions which astonish a European, though he is not asleep to similar influences of another kind. It would seem that the faculty of imagination is associated in some way with the "inner dynamism" upon which any visible display of nervous energy depends, and this "inner dynamism" in turn is connected with the muscles which control both action and expressive gesture. When the "inner dynamism" registers a specific emotion, the proper gestures tend to arise. Experiencing the emotion joy, the pupils of the eye become dilated and the muscles of the mouth relax. Then a gurgling laugh arises, accompanied, perhaps, by such a gesture as the opening and closing of the fists, or it may even be tears, as the inner dynamism reaches its highest potency.

Leigh Hunt wrote in 1807, apropos of Mrs Siddons:

"It appears to me that the countenance cannot express a single passion perfectly, unless the passion is first felt. It is easy to grin representations of joy, and to pull down the muscles of the countenance as an imitation of sorrow, but a keen observer of human nature and its effects will easily detect the cheat. There are nerves and muscles requisite to expression, that will not answer the will on common occasions; but to represent a passion with truth, every nerve and muscle should be in its proper action, or the representation becomes weak and confused, melancholy is mistaken for grief, and pleasure for delight. It is from this feebleness of emotion so many dull actors endeavour to supply passion with vehemence of action and voice, as jugglers are talkative and bustling to beguile scrutiny."

To this readiness to feel emotion must be added the general training and intensive rehearsals which make control also possible. All habits are cultivated and not least those which give rise to movement, gesture or facial expression proper to a given moment in a dramatic rôle.

Mere physical vitality may well be the source of the strange power which some actors and actresses exert and which enables them to arouse mass emotions in a high degree. In origin the power may arise from physical well-being but, equally, it may be due to the concentration of nervous energy. One of the thrills of the early years of the twentieth century was Polaire, in the sketch *Ma Gosse*. (Reference has already been made to Polaire in *Le Visiteur*.) This was first given at the Moulin Rouge, Paris, but later in London, at the Palace. As in *Le Visiteur*, Polaire's purpose was to express passion in its most primitive forms. Like some lithe beast of a tropical forest, she moved round the stage, first fascinating and then hypnotising her male prey, until, as passion possessed the man in his turn, the woman was caught up and then flung down, whence she crawled back to his feet, conquered at last.

Similar in kind is the vitality displayed by stage dancers, Fred Astaire, for example. The frenzied speed of Fred's step-dancing and its amazing precision told of physical well-being so manifest that it was a tonic, though fun might be added, as when Fred, with a chorus of sailors, danced "I'd rather Lead a Band", and tapped out drill orders with his feet. In similar fashion, Adele Astaire displayed an impish sense of humour which was infectious in a high degree, but the tonic quality of her twinkling feet and the precise rhythm which her matchless technique produced may well have had a deeper significance. Adele Astaire was of sylph-like proportions but middle-aged men and women grew younger when they sensed the vitality in those mercurial limbs and waited for the quick hitch of the skirt which enlivened her frolics. At the time, tap-dancing was becoming recognized as a new type of stage talk and a whole gamut of unsuspected stage potentialities was coming into being. The dancing of the Astaires gave rhythmic energy, not only to a song and dance, but to an entire show.

"Pep" of this sort has been a characteristic of many American plays, particularly musicals. The quality first impressed itself upon English audiences when *The Belle of New York* made her sensational appearance in Shaftesbury Avenue, at the end of the 'nineties. A generation later, *Little Nellie Kelly* came to the Oxford and had the advantage of rehearsal by the great George M. Cohan himself. To say that *The Belle* was out-speeded would be an under-statement. In *Little Nellie Kelly*, George Cohan worked his principals and chorus into something like a frenzy, until the stage was filled with figures "frantically writhing and swinging and leaping" in a delirium of excitement, an excitement which, of course, communicated itself to the audiences.

CHAPTER 16

THE PATENTLY IMPOSSIBLE AND VAIN, WITH AN EXCURSUS UPON GAGS AND GAGGING

WHAT Edward Lear called "The Lord High Bosh and Nonsense Producer" is an important figure in the theatre, though the office and its functions are not easy to define. Sid Field has told us that audiences love to watch a "big guy" coming a cropper, but the Lord High Bosh Producer does much more than invent butter slides or occasions for the throwing of custard pies. Similarly, he is more than an inventor of wisecracks, though wisecrackery is an important part of his functions. Stanley Lupino, in *Sporting Love* "a Musical Horse-Play" at the Gaiety, had to put £5,000 upon a horse for the Derby, and he got the names wrong. Instead of "Cold End", he backed "Winterbottom". This was funny, but it did not enrol Stanley Lupino among the Lord High Bosh Producers. More sustained and substantial efforts were called for; more of fantasy; more real invention.

We are nearer the real thing when we recall Harry Tate fishing. Any fortune can attend the sportsman who has the wit to cast snuff upon troubled waters, and, when the fish come to up sneeze, "hits 'em on the head with my big stick". Or, a generation later. Austin Melford, Sydney Howard and Jack Hobbs unexpectedly finding themselves in a Turkish Bath on Ladies Night. By the time the fun had been accumulating for a quarter of an hour audiences were in the mood for any absurdity. The hilarity reached a climax when Melford was placed upon a marble slab and an enthusiastic attendant imprinted a dimple upon his nether anatomy by appropriate doses of electrical treatment. Possibly an element of what psychologists call surrealism distinguishes the lesser from the greater nonsense. When an element of delirious logic is added to the "funny" the Lord High Bosh Producer is functioning fully, and this is why Hermione Gingold ranks so high. Any of her shows at The Gate or the Ambassadors in recent years would illustrate the point. Let us say, the memory of the elderly model who posed for Picasso, with an extra limb and misplaced abdominal organs in *Sweetest and Lowest*, or the same Hermione as an up-to-date Brunhilde, explaining why Valhalla had changed for the worse after

> "Ambassadors toasted my fatal allure
> And Hindenburg chased me all over the Ruhr."

The Comic Muse abstracted the quality reverence when she fashioned our Hermione, and respect for the traditional is one of the surest destroyers of the truly ridiculous, just as it is a source of many jests. However, the temptation to become high-brow must be resisted. Our point is that only when a comic situation is not only posed, but disintegrated and refashioned in the realm of the subconscious, do we recognize the product as fully comic. The final delirium lulls the critical faculty into insensibility, so that the utterly unreasonable is not only acceptable but to be welcomed.

The chapter which follows could readily be expanded into a book, but, dipping here and dipping there into memories extending over half a century, we may be able to focus attention upon an important class of theatrical effects and judge how they are arrived at.

The Function of Gagging

Speaking very generally, the Lord High Bosh and Nonsense Producer is required to do the work which the dramatist fails to do, and this is why gagging plays so large a part in his function. The gag has been defined as the line the author omitted to write. Not a few theatrical effects are unpredictable, owing to ever-changing audiences and their ever-changing moods, so gagging arises because only the man or woman on the stage can deal with the unpredictable. Be that as it may, the majority of comedians of fame have been gagsters or have become so skilled in the use of specially prepared materials that they are credited with the spontaneity which gagging implies. The expert gagster is among the best paid members of a cast just because he is not only actor but part-author.

There may have been farces and musical comedies that could be acted as they left the author's desk. Those of Arthur Wing Pinero were among them; Gilbert also was untouchable; so was Aristophanes. In general, however, a farce owes only its underlying machinery to the author; the embroidery of funny business and not a few of the amusing lines belong to the principal comedian. *The Private Secretary* is an example. Charles Hawtrey found the bare bones of the story in a German original and after a struggle collected enough money to get a cast together, with a view to production at the Prince's, with Beerbohm Tree as the Curate. Most of the business which made the Rev. Robert Spalding a figure of fun was Tree's invention. He was always adding something. On one occasion Mrs Leigh Murray, while on the stage, accidentally shed one of the skirts which loomed so largely in feminine underwear in the 'eighties. She threw it aside with a blush. Immediately after, Tree made his entrance in the second act and what he said was: "I beg your pardon. I thought I met a petticoat on the stairs."

The famous "I don't like London" was another Beerbohm Tree invention, this being an example of the repetitive gag, in which the laugh arises from the ease with which the phrase can be adapted, not only to the numerous chops and changes of a farcical plot, but to social life itself. The repetitive gag seems at first sight in contradiction to the general rule that what is all important in a "gag" is unexpectedness, but, on analysis, the unexpected is only put a stage ahead. With repetition, the familiar and expected line arouses a second and third laugh because it puts a new situation so neatly.

When Hamlet gave his advice to the Players. "Let those that play your clowns speak no more than is set down for them," he had in mind special circumstances, rather than a debate upon theatrical method as a whole. Clowning, as Shakespeare used the word, may best be described as imitative action, which transforms the serious into the ludicrous and has a history as long as comedy. Such a clown as Launcelot in *The Merchant of Venice* was the successor of the mediaeval jesters and licensed to make impromptu fun when the dramatist did not require the stage for his story-telling. As jester, the Shakespearean clown was permitted to grimace, indulge in comic gesture and mock such a principal player as Shylock. What Shakespeare, as dramatist, objected to was a popular clown invading his territory and improvising anecdotes and jests. What Hamlet was telling the Players was that they must stick to his words. I am indebted to my friend John Munro for this information. In his Shakespearean studies, John Munro has noted the importance of clowning in Elizabethan practice, Shakespeare's treatment of Malvolio being another example. Several puzzling lines in Shakespeare's comedies are easy of comprehension when we recall the mocking antics of a Shakespearean clown, filling in a scene at the expense of a leading player.

Apropos of gagging and clowning in the modern theatre, it is on record that Augustus Harris, of Drury Lane fame, was once contemplating a £100 a week engagement, a large amount in the 'nineties of the last century. Sitting back comfortably in a stall, Mr Harris issued his order. "Be funny and make me laugh for twenty minutes." This was precisely the time needed to change a big scene. Aided by £300 worth of props, the comedian earned his £100, for Augustus Harris laughed and kept on laughing.

Maisie Gay's ten minutes of dumb show in *This Year of Grace* had a similar origin. At the last moment, rehearsals of the revue suggested to Mr Cochran that laughs and not sentiment or pretty ballet were needed at a certain point. He accordingly put a very tired Noel Coward to the test. Noel protested that he hadn't the ghost of a jest left; nevertheless, during the week-end he produced the Maisie Gay sketch, "Boarding the Bus". For ten minutes Maisie, burdened with a number of toy balloons, kept audiences chuckling over her failures to make contact with the omnibus, the climax being the only word which Noel Coward wrote between Friday night and Monday morning, Maisie's impassioned, "Taxi!"

Nor is it only the farce or the musical show which may be enriched by a laugh which the author did not devise or even approve. Wilson Barrett's brother, George, was a low comedian who appeared in most of his brother's successes, including *The Silver King*. These had been modern melodramas and the comedian felt at home, but when Wilson Barrett staged the great Roman spectacle *Claudian*, George was less happy. As the jests of ancient Rome seemed sadly out of date, he set to work to modernize his lines, only to call forth a stern rebuke from his brother. *Claudian*, he was told, was a play of far-away times. The first night came and Wilson Barrett raised the audience at the Princess's to a pitch of high excitement over a great earthquake scene, in which temples and palaces fell until the stage was a mass of ruins; so much debris had to be cleared away that the next scene was laid before a front curtain, with George Barrett in full control. Wrapped in a toga with purple stripes, his patrician brow surmounted by a wreath of pink roses, George Barrett discussed the catastrophe. "Yus, it is orful, aint it? But what worries me is not so much the public buildings, as what 'as 'appened to my five white mice."

The audience at the Princess's Theatre laughed and laughed again and George's gag remained in *Claudian* until the run ended.

Gagsters of Genius

Another reason why authors frequently miss the line which earns the big laugh is that the personality of the gagster must fit the gag precisely if it is to have full effect. Only a George Graves could conjure up the shudder of disapproval with which he picked up a copy of *The Times* years ago and noted that it had been reduced from 3d. to 1d. Having shuddered his disapproval George went on:

"This isn't *The Times*, Pompey. This isn't the good old three-penn'orth I used to sleep behind at the Club."

Again only her creator could be expected to take Hetty the Hen so seriously that the bird's adventures, actual and prospective, excited Daly's audiences during the centuries-long run of *The Merry Widow*. One evening George Graves assured his hearers that Hetty had laid a door knob. A foolish neighbour had been feeding the hen with brass filings. Another peculiarity of Hetty was a capacity to lay bent eggs. George expatiated at length upon this peculiarity and his personal anxiety lest it might harm the bird. Or, in the alternative, what might happen to any member of his audience who responded to the new slogan, "Eat more bent eggs." Strange as had been the vagaries of that remarkable creature, the Gazeka, during the run of *The Little Michus*, they were outclassed by those of Hetty.

George Graves was partial to egg gags. In a Drury Lane pantomime, amid a polar setting, he spent a wealth of eloquence upon a penguin which refused to lay any egg at all. Indeed, the success of the Gazeka, Hetty the Hen, and the Drury Lane penguin resulted in a whole series of similar animal inventions, among them Dan Rolyat's Lizzie the Leech, which was lost in *Tom Jones*, and the bull which enlivened some minutes in *The Arcadians*. "Poor beast," mused Dan. "People passing through a field have only to see it swish its tail and they run for their lives; so stupid of them. Only a few months ago I was in Devonshire and saw a bull swishing its tail. Remembering the ladies, I tied a lump of lead to the end of its caudal appendage. My wife brought flowers to the hospital every Sunday, bless her heart." Nor must one forget Tonio (Lauri de Frece) in *The Maid of the Mountains*, lobster in hand, addressing Vittoria, "If they never give me my freedom, be kind to little Leonard."

Gagging of quite another order is sometimes called for to cover some stage mishap. John Gielgud recalled an example in *Strange Orchestra*, in which Laura Cowie played Vera Lyndon, the keeper of a Bloomsbury boarding-house, a slattern indeed, but a slattern with a heart of gold. On the first night Mrs Lyndon was spreading jam on toast as the curtain rose, and, inadvertently, dropped a dollop on to her stocking. Miss Cowie lazily scraped off the jam and put the dollop on to the toast once more—a superb piece of improvisation, which caused a roar of laughter in an audience which was quite unaware that the "business" was unrehearsed.

The classic example of gagging in the theatre is E. A. Sothern's creation of Lord Dundreary in *Our American Cousins*. The play was by Tom Taylor, and as the dramatist wrote the part, Dundreary had forty-seven lines. Sothern's first idea was to turn down the part, but his wife persuaded him to build it up into something good. Before Sothern finished the role of Dundreary was embodied in 800 lines. He gathered together all the wild absurdities he could discover, drawing largely upon nigger minstrel entertainments. First he changed every "R" into a "W", and thus suggested a lisp. Again, as he moved across the stage, an up-turned tack entered the sole of his shoe. "Are you going to limp as well as lisp?" asked a fellow player. "That's just what I am going to do," retorted Sothern, and the Dundreary "hop" was born.

Yet again, Dundreary counted from one to ten on his fingers and then reversing the process, continued, "Ten, nine, eight, seven, six and five are eleven." Every one had tried the trick on children, but, oddly enough, playgoers were also puzzled and amused by the curious arithmetic.

The biggest accretion to the character of Dundreary was

Mr Sothern as Lord Dundreary

Brother Sam's letter, into which Sothern thrust any jest which would not find a place elsewhere. Jack Warner adopted a similar device in his coster sketches in the *Garrison Theatre* on Satur-day nights during the second World War. Before Sam's letter was opened, the audience were made aware that it was being held upside down. Moreover, on the cover Dundreary read this note: "If you don't get this letter, write and let me know." This brought forth the comment, "That fella's an ass, whoever he is. And he's written the letter upside down. No, no! I've got it upside down."

Possibly, jesting with a familiar proverb would follow. For example, the phrase "birds of a feather" suggested this commentary to Sothern's agile fancy. "Birds of a feather! Absurd, who ever heard of a whole flock of birds with only one feather. The idea is ridiculous. Besides the poor bird that had the single feather must have flown on one side. Consequently, as the other birds couldn't fly at all, they couldn't flock together."

Thanks entirely to the craft-skill which Sothern brought to the creation of Dundreary, the character came to life as an embodiment of helpless vacuity, mingled with occasional insight. An indolent, semi-educated Victorian swell, bovine and foolish, but not unattractive, such was Lord Dundreary.

George Grossmith, the third of the clan, made a name for himself when he took the three line part of Lord Percy Pimpleton in *Morocco Bound* and gradually expanded it into the longest rôle in the musical comedy. He drew upon an infinity of short stories, many of them from the "States" and an inexhaustible supply of silly giggles. Would-be leading comedians have been doing the same sort of thing ever since.

Another example of the accretion method was the famous music-hall sketch, *A Sister to Assist 'er*, in which Fred Emney Senior and Sydney Fairbrother played in the years before the first World War. It was timed to run for thirty-five minutes, of which fifteen were "wordless", being devoted to laughter. The sketch originated in a gagging scene in *Sinbad the Sailor*, the Drury Lane pantomime of 1906. Harry Randall and Fred Emney as two elderly chars exchanged reminiscences over cups of tea, to which something had been added from a flask. The reminiscences ended in a violent quarrel. When the pantomime season ended Emney converted the gagging scene into a full-length music-hall turn, with himself as the bibulous Cockney monthly nurse and Sydney Fairbrother as his companion. Emney was continually collecting new material. Thus Emney pictured Mrs May, the monthly nurse, as in debt to her landlady, who weighed

w

in with the ultimatum, "Pay up or you go!" When Mrs May arranged that she should receive an urgent call to a case in the country, the landlady made a quick change, the new ultimatum being "Pay up, or I *don't* go." Emney's reaction to the new dilemma was to make Mrs May assume the personality of a wholly fictitious sister, whose affluence was to solve all monetary problems and incidentally justify the odd title Fred Emney had selected. Fred Emney was the victim of his sense of fun. In 1917, on the opening night of *Cinderella* at the London Opera House, he initiated a soap-suds slide on the stage in which his fellow-comics joined. Emney's fall was received with delirious laughter; in fact, it was accidental and the injuries proved fatal. Our Fred Emney, the big man with the eyeglass and the cigar, is "Mrs May's" eldest son.

The Origin of Gagging

Without probing too far into ancient history, it may be said that Fred Leslie and Arthur Roberts initiated the revolution in musical shows which substituted the gags of a comedian for the jests of an author. Of his own rôle in a show dating back to the 'nineties Arthur Roberts said, "I had a blank sheet—and a bottle of champagne." In other words, the author who was fitting Roberts with a new part was instructed "to leave plenty of room for Arthur" and thus Captain Codington of *In Town* came into being. Aware that Arthur had an immense capacity for pantomime suggestion, as well as a mercurial wit, George Edwardes and the other managers who employed the comedian were willing to offer not only freedom but licence.

But the revolution had been initiated some years earlier when full-blooded burlesque gave place to the almost plotless musical shows which George Edwardes favoured. The sources of possible burlesque had been exploited so fully that freer methods were essential if audiences were to be amused. As Clement Scott said when reviewing Fred Leslie's contribution to the vaudeville of his time, "the backbone of narrative" which had previously run through burlesque had become "gelatinous" by the time Leslie was installed as head nonsense purveyor at the Old Gaiety. Leslie did not so much "act plays" as "make them up", and this to such an extent that the playwright of burlesque was merged in the office of principal comedian. The revolution from author to actor invention came full circle in our own time when the singers of "blues" neglected the inventions of their lyricists entirely and put in any nonsense they, the singers, judged effective. Authorship is not an appropriate description for the majority of "blue" lyrics. For example:

> Love is like whisky;
> Love is like good red wine;
> If you want to be happy
> You've got to love all the time.

Fred Leslie was a master craftsman. He it was who first exploited the device of guying the prompter, or the stage-hand who was in charge of the thunder and lightning department. Leslie could make occupants of the stalls rock with merriment while he explained that the stage thunder was due to nothing except sheet iron, while the rain was due to dried peas rolling up and down in an oblong box. Or, again, accusing the stage hand who was in charge of the falling snow of throwing big lumps at him (Leslie), while he let off the heroine with a few flakes of white paper.

George Graves brought off a similar coup in a Drury Lane pantomime when he shared his calls with the scene-shifters. These popped up from all sorts of corners and a crowded house was in hysterical laughter before the joke exhausted itself. I have written "stage-hands". Those who shared the call with George may equally have been the numerous prompters who allegedly helped him with his gags and topical verses.

Wanting a competent "feed", comedians frequently call upon the conductor or the man in charge of the big drum to act as the stooge and prepare the ground for a series of wisecracks. The trick has become tedious over the Wireless. On the other hand, a comedian may devise an act which gives an easy justification for an endless series. Jack Warner's quotations from his brother's letters have been mentioned, and the stories of Bert, which figure so largely in the stage appearances of the Waters Sisters, are another example. Old-time music-hall stars such as T. E. Dunville were experts at finding justifications for wise-crackery. What device could be simpler and more satisfactory than

Dunville's melancholy telegraph boy, in the sketch, *Working for the G.P.O.* Standing on the door-step, waiting for the "reply paid" money, Dunville would fumble with one of his buff-coloured envelopes and then open it curiously, "I say. This is a bit steep. To Mrs Johnson (*reading*): 'If your daughter has chilblains, blame the chaps she has on the door-step on wintry nights.'"[1]

Those who knew Fred Leslie well say that he was not particularly quick in invention but every fresh idea was pondered and polished until it shone. One clever bit of work (this time at the expense of the audience) was a spoof imitation scene, played with Arthur Playfair, himself a mimic of high repute.

"I will now", said Playfair, "give you an imitation of Mr Fred Leslie," and he walked off the stage, as usual. When he returned, the resemblance was amazing and a snatch of a song from *Rip Van Winkle* was rendered in Leslie's best manner. The audience shouted a rapturous recall, but the deception became plain when two Fred Leslies walked on together and bowed their thanks. Leslie had made up exactly like Playfair, and "imitated" himself.

"Injury laughs" are a recognized form of laughter creators, having kinship with acrobatics. Fred Leslie's fall downstairs in *Cinder Ellen*, was a highly elaborate example of the type. This was, apparently no more than the passing of a smart servant up a flight of stairs laden with luggage, followed by an ignominious descent. But in the process the smart uniform was reduced to rags and tatters, and it seemed amazing that the actor survived. Sleeves, boots and the rest were released during the descent by the pulling of a lace and the coat, which was only held together by strips of paper, easily broke, while the struggles of Leslie as he fell were really efforts to rid himself of the clothes.

"Injury laughs" range from the simple tripping over a mat to the elaborations of Leslie's *Cinder Ellen* fall, but theatre-goers will call to mind numerous examples, not all of them funny, among the latter being Laurence Olivier's memorable staircase fall in *Theatre Royal*.

On the point of technique, Lupino Lane, after hundreds of falls in the musical comedy *Twenty-to-One*, advised players who

[1] T. E. Dunville, *The Autobiography of an Eccentric Comedian.*

wanted to fall down stairs without undue pain to drop full length
at the top and roll down backwards.

Nor was Fred Leslie a whit less inventive in respect of stage
trickery. His jumping moustache in *Monte Cristo* made its appearance years before that of Harry Tate. The moustache was of silk
and was attached to the inner part of Leslie's nose by a spring
clip. One night the spring became bent and Fred had to grip it
between his teeth, only to find that Gaiety audiences were vastly

Fred Leslie's Fall

more amused with the new evolutions than they had been when
the moustache was relatively static. With practice Leslie made
the moustache move from side to side. At last, it made a complete

circle of the comedian's mouth and disappeared (apparently) down his throat.

Leslie usually tried out his more elaborate tricks in the Provinces before facing London audiences. Thus his "blowing out the moon" was first tested in *Little Jack Sheppard* at the Prince's, Manchester. The first step was to persuade the stage-manager that a sudden extinction of the stage lights was possible and when this had been duly rehearsed the comedian proceeded to announce to a wondering audience: "I'm going to blow out the moon." And sure enough, at a puff, the lights went out and with them the stage moon. So successful was the trick that Leslie brought it to London in *Monte Cristo*.

All sorts of variants upon Fred Leslie's jest come to mind. Harry Randall's effort when he shot at a hare and brought down

Fred Leslie, E. J. Lonnen, and Nellie Farren in Monte Cristo

a tin of canned rabbit, and W. C. Fields's pistol shot which sank a battleship, to the joy of American audiences. The theatrical law seems to be that, if costume enhances a jest by a hundred per cent, funny business adds four hundred per cent to its efficiency. It was funny when George Robey, in *Johnny Jones* at the Alhambra, thought of plucking cherries from Ivy St Helier's big hat, and threw the stones with apparent dexterity among the players in the orchestra, but the big laugh came when the arrival of each stone was heralded by a bang on the big drum. When Will Rogers, on the other side of the Atlantic, used to throw off his wisecracks at the expense of the politicians, national and international, he was amusing. As he said, "I guess I wouldn't be very humorous if it wasn't for the government. I don't make jokes, I just watch the government and report the facts." But Will Rogers was careful to enhance his gifts as a political reporter with a lasso and his dexterity with the rope was fully as amusing as his wisecrackery. Indeed, given ingenuity enough, dialogue becomes almost superfluous. When the Cairoli Brothers did their clowning at the Palladium they dispensed with dialogue altogether and allowed the clarinet, the trumpet and other instruments to do the talking. Charlie Cairoli was the player with the bowler hat and Johnnie the clown with the three-cornered cap.

The locomotive "business" which George Grossmith senior introduced into the tea-pot scene of *The Sorcerer* is memorable because it is one of the very few liberties with his script which Gilbert permitted. Grossmith, singing the John Wellington Wells song, came on carrying the famous silver teapot and in a kneeling posture puffed round the stage with amazing facility. Passmore, another dancer of fame, invented a dance as a conclusion to "Here's a how-de-do" in *The Mikado*, which also won Gilbert's approval. Slithering in and out among the wings, he appeared and disappeared behind bits of scenery until Savoy audiences in the late 'nineties were delirious with laughter.

Half a century after Fred Leslie we were laughing over the inventions of Lupino Lane, among them the public house bar stool, fitted with a strong steel spring, which enabled "Nip" to swing himself at all sorts of queer angles, the while a lady-love displayed a pronounced coming-on disposition. This particular form of stage jesting is akin to the Jack-in-the-Box joys of childhood or the ride-a-cock horse and peep-bo humours of an even earlier age. Mysterious appearances and disappearances can be excruciatingly funny because they are repeated with small differences which are just marked enough to arouse curiosity as well as surprise.

Lupino Lane, in musical comedy, like his friend Charlie Chaplin on the films, is an embodiment of the Little Man. He enjoyed his first big success in the 'thirties when Snibson's *Lambeth Walk* dance went round the world. It is noteworthy that the vast majority of low comedians are small men. Leslie Henson for example. So were Dan Leno, and Teddy Payne. It may be that the element of pathos is difficult to associate with a tall man. Shuffling on with his cane, Charlie Chaplin's aim was to look dignified, but what he achieved was a combination of the tragic and the comic which his generation accepted as the embodiment of the suffering the machine age had brought upon "the Little Man".

The Stooge and the Feed

In wise-crackery, the comedian's problem is to introduce his mots quickly and yet naturally. It is one thing to invent the joke anent the Jewish parent, on the eve of a family marriage, who comments, "Vell, it don't seem right to me that I 'ave to give Rachel away," and quite another to time the jest that creates laughter. Suzette Tarri has a genius for introducing her titbits, for example, "the barmaid at the Rose and Drown, who for twenty-seven years fought a losing battle against drought". Commonly, however, the services of a feed or stooge are called for. That is why comedians usually hunt in couples, triplets or foursomes. Bud Flanagan with Chesney Allen, Teddie Payne with George Grossmith, Vera Pearce with Bobbie Howes, and Stanley Lupino with Laddie Cliff. Astute aid from collaborators was needed before Groucho Marx successfully brought off his elephant in pyjamas sally. It ran: "Did I ever tell you how I shot an elephant in my pyjamas? How he got into my pyjamas I can't say."

Apropos of the comic and his stooge, success in casting a farce or a musical show largely depends upon discovering a piquant contrast of personalities. Leslie Henson, the mercurial, set against the solemn Sydney Howard, was a winner from the start. So was the overwhelming Alfred Drayton and the long-suffering Robertson Hare, replete with bald head, woe-begone expression and, possibly, the tribulations of a jealous wife. Robertson Hare was excellent farcical material anyhow, but four-fold or eight-fold laughter-creative in company with the assertive Alfred Drayton. One of the laws governing comic expression is that some one must suffer and *that* some one must not be the person who enjoys the joke. The confusions in which Robertson Hare lost his nether garments in Aldwych farce generally involved an effort to preserve the dignity properly associated with a blameless life. Thus *Banana Ridge* was a variation upon Marryat's *Japhet in Search of a Father* and Mr Hare's bald pate, gold-rimmed spectacles, and tropical "shorts" all helped to give reality to Willoughby Pink, by emphasizing the dread seriousness of the catastrophe which assailed one who was essentially unblameworthy. But *Banana Ridge* ranks among the laughter-creators primarily because gentleness of spirit is not a characteristic of a theatre audience, any more than it is a characteristic of any other mob. We ought not to laugh, but, in fact, we do.

Robertson Hare curiously enough began his career in *Oedipus Rex* at Covent Garden and toured the provinces in dramas and comedies until he found fame and fortune in *It Pays to Advertise*. Thenceforward, he was bullied by Ralph Lynn, Tom Walls, Alfred Drayton, as it might be, in *Thark, Turkey Time, Dirty Work*, and the rest, until even the ingenuity of Ben Travers was exhausted and Vernon Sylvaine took up the arduous task of devising situations in which Robertson Hare could plausibly lose his trousers.

Again, in the feminine attire assumed by Mr Mould in *Madame Louise*, we have not forgotten Alfred Drayton's caressing, "It's my little girl, Rosebud," and the voiceless resentment of the little bald, bespectacled shopman over the endearment. Very much of Robertson Hare's resentment was necessarily voiceless. And to the doubles or trebles in Aldwych farce, add the relatively restful presence of Mary Brough ("Polly" to her friends), whose method was to "guy" but never to guy too much. Her characterizations had about the same reality as the charwomen in a Punch cartoon by George Belcher, but, as a member of a team, Mary Brough was a farcical actress of worth. Now a guardian of public morals as in *A Night Like This*, or perhaps, merely disapproving of love-

making in business hours, as Mrs Bugle did when she rebuked
Ralph Lynn in *Dirty Work*.

Born in Manchester in 1882, Ralph Lynn did not reach London until the eve of the first World War, having been acting in the
provinces for a good fourteen years. Even then eight years passed
before he reached fame with his Aubrey Allington in *Tons of
Money*. Ralph had had some success in America and Tom Walls
had had *Tons of Money* hanging about the theatre awaiting a
comedian who could get away with "blithering idiocy" and yet
make it likeable. The description comes from Tom Walls.
Directly Ralph Lynn materialized, Tom Walls and Leslie
Henson made up their mind to try the farce out, though manager
after manager had refused it. The Shaftesbury Theatre was
rented and with Ralph Lynn, Yvonne Arnaud, Tom Walls,
Mary Brough, Willie Warde, and Robertson Hare in the cast,
Tons of Money proved a winner among winners for there were
children and grandchildren until Aldwych farce became a
London institution.

If every stage jape called for fresh invention, the job of a
comedian would be a weary one. Fortunately, one jest leads to
another. Bud Flanagan, in an expansive hour, once gave a verbal
demonstration of the potentialities of a comic idea. He began
with a wooden leg—a plain wooden leg. For, example, the pun
"Where's Harry? He's fallen down. But why? Harry has a
wooden leg and it wooden go!"

A feminine twist would present the primitive jest thus: "I was
engaged to a girl with a wooden leg." "Was? Why was? What
happened?" "I broke it off." "What, the leg?" "Oh, no, the
engagement."

Or another feminine variant which Bud Flanagan admitted
was only fit for masculine audiences.

"Oh, I took a smasher out last night, and, do you know, I
found she had a wooden leg."

"But how did you find that out?"

"Look at my hand, covered with splinters."

Which explains why gags call for careful collection and
elaboration rather than what may strictly be described as invention. No great ingenuity went to the gag which Flanagan and
Allen built into a laughter-creator.

Flanagan (*dismally*): There have been seven women in my life—all told.

Allen: All told?

Flanagan: Well, one of them kept her mouth shut.

The laugh arose from proper timing.

Relatively small things make all the difference between the gag which provokes and the gag which stifles laughter. When Seymour Hicks was a very youthful actor, he played an office boy, with little more than a single line to bless himself with. This was his exit, "Good day, sir. I shall be back in an hour. I'm going to have a game of billiards." Now the phrase "good old" happened to be acceptable London slang in the 'eighties of the last century, so young Seymour ventured upon what he regarded as an improvement, the jaunty, "Good-day, sir. I'm off for a good old game of billiards."

Thanks to the trifling change, the pit laughed and Seymour considered himself hardly used when he was fined a shilling "for gagging".

Important, too, is the follow-up which so often gives the gag its real bite. When Olaf, played by Leslie Henson, in *Nice Goings On* looked into a perambulator and asked, "What are they, twins?" there were chuckles, and more followed when the nurse replied coldly, "The one on the right is a melon," but the real laugh came when Leslie continued with, "Ah, quite a fruitful marriage." The culminating come-back is what matters, that is the process stage comics describe as "topping a gag". In a certain Jack Waller production, *The Girl Friend*, Emma Haig was playing opposite George Gee and she had to inform the audience that her portrait was due to appear in the papers. Plainly, self-respecting comics could not be content with this bald observation and what came from the players eventually ran something like this:

Emma: I'm going to have my picture in the papers.

George: Your face in the papers. But what about the poor people who will have their meat wrapped in it?

The exchange of rude remarks is a recognized form of gagging, the essential in each case being the maintenance of a proper contrast in character. For example, a due cattiness is called for in

Jessie if this exchange of wit is to arouse a laugh, but Alice must also have deserved the riposte.

Alice: I didn't accept Tom the first time he proposed.
Jessie: No, dearie, you weren't there.

The requisite cattiness was preserved when a similar thrust and counter-thrust found its way into the script of that amusing Gaiety show *Theodore and Co.* The fencers were Adrah Fair and Irene Richards. Irene, as Alma, was a relatively substantial beauty; Adrah was fair, and of the type G. P. Huntley described as "filleted flapper".

Alma: I've got the legs.
Cleo: Yes, calves all the way down!
Alma: That's better than ankles all the way up.

Verbal jesting of this kind has a long history. It has always been a recognized part of the play mood, as the phrase, "a play upon words" suggests. For example.

Lola (the script girl): I'll cut your throat from ear to ear.
Cornelius (politely): Pardon me, from 'ere to there.

Gaiety lovers may remember Leslie Henson as Cornelius Crumpet, the proprietor of a troupe of performing fleas. The particular show scarcely mattered, Leslie could have found an occasion for the play upon words in a hundred situations. Add the appropriate gesture, and stalls, pit, and gallery must chuckle.

More closely associated with a specific rôle, and perhaps not strictly a gag, was Eddie Cantor's classical bit of wisecrackery. As a slave Eddie was up for sale in the market of Imperial Rome, and in the absence of bids, was frantically pleading for attention from a crowd of uninterested dealers. "I can wash dishes, I can mop floors; I can take care of the children, and if there aren't any children, I can take care of that!"

A similar perversion of history was the amusing bit of foolery in Cecil de Mille's *The Crusades*, in which Loretta Young, in the role of Queen Berengaria, had cause for dissatisfaction with Richard the Lion-Hearted on their bridal night.

Berengaria: Well, what are you doing now?
Richard (fumbling at an ankle): I always take off my spurs before I
get into bed.

Nor would one willingly forget Sydney Howard's encounter
with the French costumier in *Magic Carpet*, a Firth Shephard
revue at the Prince's. The point at issue was whether a certain
pair of breeches were "Toulon" or "Toulouse". Sydney Howard
learnt his trade playing in revue in the smaller towns of Northern
England, when there was usually no more in the script than a few
hints. The audiences were critical enough to put a premium upon
ready invention and before Sydney Howard made his first big
success in *Hit the Deck* he had mastered the art of gagging, not
only of verbal but the equally effective property gagging. In
Magic Carpet Sydney Howard, seated at a counter, made most
amusing play with the model legs which department stores use
for the display of ladies' stockings. As Miss Finchbottom, in
company with Cyril Fletcher as Miss Goosebody, he kept
crowded houses chuckling for minutes while he eased out the
crinkles. By some trick of vision, Sydney Howard managed at
times to suggest a real feminine leg of the most charming proportions, projecting from some body concealed beneath the
counter.

Property Gags and Slapstickery

The property "gags" are very varied. Who will forget the big
bath sponge which "Bill" Berry bounced so merrily in company
with Maisie Gay, when playing D. Wilkie Thorne in *High Jinks* at
the Adelphi years ago. "Bill" Berry found unusual properties
very fruitful sources of laughter. The quill pens in the musical
version of Pinero's *The Magistrate* furnish another example.

Slapstick may be defined as physical wisecrackery. It has its
name from an instrument in the hands of Clown in the old-time
harlequinade. It was not a stick but a roll of paper glued closely
together and then flattened out. A noisy but harmless spank upon
any part of the body which presented itself was therefore possible
without inflicting pain, and became the more noisy when two
thin pieces of some light wood, separated by a wedge, was sub-

stituted for the paper. Finally some bright boy added a blank cartridge and when Clown delivered his blow there was a loud report.

Almost as rewarding as the verbal gag is that in dumb show. Many a faltering ten minutes in a musical show has been filled by a comic with a gift for miming. Maisie Gay's efforts in Noel Coward's *This Year of Grace* have been mentioned. Memorable in itself and revealing in connection with the origins of the stage trick, was an effort of Leslie Henson in *Yes, Uncle*. In the cast with Henson was the then youthful Margaret Bannerman, who was entrusted with a single line: "Well, good-bye; I'm going out to buy some stuff for a petticoat."

Now it chanced that there was a sofa in the scene and on the sofa were two big bolster cushions. Leslie suddenly became conscious that one of the cushions dimly resembled a roll of silk, and without the least notion where he was going, proceeded to exploit the idea. In pantomime, he unrolled the silk, measured off a few yards and then snipped at a corner with imaginary scissors, before he tore off a length, folded it up and presented the imaginary packet to the amazed "Bunny". The "House", by this time, was fully alive to the jest and Henson whispered to Miss Bannerman, "Quick, give me some money out of your handbag."

"Bunny" duly obliged, whereupon Mr Henson proceeded to pen an imaginary bill, and sent it hurtling to an imaginary cashier by means of an imaginary wooden "ball", in which the bill and the cash were supposed to be enclosed. As the ball sped round the dress circle, in imagination, Leslie's goggle eyes followed it, and when it returned to him with the precise change, Mr Henson delightedly opened the ball, gave the money to Miss Bannerman and bowed her out of the imaginary shop. Poor Bunny! Her inexperience in those early days was revealed on the following evening, when she said, "Well, I'm going out to buy some stuff for a petticoat," and calmly tripped off the stage. Thus the most elaborate silent gag in musical comedy was lost to the audience for a night. Later, "Bunny" Bannerman explained: "I thought it was just Leslie's fun!"

She was right, it was, but inspirations of the sort are evidence of comic powers, in excelsis. Your Hensons and your Graves are distinguished from the rest by the very fact that they can improve so vastly upon anything which authors can devise, because their sense of the immediate reactions of an audience is so keen.

Leslie Henson was fond of shop-walker parts. In *Tell Me More*, with music by Gershwin, he had to satisfy a customer who was insistent that the silk on her hat should match the silk in her dress; the inventive Leslie solved his problem by snipping a bit off the back of the skirt, slipping it dexterously into the hat, and allowing the lady to pass from the stage displaying considerably more of the lower limbs than the original costumier designed.

In the light of these principles it would be pleasant to follow the careers of some of the men and women who have achieved fame by exploiting them. The temptation shall be resisted. An example will suffice, and what better than the stage story of Leslie Henson himself. Henson has related the terrors of his first London audition. It was at the Empire when George Grossmith was producing *Hullo, London*. It seemed possible that eighteen-year-old Leslie might be helpful, as the concert party known as the *March Hares* was in the show, and it included the late Davy Burnaby. Wearing eyeglasses and a blue suit and equipped with a nasty cold in the head, Leslie was required to make violent love to Millie Legarde. Small wonder that his success was small. Later, Leslie's luck changed momentarily, when he sang "Murders" in the hearing of George Grossmith. The great man asked if he (George) could introduce the song into the second act of *Tonight's the Night*. The refrain ran: "So I murdered him last Tuesday; I thought it would be best."

Leslie would have preferred to sing "Murders" himself, but assented with becoming graciousness. His own opportunity was to come, not in London but New York, at the Shubert Theatre, where he was appearing as Albert, a waiter, a one line part. Leslie has told us, "In a fit of lunacy one night I went on with some knitting I'd picked up. I'd never seen a waiter knitting. It stopped the show for a bit." When Robert Nainby, the stooge, said, "What are you doing?" instead of speaking his proper line which was "I'm only having a look to see what won the 3.30!" Leslie answered on the spur of the moment, "I'm sewing my wild oats!" This was the first spontaneous gag of Henson's musical comedy career. With Robert Nainby's aid, Leslie built up a gag scene lasting ten minutes.

Douglas Furber, the revue writer, was the fortunate instrument which brought Leslie to London and stardom. It was in September 1914, and George Edwardes was interned in Germany, having been trapped by the World War. George Grossmith and Laurillard were, thus, in charge at the Gaiety. Furber's introduction to Grossmith was followed by an audition which resulted in an engagement to play the part of the Hon. Tolly Ridgmount in *To-night's the Night*. The pay was only four pounds a week, so it is not surprising that the part consisted of a single line. Mr Leslie had to dart forward from the midst of a party of chorus girls and cry, "O Mrs Lovett-Lovett, do come and see the wistaria." However, it was a beginning, and within a year, Leslie was earning £100 a week. The little man with the gutta-percha features and the bolting eyes had "got there".

Just as authors at the Gaiety in an earlier generation had to work with Teddy Payne in mind, so the comedian who had now to be fed was Leslie Henson. His first foil was the burly Dave Burnaby. Later, Henson became the leader in a famous trio, his companions being Fred Emney Junior and Richard Hearne. One of their ventures has been mentioned. In *Running Riot*, a Douglas Furber invention with music by Vivian Ellis, the trio were partners in a travelling show, which specialized in performing fleas, and they (the trio, not the fleas) were unwittingly involved in a super-film production. In one episode Cornelius Crumpet and his two friends gate-crashed into an East End opium den in search of the heroine. The opium provoked a flood of reminiscences by Henson and Emney, which included a discussion upon the ingredients of porridge. The opportunities proved endless and not a few involved that substratum of surrealism which we judge important in what abides in boshery.

Swing Along was another Gaiety venture in which Leslie Henson was supported by the burly Fred Emney, and the less than burly Richard Hearne. Leslie will be remembered for his appearance in the fetching lingerie of a can-can dancer. He donned this after he lost the more essential parts of his wardrobe through risking them upon errant numbers at the Casino tables in Monte Carlo. It was an unhappy situation.

Leslie: I'd take poison, if I had some poison.

Fred Emney (gently but decisively): I've got some poison, and sweeties to take the nasty taste away!

Memorable, too, was Leslie's costume a little later, when he was about to retire for the night, momentarily posing as Madame Zabiski. It was in this rôle that Leslie exhibited his dismay when the leader of the No Shirts assured him that his men did not make war upon women. "What, no atrocities?" asked the disguised and disgusted Leslie.

And, again, in the photographer's studio, with the anxious Richard Hearne in charge of the photographic apparatus:

Hearne: What kind of photo do you want? A bust up?

Leslie (puzzled): A bust up?

Hearne: Yes, from the bust down, or the bust up?

Leslie: It's imperial to me.

Going Greek was another vintage piece, in which the Henson, Emney and Hearne brand was served, together with such sweets as Roy Royston and Louise Browne singing, "A Little Co-operation from you." The trio were funny as Greek bandits, but their triumph was an appearance as schoolboys—embodiments of the unhappy Bultitude in *Vice Versa*. Like Mr Anstey's book, this scene from *Going Greek* was "a lesson to fathers".

At the Winter Garden in the early 'twenties, working for George Grossmith and J. A. E. Malone, Leslie was paired with Heather Thatcher, another partnership with pleasant memories. Thus, in *The Beauty Prize* (1932) he was Odo Philpotts in love with Lovey Toots (Miss Thatcher). As one scene was laid on shipboard, ship sports loomed largely in the fun, and they included a three-legged race on deck with Odo Philpotts and Lovey Toots in partnership. And when he chose, Leslie like all good comics, could be properly pathetic, an example being the hour when he wooed Sally the Foundling (Dorothy Dickson) by offering to help wash the dishes at Alley Inn, while both were looking for "the silver lining" and trying to find the sunny side of life. In *Kid Boots*, Leslie Henson was as near to being his pleasant self as his art allowed. His rôle was that of a golfer and very spruce he looked in his chequered costume. The inevitable sufferings began

x

when the exigencies of the plot handed Boots to an over-ener-
getic masseuse, who added to her handiwork treatment in an
electric chair which was as near to capital punishment as might
be.

Diana Wilson (at the switch): What's the matter—wrong side?
Leslie (in the electric chair): No—wrong place.

Leslie's facial play on the operating table was equalled, if not
eclipsed, a generation later in *Bob's Your Uncle* (1948), when the
comedian experimented with a seidlitz powder. First, he swal-
lowed the contents of the blue packet, neat; then the contents of
the white, also neat. When the water was added the joke reached
a climax, the finale being an explosion "off". Grimacery is a
recognized branch in the business of a low comedian.

And, lastly, in justification of our opening proposition regarding the element of surrealism in the more intriguing forms of
stage fun, the ladies shall have full recognition. A final tribute to
Hermione Gingold, of the Ambassadors, where the *Sweet and
Low* revues were staged between 1945 and 1948. No one will ever
estimate with accuracy Hermione's personal contribution to the
record-breaking revues. If she did not actually write her more
telling lines, she inspired them. Recall that wicked reminder of
Camille Clifford as the Gibson Girl. With a background of New
York Central Park and wearing the costume of 1900, Hermione
sang of

> That filly of fable, adorable Mabel,
> The horse with the hansom behind!

Or again, Hermione Gingold thrusting this stanza upon the
stalls at the Ambassadors at a time when not a few American
soldiers were still in Britain:

> Thanks, Yanks! for that rather nice boy,
> From old Illinois,
> Who led an attack on my flanks;
> The least I can say is, "Thanks!"

Yes, Hermione Gingold was "It". And Rosie Boote singing
"Maisie" in the Paris Exhibition scene of *The Messenger Boy*,
pretty Ethel Haydon, fresh from Australia as La Favorita in *The
Circus Girl*, George Grossmith, Junior, singing "Yip i addy i ay",

with the chorus of girls, and John le Hay in *My Girl*, as Alexander McGregor of the Mulct'em in Parvo Stock Exchange. Or Julie James, with her Titian red hair, when she sang "Widows are Wonderful" in *Yes, Uncle*, assisted by a chorus of male admirers, and Winifred Barnes who graduated in the chorus of *Our Miss Gibbs*, and, very wisely, decided that her singing voice was far from adequate. Lessons with Jean de Reszke in Paris helped to make her a star in *Betty*; Mabel Russell's wink to the gallery, too, as she sang "I'm afraid to go home in the Dark."

These from the distant past. In more recent times Mary Ellis in *Music in the Air*, a Hammerstein and Jerome Kern show of the 'thirties, in which Miss Ellis lighted upon a delightful foil in the unsophisticated Sieglinde (Eve Lister). Or Vera Pearce, singing "Vive L'Amour" at Les Folies-Bergère in *Wild Oats*, in a Mistinguett costume which was in such magnificent contrast to the cricketing flannels of Vera's opening scene, in which she captained the Little Giggleswick Ladies, though her Patsy Beresford, singing that pathetic ditty "The Girl the Soldiers always left behind" in *Yes Madam*, is an equally satisfying memory. Nor would one omit Pat Kirkwood, with the wink and the outsize smile which accompanied "My Heart Belongs to Daddy" in *Black Velvet*, or Claire Luce, preferably as the faithful Bonny in *Burlesque*, in company with Nelson Keys. And the Alhambra, on the evening Fred Emney and Jack Buchanan appeared in *The Flying Trapeze*, Emney being the big ventriloquist and Jack the doll on his knees. And if Jack, why not Elsie Randolph, in the bewitching white breeches she wore while singing "You've got the wrong rumba" in *This'll Make You Whistle*, or Bea Lillie, struggling with "two dozen double damask dinner napkins" at the department store in *At Home, Abroad*.

The memories arise all too quickly. There is nothing for it but to close this chapter and my book.

BIBLIOGRAPHY

Who's Who in the Theatre, edited by John Parker, 10th edition, 1947
Bibliographies, British Drama, issued by the National Book Council
The "Stage" Cyclopaedia, Bibliography of Plays, compiled by R.
Clarence
French's *Catalogue of Plays*, published by Samuel French
Bibliography of Community Drama, including Production, Scenery,
Costume and Make-up, compiled by the British Drama League

Building the Modern Theatrical Tradition

Manzius, Karl	*History of Theatrical Art* (6 vols.)
Nicoll, Allardyce	*Development of the Theatre*
The Greek Dramatists	Translations by Gilbert Murray
Chambers, Sir Edmund	*The Mediaeval Stage*
Chambers, Sir Edmund	*The Elizabethan Stage*
Lawrence, W. J.	*Old Theatre Days and Ways*
Dobrée, Bonamy	*Restoration Comedy; Restoration Tragedy*
Brereton, Austin	*Henry Irving* (2 vols.)
Darton, H.	*Vincent Crummles; his Theatre*
Reynolds, Ernest	*Early Victorian Drama* (1830–1870)
Martin, Sir Theodore	*Life of Helena Faucit*
Calvert, Mrs Charles	*Sixty-eight Years on the Stage* (reminiscences of the old-time stock companies)
Shaw, G. Bernard	*On the old-time stock companies*, in his Preface to Ellen Terry's Letters
Bancrofts, Marie and Squire	*The Bancrofts*
Dark, Sidney, and Gray, R.	*W. S. Gilbert*
Simonson, Lee	*Theatre Art Progress through Four Centuries*

The Playhouse

Sherson, Erroll	*London's Lost Theatres of the Nineteenth Century*
Mason, A. E. W.	*George Alexander and the St James's*
Williams, Harcourt	*Four Years at the Old Vic*
Baylis and Hamilton	*The Old Vic*
Maude, Cyril	*The Haymarket Theatre*

Playfair, Nigel	*Hammersmith Hoy* (story of the Lyric Theatre)
Goldie, G. W.	*Liverpool Repertory Theatre*
Adam, Ronald	*Overture and Beginners* (1938)

The Dramatist Gets to Work

Reynolds, M. E.	*Galsworthy, Life and Letters*
Coats, John	*Galsworthy as a Dramatic Artist*
Jones, D. A.	*Life and Letters of Henry Arthur Jones*
Cordell, R. A.	*Somerset Maugham*
Maugham, Somerset	*The Summing Up* (an autobiography)
Druten, J. van	*The Way to the Present* (autobiography)
Thompson, A. R.	*The Dry Mock. A study of Irony in Drama*

Theme and Plot-making in the Drama

Barrett, T. K. P.	*Themes of Modern Drama*
Koht and Jaeger	*Life of Henrik Ibsen; In Ibsen's Workshop*
Tennant, P. F. D.	*Ibsen's Dramatic Technique*
Björkman, E.	*Plays by Strindberg*, translated with introductions
Shaw, G. Bernard	*Dramatic Opinions and Essays*
Archer, William	*Playmaking* (1913)
Polti, Georges	*Les Trente-six Situations Dramatiques* (*1895*)
Ervine, St John	*How to Write a Play*
Hamilton, Patrick	*Rope* (with a Preface on Thrillers)
Munro, C. K.	*Watching a Play*
Barker, Harley Granville-	*On Dramatic Method* (Clark Lectures, 1930)
Balmforth, R.	*The Problem Play*
Campbell, Mrs Patrick	*My Life and Some Letters*
Priestley, J. B.	*Three Time Plays* (with Preface); *Johnson over Jordan*

The Faculty of Laughter

Agate, James	*Buzz-Buzz*
Pemberton, T. E.	*E. A. Sothern* ....
Jacob, Naomi	*Our Marie* (Marie Lloyd)
Short, Ernest	*Fifty Years of Vaudeville*
Vincent, W. T.	*Recollections of Fred Leslie*
Hollingshead, John	*Gaiety Chronicles*
Randall, Harry	*Old-time Comedian*

Roberts, Arthur	*Fifty Years of Spoof*
Merson, Billy	*Fixing the Stoof Oop*
Cochran, Charles B.	*I Had Almost Forgotten; Cock-a-doodle-do*
Robey, George	*Looking Back on Life*
Lane, Lupino	*How to Become a Comedian*
Dunville, T. E.	*Autobiography of an Eccentric Comedian*

Plays of To-day and To-morrow

Nemirovitch-Dantchenko	*My Life in the Russian Theatre*
Stanislavsky, Constantin	*My Life in Art*
Vittorini, D.	*Pirandello*
Eliot, T. S.	*The Family Reunion; Murder in the Cathedral*

Irish Theatre

O'Casey, Sean	Published plays, including *Juno and the Paycock, The Silver Tassie,* and *Within the Gates, I Knock at the Door* (autobiography, 1939)
Gregory, Lady	*Irish Folk Plays* (2 vols.)
Robinson, Lennox	*The Irish Theatre* (1938)
Fermor, U. Ellis-	*The Irish Dramatic Movement* (1939)
Fay, W. G., and Casswell, C.	*Plays of the Abbey Theatre*

Only Acting. Enter the Players

Kemble, Frances	*Autobiography*
Ashwell, Lena	*Myself a Player*
Terry, Ellen	*The Story of my Life*
Kendal, Dame Madge	*Dame Madge Kendal* (1933)
Bolitho, Hector	*Marie Tempest*
Millward, Jessie	*Myself and Others* (1923)
Lanchester, Elsa	*Charles Laughton and I* (1938)
Maurier, Daphne du	*Gerald, a Portrait*
Benson, Sir Frank	*My Memories* (1930)
Benson, Lady	*Mainly Players*
Neilson, Julia	*This for Remembrance*
Lang, Matheson	*Reminiscences*
Tree, Sir Herbert	*Thoughts and Afterthoughts* (1913)
Pemberton, T. E.	*Sir Charles Wyndham* (1904)
Kerr, Fred	*Recollections of a Defective Memory* (1930)
Asche, Oscar	*Oscar Asche, his Life*
Beerbohm, Max	*Herbert Beerbohm Tree and Others*
Robins, Elizabeth	*Theatre and Friendship*

Hicks, Seymour	*Me and My Missus*
Terriss, Ellaline	*By Herself*
Compton, Fay	*Rosemary*
Gielgud, John	*Early Stages* (1939)
Seyler, Athene, and Haggard, S.	*The Craft of Comedy*
Vanbrugh, Irene	*To Tell My Story*

Production and the Producer

Heffner, Selden, and Sellman	*Modern Theatre Practice* (1936)
Craig, E. Gordon	*The Art of the Theatre*
Komisarjevsky, Theodore	*Myself and the Theatre; Theatre and a Changing Civilization*
Komisarjevsky, and Simonson	*Settings and Costumes of the Modern Theatre* (1933)
Simonson, Lee	*The Stage is Set*
Barker, H. Granville-	*The Exemplary Theatre; Prefaces to Shakespeare*
Fuerst, and Hume,	*Twentieth-Century Stage Decoration* (1929)
Browne, E. Martin, and others	*Putting on a Play*
Zinkeisen, D.	*Designing for the Stage* (1938)

Creating a Star. How a Player Makes Good

Fairbrother, Sydney	*Through an Old Stage Door* (autobiography)
Moore, Eva	*Exits and Entrances* (1923)
Collier, Constance	*Harlequinade*
Gay, Maisie	*Laughing Through Life*
Coward, Noel	*Present Indicative* (autobiography)
Lawrence, Gertrude	*A Star Danced*

Voice and Gesture in the Theatre

Coquelin (*Aîné*)	*The Art of the Actor* (translated by E. Fogerty)
Baring, Maurice	*Sarah Bernhardt*
Aitken, Dr W. A.	*The Voice*
O'Neill, R. M.	*Science and Art of Speech and Gesture*
Guilbert, Yvette	*Struggles and Victories*

The Function of Criticism

Walkley, A. B.	*Dramatic Criticism* (Royal Institution Lectures, 1903)
Scott, Clement	*The British Stage* (1850–1900)
Archer, William	*The Theatrical World* (1895 onward)
Shaw, G. Bernard	*On Theatres in the 'Nineties* (3 vols.); *Prefaces to Plays* (1 vol.)
Orme, Michael	*J. T. Grein*
Dukes, Ashley	*The Youngest Drama*
Littlewood, S. R.	*Dramatic Criticism*
Ervine, St John	*The Theatre in My Time*
Darlington, W. A.	*Literature in the Theatre*
Agate, James	*The Amazing Theatre* (1937–9); *The English Dramatic Critics*, etc.
Hardwicke, Sir Cedric	*The Drama To-morrow* (1937)
Palmer, J.	*Future of the Theatre* (1913); *Studies in the Contemporary Theatre* (1927)
Walbrook, H. M.	*A Playgoer's Wanderings*

INDEX

350

Y